★THE SPORTS PAGES★

A Critical Bibliography
of Twentieth-Century American Novels
and Stories
Featuring
Baseball, Basketball, Football,
and Other Athletic Pursuits

by
Grant Burns

The Scarecrow Press, Inc.
Metuchen, N.J., & London
1987

Library of Congress Cataloging-in-Publication Data

Burns, Grant, 1947–
    The sports pages.

    Includes indexes.
    1. Sports stories, American--Bibliography.
2. American fiction--20th century--Bibliography.
3. Sports stories, American--Stories, plots, etc.
4. American fiction--20th century--Stories, plots,
etc. I. Title.
Z1231.S66B87 1987   016.813'5'080355   86-31388
⌊PS374.S76⌋
ISBN 0-8108-1966-X

For Stephanie

(my favorite swimmer)

CONTENTS

v

PREFACE

The fiction of American sport in the twentieth century is rich with implications for a deeper understanding of American life. The reader will find in this fiction both a great many enjoyable novels and stories and numerous insights regarding the attitudes, aspirations, hopes, and fears central to our national character. My objectives for this bibliography, then, are to lead the reader to both pleasurable literature and to literature that will help reveal the heart of our society.

Works discussed in the bibliography include the best as well as the most representative American sports fiction of the century. I have read in their entirety the short stories described here, and have done the same with a large number of the novels. Of the remaining novels, I have tried to read sufficient portions to obtain a feel for their characters and a critical sense of their quality.

The short stories have been drawn from a wide variety of popular and literary magazines and anthologies. Most of the items cited will be available to readers with access to large academic or public libraries with strong collections in American fiction, and many of the works will turn up even in libraries of modest size.

In any selective bibliography, the reader will note bothersome omissions. I considered for inclusion at least twice as many candidates as eventually appeared in the list. No doubt if I re-evaluated the lot, some of my decisions would have been different. If your favorite author is not here, his or her absence is not necessarily due to my dismissing the writer's work as unimportant or to my obliviousness to its existence. Some readers might wonder, for example, why P.G. Wodehouse's sports stories are missing. They are not here because the author of such tales as "The Pitcher and the Plutocrat," in spite of his lengthy stays in the United States, remained English to the bone, not only in his sensibility, but in his literary niche as evidenced in numerous authoritative guides. On the other hand, I have included a few foreign writers whose work seems solidly in the mainline of American fiction. The most notable of these authors is probably W.P. Kinsella, a Canadian whose baseball fiction is rooted firmly in the midwestern soil.

DEFINING THE FIELD OF PLAY

Deciding on the boundaries for a sports fiction bibliography presents some problems. No matter where we put the lines, we cannot set up a field as neat as those employed in football or tennis. The field laid out here is more like those found in sandlot baseball, full of odd corners, vague fences, and annoying imperfections. No matter the shape of sandlot fields, the rule of three outs per at-bat remains. Likewise, this bibliography does observe some fairly rigid boundaries:

1) There are no entries for fiction specifically intended for juveniles.

2) With few exceptions, mystery stories are absent.

3) Works in which a sports setting, however grandiose, serves as no more than a backdrop to other goings-on, such as Thomas Harris's Super Bowl terrorism novel Black Sunday (Putnam, 1975), do not appear.

4) I have omitted fiction about motor sports. The only justifications I can offer for this act are that I find these sports terminally boring, and, fortunately for the sake of my prejudices, not abundantly represented by good fiction.

5) I have also omitted works dealing with hunting or fishing primarily from a non-sport perspective, such as Hemingway's The Old Man and the Sea.

6) Works whose focus on sport is not of primary, and preferably continuing, importance, do not appear. This qualification eliminates many novels, including work by James T. Farrell, Thomas Wolfe, John Updike, and others who have used sports in passages in the context of other interests. The reader may find this restriction dismaying, and I share this reaction to a degree. No matter how we approach them, however, these works cannot be defined as "sports fiction." James Jones's From Here to Eternity is no more sports fiction because Robert Prewitt is a boxer than it is music fiction because he blows a good bugle. Thomas Wolfe's Nebraska Crane was an interesting creation as a baseball player, but a few pages from the hundreds comprising The Web and the Rock and You Can't Go Home Again do not turn those novels into sports fiction.

If we refer to a few obvious excerpts, moreover, we open the door to the entire domain of American fiction that lies beyond the sports genre. If Jones and Wolfe, why not a hundred others who never wrote sports fiction but who may have included sporting scenes in their work? There may be good reasons to compile an analytical guide to sports excerpts in non-sports genre novels, but that is not my purpose here.

WOMEN IN SPORTS FICTION

As alert readers would probably see without being put on notice, American sports fiction is very much a man's world, and not infrequently one whose vision is resoundingly sexist. The overwhelming majority of the stories and novels discussed here feature males as their central characters, and males as their authors. Women generally appear as vehicles for plot manipulation or as a kind of scarcely detectable background noise. They serve as objects either of sweet romance or romantic frustration rather than as complex human beings. Exceptions do exist, with greater frequency as the century moves on, and I have tried to note such exceptions in the annotations. Many of them come from the pens of women writers, but there are also some good representations of women as whole characters by men.

While preparing the thematic index, I gave prolonged consideration to the advisability of including an index entry for "Women." This heading would, I hoped, allow the reader easy access to items illuminating the changing roles of women as revealed in sports fiction. I abandoned this index option as unworkable. The entire body of this fiction illustrates the roles and perceptions of women in our society since the turn of the century. Even works that ignore women reveal historical attitudes toward the sex because of its absence. An index entry for "Women" would thus be misleading either because it focused only on work that pointedly dwelled on women, or because it included nearly everything in the bibliography. I have provided some index entries pertinent to women, such as "Marriage," but these obviously address only very narrow aspects of the overall roles of women.

The treatment of women in American sports fiction offers some of the genre's most provocative ground for further study. It would be easy to go off on a tangent here in an attempt to analyze this treatment, but I will confine my remarks to the annotations. I hope that others will accept the challenge that lies in this area.

SPORTS FICTION AND AMERICAN CULTURE

American sports fiction has come of age in this century. It has made the difficult transition from innocence to experience that so occupied William Blake, and that consumed Mark Twain in his story "The Man That Corrupted Hadleyburg." The innocence of our early sports fiction was an innocence untested by the real world, full of assumptions about American righteousness and destiny. As we edge nervously toward the next millennium, the arrogant anticipation embodied in Henry Luce's vision of the "American Century" has long since melted away. The innocence of our early sports fiction, like our national innocence, was a false one.

The reader who ranges through our sports fiction will find some profound changes in the stories that we have turned to for entertainment, for affirmation of our values, and finally for criticism of our values. The easy optimism of the century's opening gives ground to confused perceptions and mixed expectations. The genre's palette has been gradually darkening with the sobering influences of the century's wars, economic catastrophes, widespread social upheavals, and the anxiety-ridden currents that drive our contemporary life. We still find some sports fiction with a warm measure of tender mercies, but as in most mainstream fiction these are private mercies up against the tide of public hostilities. They recall Matthew Arnold's poem "Dover Beach," in which the speaker surveys a world that once looked so promising, but which now offers no certitude or peace. It is a place

"Swept with confused alarms of struggle and flight,
Where ignorant armies clash by night."

Those alarms have become clearly audible to many writers of sports fiction.

OTHER BIBLIOGRAPHIC LEADS

The bibliographic record for sports fiction has been spotty. The best single effort that I have found is Michael Oriard's "A Checklist of American Sports Fiction," a lengthy appendix to his excellent study, Dreaming of Heroes; American Sports Fiction, 1868-1980 (Nelson-Hall, 1982). Oriard's list is, perhaps, overloaded with citations to juvenile fiction, and generally ignores short fiction, which contains much of the genre's best work. Suzanne Wise's lightly-annotated Sports Fiction for Adults (Garland, 1986) is sometimes useful, but its selection criteria led to the inclusion of many works with little or no real emphasis on sport. Its attention to short fiction is also slight. Anton Grobani's Guide to Football Literature and Guide to Baseball Literature (both from Gale, 1975) contain chapters listing works of fiction, though the emphasis is too much on juvenile fiction and annotations are scant. Regardless of their drawbacks, I found all of these works of assistance in identifying candidates for this bibliography.

The world is a serious, dangerous place, and American sports fiction reflects this fact. The world is also a place with certain opportunities for joy; it is the setting for all the fun we are likely to have. Having fun is still the best reason to play sports, and to read about them. I hope that this bibliography will help its users toward that objective.

G.B.
August 1986

x

I. BASEBALL

1. Ade, George. "The Fable of the Base Ball Fan Who Took the
Only Known Cure." In The America of George Ade, 1866-1944,
p. 55-56. Edited by Jean Shepherd. Putnam, 1960.
Ade, a Chicago reporter, began writing his brief "fables" in
1897. They are characterized by the conciseness required for daily
paper form, by a sure feel for character, and by a sense of humor
edged with darkness. Ade's work in the last respect sometimes foreshadows that of such writers of sports fiction as Ring Lardner and
Nelson Algren. In this example, a loyal fan lies on his deathbed in
"his Ninth Inning," and delivers a final plea to his wife. The plea
makes the story.

2. Alexander, Holmes. "Five Inning Wonder." Saturday Evening
Post 219 (Aug. 24, 1946): 24-25+.
Veteran pitcher Tony Westbrook has recently returned to his
team from a stint in the Army Air Force, where he sustained frost-
bite to his pitching hand in courageous service. His hand now loses
feeling after four or five innings. With the team slumping and desperate for a pitcher who can go nine innings, Westbrook receives an
ultimatum: pitch a complete game, or be gone.
Most of the story relates the crucial game's events. It is a tense
production, full of knockdowns, insults, and injury. When Westbrook
cuts his nails to the quick and rasps his fingertips against the bench
to bring back some feeling, the reader cringes. It is a foregone conclusion that Westbrook will go the distance, but what else could a war
hero do in the Post in 1946?

3. Anderson, Poul, and Dickson, Gordon R. "Joy in Mudville."
In The Infinite Arena: Seven Science Fiction Stories About
Sports, p. 11-42. Edited by Terry Carr. Nelson, 1977. First
published in the Magazine of Fantasy and Science Fiction (November 1955).
In the distant future, baseball has spread not only across the
Milky Way, but across the species of intelligent life. The Interbeing
League plays a season whose length is in keeping with the duration
of its road trips. Sociologists estimate that the Galactic Pennant playoff will occur in about 500 years. The story climaxes with a parody
of "Casey at the Bat." The plot is thin, but the atmosphere is thick
and funny.

4. Apple, Max. "Understanding Alvarado." American Review, no.
22 (1975): 258-272. Also in the author's The Oranging of America,
and Other Stories. Grossman, 1976.

Alvarado, a former big-league star, now lives in Cuba as a re-
spected comrade-in-revolution. The question: will he leave Cuba,
even briefly, so that he may collect his baseball pension? The issue
is resolved in a contest with Fidel Castro himself on the mound, chal-
lenging with a sidearm fastball the man who has come to take Alvarado back to the States. A nifty finale saves the story from its
early immersion in too much talk.

5. Asinof, Eliot. Man on Spikes. McGraw-Hill, 1955. 276 p.
Outfielder Mike Kutner has escaped the coal fields, but his niche
in pro ball has been an uncomfortable one at the Triple-A level. In
his mid-30s, he has little to look forward to in the game. When he
finally plays his lone big-league game, he takes his turn at bat, then
leaves for oblivion.
One of the first baseball novels to step free of tired formulae,
this book still deserves the reader's time. Asinof knows the territory, having played minor league baseball himself in the Phillies organization. His experience comes out in his evocation of the hard
life in the minors, along with his perceptive depiction of the frustration that attends the goal of playing in "the bigs."
Asinof is also the author of Eight Men Out (Holt, 1963), one of
the best accounts of the Black Sox scandal of 1919.

6. _____. "The Rookie." In Fielder's Choice; An Anthology of
Baseball Fiction, p. 256-270. Edited by Jerome Holtzman. Harcourt, Brace, Jovanovich, 1979.
Those who would rather not read all of Man on Spikes can read
the story's major crisis here. It focuses on a single at-bat during
an important game, and makes an interesting psychological study in
itself.

7. Babitz, Eve. "Dodger Stadium." In her Slow Days, Fast Company: The World, the Flesh, and L.A.: Tales, p. 43-55.
Knopf, 1977.
This story of a woman who goes to her first baseball game (Dodgers vs. Giants) with her lover is so light it nearly floats off the
pages, but it is worth the space it takes if only for one paragraph
that records the woman's first impression of the field from high up
in the stands.

8. Baer, Arthur. "The Crambury Tiger." Collier's 110 (July 11,
1942): 19+. Also in Great Baseball Stories. Edited by Jerry D.
Lewis. Tempo Books, 1979.
A witty literary outgrowth of the legendary one-game strike by
the Detroit Tigers in 1912. The team elected to sit it out in sympathy
with Ty Cobb, who had been suspended for assaulting an abusive fan.
Detroit management fielded a squad of semi-pro and college players to
face the Athletics, who drubbed them 24-2. Half the story covers
the strikebusters' performance (complete with actual boxscore); half
follows the fictional sandlotters into further baseball exploits. An
interesting fictional use of an historical curiosity.

9.   Bahr, Jerome. "The Ball Game." In his <u>All Good Americans</u>,
      p. 93-116. Scribner's, 1937.
      A good satirical attack on small town egotism, overblown "patri-
otism," and simple, old-fashioned greed.
      The annual ball game between the towns of Freedom and Hillon
has taken on the aura of a religious rite. Indeed, the local drunkard
condemns "the religion of sport," claiming that athletic competition is
"A time-old substitute for people who don't live creatively, who can't
get the opportunity to do the things they want." The game is a
focus for the flag-waving pride of both towns, which are heavily
populated with ethnic types. Winning the ball game apparently gives
greater force to one's claim to be a real "American." There is more
at stake than victory for the teams or the towns; one of the umpires
--both of whom are corrupt--hopes to parlay his officiating into
enough votes to elect him town marshal.
      Shortly before gametime, the drunkard surfaces in the stands
with a speech parodying the Gettysburg Address. He scores the
public's eagerness to trade a life of creativity for one of competition,
and contends that baseball is the symbol of this bad bargain. The
crowd stupidly misses his point, and applauds him for the wrong
reasons.
      The game is a fiasco, closing with one of the umpires holding
the maddened crowd at bay with a pistol. Bahr gets in a lot of accurate satiric shots here, from those taken at the crooked umpires to
the news correspondent on the make to the town mayor who calls for
unity so the citizens can "fight the cities." In his introduction to
the collection, Ernest Hemingway says that Bahr writes "very good
stories." This is one.

10.   Baumbach, Jonathan. "The Fields of Obscurity." <u>Iowa Review</u>
      6 (Summer/Fall 1975): 1-10. Also in the author's <u>The Return</u>
      <u>of Service</u>. University of Illinois Press, 1979.
      A wonderful, crazy story informed by a delightful sense of hu-
mor, with an underlying heads-up awareness about the difficulty of
being what one is not. Lawrence Rocco Kidd is a sometime left-fielder
in the majors; his smarter-than-he-is wife tells him he can get what
he wants if he wants it enough; obviously the reason he has trouble
with the curve ball is that he doesn't want to hit it enough.
      Kidd hits a game-winning homer in one of his infrequent at-bats,
but in a post-game interview says some unpleasant things about the
fans. The Commissioner takes Kidd's home run away from him and
awards it to the rookie Hatchmeyer. From this point, the identities
slide around like watermelon seeds on a wet plate. Kidd assumes
Hatchmeyer's, Hatchmeyer confuses himself with Kidd, Kidd goes on
a batting tear pretending to be Hatchmeyer after he disables Hatchmeyer with a bat upon finding him at his supper table with his
(Kidd's) wife one day.
      This is only part of it. A witty and highly original story.

11.   Beatty, Jerome. "Oh, You Robber!" <u>McClure's</u> 47 (Oct. 1916):
      12-13+.

An honest umpire's dedication to justice wins him back the heart of his girl. Umpire Tim Patterson has asked his girlfriend Nettie to marry him, but this sweet child's head has been turned, first by the big city of New York, then by a detective, "one of those Broadway guys that changes his shirt every day," and then by baseball. Nettie has become an avid Giants fan, and, like many of the serious "bugs" in the stands, is convinced that all umpires are born criminals, existing only to spoil the rightful victories of her team.

Patterson observes a burglar in a crowd one evening, but cannot reach him. The following day, he hears the burglar's loud voice during a Giants-Cubs game. Assuming that the felonious bug will be back for the next game, Patterson conducts a clever ruse that leads to the culprit's apprehension and to Nettie's arms.

Of interest chiefly for the portrait of the ball-park scene at a time when umpires were less generally regarded as impartial arbiters than they are today.

12.   Beaumont, Gerald. "The Crab." In The Omnibus of Sport,
       p. 141-155. Edited by Grantland Rice and Harford Powel.
       Harper, 1932. Also in the author's Hearts and the Diamond.
       Dodd, Mead, 1921.
       A sour-tempered third-baseman in the Coast League finds his acumen in the field temporarily short-circuited by his astounding marriage to a singer known as "The Smile Girl." Sentimental but amusing.

13.   Beckham, Barry. Runner Mack. Morrow, 1972. 213p.
       This novel presents the black struggle in America in the sym-bol-laden context of the national game (or what once was that game). The central character is a young black man, Henry Adams, who leaves the small-town South behind and heads north to find freedom and fame in the big leagues. Untoward intrusions, including a draft notice, derail Henry's pro ball ambitions. Instead of taking the field for the Stars, he takes to the battlefield for the Stars & Stripes, to help fight a bizarre war in Alaska.
       Runner Mack, a black revolutionary, educates Henry Adams in the philosophy of guerrilla action against the U.S. government, and enlists Henry's aid in a bombing attack on the White House. As the ultimate symbol of white America, what other house could do?   .
       The adjective "Kafkaesque" is too often applied too easily to surreal studies of contemporary life, but this novel is worthy of the term. It is a rich, black-humored, and terrifying rendering of existence pursued for incomprehensible purposes and ever-receding goals. Beckham works in his baseball metaphors in a consistently interesting and thoughtful way. (Readers of Robert Coover's The Universal Baseball Association might want to compare Coover's sex-as-baseball conceit with Beckham's).

14.   Boyle, T. Coraghessan. "The Hector Quesadilla Story." The
       Paris Review 26 (Fall 1984): 253-266. Also in The Pushcart

Prize, X: Best of the Small Presses. Edited by Bill Henderson. Pushcart Pr., 1985.

Theoretically, a baseball game can last forever. In this fantasy, we see the theoretical become real.

Hector Quesadilla, formerly of the Mexican League, has been a ballplayer for many years. He has compiled a .296 lifetime average in a career that has hop-skipped through several teams before bringing him to gimpy-legged rest with the Dodgers.

The game in question begins auspiciously in a dream: Hector envisions that he will be the hero of the coming contest against the Braves. He will pinch hit late in the game against an old nemesis, and drive the ball from the park. His dream eludes him, but the game turns into something out of the reach of simple heroics. It goes on 15, 20, 30 innings, the players dragging themselves around the field like extras from "Night of the Living Dead." Hector is the goat, then the hero, then the goat, and hero again as the game does indeed go on forever.

A good story of time and dreams, with a fine title that plays off the most shopworn of all athlete-biography titles.

15. Bradbury, Ray. "The Big Black and White Game." American Mercury 61 (August 1945): 227-235. Also in the author's The Stories of Ray Bradbury. Knopf, 1980.

One of Bradbury's small-town stories, this one is set for the most part at the annual baseball game between the town's white team and a black team composed of laborers, servants, and dance-hall workers. The narrator, a young boy, is sympathetic to the black players, and comments on their grace and lack of self-consciousness, as opposed to the stiff, ungainly style of the white players.

The black team is on the way to a lopsided win when a violent incident on the field precipitates a near-riot. The game breaks up, and none of the local white folk attend the fabulous dance scheduled that evening by the blacks.

As usual, Bradbury tunes in accurately on small-town ways and boyhood perceptions.

16. Brashler, William. The Bingo Long Traveling All-Stars and Motor Kings. Harper & Row, 1973. 244p.

An entertaining recreation of the era when black barnstorming teams carried baseball to some surprising places.

It is the late 1930s. Bingo Long, catcher and slugger, leads his team of "All Stars" from the clutches of a mercenary owner to the barnstorming road. The book winds down into the All Stars' dissolution when the majors begin signing black players to minor-league contracts. The career of the great pitcher Leon Carter brings the story full circle in a neat fashion. When the book opens, Carter is pitching for the Stars, performing that classic trick of the exhibition pitcher: he throws the first pitch of the game to a superb batter, with catcher Long the only other Star on the field. In the end, Carter's arm is dead after 25 years of work. In his announcement that he is quitting the game, Carter sums up the driving force

of black baseball when he says, "We been playing this game all our
lives, Bingo. Hustling and scrambling for every little bit of meat
been dangled out front of our noses ... if we don't, you know
there's some fool out there dying to take it from us because he
ain't had a meal since week before last."

Bingo, Leon, and their kind are gone, but the memories of
the great black leagues and barnstorming players endure. This
novel is one of the best literary tributes to them. The 1976 film
version of the book, with the same title, is a very good adaptation.
For those interested in pursuing the history of black baseball before Jackie Robinson broke the color line, the best place to start
may be Robert Peterson's Only the Ball Was White: A History of
Legendary Black Players & All-Black Professional Teams (Prentice-
Hall, 1970).

17. Broun, Heywood. "In the Heart." Collier's 98 (Aug. 22,
    1936): 24+.

This story lightly addresses the conflict between baseball and
religion. Baseball wins. Fred Bay is a seminarian who refuses to
play ball for the Yankees on Sunday. He plans to leave the team
on September 1 to serve as a missionary in China. Since he was a
small boy, this is the "call" that has been pressed upon him.

Fred spends his Sabbath afternoons sitting on the bench, his
head bowed. This piety unravels one Sunday when the Yanks need
a pinchrunner to help them win a big game. The call of the diamond
proves more powerful than that of "heathens" craving conversion,
and the devout Mr. Bay runs out to raise hell on the basepaths. A
good story for our times, when too many players cross themselves
before taking their batting stances.

18. _____. "The Last Signal." Collier's 98 (Aug. 1, 1936): 19+.
    Also in Great Baseball Stories. Edited by Jerry D. Lewis.
    Tempo Books, 1979.

Chauncey Frothingham Wigglesworth, Jr., flunks out of Harvard
and slips into the Yankees' pitching rotation. The boy has a lot to
learn, but under the guidance of the gnarled old catcher Hardcoal
Haggerty, he learns well. To repay Haggerty, he tutors him in
reading and writing through a creative system of pitch calling.
Broad, effective humor.

19. _____. The Sun Field. Putnam, 1923. 204p.

The noted reporter works up an unusual situation in this novel
focusing on the marriage of a radical reformer and an American
League slugger without a surplus of brains. The marriage between
Judith Winthrop and Tiny Tyler is one of intellect and brawn, and
is thus unbalanced and unsatisfactory. In spite of their mental in-
compatibility, Tiny's awesome physical appeal retains Judith's interest. Tiny tries to fit himself into her vision of him as classical
sculpture come to life, with unfortunate results. Judith cannot accept Tiny as a ballplayer, or even as a man, only as an object of
lust with an echo of Antiquity. Broun might have made more of the
novel; its execution is not up to its dramatic potential.

20. Brown, Frederick W. "Baseball at Bangalong." Harper's
    Weekly 51 (Dec. 14, 1907): 1826-1829.
        U.S. Army Sergeant Hook tells one of his buddies a whopper
    about a baseball game he and his men played in the Philippines
    against a team of locals. The game itself is not interesting, but the
    sociology is. The U.S. moved in on the Philippines during the
    Spanish-American War. One of the notable phenomena of that war
    was the way in which American attitudes toward the other partici-
    pants shifted as the war progressed. The initial loathing for the
    Spanish gave way to dislike for the dark-skinned Cubans, for whom
    the U.S. was supposedly fighting. Racism had its way, and it has
    its way in this story. Sgt. Hook casually refers to the Philippine
    natives as "black and tans," "niggers," "Indians," "brown brothers,"
    and so on. He portrays them as sneaky, thieving, and violent but
    ineffectual ("one of us was equal to about six o' them.") The author
    intends all this as funny. It isn't funny, but it is an instructive
    and embarrassing portrait of the imperialist mindset.

21. Buck, Ashley. "A Pitcher Grows Tired." Esquire 2 (July
    1934): 61+.
        Rodkin, a star who remembers pitching to Ty Cobb and Tris
    Speaker, has just pitched another good game, but he knows that
    the trainer is right: he pitched the game with his head, not his
    arm. The arm aches; his whole body aches, and, although he wants
    to pitch until he dies, he realizes that like those long-gone stars,
    he too must leave the game. The sense of fatigue and regret is
    strong.

22. Bulger, Bozeman. "Big-League Promise." McClure's 47 (May
    1916): 30-32+.
        Bob Pressley, scion of a landed Texas family, hankers after
    big-league fame. Because he helped break down the social barriers
    against the Bluelegs in the small town where the team trains in the
    spring, the Bluelegs' manager lets Pressley play with the team, his
    salary secretly supplied by generous townsmen. Pressley has no
    real talent, and it falls to a scheme between his sweetheart and the
    manager to point this out to him.
        The story's most interesting aspect is its emphasis on social
    class: although Pressley has helped the ballplayers overcome some
    of the antipathy that surrounds them (major leaguers were not such
    a gentlemanly lot in 1916), he still welcomes the collusion between
    his fiance and the Bluelegs' manager that shows him where his true
    "place" is.

23. Carkeet, David. The Greatest Slump of All Time. Harper &
    Row, 1984. 232p.
        Slumps, whether team or individual, can be mystifying and
    engrossing, particularly when they happen to talented players.
    Carkeet's novel is a good picture of a slump affecting a major-
    league team. The irony of this slump is its location: it takes place
    not between the foul lines, but inside the players' heads. Few

probes of The Slump have done a better job of illustrating the inexplicable sense of doom that hangs over a slumping team. Carkeet
also shows a good touch, on occasion, for team relationships, and
the distance he keeps between himself and his characters allows
considerable ironic humor.

24. Charyn, Jerome.   The Seventh Babe.   Arbor House, 1979.
    347p.
    This is the depiction of an odyssey that begins in 1923 when a
millionaire's son passes himself off as an orphan for a tryout with
the Boston Red Sox. It ends over a half-century later, with the
same man still playing third base for the land's last black barnstorming team.
    Under the assumed name of Babe Ragland, young Cedric Tanne-
hill takes up with the sad-sack Sox, who have recently gutted their
team by sending some of their best players, including Babe Ruth,
to the Yankees. Ragland becomes one of the few Sox stars. He
plays a left-handed third, defying the old claim that only righties
can master that position. With his first Sox season begins a long
series of adventures, some funny, some terrible, some pathetic.
    Ragland's best friend is a hunchbacked bat "boy" who is a
former lumberjack. A bad marriage provokes Ragland to hostile
acts, and the refusal of the team owner to trade him infuriates him.
He supplants Ty Cobb as the man most likely to beat opposing
players senseless with his fists, and, if not the opposition, then
his teammates. After his first season, Ragland tours with the Cincinnati Colored Giants, a white infielder strangely at home on an
otherwise all-black team. After Ragland's victimization in a gambling
set-up, Commissioner Kenesaw Mountain Landis bans Ragland from
the majors for life.
    Unfazed, Ragland joins the Colored Giants on a permanent
basis, and through the decades handles third like a magician. In
the final pages he proves to some Amherst boys, with the aid of
his Colored Giant confederates, that he really is, even in his 70s,
the best third baseman of all time.
    The novel's progress is toward mythology, and it is a long,
strange, entertaining trip.

25. Cheever, John. "National Pastime."   New Yorker 29 (Sept.
    26, 1953): 29-35.
    Eben, the narrator, is speaking of his belief that his father
Leander should have helped him learn to play ball as a boy; it was
"as if parental love and baseball were both national pastimes." As
he grew up, Eben found that he had no aptitude for the game. A
desultory catch with his father left him unconscious when the ball
beaned him, and gave him a longstanding dislike for the sport, notwithstanding his former conviction that he would grow up to be a
professional player.
    Wherever he went, baseball followed and tormented him, from a
private school where he lost his job because of a base-running blunder, to a company team in the Middle East oil fields. At one point

he hid under a shed to avoid a game; at another, he buried a
friend's baseball to prevent one from taking place.
It is a melancholy story in spite of its amusing passages until
near the end. Not until Eben takes his own children to a game at
Yankee Stadium, where he makes a good barehanded catch of a foul
ball, does he finally lay to rest his lifelong bad relationship with
his father.
Cheever effectively addresses several themes of sports fiction
here, especially the matters of individual dreams and the conflict
between youth and age.

26. Clark, Philip. "Grandstand Player." American Magazine 150
    (Oct. 1950): 32-3+.
    Burk Stoddard (certainly christened from that pool of athletes'
names that sound like athletes' names) pitches for the Blue Sox,
and, although he plays well, he does not play happily. He spends
most of his time thinking about how his fine record will get him a
job with another team, away from the hapless Sox. He is convinced,
moreover, that his manager's apparent dislike for him accounts for
the manager's daughter's rejection of Burk's marriage proposal.
    In a popular moral tale of this sort we know that youth going
astray will bow to the wisdom of the experienced. This piece packs
a lot of stereotyped situations into a few pages: there is the al-
ready-cited conflict between youth and age; there is the frustrated
romance (a staple of many popular sports stories); there is the
selfish athlete who learns the value of team play, and there is even
the temptation offered the talented but dissatisfied player by an
organized-crime representative, and the young man's stalwart behavior in the face of this temptation.

27. Cobb, Irvin S. "Persona au Gratin." In his Local Color, p.
    368-407. Doran, 1916.
    J. Henry Birdseye's vocation is that of travelling salesman,
but his real love is baseball. He knows all the statistics, all the
names. When a big-league team, the Moguls, is about to appear in
town on its way north from spring training, J. Henry believes that
this is his chance to impress the townsfolk: he'll slip aboard the
train up the line, ingratiate himself with the team, and astound
his friends when he steps off the train with the big leaguers. J.
Henry does get on a train, and mixes with the boys, but they are
not quite the boys he had in mind. A funny account of a know-it-
all's come-uppance.

28. Cohen, Octavus R. "False Alarm." Collier's 55 (April 17,
    1915): 10-11+.
    The human chemistry of ball clubs is almost always a topic of
interest, and this story of an outstanding rookie pitcher's influence
on a major-league team--the Vultures--is not far from believable,
though marred by a weak conclusion.
    Dan Borton is a muscular, self-confident specimen. He con-
siders himself assured of a starting job before he begins spring

training and demands a raise before he has thrown a pitch. Borton
proves that his boasting rests on a strong foundation: a few warmup throws show that he is "a corker."

As the season gets under way, Borton inspires hatred. The
whole team detests the rookie for his patronizing airs, but they play
well behind him, too proud to let him show them up. A thaw in the
team's cold war produces ironic results. Borton, in his mates' good
graces, loses concentration, and he and his fielders kick away a
long string of games. Only when hatred is the prevailing team emotion does victory follow them off the field.

It is unfortunate that Cohen did not pursue his story a little
more energetically, for there is enough raw material here, including
a bloody fistfight between Borton and a teammate, to have produced
something better. Cohen lays out the dynamics acceptably, but
hobbles his theme with a silly romantic resolution.

29. Connell, Richard. "Big Fella." American Magazine 125 (April
     1938): 30-31+.
     The "Big Fella," known on his paycheck as Frank E. Reed, has
been a big-league homerun slugger for close to twenty years. This
spring brings him some competition for his right-field post in young
Gene Geary, a California lad who has left his dear mother to manage
their orange grove alone.

Strange things happen. The Big Fella seems to have lost both
his batting eye and his legs, and Geary shows none of the skill he
displayed in the minors. And why does a hard-boiled guy like the
Big Fella take Geary under his wing, when the kid's ambition is to
take his job away?

Enter the Good Fairy. Geary, we learn, is actually the Big
Fella's son, and B.F. is deliberately yielding his position to the boy
preparatory to returning to California, where he will resume his
long-interrupted relationship with citrus entrepreneur Molly Geary.

A juicy slice of make-believe for the Depression's tail end.

30. Constans, L. "My Baseball Debut." McClure's 28 (April 1907):
     677-684.
     A middle-aged man on vacation in the country grows bored
with the tranquility. When he hears a group of boys preparing for
a ball game, he joins them, to their confusion. "The Old Man," as
the boys call him, shows plenty of enthusiasm, but a couple of innings also show one minor failing: he cannot play a lick. Not only
is he inept, he is ignorant. When called upon to judge a disputed
point, he decides blithely and mistakenly against his own team.
The game ends with the "Old Man's" team winners by a 28-23 score,
in spite of his inglorious contribution. A mildly entertaining story
that would have worked better had the author not insisted on giving
the Old Man, who narrates, an overly literary tone.

31. Coover, Robert. "McDuff on the Mound." Iowa Review 2 (Fall
     1971): 111-120.
     An outrageous prose verison of Ernest Thayer's "Casey at the

Bat" told from the viewpoint of McDuff, the opposing pitcher.
McDuff is an inordinately nervous, doomful man. Having disposed
of the first two Mudville batters in the ninth, his 4-2 lead no per-
ceptible threat from the lightweight Flynn and Blake, McDuff should
be breathing easily, but, as "Flynn bounced insolently and made
insulting noises" after reaching first on a blooper, McDuff comes unglued.

Blake is totally incompetent, a clown, a turkey ("Gobble,
gobble!" cry the fans) who can barely lift the bat to his shoulder.
Yet, as in the poem, he rips the cover off the ball. He and Flynn
then comport themselves on the bases like two of the Three Stooges,
cavorting with chocolate pies and water pistols.

Then Casey, Mighty Casey, comes to the plate. Is it true,
speculates McDuff, that his name is a transliteration of the initials
"K.C." standing for King Christ? Or maybe King Corn? So unhinged is McDuff at the threat of Casey that he can do nothing but
groove three fat pitches. We know the end: "some saw light, and
some screamed, and rain fell on the world."

Loony and delightful, this is a story that anyone familiar with
the original poem will savor. Coover even has the nerve to use internal rhyme in one paragraph, and it works. Great fun.

32. _____ . The Universal Baseball Association, J. Henry Waugh,
Prop. Random House, 1968. 242p.

"J. Henry" seems to be a popular name among fanatic baseball
followers. Coover's J. Henry is much further gone than Irvin S.
Cobb's, however. J. Henry Waugh is a near-friendless accountant
whose only real "living" takes place in his fantasies. He has designed an elaborate baseball game that he plays with dice. Night
after night he sits down with his dice and his paper records and
rolls through a few more games. The games play vividly in Waugh's
head and on the page. The players and managers all have distinct
personalities and histories, and it is easy for the reader to become
as caught up in the fantasy as is Waugh.

As the book goes on, Waugh's involvement in tangible reality
slips away bit by bit. He loses his job, alienates his few acquaintances, and is consumed by his game. A young star pitcher, Damon
Rutherford, is the focus of much of Waugh's obsession: he regards
the imaginary diamond hero as a son. A tragic throw of the dice
destroys Damon, and with him Waugh's remaining control. He is no
longer the proprietor of his league, but its puppet. Once scrupu-
lous in his observation of the rules, he begins to cheat, seeking
vengeance on the team "responsible" for Damon's loss. This cheating
and vengefulness only highlight Waugh's eroding control of the
game, and of his fantasy itself. At book's end, the game remains--
but whether J. Henry Waugh remains is another question.

This is a compelling and utterly involving story of one man's
attempt to create meaning and order in a chaotic, absurd world.
Waugh's choice of baseball as the vehicle for this attempt is as fitting
as it is crazy, for no other sport is so committed to, and embedded
in, rule, order, and continuity.

33. Damon, Philip. "Al Guard's Night of Nights." Iowa Review 3
    (Spring 1972): 55-66.
    A clever, funny, and yet tense story of a baseball announcer's
dual identity.
    The narrator is Asa Weingarten, and we know he's in trouble
from the opening sentence: "I know my rights." Asa addresses
this to the legal authorities to whom the entire tale is ostensibly
directed. Asa is a former announcer for the Gothams, a fixture in
the television booth for fifteen years, and one of the smoothest play-
by-play men in the league. When he was a boy, he was stocky and
slow, and as a man crooked-toothed, nearsighted, and sparse of
hair. When he became "Al Guard," voice of the Gothams, he assumed
not only a new name, but a new look achieved through capped teeth,
contact lenses, a hair transplant, and a low-calorie diet.
    When the Gothams gave Al/Asa the axe to make room for a for-
mer player (who proved a bad announcer, as most former players
do), Al/Asa began a journey of retribution. He trained himself to
be a crack shot with a high-powered rifle, studied the rudiments of
mountain climbing, and learned enough about electronics to patch
himself into the Gotham broadcast system.
    On the night referred to in the title, Al/Asa suspends himself
high in the girders in the Gotham park, his rifle and his patch cord
to usurp the play-by-play at hand. Late in the game Asa Weingarten
cuts into the Gotham broadcast to introduce Al Guard, and to de-
clare the evening "Al Guard Night." Weingarten backs up this declaration with rifle fire, some of it lethal.
    A novel idea, nicely played. Not until near the end of the
story does the Asa/Al split become clear, which lends extra punch.

34. Davies, Valentine. It Happens Every Spring. Farrar, Straus,
    1949. 224 p.
    This book is light entertainment; its themes will not keep the
reader pondering the verities of life and death long after turning
the final page. Yet it is not mere throwaway diversion either, since
it touches base firmly with some human universals, including the desire to see one's favorite dreams brought to reality, and the yearning of the obscure but dedicated for public acclaim.
    Chief character Vernon Simpson is a mild-mannered, baseball
loving chemistry professor working on a project involving a technique
which he hopes will enable plants to repel harmful bacteria. One day
a baseball crashes through Simpson's window, ruining his work, and
landing in his experimental solution. The stuff may not repel bacteria, but for Simpson's purposes its effect is even better: it re-
pels wood. Soon Simpson has converted an ability to simply throw a
baseball more or less straight into an unbeatable pitching style, secretly fueled by applications of his formula to the ball. There are
complications, of course. The book is fun, and so is the 1949 movie,
with Ray Milland in the lead role.

35. Dawson, Fielding. "The Next Turn of the Wheel." In his
    Krazy Kat & 76 More: Collected Stories 1950-1976, p. 94-95.
    Black Sparrow Pr., 1982.

A short, short story that contains the power of a good poem
within its lines, yet which escapes descent into that often dread
category, the prose-poem. The narrator recalls how one May evening
as a boy he went to the American Legion carnival in town. He had
attended baseball practice, and his new glove stuck out of the back
pocket of his Levis. On his way home, he missed the weight of the
glove, reached back, and found it gone.

The above events occur in two short paragraphs. Two longer
paragraphs lay out the great emotional and philosophical significance
of the lost glove, a gift from the boy's favorite uncle. The glove
was a first baseman's mitt, and the boy, in defiance of everything
his body told him about where he belonged on the ballfield, was
forcing himself to play first. The boy admired the "oblique and
powerful style" of the good first baseman, but he only felt right in
the outfield.

Much could be made of this brief story's conclusion, in which
the "darkness and power" of the nearly-black glove "has taken the
more strict form of myself, clawing and hurting and forcing strength
into me. Strength! For the fateful moments of purpose without accident...." Frightening and mysterious, this story walks through
territory seldom stepped upon by stories of baseball.

36. Dickson, Margaret. "Can Ball." Antioch Review 42 (Winter
      1984): 93-102.

An emotional story that could easily have strayed into sentimentality, but does not. Set in rural Maine in the early 1960s, its
two main characters are a former semi-pro ballplayer named Red
Brody, and Stewart Smith, a neighbor boy perhaps ten years old.

It is a summer of hardship. Drought has taken over, Stewart's
mother cannot find work, and his father is dead, a suicide in the
spring. Money is so scarce that when Stewart and Red get together
to play catch and hit flies to each other, they use Carnation milk
cans instead of a baseball. Red and Stewart play for hours, driving
away their separate sorrows.

Stewart's paternal grandfather, a baseball lover, is dying. He
and his wife visit Stewart one afternoon, driving out in their rusty,
beat-up old car. The boy sees a bulge in one of the old man's
pockets: it proves to be a new baseball, and a good one. After
his grandparents leave, Stewart and Red play catch into the twilight.
Red gives the boy his cherished black first baseman's glove, and instructs him to sleep with it under his pillow, the ball tucked into
the pocket. Disaster nearly strikes when Red foolishly hits the ball
across a road and into high weeds; he and Stewart search for it into
the night.

The author shows a subtle feeling for healthy relationships in
this story, conveyed with some nice touches, e.g., when Stewart
watches his grandparents drive out of sight before he begins playing
with the ball. She also demonstrates how small material objects can
mean a great deal in an atmosphere full of love, free of greed.

37. Dubus, Andre. "The Pitcher." North American Review 264

(Spring 1979): 18-24. Also in the author's Finding a Girl in
America: Ten Stories & a Novella. Godine, 1980.
    A lot of distance lies between this story and many of the earlier
ones noted here. It is a distance of time, but more so of attitude.
If a story like "The Crab" (item 12) represents an innocent vision of
baseball, the sport untouched by real life, its "problems" those of
brief and comical duration, "The Pitcher" represents innocence departed, and the demands of real life, not just those of the game itself, always threatening to cut into a man.
    The title character is a 19-year old with a good future ahead
of him in the majors, but while he has been compiling a good first
year in the minors, he has been losing his wife to a dentist. "How
can you be married to a ballplayer and fall for a dentist anyhow?"
he asks.
    Losing his wife to the man who repaired her lost filling provokes
the pitcher to foresight of his future loss, the loss of his pitching
arm "when the pitches that created him would lose their speed ...
become hits in other men's lives...." A serious story, well told;
the main action, and the pitcher's reflections, take place during an
important game.

38. Edmunds, Murrell. Behold Thy Brother. Beechhurst Pr.,
     1950. 80 p.
    This brief, fast-paced novel of one baseball team's racial inte-
gration is a good story, but it is now of more interest as an historical artifact than as a work of fiction.
    The Eagles are in a tight race for the pennant in 1945, and, as
most teams were during WW II, are hurting for capable players.
Their pitching staff is especially thin, with the team's one reliable
pitcher overworked and in danger of burning out. The promise of
relief arrives in a letter from the owner's son, announcing the
signing of a young man "as fast as Bob Feller" who has recently
been discharged from the Army. When the rookie shows up at the
park, it is clear that the letter slid over one prominent fact: this
left-handed pitcher is black.
    On a team with a number of members from the deep South,
complications follow. The manager is awed by Washington Hurt's
pitching prowess, but is afraid to use him, lest the team be torn
apart by racial antagonisms. The reader knows that Hurt will pitch,
however, and when he does, his superlative performance quashes
even the hostility of his Mississippi-born teammates.
    Jackie Robinson, the first black player to reach the majors (in
1947), was selected by Dodger general manager Branch Rickey as
much for his ability to maintain a cool demeanor under racist abuse
as for his baseball skills. Today, when no team would be likely to
think twice about a player's color, the idea that a black player must
be a superman in any respect is incomprehensible, unless one looks
back at the context of baseball's initial venture into integration.
Washington Hurt is a superman, with speed, a great curve, and a
baffling change-up, all mastered at a tender age. Readers may argue that it isn't fair for Hurt to have to pitch like a giant of the

diamond. It isn't, but neither was it "fair" for Jackie Robinson and
other early black players in the majors to have to be more than
average. Only by being more than average could they have led the
majors to a more racially equitable footing.

Behold, Thy Brother, then, is quite true to the historical
record. It also contains some exciting game action. Its one false
note is the author's wishful thinking that by simply playing well,
Washington Hurt could win the hearts of his teammates.

39. Effinger, George. "Naked to the Invisible Eye." Analog 93
     (May 1973): 58+. Also in Fielder's Choice: An Anthology of
     Baseball Fiction. Edited by Jerome Holtzman. Harcourt, Brace,
     Jovanovich, 1979.

It happens down in the low minors. A young Latino pitcher
throws the ball accurately, but his real talent lies in his ability to
cloud batters' minds as they wait for his pitches. They wait so long
that they forget to swing at them. Rudy Ramirez soon appears on
the covers of national magazines; Playboy calls him the greatest natural talent since Grover Cleveland Alexander. An entertaining and
nicely written bit of fluff.

40. Einstein, Charles. "Last Inning." Collier's 131 (June 20,
     1953): 22+.

Another entry in the spirit is willing but the legs have had it
column. Thirty-five-year-old Wally Voss played a distinguished
major-league shortstop for over fifteen years, but has recently been
on the yo-yo route, spending most of his time in the minors, going
back up to fill in for brief spells in the bigs when someone gets hurt
or goes into a slump. His tired legs keep him from covering the
ground he once did, but his experience allows him to play his position with leg-saving anticipation of the batter's work. Wally also
runs a thriving taxi service for expectant mothers (plenty of those
in 1953), and, at the same time as he falls in love with his secreta-
ry, receives his final summons to the majors.

Lightweight, but representative of those ceaselessly repeated
themes of popular sports fiction: the end of the athletic road, insistence on going out with dignity, and a healthy love interest.

41. _____. "The Long Out." Collier's 132 (Oct. 2, 1953): 48-
     49+.

Called up from the minors near the end of the season to help
settle the young players on the American-League leading Badgers,
Ray Lane does just that. At the age of forty he can no longer
cover much territory at first, but he knows the game's technical
points instinctively, and eases out the rough spots for several
players through his unobtrusive example. The Badgers win the pennant and face the Brooklyn Dodgers in the Series. Lane's great desire is to hit a home run, in this his first, and obviously last,
Series. He still swings a good bat, and drives the Dodger outfielders to the walls several times, but cannot put one out of the
park. When his chance finally comes, on a pitch thrown badly,

he does the admirable thing: instead of swinging from his heels,
he slaps the ball into left field to advance the baserunners.

A tidy little moral tale in which personal ambition bows to the
welfare of the group.

42.   _____. "Reflex Curve." Collier's 129 (June 14, 1952): 26-
27+.

Sam Lewis, a pitcher of talent, cannot make it through the
sixth inning. For several games in succession he tries to get
through tight sixth-inning spots with his curve, but the batters
wait for it and hit it to distant locales when Sam dishes it up. Disgusted with Sam, his manager sees that Sam is traded to another
team. Before he leaves, he falls in love with a sleek young reporter.
She suggests that Sam try a different pitch, and when Sam takes his
first turn against his old team, he remembers her advice.

This story is more interesting for the sex than for the baseball.
Though under necessary restraints, the former is still evident in a
way much more sensible than in baseball tales of previous decades.
When the reporter interviews Sam in his hotel room, they "accidentally" tumble into bed together, albeit fully clothed. And what we're
to make of Sam's dream that he strikes the young woman out "with
a slow ball" cannot have escaped the author's calculations.

43.   _____. "The Wrong Pitch." Saturday Evening Post 225
(May 2, 1953): 24+.

Walter Meers, now a catcher with the doormat St. Louis Stars,
reflects on the circumstances that brought him to St. Louis from
his former team, the Philadelphia Robins. As a Robin, Meers was
the goat in a critical game the past season. He offended a young
pitcher, who then deliberately threw a pitch that Meers had not
called. Meers couldn't handle the pitch; it got by him, two runs
came in on what the scorer called a passed ball, and the papers
tagged Meers with the blame for the loss.

Meers kept quiet, refusing to blame the pitcher; when he
started a fight in a restaurant (a fight set up by the same pitcher),
he looked worse than a bad catcher when the next day's papers re-
lated the details of his night in jail.

The reactions of fans and newspapers may seem a bit much,
but the story's conclusion, with Meers playing against the Robins
and his old antagonist pitching, has a well-planned twist which
avoids the irritation of the expected pat ending.

44.   Elkin, Samuel. "The Ballplayer." In Cross Section, 1945; A
Collection of New American Writing, p. 99-112. Edited by
Edwin Seaver. Fischer, 1945.

Phil Rossof, a good player, is cut by a minor league club when
he refuses to participate in a stupid brawl provoked by teammate
Mike Deegan. Rossof catches on with another club, and on the first
meeting with his former team, Deegan pushes the normally civil
Rossof to a savage attack on him. The story ends with Rossof alone
in the locker room, ejected from the game, thinking sourly about his

failure to live up to his own standards of conduct. An arresting
story, with equal doses of adrenalin and moral interest. The author
was a pro ballplayer before serving in WW II; it is fair to assume
that the cruelty of the war, and the author's reaction to it, find
their way into Elkin's story.

45. Ellison, Harlan. "The Cheese Stands Alone." In Magic for
    Sale, p. 87-99. Edited by Avram Davidson. Ace, 1983. Also
    in the author's Stalking the Nightmare. Phantasia Pr., 1982.
    Baseball receives only a paragraph's mention in this story, but
it is the critical paragraph, the story's heart, and it is a striking
paragraph.
    Cort, a man in his mid-30s, visits a unique rare book store in
Monterey, California, whose customers receive certain revelations
when they peruse the stock. Cort himself receives one when he
examines a particular Big Little Book. It would be a disservice to
the reader to describe the story's details further, but anyone interested in baseball, magic, or the passage of time and dreams will enjoy it.

46. Farrell, James T. "Jump to Chicago." In his Childhood Is Not
    Forever, p. 101-107. Doubleday, 1969.
    A look at one of baseball's necessary travelling companions, the
press. The scene is on a train, rolling from St. Louis to Chicago
after the team has taken a sloppy game from the Cards. The sports
writers are gathered for post-game drinks and dinner, but one of
them, Pat Donnelly, makes too much of his drinks. It becomes clear
from other writers' talk that Pat is well into alcoholism; from Pat's
own ruminations, it is also clear that his life has lost all of its savor,
except for the comforting blur furnished by liquor.

47. _____. "Monologue of an Old Pitcher." Ibid., p. 183-187.
    A morose little story in which an aging former ballplayer
grouses about contemporary players whose hearts are not really in
the game. Ah, but back in the '20s, he assures us, that was the
time to be young and a ballplayer, when the "Big Fellow" (Babe
Ruth, apparently) set the tone for the whole game. No doubt
nothing looks as good as the best of one's long-gone youth, but insistence that looks equal reality can wear thin quickly.

48. _____. "They Ain't the Men They Used to Be." In his
    French Girls are Vicious, and Other Stories. Vanguard, 1955.
    Also in Great Baseball Stories, p. 206-216. Edited by Jerry D.
    Lewis. Tempo Books, 1979.
    One of the saddest baseball stories of all. An elderly man, a
railroad ticket agent, goes to an old-timers' game at Yankee Stadium.
There he sees once again the men who meant so much to him in his
prime, playing a little two-inning game. He is glad that he has
come, but he is sad, too, for the old-timers' game is a strong reminder of how his own life, along with those of his former heroes,
is slipping away. The last long paragraph is especially moving:

"...You don't like to think of the umpire in his blue suit and blue
cap calling the last out in the last of the ninth, but he has got to
call it. Then the shadows fall like they fell across the green outfield, and the sun goes down, and the stands are empty, and there
is no more cheering and no more roaring of the crowd."

49. _____. "Yellow Streak." In his An American Dream Girl,
    p. 253-265. Vanguard, 1950.
    Eddie Hynes is a mediocre student, but he shows promise of
becoming a good athlete. He has fine form in various sports, including baseball, and always shows up early to put in enthusiastic
practice.
    Two problems spoil Eddie's promise: his good form obstructs
his spontaneity, and he leaves his game on the practice field. When
a real game begins, Eddie is erratic, sulky, out of synch with his
teammates. Only when his team is hopelessly out of contention does
Eddie relax and play well. His peers think that Eddie has a cowardly
streak, and maybe he does; the answer to the enigma of Eddie may
also be more complicated than that. A worthwhile study of an athlete whose emotional problems deny him the opportunity to play up to
his physical potential.

50. Foster, Alan S. Goodbye, Bobby Thomson! Goodbye, John
    Wayne! Simon & Schuster, 1973. 190 p.
    A good contribution to the school of athletic disillusionment, of
disgust with sport that has been perverted to serve the purposes of
politics, ideology, and fanaticism.
    The novel opens in 1951. Pete, the narrator, attends a Giants-
Dodgers game. Only gradually does the reader realize that this is
one of the most memorable ball games of all time, the Giants come-
from-behind pennant winner fueled by Bobby Thomson's dramatic
homerun. Pete and his father are at the game with the death of
Pete's brother in Korea fresh in mind. Baseball now seems a trivial
thing to Pete. He has told his father that he plans to join the Army
rather than continue his college career at Ohio State, where he has a
football scholarship. Through the twist of fate that deposits the
Thomson blast in the stands, Pete's decision to join the Army falls
through.
    Following Ohio State, Pete's pro career with the Cleveland
Browns is cut short by a broken leg; upon healing, he joins the
Army anyhow, which stations him in Germany. While in Europe, Pete
executes a fairly ridiculous grandstand play to rescue a Hungarian
farmer under fire from Soviet troops near the Hungarian border.
    Pete returns to the U.S. to resume his football career. It is
only the assassination of John F. Kennedy that finally awakens him
to his lifelong involvement in the most juvenile aspects of American
sport, and to the violence in his life as a football player that seems
to mirror the violence in society at large. The Kennedy assassination passage is one of notable subtlety, and, although the animating
idea is hardly fresh (i.e., sports violence fits hand-in-glove with
cultural illness), the presentation is effective. The book's most ef-

fective section by far, however, is the opening fifty-plus pages, in
which Foster does a beautiful job of interweaving young Pete's agonizing over his brother's death with the details of the Giants-Dodgers
confrontation. It is this section that led to the book's entry in this
bibliography's baseball rather than football section.

51. Fox, William Price. "Leroy Jeffcoat." In Fielder's Choice:
    An Anthology of Baseball Fiction, p. 71-80. Edited by Jerome
    Holtzman. Harcourt, Brace, Jovanovich, 1979. Also in the
    author's Southern Fried Plus Six. Lippincott, 1968.
       Leroy Jeffcoat, a housepainter, is a dedicated but clumsy
    player for a bush-league South Carolina team. Never out of uniform,
    game or not, he is always ready, even in hurricane season. Leroy
    does enjoy one moment of glory, detailed here in an account of his
    team's taking on a prison nine, in the prison yard itself. A happy
    story with amusing characters.

52. Frank, Pat. "Last Time Around." Collier's 109 (June 13,
    1942): 19+.
       A tight little story that follows a 40-year old infielder around
    the diamond in his last at-bat in the game. His release from the
    team takes effect when the game is over. He has a bit to say with
    each of the basemen on the opposing club; most of the conversation
    focuses on the inevitable end of a ballplayer's career. Published at
    a time when the big leagues limped along on the tired legs of men
    too old for the service, or too unsound to pass induction physicals.

53. Frank, Stanley. "The Name of the Game." In Fielder's Choice:
    An Anthology of Baseball Fiction, p. 304-320. Edited by
    Jerome Holtzman. Harcourt, Brace, Jovanovich, 1979.
       In spite of a little too much in the way of clichéd lingo, this is
    a fairly serious story of evil almost triumphant and of good barely
    holding on. The evil is embodied in Gaban, a big-league player-
    manager who thinks nothing of endangering a player's career for the
    sake of a single victory, who fills his team with arrogance but leaves
    it short of pride, and who as a rookie was a sneak thief. Told from
    the perspective of an aging pitcher whom Gaban distrusts because of
    the pitcher's knowledge about his real character, which is that of a
    cowardly fascist. Considering that the story is set during WW II,
    that is probably not an accidental move on the author's part.

54. Fullerton, Hugh S. "The Insignificant Dub." American Maga-
    zine 86 (Oct. 1918): 28-31.
       Students of advertising will find a chuckle in this one. The
    narrator, a baseball scout for the Greens, signs a 2d baseman named
    Rubby playing for a minor-league outfit in Des Moines. Rubby is a
    plodder: "He played the game as if baseball and plowing were the
    same kind of work." He is steady, though, and with the big team's
    regular 2d baseman injured, he fills in capably for a few weeks.
       Capably but invisibly. Rubby is one of the most colorless,
    anonymous players to set foot on a field. No one notices his absence

upon the regular's return. Rubby the invisible disappears for
three years, but when injury again leaves an opening, Rubby is
ready, and this time around he puts into play certain elements of
personal drum beating, not to mention fife playing. A funny story
told in a comfortable, colloquial style.

55. _____. "Li'l Ol' Dove of Peace." American Magazine 85
(April 1918): 38-41+.
      Mike the scout relates a tale of big-league nonsense. A new
catcher named Doug joins the club, and soon leads the team in more
ways than one. He is steadfast on the field, but is a post-game
terror. Within weeks he has most of his teammates run ragged trying to keep pace with his saloon-hopping, and manager Slough is
infuriated. One of the few men on the team not reeling from Doug's
unwholesome influence is outfielder Whitmore, a man--he says--of
peace, much given to squaring conflicts and putting differences
among men to rest. Whitmore reveals the ultimate short-circuit in
his doveishness in a hotel room one night. Doug and Slough have
destroyed the room during a wild fistfight, and Whitmore, whose
"conscience dictates that I must spare no effort to maintain friendship between all humankind" dictates terms of peace in a most authoritative way.

56. _____. "The Man Who Made His Bluff Come True." American Magazine 88 (July 1919): 26-28+.
      For the postwar crowd about to embark on the financial empire-
building of the 1920s, stories of this sort must have served as
starter-fluid.
      Fullerton's favorite scout-raconteur tells us here about Jerry
T. Coonihan, "the fellow in the big blue limousine." Coonihan joined
the Greens upon their discovering him in the hinterlands of Illinois,
where "he pitched baseball as if he enjoyed it." It takes him a long
time to get a chance to pitch for the Greens, and as he looks forward
to his first start, worry assaults him. The scout advises Jerry to
pitch as though he didn't need the job. The strategy works so well
that Jerry soon learns how to let not only opposing players, but the
press and public, believe him far wealthier than he really is. Illusion becomes reality--like stock bought on margin building quick
fortunes--as Jerry turns public perception to his own profits. Given
its timing, a fascinating glimpse into the makings of a generation's
vision of money and success.

57. _____. "Nut from Pecan University." American Magazine 82
(Aug. 1916): 7-11.
      A funny--sometimes very funny--romp reminiscent of the Marx
Brothers in "Horse Feathers." The old scout is combing the minors
for a pitcher with control. No one on the Greens can get the ball
over the plate, and manager Slough is eating his cigars in anxiety.
On a trip through Michigan the scout turns up one Shrapnel Stevens,
a former Green now pitching under an assumed name, and masquerading as a college man. Shrapnel pitches well, but because Slough

can't stand Shrapnel, the college ruse, complete with gaudy clothing,
a preposterous college yell, and makeup, continues. Slough is not
impressed. Referring to the "new" man's ludicrous style, he says,
"College manners, hell! ... That guy must have roomed with all the
squirrels on the tree of knowledge." And what does a college man
do in the evening? First, "he fills up on beer, then he goes to a
theater and pulls chorus girls off the stage and drinks wine out of
their slippers, and licks two policemen and a cabman and sets fire
to a church."
     Shrapnel Stevens wins the big ones (of course), and Slough
eventually sees through his ploy, as we knew he would. Knowing
the inevitable does not in this case spoil the trip.

58.   Gallico, Paul. "Saint Bambino." In his Further Confessions
      of a Story Writer, p. 317-332. Doubleday, 1961.
     There may be more sentimental baseball stories that are worth
reading, but it would take some time to find them. Here Babe
Ruth, designated Saint (believe it or not!), drops by to give a
boy who doesn't care about baseball a little spiritual talking-to.
Well, what can the kid do but change his ways and become cleanup batter for his team? Yes, the corn is as high as an elephant's
eye, but the Babe's remarks to little Jimmy on why baseball is a
great game are not without merit.

59.   Graham, John A. Babe Ruth Caught in a Snowstorm. Houghton
      Mifflin, 1973. 280 p.
     This novel opens with a bang--several of them--in a brief chap-
ter describing a bloody brawl on some unnamed baseball field. Fans
and players alike are going at each other with fists, bats, a few .22
caliber revolvers and one "tactical defense utensil," i.e., a machine
gun. What is going on here, and why?
     A wealthy Mr. Slezak has recruited a team based only on the
members' desire to play. Ability is beside the point. The Wichita
Wraiths, whose home is Braintree, MA (why not?) have been founded
for one main purpose: "to give the players spiritual gratification
through good clean exercise."
     The title refers to Slezak's most prized possession, a figurine
of the Babe inside a glass ball filled with fake snow. He has carried
it with him most of his life. The Babe in the snow represents a
complex yearning for simplicity, innocence, youth, and fun, all to
be achieved through the Wraiths.
     The Wraiths take on local teams, and soon show such unexpected
skill that the Boston Red Sox seek to play them in an exhibition
game. The Wraiths defeat the Sox, and receive a franchise offer
from the National League. Things go well at first for the Wraiths in
their new professionalism, but it seems that a dream realized is too
great a burden to bear. Petty squabbles, stupid controversies, and
general dissension tear at the team; at one point they have lost 29
straight games, staged a player strike, uttered and published vile
accusations against Slezak; a star player commits suicide by burying
himself in the field--and the team's final game turns into the raging
travesty that opened the book.

When the indictments have been handed down and the bodies
hauled away, Mr. Slezak still has dreams of hardball glory, and is
speculating on the possibility of re-establishing the team under a
different name (though, alas, under the same management) somewhere in Central America.

This is a funny novel, with many out-loud laughs in its pages,
but it also points out one of the truths of cherished dreams; they
are often better cherished than brought to fruition.

60. Greenberg, Alvin. "Game Time." In his Delta q: Stories,
     p. 23-37. Univ. of Missouri Pr., 1983.

The low-keyed surrealism of this story nicely evokes the time-
lessness of a baseball game. A barnstorming team travels through
the South and into the Midwest, stopping, according to schedule,
to play intrasquad games, with or without--and more often without--
an audience. Most of the action takes place on a diamond in the
middle of a sun-baked Iowa cornfield. Seen through the eyes of
rookie Jesus Caracas, the game takes on qualities of slow motion,
even of eternity; the sun itself seems to stand still in the sky as
Caracas moves to catch a pop fly. The pace of the narrative effectively matches these impressions of time slowed down.

A good story, not just for the treatment of "game time," but
for the implication that the game stands somehow outside of the flow
of human events in a self-contained world of its own.

61. _____. "The Real Meaning of the Faust Legend." In his
     The Discovery of America, and Other Tales of Terror and Self-
     Exploration, p. 87-99. Louisiana State Univ. Pr., 1980. Also
     in Best American Short Stories, 1973. Edited by Martha Foley.
     Houghton-Mifflin, 1973.

"Who is there who isn't peddling himself to the devil in some
way?" This, the opening line in the story, is also its most important. A veteran minor leaguer (and college graduate with an M.A.)
didn't know what he wanted when he left school, but he found out,
and then he did it. He wanted a lifetime batting average of .368.
Greenberg does not tell us, but this is one point higher than Ty
Cobb's all-time best major-league lifetime average.

The player has never been able to catch on in the majors, but
with lowly Muncie he has, year in and out, hovered right around
his target average. On the day he learns that after these many
years his cumulative average is .36802, he quits the game. "I know
I got exactly what I peddled myself for," he concludes. "Who
doesn't, as long as he's willing to go all the way with it?" Many
don't, no matter how far they're willing to go, but this is a story
that will lead to some perhaps useful reflections by its readers.

62. Greenberg, Eric R. The Celebrant. Everest House, 1982.
     272 p.

This novel, as good as it is offbeat, stands with Harry Stein's
Hoopla (item 146) as one of the finest recreations of baseball and
American society in the early twentieth century. It is easy to call

a book "offbeat" if it departs from convention in any way, but the term seems fair when applied to The Celebrant. Of the relationships in sports fiction, few could appear more unlikely than that of Christy Mathewson, the great pitcher who came to the New York Giants from Bucknell College, and Jackie Kapp (born Kapinski), a Jewish immigrant who designs jewelry to fulfill his part in his family's business.

Kapp, a once-promising pitcher who had to abandon the game with a sore arm and under family pressure, sees in the brilliant, dignified Mathewson something he might have been himself, if only. The novel dwells in great and thoroughly researched detail on some of Mathewson's most notable games. Following a Mathewson no-hitter, Kapp commemorates Matty's achievement with a specially-designed ring that he gives to the pitcher. He follows this ring with several more to mark important points in Mathewson's career.

In spite of this homage, the two men rarely meet, and one would not call them friends. Yet Kapp identifies powerfully with the pitcher; he acknowledges this himself early on, but not until much later does the intensity of his sense of oneness with Mathewson become clear to him when a sportswriter friend compares Mathewson to Christ. The ballplayer is followed by multitudes who worship him, but at the same time secretly hope for his failure, that they may be free of the need to follow him, free of any obligation to try to imitate him in his dignity, his excellence, his glory.

Mathewson himself refers to Kapp as "the celebrant" of his works, and at last makes it plain to Kapp how much the jeweler's exquisitely-designed rings have meant to him as symbols forever keeping the past alive.

The novel ends in darkness, with the slowly dying Mathewson cast unmistakably as a Christ figure determined to drive the corrupt money changers of the Black Sox scandal from baseball's temple.

The Celebrant works so well in so many ways that its reading is consistently pleasurable and instructive. The college-educated Mathewson allows Greenberg to use some dialog insightful far beyond the ordinary range of baseball players' discourse; Greenberg's re-creation of the games, for all its diligently studied foundation, is never dull; his employment of real-life players is the equal of Stein's (consider, for example, his portrait of the famed--and notorious-- Giants manager, John McGraw), and his overall picture of what was a much more innocent United States, the Black Sox notwithstanding, is closely-observed, exciting, and informative. The phrase "must reading" is as easily tossed about as "offbeat," but having used the latter, why not the former? Read this book and see where legends are born.

63.   Grey, Zane.   The Redheaded Outfield, and Other Baseball
      Stories.   Grosset & Dunlap, 1920.   238 p.
      A collection of stories strictly for fun, with a lot of emphasis
on play-by-play action. The title tale concerns the antics of three red-headed minor-league outfielders; several of the stories, including "The Rube," "The Rube's Waterloo," and others focus on Whitaker

"Rube" Hurtle, a pitching phenom in the Worcester Eastern League.
The most interesting story may be the book's last, "Old Well-Well,"
about a fan who dies rooting his team on.

64.   Hall, James B.   "Yates Paul, His Grand Flights, His Tootings."
      In Stanford Short Stories, 1962, p. 27-43.   Edited by Wallace
      Stegner and Richard Scowcroft.   Stanford Univ. Pr., 1962.
      Thirteen-year old Yates works as an assistant to his father,
a photographer, and wants to impress Jane, his father's helper.
Jane is a grown woman.   Under the self-induced impression that
Jane will go for the athletic type, Yates buys his way onto an inept
local baseball team by promising to take publicity shots of the players.   Yates is pitifully ignorant, until the story's last paragraph,
of how distorted his perceptions are, as distorted as the out-of-focus
team in his old Speed Graphic's view finder.   A funny story, but a
sad one, too; it really is not much fun to watch Yates make a fool
of himself in his career as a young Walter Mitty.   That he has some
insight into his behavior may mean that he will not grow up to become an adult Mitty.

65.   Hanson, Nels.   "Homer."   Antioch Review 38 (Fall 1980):   449-
      461.
      This story's blend of realism and fantasy creates an eerie,
mysterious mood.   Collins, a minor-league outfielder, narrates.   He
describes the final game of the season, a sloppy contest in which
both teams score in double figures.   The team's manager is an abusive, repulsive lout who berates his players far beyond reason, from
batting practice to after the game.   Collins hates the man, but the
team's veteran, a former Yankee named Albie Gambo, gives Collins
some advice on keeping his composure in spite of the manager's obtuse tirades.
      The final game stumbles along until, with Collins and Gambo
in the outfield, an opposing batter hits what looks like a blooper.
Both Gambo and Collins run for it, but the ball unaccountably picks
up speed and height, and disappears over the stands for a homer.
"Like in Cincinnati," says Gambo cryptically.
      Long after the game, Collins retrieves the inexplicable ball; it
has come to rest nearly a mile from the stadium.   Seeking a ration-
alization of this event, he visits Gambo, who has been drinking.   The
old outfielder responds obliquely: "You hit the ball ... you catch
the ball, you slide, you run the bases.   You do it every day, not so
it gets easier, but so it gets harder, so anything you get you're
thankful for.   No matter how well you hit, a single or a homer, you
remember the ball has a mind of its own."
      "You can't live that way," says Collins.   "I know," says Gambo.
      A story dense with points of departure for analysis, only a few
of which are hinted at here.

66.   Harris, Mark.   Bang the Drum Slowly, by Henry W. Wiggen.
      Knopf, 1956.   243 p.
      Harris's second novel in the Wiggen manner, this has become

his best known through excellent motion picture and television adaptations. It is easy to see the reasons for the story's appeal, both for a popular audience and for directors searching out a piece with plenty of emotional impact.

Wiggen presents an account of substitute catcher Bruce Pearson's final season. Pearson, a holdover from The Southpaw, receives a diagnosis of Hodgkin's Disease before the season starts. His doctors tell him that the disease may kill him in six months. The first man he informs of this affliction is Wiggen, his roommate. Wiggen insists that his contract include a clause requiring that he and Pearson be treated as a package. They must play together, be traded or sold together. Management, in the dark about the pitcher's motives, agrees. Wiggen is, after all, their star southpaw.

What follows is a drama of life asserting itself before certain death, and not only Pearson's death, but the inevitable end for all. Long a sub-mediocre catcher with a few good physical tools, Pearson finally bears down, takes some counsel, and extracts a maximum from his limited talent. When word of his illness spreads among his teammates, the knowledge becomes a catalyst for greater team unity.

Pearson's salvaging of dignity and achievement in his final year, when he could easily have given up and gone home to die, is an act of courage. Harris does not press the issue, but Pearson does stand for everyman. To live bravely, we must live the best we can, without knowing whether we are to be granted six months, fifteen years, or eight decades. As easy as it would be for Pearson to fold up and do nothing, it would be equally easy for Harris to give in to sentimental wallowing in this novel. He doesn't, and neither do his characters. Harris plays the drama out with a spare hand, and his restraint enhances the honesty and depth of the story's effects. Aside from the book's other virtues, the continuing device of Wiggen as "author" (and indeed, "Author" is his new nickname) carrying on after his work The Southpaw is nicely managed.

67. _____ . It Looked Like For Ever. McGraw Hill, 1979. 276 p.
Readers who want to follow pitcher Henry Wiggen, lead character and "author" of the other Harris novels noted here, will see him at the end of the baseball line in this one, close to two decades after he entered the majors.

The novel opens with Henry receiving news that his old manager has died on the golf course. Henry not only does not get the offer he expects--and wants--to manage the club: he gets his release. The question is, what to do? The answer does not come easily. Wiggen bounces around from a flirtation with Japanese baseball to a brief job as a television announcer. At nearly forty, he has lost his fast ball, but he is a craftsman and can still retire batters. He catches on in mid-season as a short relief specialist for a California team. All goes beautifully for a month or so, but Fate has a card up her sleeve for Mr. Wiggen.

This novel falls a bit short of Harris's finest in the Wiggen manner; it comes fully alive only when Wiggen pulls on a uniform, and in most of the book he wears what athletes like to call "street

clothes." There are, however, some good passages. An irritated
Wiggen throwing as hard as he can to aged men in an old-timers'
game is one; another is his amused and almost fatherly description
of the "young savages" that make up his new ball club. Wiggen is
an easy character to like. He's talented, smart, a hard worker,
and, in spite of his saying otherwise, he is a "gentle man." He
writes a good account of himself, too, with Harris's help.

68. _____. The Southpaw, by Henry W. Wiggen. Bobbs, 1953.
        350 p.
    The first of Harris's books "credited" to pitcher Wiggen, The
Southpaw is a winner on all counts. It is a consistently enjoyable story
of growing up, not just of a young ballplayer's growing into a star, but
of a boy's growing into a man. With a good heart and a hefty amount
of well-described game action, the book will please any baseball fan.
    It is a relatively episodic book, but the episodes are like those
of life itself, weaving seamlessly one into another. The chief dramatic matter is Henry's decidedly peaceful attitude. At the height of
the Korean War, he has been rejected for military service because
"fighting roils my bowels." He accuses the Koreans, the Chinese,
the Russians, and the Americans ("and all the rest") of making fools
of themselves with their warlike conduct. An obnoxiously "patriotic"
sportswriter uses the fact of Wiggen's humane reaction to war
against him in a particularly offensive column.
    Henry's political and humanitarian sensibilities aside (though
they should not be tossed aside easily; until Henry Wiggen's debut,
rare was the athlete in fiction who received credit for a mind of his
own), The Southpaw contains some delightful parts. Wiggen's memories of backyard ball--he pitched "about 5,000 games of baseball
against the back of a house with a rubber ball"--will evoke memories
in many readers as they look back on their own unique ground rules
taking into consideration the placement of the clothesline, the at-
tribution of base hits by bounces, the difficulty of explaining bad
hops into the neighbor's flower bed. There is a nice scene in which
Henry's father, himself a talented player, instructs Henry in pitching's fine points in a vacant lot across the street from their house.
And there is Henry's account of his first visit, at sixteen, to a big-
league game: "In the morning I woke up, and it was like I dreamed
a dream so fine that you want to go back and dream it again...."
    Those who have looked with fresh eyes at the magnificent pic-
ture presented by a major-league ballpark will have no trouble understanding the fineness of Henry Wiggen's near-dream, nor will they
regret spending time with The Southpaw. It is one of baseball's
best novels.

69. _____. Ticket for a Seamstitch, by Henry W. Wiggen; But
        Polished for the Printer by Mark Harris. Knopf, 1956. 143 p.
    Henry Wiggen's problem in this enjoyable if rather attenuated
novel is new catcher Piney Woods, who, next to the dead Bruce
Pearson, is a fairly unappealing character. Woods has not only a
long way to go to grow up; his peculiar romance via the mails with

a seamstress from the West Coast is interfering with Wiggen's pitching. This interference is especially vexing since Wiggen is on the
verge of supplanting Hall of Famer Carl Hubbell as possessor of the
longest winning streak in major-league history.

Harris knows and loves baseball, and, luckily for the reader,
he also knows human character and writes of it with warmth and
tolerant humor here as in his other Wiggen books.

70. Hays, Donald. The Dixie Association. Simon & Schuster,
     1984. 384 p.

Hog Durham, "a thirty-year-old minor-league-rookie with a
smart mouth and a record of armed robbery" is the narrator of this
funny, serious novel. The story begins with Hog packing his
meager possessions in a cardboard box in preparation for his departure from the Oklahoma State Prison. The most valuable item
among his goods is a $600/month contract sent him by Lefty Marks,
the notorious one-armed Marxist manager of the Arkansas Reds,
Little Rock's franchise in the Dixie Association. The novel follows
Hog through a turbulent season with the Reds. During the year he
engages in a running battle with the authorities; his parole officer
wants to put him back behind bars, and detests Hog's decision to
play for the Reds. It seems the officer had persuaded the city library to offer Hog a pleasant, respectable job driving a bookmobile.

"It's why I went into crime in the first place," says Hog.
"To get enough loot to set up a library of my own. Hog, the librar-
ian. Got a nice ring to it, don't it?" Disdaining the library business, Hog, a natural power hitter, joins the Reds. The Reds are a
colorful (bizarre?) collection of players featuring Bullet Bob, a beer-
swilling old knuckleballer; a couple of Cherokee Indians; a female
first baseperson; some Cuban players on loan from Castro, and a
diverse group of oddballs and misfits.

The book's true topic is the conflict between state-sanctioned
repression and the individual desire to be free. Hog serves as the
focus for the struggle, made unmistakable in his decision to play
ball at the risk of going back to prison. The novel also concerns
personal loyalty and responsibility, and in it we see Hog change from
an almost solipsistic attitude to one far more in sympathy with others.
When he and his lover Pansy begin trading lines that recall Matthew
Arnold's "Dover Beach" ("Right now it's just me and you and the
darkness left and all the light there's going to be is what we can
make on our own,") we know that there has been a sea-change in
Hog's point of view.

This is a fine serious novel, then, but it is also one great
baseball story, with some of the best game action ever put down on
paper. Choices of the outstanding game passages are hard to make,
but one of the best describes the superb old Indian Eversole's perfect game, pitched before a Police Night crowd fired up with Hymns
to Jesus and visions of Law & Order: "It was pure baseball, pure
art ... when a man's right arm delivered us all for a while from our-
selves and the mean world made by men who, in the name of God
and money, conspired to keep us at one another's throats."

The Dixie Association belongs near the top of the list of American sports novels.

71.   Heinz, W. C. "One Throw." Collier's 126 (July 15, 1950):
      38+.
      A neat twist at the end of this little story of an aspiring minor-
league infielder gives the reader a pleasant, value-affirming moment.
The infielder, Maneri, is playing very well, but is down-in-the-dumps
because, he believes, the parent major-league team is ignoring him.
He learns otherwise.

72.   Hemphill, Paul. Long Gone. Viking, 1979. 213 p.
      In 1956, Stud Cantrell hits bottom. His eyes are bleary, one
shrapnel-loaded leg hurts all the time, and he can't sleep. He has
been summoned to manage the woebegone Graceville Oilers in the
lowest of the minors, the Class D Alabama-Florida League. The
Oilers "were determined to become the most pitiful club in the history
of organized baseball." For a grand $475 a month, along with a gen-
erous buck and a quarter a day meal money, Cantrell is privileged
to put up with whatever losers life in the sub-basement of organized
ball can throw at him.
      And there are some out of the odd lot here, not the least of
which is Q. Talmadge Ramey, Oiler owner, used-car dealer, and
homosexual evangelist announcer for station WGOD, booming its message to the heart of metropolitan Graceville, to all 1,600 of its residents.
      As must happen in stories of this sort, whether serious or
popular fluff, the arrival of the Savior from Nowhere cannot be far
away, and here the Savior comes dressed as Venezuelan catcher
Jose Brown, a mountainous man who bats over .400 and hits homers
at a marvelous rate. Jose's real name is Joe Louis, and Joe is black,
but not Venezuelan; certain parties in the Florida Panhandle were
not ready in 1956 to deal in a civil way with a black ballplayer, no
matter how many homers he hit. A little confrontation with the Klan
demonstrates the judiciousness of Joe's decision to assume a new
identity.
      With the help of Brown/Louis, a teenage 2d baseman, and a
group of has-beens and may-bes, Cantrell brings the team to within
a whisker of the league championship, only to be denied it through
blackmail.
      This is a bawdy, funny book. Hemphill has a good touch with
his characters, especially with Cantrell, who, in addition to working
as a player-manager of phenomenal ability, also epitomizes a down-
home philosophy in which baseball represents the pinnacle of
democracy. The aim is to hit the ball and "run like hell," and the
victory goes to the best players. Unless, of course, someone cheats,
as happens even in allegedly democratic institutions.

73.   Herndon, Booton. "The Big Inning." Saturday Evening Post
      225 (July 12, 1952): 31+.
      A story of minor-league exploits set in a small North Carolina

town, "one of those red-hot little baseball towns which make up the
Tarheel League." Manager Ab Walker's hair is thinning, and his
team's performance isn't helping the cause. His cleanup hitter is
in a slump, his shortstop plays as if in a dream, his pitchers are
erratic, and the local paper is basting him with vitriol in each
morning edition. Taking the paper's cue, the fans are howling for
Walker's dismissal.

Walker ponders his future as it would be without baseball. It
would prove pretty grim. He knows nothing but the game; all that
would remain to him would be unskilled factory work.

Is Walker going to pull out the big game and save his job? Do
they grow tobacco in North Carolina? Of course he is, and he's
going to do it not only by managing his team with the creativity of
a Harvard M.B.A., he's going to substitute at third base himself!
Makes a case that in popular sports fiction the most important quality
is honest, yet heroic, desire.

74. _____. "The Rube Nobody Could Hit." Saturday Evening
Post 225 (June 6, 1953): 76+.

At 36, Rudolph Kitchen no longer harbors any dreams of what
could be a pitching career in the majors. He has had some chances,
but luck has not been with him. Illness or injury or parental ob-
jections or a death in the family have all conspired to cut short
Rudolph's chances; now it doesn't look as though he will succeed at
anything more glamorous than running a service station or trying to
pull a few more harvests from the washed-out old family farm.
Rudolph is not bitter, but says wistfully, "I never really wanted to
be somebody; all I wanted to know was if I coulda been."

Rudolph does get one more opportunity to find out what "coulda
been" when his hometown Emporia team faces the Camp Amory team
in the state semi-pro tournament. Emporia is far behind when his
manager sends Rudolph to the mound in the second inning, but in
the remaining innings, against a team loaded with a half-dozen big-
leaguers in the service, Rudolph shows everyone, including himself,
what he might have done had fate not crossed his path unkindly.

Like several stories noted here (see item 45, for example),
this one concentrates on a single moment of athletic glory that saves
the life surrounding it from banality. It is a provocative psychological issue, and this is a good story.

75. Herrin, Lamar. The Rio Loja Ringmaster. Viking, 1977. 305 p.

Starts with popping fastballs, weakens in the middle innings,
and staggers from the mound in the ninth. The novel belongs to
Richard Dixon, a thirty-year old veteran of the majors, a pitching
star, conqueror of the Yankees in the World Series on behalf of the
Cincinnati club.

When the book opens, we find Dixon inexplicably pitching in the
Mexican bush leagues, struggling to finally obtain that coveted jewel
in the pitcher's crown, a no-hitter. As the game against a group of
semi-pros proceeds, Dixon's achievement of his long sought goal
falls in jeopardy.

This opening chapter is full of promise, with lively language, a sense of humor, and a good mythical reference. The book's title is an allusion to an ancient Aztec ball game in which, provided a player performed a certain extremely difficult feat, opposing players and officials would stop to sing a hymn of praise to the happy hero as a prelude to riot.

The whole does not work. After the opening, confusing chronological sequences and shifts in narrative voice are impediments to the story; Dixon himself grows less interesting, and the novel's end is a disappointing effort to restore some excitement. Very good in parts, however, and worth reading for those.

76. Heuman, William. "Brooklyns Lose." Sports Illustrated 1
     (Sept. 20, 1954): 31-33+.

Ted Kluszewski beats the Dodgers in the ninth with a home run, and the loss settles with ill effect on one of the Bums' most committed fans, Joe Armbruster. He snaps at his wife and son and can barely eat his supper. His Uncle Nathan says, "You gonna slit your throat tonight, Joe, because the Dodgers lost?" With the help of sympathetic neighbors, Joe pulls himself together and looks forward to the next game. A nice portrait of the impact on individuals and community of a beloved athletic team--and an unintentionally ironic one, since the Dodgers left Brooklyn not long after this story appeared.

77. _____. "A Real Flatbush Finish." Saturday Evening Post
     227 (July 10, 1954): 24+.

A touching and insightful story, one of the best entries from the Post included here. Manny Keefe, a Brooklyn garment worker, has to leave the shop early: his union has voted to strike. He comes home to his wife of thirteen years and his two children, and, as one might expect, the home front is short of sweetness and light. Manny and his wife, Mabel, have a hot argument over his role in the strike. It is one of those "I told you five years ago you should have done thus and so" exchanges that leaves a sour taste all around.

Manny seeks escape with a friend at that afternoon's Dodgers-Cards game. As the game moves along, the Dodgers getting the worse of it, Manny sinks into a miserable imagined scenario. This is it, he thinks. His wife is going to leave him. O.K. for her if that's what she wants. He'll rent a lonesome room in Flatbush. The kids will be ruined. They might turn out to be gangsters; those things happen.

Manny's mood turns with the Dodger's game: they pull it out in the ninth, and Manny goes home elated, winner of a small bet. He greets Mabel amiably, barely remembering what not so long ago looked like a serious fight.

The fan's life can be closely tied to the exploits of his or her favorite team, and this story is a compassionate illustration of how this dynamic works for one average working man.

78. Hoban, Albert J. "On Account of Darkness." <u>Esquire</u> 23
    (June 1945): 50+.
    A marine sergeant tells a fellow train traveler about a baseball
    game conducted in a Japanese prison camp between a scraggly group
    of American prisoners and a specially-imported team of Japanese pro-
    fessionals. What the American team has going for it is its pitcher,
    a former college standout; his clever maneuver in the fading light
    brings disgrace to the Japanese camp commander.
    An interesting propaganda exercise, and the tension building
    toward the end is adeptly created.

79. Honig, Donald. <u>The Last Great Season</u>. Simon & Schuster,
    1979. 384 p.
    Allie Brandon is a New York theatrical producer and ball club
    owner. He is brusque, impulsive, and convinced that this year,
    1942, is the year his team, the New York Lions, will be "a big,
    smashing, goddamned winner." He sleeps with a .38 revolver at
    hand, as well as a mistress whom he has promised he will stand by
    properly "after the season" when his head is clear enough to "ex-
    plain things" to his wife.
    Brandon is also a philosopher of sorts, and his conversation
    early in the book with a sportswriter about victory in sports as a
    manifestation of human supremacy over all the forces standing
    against us is worth reading. The speech ends with a vulgar but
    effective metaphor that reveals Brandon's character as well as his
    philosophy: "Winning puts you just a little closer to the stars.
    Losing? Losing gets flushed down the toilet."
    Brandon's meddling with the Lions is strongly reminiscent of
    George Steinbrenner's sometimes eccentric handling of the New York
    Yankees, but Brandon is more fun to watch. There are some funny
    vignettes here, including one in which Brandon dickers with another
    club owner for a first baseman. Brandon offers a straight cash
    deal, then, to sweeten the pot, throws in (from the deep recesses
    of his memory) a totally unknown high school player named Vernon
    Keek, whom Brandon ballyhoos as "the greatest natural talent to
    come out of New York since--since--Gehrig." The book's other
    chief character is Todd McNeil, a young writer who becomes per-
    sonally involved with the Lions as he covers them for his paper.
    The catalyst for much of the book's drama is the fate of a rookie
    centerfielder, a gifted player victimized by beanings. McNeil rages
    over the continued insertion of this man in the line-up, and, as he
    rages, loses the innocence that previously characterized his under-
    standing of the game.
    <u>The Last Great Season</u> is an enjoyable, thoughtful novel.
    Honig has written several well-received nonfiction books on baseball,
    and his understanding of the game, which is thorough and not in-
    nocent (but not jaded, either) comes through very well.

80. Hough, John. <u>The Conduct of the Game</u>. Harcourt, Brace,
    Jovanovich, 1986. 340 p.
    "The umpire shall be responsible for the conduct of the game

in accordance with these official rules and for maintaining discipline
and order on the playing field."
     This prime rule of umpiring becomes the call answered by Cape
Cod youth Lee Malcolm. Shortly after graduating from high school,
Lee spurns college for a professional umpire school in Florida, where
he is a star pupil realizing the promise of his first impressions behind the catcher in an amateur game: "It was my game," he says.
"Mine to ruin or to make right--the difference between noise and
music, between a free-for-all and the pretty game of baseball."
When played and officiated well, baseball is a pretty game, and Lee
Malcolm does his best to insure that his contributions add to the
game's beauty.
     It is not easy. His initiation to professional umpiring is made
doubly difficult by his big-brothering relationship with Eddie Snyder,
a hothead whose penchant for making and inviting trouble, whether
with a blown call on the field or with a pointlessly offensive remark
to a night-club stripper, is of award-winning quality.
     Lee Malcolm's talent takes him to the majors, where he becomes
embroiled in an ultimately tragic situation involving another umpire.
The event forces Lee from the game. This is a less than lighthearted
ending, but this is not at all a sad book. It is a story of considerable human dimension, one of depth and vivid characterization, of
growing awareness and growing up. There are some very moving
passages. An early one portrays the class outcast Lucinda Fragosi's
awkward comforting of Lee after the death of Lee's brother. Another
is the almost pitifully tender description of Lee's first passionate embrace with his girlfriend. The honesty of feeling and excellence of
narrative in these passages is present throughout the novel. One
for the heart.

81. Johnson, Nunnally. "No Hits, No Runs, One Error." Saturday
     Evening Post 204 (Dec. 19, 1931): 14-15+.
     A dose of Lardnerian cynicism carries this one along, with the
attitude supplied by the story's narrator, sportswriter Mapes of the
New York Globe. Mapes relates the intense week-long affair of New
York Maroons part-time outfielder Pep Howard. Howard meets a
chorus girl named Dotty through Mapes, and immediately falls for
her. Howard is even more stuck on himself than on Dotty, and laments his manager's refusal to play him against right-handed pitchers. Surely, he believes, he will show Dotty what a hero he is
if he gets a chance to play while she watches from the stands.
     He does get his chance, but while dancing around near second
base to impress Dotty, manages to get himself picked off for a rally-
killing out in a game against the Dodgers. Howard's rock-headed
play costs him a fine and a suspension, but Dotty's head is as dense
as Howard's: she thinks that the great noise from the pro-Dodger
crowd that greets Howard's faux pas means Howard has committed a
noble feat.
     "'Oh, Pep!' she bubbled. 'I was so proud! I thought you were
the cutest thing that ever lived on earth!'"
     Lardner himself could not have dissected mutual stupidities with
a much keener blade.

82. _____ . "Private Life of the Dixie Flash." <u>Saturday Evening</u>
<u>Post</u> 200 (June 2, 1928): 20-21+. Also in the author's <u>There</u>
<u>Ought to be a Law, and Other Stories</u>. Doubleday, 1931.
The "Dixie Flash," also known as Eddie O'Neil, ordinarily leads
a simple life. He goes to the ball park, collects a couple of base
hits, and chats with his wife Lila over supper about how the opposing players "ain't got a thing." After eating, he and Lila join teammate Charlie Bradley and his wife Ruth for a movie or a show.
Trouble comes with a slump. Eddie goes a wretched 1 for 27,
and life turns sour. When Lila suggests that he has been crowding
the plate, he sulks. What does she know? Eddie insults his friend
Charlie, questions his ability to play the infield, and retreats to a
speakeasy. What began as an apparently light domestic satire takes
on darker shades when we watch Eddie about to fall victim to a
blackmail scheme in the speakeasy. Eddie steers away from the set-
up by taking his wife's advice at the plate. All ends tenderly, but
it is plain that the moment's sweetness owes only to Eddie's present
success at the batter's box. Beneath the happy veneer lurks back-
biting, jealousy, and the fear of failure.
Johnson makes his points well, and slips in some nice details,
too, such as a bar girl's waiting for Eddie, "a confession magazine
in her hand to offer a literary touch to the scene."

83. _____ . "The Rollicking God." <u>Saturday Evening Post</u> 197
(Oct. 11, 1924): 8-9+.
"There's too damned much aesthetics going on round here!"
This is the final, despairing cry of slugging Smack Riley of the
New York Grays, delivered seconds before he clobbers a sportswriter with a bat. The writer, one Marshall Mount, has through
his pretentious analysis of Riley's performance persuaded Riley that
the latter is a--pardon the cliché--diamond in the rough, a veritable
Greek god. So caught up is Riley in Mount's lunatic insistence on
his classical virtues that before the season is far along he poses for
art magazines, and even takes a role as "the rollicking god" in a
Greenwich Village play. This foolishness could have only one end,
and it isn't a good one for the Grays.
A funny, nearly slapstick tale by the future filmscript writer
of "The Grapes of Wrath." Smack Riley's dance debut in the Village
is by itself worth the time it takes to look this one up in the library.

84. Jordan, Eileen H. "The Little League." <u>Good Housekeeping</u>
139 (July 1954): 46-47+.
Here is an example from a 1950s point of view of the wise woman
who knows her own husband. Joey Powell, eleven years old, is
overjoyed when former big-league pitching star Dusty Hawkes moves
in next door. Joey's parents know nothing about baseball, but Joey
knows the game in great detail, including the minutiae of Dusty's
career. A lefthander like Dusty, Joey wants to be a pitcher, and
enlists the former star's help in learning how to throw the ball.
Dusty also organizes a Little League team. The first sign of
trouble is Dusty's wife's pointing out that Joey has no fastball.

Come tryout time, Joey's pitches--the ones he delivers near the
strike zone--go rocketing off the bats into all sectors of the park.
Dusty is merciless in his appraisal of Joey's ability: "All that time
I wasted on you, and you weren't no good at all." Joey takes this
crushing evaluation in near silence.

It is up to Baby, Dusty's wife, to awaken Dusty to his shabby
treatment of the boy, and through her intervention Joey becomes
the official chronicler of the team. How does Baby effect Dusty's
eye opening? Well, she's a woman. "There's something special in
women; maybe it's the alien rib. Whatever it is ... it makes them
just naturally worry about men." And also, evidently, makes them
naturally cleverer than the objects of their worry. Thus what
could have been a good story of hero worship gone awry slips into
conventional sex-role stereotyping.

85. Kahn, Roger. The Seventh Game. New American Library,
     1982. 321 p.

Johnny Longboat, after a Hall-of-Famer's career, is pitching in
what will probably be his last time in the World Series' seventh game.
At the age of forty-one, his arm cannot take much more; whether it
will take him and his team, the New York Mohawks, through this
game is far from certain. The arm hurts all the time, but as Longboat goes through one scoreless inning after another, he ignores the
pain.

Between segments of the game, the novel goes on digressions
into Longboat's past and into the lives of those for whom Longboat
has been important. These include wife, lover, sportswriters, the
Commissioner of Baseball (who is a patent fraud), Longboat's dead
father (a poor Oklahoman) and his mother, an Indian. These inter-
ruptions of the game contain some interesting stretches, but one
often reads them more dutifully than eagerly, for the game is the
thing--and what a game it is, with Longboat crafting a near-perfect
game against a young black pitcher with a fastball that threatens
100 miles per hour. Neither pitcher has allowed a run when Longboat is working with the bases loaded in the ninth.

The baseball action in The Seventh Game is among the best in
any novel. Kahn makes the old saying come alive: he is very much
"a student of the game," not only of tactics and strategy, but of
personality and history. Johnny Longboat is a thoughtful, articu-
late character, likely to lead most readers to sympathetic responses,
either when he is striking out the neighborhood kids as a boy back
in Oklahoma, when he is trying to complete the seventh game,
white-hot pain streaking down his arm with each pitch, or when he
learns that he is a financial ruin on the verge of his retirement.

86. Kaylin, Walter. "Blaze of Glory." American Magazine 160
     (Aug. 1955): 30-31+.

A little moral lesson with the familiar elements: a cocky rookie
who thinks of little but himself, a veteran third baseman playing out
his last season, and a World Series showdown.

Joe Ferris has been called up from the American Association to

the parent club to provide an occasional breather for The Sailor,
for many years the best third baseman in the league. Ferris comes
from the minors with a fat batting average and a head to match.
He quickly sees that The Sailor has to push himself to get through
a game. Inevitably, Ferris starts at third, and, equally inevitably,
The Sailor shows what a gentleman he is by providing Ferris with
valuable tips on fielding and hitting. Ferris shows that his earlier
unpleasant attitude was probably no more than a cover for insecu-
rity; The Sailor's generosity humbles him and starts him down a new
path.

Similar in some respects, especially in the young athlete's offensive conceit, to Frank Rooney's "Loser Take All," item 252.

87.   Keefe, Frederick L. "Mama Drobeck and the Great American
      Game." New Yorker 27 (Sept. 15, 1951): 94+. Also in the
      author's The Bicycle Rider & Six Short Stories. Delacorte, 1970.
      A company of American soldiers is stationed near Pilsen, Czecho-
slovakia, shortly after the end of WW II. There is little to occupy
them save a baseball league they have organized. The main force
behind the league is Captain McCall, a pro ballplayer as a civilian.

One obstacle obstructs the games: the playing field doubles as
an area for a hard-working cleaning woman, Mama Drobeck, to hang
her laundry. It is not so bad when a couple of outfielders run
through the sheets and shirts chasing flies, but Mama Drobeck sees
red when an errant ball mortally strikes her favorite goose.

Through an interpreter and a new goose, Captain McCall makes
peace with Mama Drobeck. The chief part of his appeal, he thinks,
is his invocation of the President of the United States, and baseball's status as the American national sport. Mama Drobeck is quite
touched, but Captain McCall learns from the interpreter that his
airy patriotic defense was not delivered quite as he meant to put it.

A wise story of cultural collision.

88.   Keillor, Garrison. "Around the Horne." In his Happy to Be
      Here, p. 115-124. G. K. Hall, 1983.
      The manager of a hapless baseball team known as The Flyers
writes a guest column for the local paper ("Bill Horne is sick. Today's column is by Ed Farr.") in which he approaches his team's
dreadful performance with the outlook and jargon of a pop psychologist. Why did the catcher Milt have so many passed balls? Owing
to catching practice as a child with his father, Milt now regards a
fast pitch "as an attack on his masculinity.... With more counseling
and perhaps more protective equipment, I feel that Milt can make a
real contribution this year." The rest is in the same vein; the only
readers who won't laugh are pop psychologists themselves.

89.   Kinsella, W. P. The Iowa Baseball Confederacy. Houghton
      Mifflin, 1986. 310 p.
      Kinsella, a Canadian, spends much of his time in Iowa. He
returns here to the Iowa heartland he explored in Shoeless Joe, and
to a fantastic performance that goes beyond that novel in stretching
the boundaries of belief.

The Iowa Baseball Confederacy, a six-team league that flour-
ished in the 20th century's first decade, has been known to only
two men since 1908, Matthew Clarke and his son, Gideon. Gideon
"inherited" the knowledge from his father, who came by it in the
most natural of ways: lightning struck him, and when he recovered
his senses, he found that "the complete history of the Iowa Baseball
Confederacy was burned in, deep as a brand, vivid, resplendent,
dazzling in its every detail." That no one else has ever heard of
the IBC makes no real impression on the Clarkes, except to fill
them with a determination to bring to light the truth of the league's
existence. Matthew Clarke even writes a graduate thesis on the
league; his faculty advisors consider it a nice piece of fiction.

The Clarkes' "memories" of the league cut short in 1908, the
year the IBC All Stars played an exhibition game with the Chicago
Cubs, a team featuring the then-peerless double-play combination
of Joe Tinker, Johnny Evers, and Frank Chance, along with pitching
great Three Finger Brown. The game took place at a field outside
Big Inning, Iowa; Big Inning is now Onamata, and no one remembers
it as anything else.

In a novel unfettered by conventions of time, place, or logic,
the obvious way to find what happened in Big Inning that summer
of ought-8 is to slip through a crack in time to make a personal investigation. Without much to-do, then, Gideon and his brother
Stan, a long-struggling minor leaguer, take a little hike one night
up an Onamata railroad spur to the site of the old Big Inning ball
field. From there, they materialize in Big Inning on the outfield
grass, the night before the Cubs' arrival. Big Inning is in a tizzy
of anticipation; Stan and Gideon fit right in, to the extent that the
IBC All Stars adopt Gideon as a good-luck mascot (he looks like an
albino), and put Stan in the line-up.

When the game gets under way and goes into extra innings,
Kinsella runs wild and leaves the reader breathless. We learn that
an Indian named Drifting Away "tampers with the reality of Johnson
County, Iowa," and is manipulating the game for his own purposes.
The game goes on, inning after inning, day after day; by the time
the winning run crosses the plate, the players have been at it for
over 2,000 innings, most of them in a steady rain that washes away
the town and rots the players' clothes on their bodies. Reality as
we know it disintegrates completely. An outfielder runs to New
Mexico after a fly ball. A statue plays as a substitute; a Cubs infielder plays while lying on a cot. Other players are shot, struck
by lightning, and lifted to Heaven. Leonardo Da Vinci comes by in
a hot air balloon.

There are several messages embedded in the novel. The most
important may be the inadvisability of sticking to one's perceptions
and commitments, no matter what. Insistence becomes obsession too
easily. The Iowa Baseball Confederacy is an often amusing, generally entertaining book; it would have been better without the hokey
religious symbolism that runs through it. Was it really necessary,
for example, that the big game last 40 days and 40 nights? Did
Gideon really have to come to Big Inning equipped with a trumpet?

Despite its excesses, the book is an engaging novel of baseball, time travel, and history, and will furnish a few afternoons' relief to readers overdosed on the contemporary world.

90. _____. Shoeless Joe. Houghton Mifflin, 1982. 265 p.

Shoeless Joe precedes The Iowa Baseball Confederacy by a few years, and shows the direction Kinsella longs to travel, back in time. His characters do this literally in the second novel; here, historic figures come to the present to regain the lives that a hard world denied them.

The novel's narrator is Ray Kinsella. We can pardon the cuteness of Ray's surname, although we hardly needed to be hit quite so bluntly with the close connection between the fictional Ray and the real-life author. Fortunately on this count, "Ray Kinsella" is the name of a character in a J. D. Salinger story ("A Young Girl in 1941 With No Waist at All"), and Salinger plays a prominent part in this novel.

Ray is a goodhearted Iowa farmer who builds a magical ballpark in one of his cornfields. Soon the players from the 1919 "Black Sox" appear on the field, led by Shoeless Joe Jackson himself. Ray's field is a good, pure country place where the old-timers' suspension by Commissioner Landis cannot hold. The corrupt power of the gambling interests cannot hold sway over Ray's innocent motives and the sweet country air.

Ray's mystic baseball mission is not yet complete, however. The same "voice" that instructed him to erect his cornfield park sends him on a quest to New England to ease the pain of the reclusive Salinger. In a good section of the story Ray "kidnaps" Salinger and drives him over 100 miles to attend a Twins-Red Sox game at Boston's Fenway Park. The meeting between Salinger and Ray is comical and almost believable, and leads in a rather roundabout way to Salinger's "rapture" back at Ray's park, where Shoeless Joe & company invite J. D. to go "out" with them after a game. The question is, "out" where?

Like The Iowa Baseball Confederacy, Shoeless Joe walks a narrow line between convincing fantasy and hybrid corn. Few will come through the book without spotting a strand or two of silk on their shoulders. The novel is good fun, though, moving in many places (Ray's relationships with his wife and daughter are particularly so), and has a fine sense of the game's mythic dimensions.

91. Koch, Claude F. "Clayfoot." The Antioch Review 23 (Summer 1963): 221-230.

A man's fourteen-year-old son makes an odd remark about pitchers: they "aren't the same any more"--and it sends his memory wheeling back to his own youth, when he and his friends were far from affluent baseball fans in the suburbs of Philadelphia. The boys could seldom afford to see their gods, the A's and the Phillies, but the semi-pro sandlot players from the surrounding towns were their flesh-and-blood heroes. Of all those men, one stands out in the narrator's memory, and that is the "Old Man," Clayfoot. Clayfoot was touched by grace, for he had years ago been given a pitching tryout with the Yankees. He hurt his arm in the tryout, and saw his big-league promise evaporate on the spot, but he continued to bear himself with an air of consummate professionalism, even on the dusty sandlot fields.

The narrator and a friend, Peanut, worked as batboys at the games. The most memorable game they worked was the game in which Clayfoot threw his last pitch. Late in the game, obviously hurting, Clayfoot tried to put extra stuff on the ball in a difficult situation. The pitch fooled the batter, but it ruined Clayfoot's arm for good. The batter tapped back to him, but he couldn't toss the ball to first for what should have been an easy out.

Clayfoot walked off the field, his dignity preserved, and hugged the narrator. He gave his glove to Peanut. The boys understood that they had witnessed something momentous, beyond the words at their resources to describe. Back in the present, the narrator decides to ask his son to explain his curious remark, for "One never knows what a child has come up against, and how words have failed him."

A moving and enlightening story, well told.

92. Lardner, Ring. "Alibi Ike." In The Best Short Stories of
     Ring Lardner, p. 35-52. Scribner's, 1957.
     Alibi Ike (born Frank X. Farrell) is one of the classic characters of American fiction. Ike is a pro ballplayer, and a highly talented one, but he cannot do anything without apologizing for it or excusing himself. A teammate jokes that Ike's middle initial must stand for "excuse me." If Ike makes a great catch, he would have been camped under it but he couldn't pick up the flight of the ball. If he takes a called third strike, it's because he thought he only had one strike on him. If he decides to go to bed, it isn't because he's sleepy: it's because "I got some gravel in my shoes and it's killin' my feet." Alibi Ike cannot be straightforward about anything, not even about the girl he loves. He can't admit that he loves her; instead, he claims to feel "sorry" for her. This widely anthologized story is on sports fiction's required reading list.

93. _____. "Harmony." Ibid., p. 149-166.
     An aging big-league outfielder's one real joy is singing barbershop quartet harmony pieces with a group filled out by his teammates. He grows moody on and off the field when one of the four, a washed-up pitcher, goes down to the minors. Salvation appears, after a couple of miserable seasons, in a rookie whose voice is as strong as his arm. The most amusing, and at the same time most pathetic, aspect of this enjoyable story is the outfielder's long and obsessive denial of the obvious, that his old singing partner can't throw the ball any more.

94. _____. "Horseshoes." Ibid., p. 205-226.
     It's just after the World Series, and Grimes, the ballplayer who made a game-saving catch and hit the winning homer in the finale,

fills in a sportswriter on "what really happened" to the opposition's
star player, Speed Parker. Parker and Grimes go back a long way,
to schooldays, when a prank of Parker's resulted in Grimes's expulsion. Since then Parker was blessed by incredible luck, while
Grimes had to scramble for everything. They faced each other in
the Series, Parker a "star" more by luck than skill, Grimes a fringe
utility man. The title of this piece, surely one of Lardner's funniest stories, is an old epithet hung on players deemed more lucky
than talented. Parker makes the big mistake of bestowing the title
on Grimes, and through Grimes's rage justice at last prevails.

95. _____. "Hurry Kane." Ibid., p. 87-107.
    The narrator, a catcher, speaks straight to the reader, saying
"If you wasn't the closest-mouthed bird I ever run acrost, I wouldn't
spill this to you." The tale he tells concerns "Hurry" Kane, a farmboy pitcher whose fastball makes the legendary Walter Johnson's
look like a change-up. Kane leads his team to the pennant and a
World Series victory, in spite of romantic troubles and a brush with
the bookies. Though not up to the standard of Alibi Ike (how many
characters are?), Kane, "a bone-headed sap," is still a memorable
creation.

96. _____. Lose With a Smile. Scribner's, 1933. 174 p.
    "This pm we got a game with a club called the House of David
witch aint in no league but they are members of a religious sex in
Michigan and Stengel says Jack Quinn will pitch the hole game for
our club because the other club all wears beards and he says they
have got 4 pitchers name Mathews Mark and Luque and John and
Mathews is a left hander." Whew! This excerpt from one of Danny
Warner's letters to his sweetheart Jessie is typical for its novel
abuses of the language. Danny, also known as "Rudy" because he
sings like "Rudy Valet," is breaking in with Brooklyn in the National
League.
    Danny is no sparkling intellectual, and he seldom thinks ill of
himself, but he isn't nearly the graceless clod that Jack Keefe is in
You Know Me Al. It is easier to be sympathetic with him in his
struggle to stick with the Brooklyns. Unlike You Know Me Al,
which consists only of Keefe's letters, Lose With a Smile features a
balanced exchange of correspondence between Danny and his girlfriend, a shy, insecure, self-effacing young woman. Their letters
to each other are full of frustration and hope. The final two letters,
written on the same day, suggest that maybe these two souls will
work out their frustrations together. But it is only a maybe.
    As in some other Lardner fiction, characters from real life ap-
pear in prominent roles. Here Casey Stengel plays a leading part.
Lose With a Smile lacks the freshness of You Know Me Al; the
epistolary approach is wearing a little thin. It is a more compassionate book than the earlier one, however.

97. _____. "My Roomy." In The Best Short Stories of Ring
    Lardner, p. 283-302. Scribner's, 1957.

The narrator tells us why he stopped hitting during the past
season. It isn't because he lost his batting eye. No, the blame is
his roommate's. His roomy, a left-handed slugger from Michigan,
is completely insane. Elliott, the madman, is a fearsome pinch-
hitter but impossible to live with. He likes to let the bathwater
run all night, shaves in the middle of the night, and takes elevators
on joyrides, among his other eccentricities. This is an interesting
story for the undercurrent of violence running through it. Even
when Elliott is cutting up in amusing fashion, there is a sense that
this man is something more dangerous than a mere baseball flake.
A chilling scene when he smashes a mirror with his fist gives some
warning of the gruesome information Elliott sends his old roomy in a
note at story's end. A topnotch piece; there is always more and
darker business going on in it than shows clearly through the story's
initially humorous surface.

98. _____. "Women." In his Love Nest, and Other Stories,
      p. 83-104. Scribner's, 1926.
      During a ball game, the conversation on the bench turns to
claims of what could have been, if only.... It is a funny story,
with some clever come-backs from the players, but it also contains
the characteristic Lardner acid. A young player whines because he
isn't playing; an older player goes on at irritating length about what
a wonderful star he would be if only women had not held him back.

99. _____. You Know Me Al; A Busher's Letters. Scribner's,
      1925. 247 p.
      Jack Keefe, one of sports fiction's most unforgettable charac-
ters, tours the American League and sends regular letters home to
his friend Al Blanchard. Keefe pitches for the White Sox. He has
a good fastball and a fair spitter; he also leads the league in ego-
tism and stinginess. Keefe never loses a game because of his own
mistakes: he loses because of "rotten support" by the Sox or because some "lucky stiff" got a hit off him by swinging the bat with
his eyes closed.
      Keefe's letters are riddled by a fixation on money, both on how
much he plans to make and on how much he has spent. He sends
Al detailed lists of his expenditures, down to two bits for tobacco--
"both kinds."
      Keefe claims to be "the happyest man in the world" over his
marriage to a woman of his brief acqaintance, but his only real love
object is himself. He's a blowhard, an alibier, a tightwad, and a
knucklehead. With such a fundamentally unattractive character as
its centerpiece, how does the book hold the reader's tolerance, let
alone interest? It does, and Lardner's genius accounts for it.
Keefe's letters constitute the entire book, and Lardner did an inspired job of using them to reveal Keefe for what he is, not only
through his petty and selfish concerns, but through his fractured
grammar and peculiar spelling.
      You Know Me Al also nicely evokes the atmosphere of big-
league baseball and American culture in the early 20th century.

Many real-life players turn up in Keefe's letters. His comments on
the hotels, restaurants, and other trappings of the sporting life
become more valuable the further the times in question recede into
the past. The book has worn well; it invites re-reading, and should
continue to do so as long as the game endures.

100.   Lewis, Orlando F. "Old Peter Takes an Afternoon Off."
       In O. Henry Memorial Award Prize Stories, 1922, p. 177-195.
       Edited by Blanche C. Williams. Doubleday, 1923.
       A gentle, good-feeling story about a former star pitcher who
has become a Latin instructor for his old college, and an expert but
unpublished authority on the local moundbuilders. Peter Simpkins,
also known as Old Peter or, behind his back, as "Old Simp," has
reached middle age with, it seems, all his triumphs well behind him.
No publisher wants to take a chance on his moundbuilders book; he
is frustrated, lonely, and laughed at.
       One afternoon he attends a Yankees' game after another dis-
piriting interview with a New York publisher. Several remarkable
events happen to Old Peter in the stands, culminating in an act of
gallantry that wins him first a night in jail, but then some well-
deserved recognition.
       The story gives a good picture of crowd behavior in the
Yanks' glory days, and when Old Peter takes his seat, who is up at
bat? Why, Babe Ruth himself! (First published in the Popular
Magazine in 1922.)

101.   Lowry, Robert. "Little Baseball World." In Great Baseball
       Stories, p. 149-168. Edited by Jerry D. Lewis. Tempo Books,
       1979. Also in Best American Short Stories, 1947. Edited by
       Martha Foley. Houghton, 1947.
       Nineteen-year old Helen has been a devoted radio follower of
th Reds for the past two years. Game after game she huddles with
her radio, letting Red Barber describe the action to her. She turns
his accounts into larger-than-life mental images.
       Like many fans, Helen turns to sport to make up for an empti-
ness in her own life. She has a badly crippled hand that she hides
with a glove whenever she goes out, and her outings have become
less frequent as her baseball obsession has intensified. She fears
the outside, and is sure that the world will find her ugly. She can
better manage her little baseball world, so personal, so private.
       The change comes when she attends her first game in person
with her brother. The field and the players are so much smaller
than they have appeared in her mind's eye; smaller, yet so public
that she rebukes the little world she had made from the radio broadcasts and, in the end, rebukes her reclusive way of life. A fine
story for its insight into a fan's life and for its portrait of a young
woman coming to terms with herself. (First published in Mademoiselle in 1946.)

102.   McCullough, David. "The Baseball Business." In Stanford
       Short Stories, 1960, p. 55-65. Edited by Wallace Stegner and
       Richard Scowcroft. Stanford Univ. Pr., 1960.

Floyd Wither graduates from high school and leaves Iowa for the first time. His destination: umpire school in Florida. Floyd admires baseball's history and its "science," but he is not overfond of the players themselves. Although given the thumb at umpire school because of his height (he's a full five-feet one), Floyd nevertheless gets "the Call" to become an umpire--any kind of umpire--during a revival meeting at Yankee Stadium. Why not? When he exits, he's on his way to Little League ump school in Scranton. Serious undertones concerning freedom and responsibility underlie the laughs here.

103. McGeehan, W. O. "Baseball Betty." Collier's 74 (Sept. 6, 1924): 6-7+.
    An odd story in which a young woman functions as a sort of angel of compassion and justice. She makes her first appearance in the press box where the writers cover the New York Mastodons. There she gently corrects the official scorer's mistaken call during a previous game, urges a caustic writer to reconsider his mean treatment of a slumping player, and congratulates another writer for a "splendid denunciation" of Umpire Burkett.
    Betty nearly disappears from the story as the author describes an important late-season series. She resurfaces when a street mob, angered unjustifiably by one of Umpire Burkett's calls, threatens his life. Betty steps into the ugly scene and deftly extricates Burkett. Later, she and Burkett marry.
    The author's motive, presumably, is to show how the feminine influence can allegedly bring tenderness and compassion to the sweaty dens of sport.

104. McMorrow, Tom. "The Most Valuable Louse in the League." Saturday Evening Post 230 (Sept. 7, 1957): 30+.
    The title character is Big Sam Cromwell, an American League relief pitcher who, like most good relievers, has one great pitch. Sam's is a bewildering change-up that floats up to the plate, slow, fat, unhittable. Sam's temper is quick, however. He gets along well with no one, including his catcher, Strobski, who tells the story. A crabby attitude usually proves no big problem for a relief pitcher; sometimes it helps. Sam has another problem: he fancies himself an incipient fastballer, and the winter after he wins the Most Valuable Player Award on the strength of his change-up, he develops a "new" pitch. His new pitch, a fat, slow, eminently bashable "fast" ball, earns him a ticket to the minors. There he rejoins Strobski, who has been cut from the team but rewarded with a farm-team manager's job. It will be up to Strobski to restore Sam, if possible, to his former status as obnoxious bullpen ace.
    A fairly entertaining story; catcher Strobski's character is friendly and appealing. The story also features a brief description of Sam's sad faring against a Yankee team including Mickey Mantle, Yogi Berra, and Bill Skowron.

105. Magnuson, James. The Rundown. Dial, 1977. 207 p.

The Rundown opens with a nice passage in which New York
Warriors scout Ron Price and a couple of his colleagues are sitting
in the stands in some Midwest stadium, watching one of the young
local heroes toss a no-hitter. Price knows the boy would walk
batter after batter in the majors, where the hitters would lay off
his high fast ball, but he and his cronies enjoy the spirit of the
game, and Price allows that the pitcher is, at least, a prospect.

Price, a former folk hero in New York (he starred in a World
Series game with a home run his only season in the majors), has
accepted his retirement from play with grace, in spite of the two-
faced treatment he received from the Warriors owner, Fred Brennan.

Following the no-hitter, a phone call changes Price's life. It
is Brennan, all but begging Price to return to New York; he wants
Price to protect his twenty-year-old daughter Carrie from unspecified
malefactors. Brennan's concern looks well-grounded; Carrie has recently taken a beating at the hands of abductors.

Price takes on the job, and finds himself immersed in a quag-
mire of suspicion, double-dealing, and violence, including the late-
night murder in a corner of the Warriors outfield of the team's
premier player.

Of more interest than who did what to whom, and why, is the
personality of Fred Brennan, a sports tycoon with a heart as big
and pure as a very small rhinestone. Through Price's observations,
Magnuson shows how an owner with a cold style can all but destroy
a good team. A passage aboard an airliner in which a young pitcher
comes unglued after a tough loss is striking, as is Brennan's pitiless
reaction to the player's outburst.

Not near the top of the baseball novel heap, but often interesting, and sometimes quite gripping.

106. Malamud, Bernard. The Natural. Harcourt, Brace, 1952.
     237 p.
     Few can be unfamiliar by now with the Roy Hobbs story, thanks
to the excellent film adaptation starring Robert Redford. Beware,
however: the film takes a far more optimistic view than the novel,
which points to darker, sadder territory.

Hobbs does double duty in the book, serving as both the "natural man," an innocent, almost a primitive (like so many rubes)
thrown into the corrupting influences of society, and as a vehicle of
mythic exposition. As King Arthur drew Excalibur from the stone,
so Roy Hobbs, by the power of his own hands, draws his magical
bat Wonderboy from the heart of a tree split by lightning. As Arthur
led his Knights of the Round Table, so Roy Hobbs leads those warriors of the Big Apple, the New York Knights, through the enemy
parks.

There is a lot going on in this novel. Maybe there is a bit
too much happening, especially on the mythical level, for the story
to settle into a comfortable, sweet-swinging groove. Yet the occasional strain for significance does little to spoil a highly-involving
story of innocence lost and redemption nearly obtained. Malamud
draws frequently from the well of baseball lore, giving the novel an

historical sense of great depth. His descriptions of baseball action
are as far beyond the pedestrian norm as Wonderboy is beyond the
standard Louisville Slugger.

When young Roy first displays his pitching skill against the
Whammer, a Ruthian figure who takes on Roy at a county fair, "The
ball appeared to be a slow spinning planet looming toward the earth.
For a long light year he waited for this globe to whirl into the or-
bit of his swing so he could bust it to smithereens that would settle
with dust and dead leaves into some distant cosmos." Here as elsewhere, Malamud's syntax shines. In its penetration of the batter's
vision, in its grand excesses of universality, in its anticipation of
the sudden outburst from stillness that is so much at the soul of
the game of baseball, and in its juxtaposition of high-flown language
with down-home lingo ("bust it to smithereens"), this passage and
its kin do a rare job of reaching for, and grasping, the sport's most
essential characteristics.

Exaltation of baseball is not the final name of Malamud's game.
The book closes in sorrow, with a boy's pathetic plea to Roy echoing
that of the boy who long ago, they say, begged Shoeless Joe Jackson
to "Say it ain't so, Joe!" when word of the Cubs star's role in
Series-fixing became public. Facing his own hard question, Roy
"wanted to say it wasn't but couldn't, and he lifted his hands to his
face and wept many bitter tears."

No one who cares about baseball, or about contemporary
American fiction, should let this novel go unread.

107.   Marsh, Howard R. "The Cactus Pitcher." American Magazine
        114 (Sept. 1932): 52-55.

Shades of Iron Man McGinnity, the indefatigable pitcher who
worked both ends of doubleheaders in the early 1900s. From out of
the sagebrush comes a long, lean pitcher who not only leads his
team to the pennant, but pitches the final three games of the season
to do it.

It begins on the Terrapin Rancho, a dude ranch where Buster
Noyes, also called the Sheik of Swat, spends his post-season vacation.
He hires Vic Williams to pitch batting practice to him on a daily basis, three hours a day. Noyes laughs at Williams when the job makes
the boy's arm almost too sore to lift. Williams presses on, though,
and even after Noyes leaves the ranch, Williams forces himself to
throw hour on end, day after day. His dedication wins him a major-
league tryout, and, as irony must have it, who but Noyes can be the
batter Williams faces at the climactic point in the pennant-clinching
game? When life is like this, no one believes it, but this story in
the Horatio Alger "bound to rise" vein is still fun.

108.   Mazor, Julian. "Jack Kelsey's All-Stars, 1941." In his Wash-
        ington and Baltimore, p. 123-154. Knopf, 1968.

Billy John Lansdowne, not yet fifteen, has just finished a summer playing with Jack Kelsey's All-Stars, a barnstorming team that
plays in the North. All-Stars team members come from the Carolinas,
Virginia, and Maryland.

Kelsey was a little doubtful when he met Billy, owing to the boy's inexperience, and Billy was somewhat astonished to learn that he would be playing for money, not for fun. As Billy relates the past summer's events in a guileless way, it becomes apparent that Kelsey, who is in his mid-60s and has seen it all, took Billy on as his personal charge. In spite of a sometimes harsh manner, Kelsey showed that he cared personally not just for Billy, but for even the most difficult young men on his team. It is in Kelsey's treatment of Luther Breen that his concern shows in depth. Breen is a seventeen-year old with great potential and a bad attitude. Kelsey keeps a tight rein on him, and Breen chafes under it.

The crisis comes after a morning when Kelsey has driven Breen and Billy around Washington, D.C., on a sight-seeing trip. He leaves them in the afternoon with instructions to go back to their hotel to rest before the game scheduled for Griffith Stadium that evening. Breen, however, knows Kelsey's next destination, a D.C. brothel, and drags Billy off to see the place. The two blunder in on Kelsey at the house; the subsequent events reveal Kelsey's compassionate attitude toward his boys in an interesting and subtle fashion. The game at Griffith Stadium is rained out, but at least two of Kelsey's players win something more meaningful than one more game.

109. Meyer, Robert. "The Blonde Who Attracted Baseballs."
     Collier's 132 (Sept. 4, 1953): 38+.
     With some exceptions, popular baseball fiction in the 1950s was in approximately the same condition as the magazines that carried it: tired, run-down, and exhausted of ideas. This story indicates to what futile lengths a writer would go to break away from the standard formulae that had lost all their fizz.

The premise here is the inexplicable ability of a young lady named Celinda to draw baseballs to her person, provided they come off the bat of Petie Katosh, a rookie with Brooklyn. No matter where she sits, Petie hits the ball straight to her. One deduction leads to another, and soon the Brooklyn management stations Celinda in the centerfield bleachers. Petie collects over 40 home runs by July, and opposing teams are helpless--until Petie faces Six-Fingered Grogan, so named for the extra thumb he sports on his pitching hand.

The rest deserves silence. The story doesn't work as satire, science fiction, or fantasy, but it does point to the unpleasant residue at the bottom of the formula barrel. Like popular music of the early '50s suffocating on a diet of "How Much Is that Doggie in the Window" claptrap, baseball fiction, and sports fiction in general, is waiting for a new wave to roll it out of the doldrums.

110. Molloy, Paul. A Pennant for the Kremlin. Doubleday, 1964.
     185 p.
     Infuriated at the U.S. government because of what he considers its brainless intransigence in disarmament negotiations, Armistead E. Childers, president and owner of Childers Hotels of Dis-

tinction, tears up his will and dictates a new one leaving all his
property to the Soviet Union. This property includes the Chicago
White Sox. Childers promptly dies, and the Kremlin takes over the
Sox, in third place that July.

The response of officials, public, and players is less than
enthusiastic. "Anybody thinks we're going to work for a bunch of
Commies, they're crazy," announces Sox player representative Bunny
Beadle.

Mikhail Deborin comes from Russia to manage the Sox; he bones
up on the game by studying baseball cards on the trip. Deborin
soon offers the players incentive bonuses, forbids sign-stealing and
product endorsement, and brings along his beautiful daughter Tasia
to help demonstrate his humanity. Bunny Beadle, the team's principal Bolshevik-hater, falls for Tasia, and before the book's end has
proposed to her. And, before the season's end, baseball turns from
national game to international crisis involving Cuban defectors, the
CIA, the Soviet Ambassador, the United Nations, and a seventh game
of the World Series played in a snowstorm--climaxed by an unprecedented play that leaves Deborin anticipating an excursion to Siberia.

This novel is both amusing and seriously motivated by an
interest in better U.S.-Soviet relations. The Russians' naivete
about the U.S. may be a touch overstated--they plan to employ body-
guards as protection against Chicago mobsters, for example--but
given the rampant distortions both nations routinely entertain about
each other's daily affairs, this badly-informed approach may not be
far from what the truth would prove.

111. Morgan, Gerald. "Back of Third Base." Harper's Weekly 58
      (Aug. 16, 1913): 18-20.
      Romantic tomfoolery and thuggish skullduggery combine in this
little piece of New York City big-league color. The heroine is the
lovely Miss Smith, daughter of a Wall Street tycoon. She takes in
ball games as often as possible, preferably from a spot behind third
base. Miss Smith is a lady not only of wealth but of generosity, as
the snack vendors in the stands have found when she tips them.

The hero is Cliff Gordon, rising young pitcher for the home
team, a man "good in the pinch." The go-between is one of the
park police, who introduces the sweet, rich girl and the clean,
humble pitcher to each other. Can it come as a shock that the two
find themselves in love?

The villain is a lowlife cur named Louie Kelly, a gambler, maybe a pimp, and an abuser of women. Kelly hatches a plan to wrest
Miss Smith away for his own nefarious purposes, but Cliff Gordon
intervenes in heroic, two-fisted style.

There are no literary pretentions here, but the story will
help interested students of American culture track the popular taste,
and psychology, of the times.

112. Morgenstein, Gary. The Man Who Wanted to Play Center Field
      for the New York Yankees. Atheneum, 1983. 288 p.
      What baseball fan who has watched a "fleet" centerfielder race

to the fence to backhand a line drive--one of baseball's prettiest,
most poetic plays--has not wanted, at least for a moment, to be that
center fielder? The dream of the everyday man to take his place in
the ballfield sun is a powerful one that turns up persistently in
baseball fiction. In It Happens Every Spring, The Year the Yankees
Lost the Pennant, and even in The Universal Baseball Association,
the dreamer takes the field. It happens again here, and as is often
the case, making the dream flesh is an act with some unexpected
costs.

Danny Neuman is a New York writer who devotes his time to
an auto mechanics journal, his earlier dreams for a law or a medical
career so much scrap. His marriage is a trial. His former liberal
concerns have floundered in the struggle for the legal tender. He
is only in his thirties, but the promises of his life are winking out,
one by one. His last chance for self-redemption, so it seems, is to
become the Yankees' next center fielder.

After following a vigorous conditioning program administered
by a couple of transvestite neighbors, Danny shows up for an open
tryout with the Yanks. Recognizing the fan appeal in catering to
Danny's aspirations, the Yankees sign him up, and ship him off to
the lower reaches of their farm system. When Danny finally comes
back to the big leagues, he gathers some notable insight into the
price of dreams realized.

113. _____. Take Me Out to the Ballgame. St. Martin's, 1980.
320 p.

In Coover's The Universal Baseball Association, defeated-in-
real-life J. Henry Waugh determines the lives and deaths of imaginary
players who are far more substantial than Waugh's three-dimensional
acquaintances, and perhaps more substantial than Waugh himself.
Here Cal Fleisher, an obscure chicken factory worker, conducts himself like J. Henry, but without Waugh's imagination.

Fleisher's worklife is a dud; his sex life is, like Waugh's,
equally unsatisfactory. His one delight is his status as the number-
one fan of the National League's Buffalo Matadors, a team who play
ball in a manner that lives up to their nickname, "The Mats." No
matter how miserable the Mats, Fleisher follows them with slavish
loyalty. Things heat up when a promotion-minded owner takes over
the team. The Mats start winning, and Fleisher leads his fellow
true-believers in fan worship that resembles a prologue to fascist
paradise. One demented step leads to another, and when the Mats'
scoreboard flashes a message urging the fans to dispose of a particularly nettlesome rival, Fleisher takes the cue seriously.

A dark satire on the too-frequent compulsion of sports fans to
live vicariously, and on the unprincipled team owners who manipulate
these neurotic individuals' errant devotion.

114. Morris, Henry. "Lillian." Story 9 (Aug. 1936): 63-71. Also
in That's What Happened to Me. Edited by Whit Burnett. Four
Winds, 1969.

The narrator, a high school sophomore, attempts to impress

his girlfriend Lillian by taking her to a pro baseball game. In spite
of an initial hitch at the gate, things go well, until a loudmouthed
fan provokes the boy to a surprising act. A funny but sensitive
story.

115. Needham, Henry B. The Double Squeeze. Doubleday, Page,
     1915. 249 p.
     A quartet of baseball stories, two of novella length. In the
title piece, one of the two long ones, the Giant-Killers, managed by
one Tris Ford (who strongly resembles Connie Mack) are in the
World Series versus the Phillies. Gamblers have arranged for the
disappearance of Ford's star player, infielder Win Shute. Shute
wakes up from a drugged sleep the day of the opening game to find
himself aboard a ship bound for Naples. The Jinx features Giant-
Killer pitcher Smoky Bill Dart with a dead arm. Farcical events
follow the demise of Dart's arm, including the apparent drowning of
Dart when he drives his car off a ferry, and--this is a nice mythical
touch--his "burial" beneath the pitcher's mound, in accord with his
last wish, in the Giant-Killers' home park.
     Two short stories, "A Treeful of Owls" and "Releasing the
Film Princess," complete the volume. This is light work, though no
more so than most sports fiction of its time. Perhaps the most interesting aspect is the book's introduction written (or at least
signed) by Connie Mack, in which the famous Athletics manager
describes author Needham's travels with the Philadelphia club preparatory to writing a series of magazine articles on baseball.

116. Neugeboren, Jay. Sam's Legacy. Holt, Rinehart & Winston,
     1974. 370 p.
     Small-time gambler Sam Berman, in trouble with hoods for
debts he cannot cover, has an unusual fascination with athletes who
have faced great physical tragedy bravely and resourcefully. The
book opens with Sam in attendance at New York Knick Dave Stall-
worth's return to basketball after a life-threatening illness; later
Sam recites in almost a litany the names and ailments of such athletes
as Monty Stratton, Herb Score, Lou Gehrig, Pete Reiser, and others.
     Interspersed through the novel are chapters from a memoir by
Mason Tidewater, a former star pitcher, now a janitor. The memoir,
titled "My Life and Death in the Negro American Baseball League:
A Slave Narrative," is ingeniously set in an antiquated typeface that
recalls dusty, long-forgotten novels, forgotten as thoroughly by most
of us as the world Tidewater's memoir describes. The memoir re-
counts the career of a black player motivated in large measure by
fury; it is enough to make the book worth the reader's time, and is
in some ways more interesting than the novel surrounding it, which
packs too much brooding significance onto the backs of rather insignificant characters. An ambitious book, but aside from the Tidewater
narrative not up to the author's best.

117. _____. "The Zodiacs." Transatlantic Review, no. 20
     (Spring 1966): 84-95. Also in the author's Corky's Brother.
     Farrar, Straus, & Giroux, 1969.

Louie Hirshfield is the worst athlete, and the best student, at Brooklyn's P.S. 92. Louie, a great baseball fan, has a fine collection of player autographs. He appoints himself, in effect, "general manager" of a baseball team composed of his friends and acquaintances, including a fastballer and small time punk named George Santini. An enjoyable story, complete with team dissent, rumbles, and triumph.

118. Norris, Hoke. "Voo Doo." Georgia Review 22 (Summer 1968): 222-235.

A couple of gifted "hillbilly" ballplayers, identical twins, with thin lips, cold eyes, and a taste for revenge, devise a unique scheme to insure that their talent carries them beyond normal limitations. Narrated by a weak-hitting outfielder who becomes the twins' co-conspirator. A nice ploy: the outfielder's "literary aspirations" allow some good satire of baseball cliché-mongers.

119. O'Connor, Philip F. Stealing Home. Knopf, 1979. 308 p.

This book is two novels, not one. One of them is very good, the other is little but high-toned afternoon television set out on the page. The good pieces almost all take place in or around Pee Wee league baseball fields in Ohio, where Benjamin Dunne has taken on the job of coaching his son's team. It is a mixed bag of early adolescents, but they share a common obnoxiousness that Dunne labors to overcome. The most offensive of the lot is his own son, Bobo, who treats his father like a dolt.

When the book opens, Dunne harbors homicidal fantasies about Bobo. His business is not going well, his wife is about to go off on an absurd arts & crafts tangent, and his daughter Suzie seems to be headed for a crack-up. Dunne ponders the desirability of fading away to a remote corner of the country with nothing but the clothes on his back and a few dollars cash.

The bad parts of the novel include most of the domestic to-do, some of which, like Marilyn Dunne's plunge into therapeutic costume design, is so overdone that it isn't believable, and fails as satire. Skip those parts. When the action moves to the field, the book takes off. Dunne knows the game, has a good sense of how boys comport themselves, and can enlist a reader's sympathy--or antipathy--toward a character with a few effective strokes. Any baseball fan will delight in the game descriptions. A high point comes when, using a toy whistle and a lot of imagination, Dunne settles a riot that has broken out due to incompetent umpiring.

120. O'Hara, John. "Bread Alone." In his Pipe Night, p. 80-85. World, 1946.

Mr. Hart, a car-washer from Harlem, wins $10 in the company baseball pool. He decides to treat himself and his thirteen-year old son to a game at Yankee Stadium, the first game he has attended in two decades. By mid-game he is miserable, lost in guilt as he ruminates over what the money could have done for his family's tight finances. Worse, his son doesn't really seem to be enjoying the

game, either. It requires a foul ball from Joe DiMaggio's bat to
turn the day around for both Hart and his son.

Hart is a hardworking, responsible person, and like so many
who fit that description, he has an extremely hard time indulging
himself in even a simple pleasure. The story's title indicates its
lesson, and it is a sound one, well presented.

121. O'Rourke, Frank. "Close Play at Home." Saturday Evening
     Post 227 (Jan. 1, 1955): 18+.

The Eagles are a listless baseball club, buried in last place at
mid-season, scarcely going through the motions. Hardly anyone
comes to the park, and financial disaster looms for the owner. The
owner changes managers at this point, bringing in old Si Collins, a
throwback to baseball's rough and tumble infancy. Collins inspires
the team through his knowledge of the game and his leadership, and
the players begin to produce. By the end of the season, the
Eagles are tied with the Giants for first place, and the season's final game, played out here in an exciting way, determines the pennant
chase.

Some will scoff at the notion of a team over twenty games behind at mid-season threatening to win the pennant, but it has been
done. Readers who remember the Giants of the mid-'50s will get a
kick out of the last game; O'Rourke adroitly works characters from
real life, including umpires, into his story.

122. _____. "Flashing Spikes." Saturday Evening Post 220
     (May 29, 1948): 32-33+. Also in Great Baseball Stories.
     Edited by Jerry D. Lewis. Tempo Books, 1979.

Don't be put off by the melodramatic title. It makes this one
sound like stereotypical heroic eyewash, but it is a sound story,
and one of historical interest. The action takes place in some mid-
American town on a hot afternoon in 1936. The town team takes on
a barnstorming group of old pros. The old players have lost the
speed and strength that carried them to the majors or Triple-A ball,
but they know the game so well that they handle the town's best
youngsters with ease.

The chief interest in the story is the presence of shortstop
Dane Bjorland, a member of the infamous Black Sox, whose character
could be based on the real-life Buck Weaver. Bjorland is playing
out the string in the bushes, taking terrible razzing and enduring
the self-righteous spiking of historically ignorant schoolboys.
Bjorland is presented with great sympathy as a tragic figure. It is
a moving story in spite of a sentimental conclusion. For a detailed
look at Buck Weaver, see Harry Stein's Hoopla (item 146).

123. _____. "The Last Out." Saturday Evening Post 220 (Jan.
     31, 1948): 29+.

Fifty-year old Sam is, and has been for many years, a clubhouse man for a bottom-rung minor-league team. Sam knows more
about baseball, and is a better judge of talent, than anyone around
him, including the team's manager, twenty years Sam's junior. But

who will heed a man who earns his keep cleaning the shower room
and gathering foul balls?

Who but Babe Bricker, a big-league scout in whom Sam recog-
nized the promise of stardom in spite of Bricker's early rough and
unlikely play? On the night of the story, Bricker is in the crowd
to scout the team. After the game, he meets Sam in the empty clubhouse, where he acknowledges Sam's exceptional player judgment
and brings him an offer of a scouting job.

O'Rourke makes the most of his material and the obligatory
happy ending. He very nicely recreates the impressions of the clubhouse, the chipped cement floor, the banged-up lockers, the sweaty
smell of the players' quarters, and, as in the best popular literature of this genre, makes even the predictable ending satisfying because of the sympathy he develops for his main character.

124. _____. "Last Time Around." Collier's 129 (March 29, 1952):
18-19+.

A good example of the aging-player theme. Kit Morgan has
played for thirteen years, a decade of those in the majors. Now in
his mid-30s, he recognizes in spring training that he has lost "a big
step" in his ability to cover his position. With a roster full of
talented young players, his team has no choice but to release him.

Morgan knew it was coming, but the knowledge does little to
cushion the impact of this moment of truth and time. He keeps up a
front of good cheer around his former teammates, but back in his
hotel room he sits on the bed and stares at his hands. The story
ends with Morgan in better shape, claimed on waivers by another
team, and given the promise of a coaching job in the minors the next
season. He knows that he has beaten the Reaper only by a whisker,
and this season will truly be his last time around.

125. _____. Nine Good Men. A. S. Barnes, 1952. 215 p.

Literature for the hard-core fan who doesn't want his or her
athletic fiction cluttered with gratuitous off-the-field trappings.
O'Rourke furnishes action, and plenty of it.

Nine Good Men tells the story of the National League Blues and
their manager, Don Shelby, during a trying season following the
Blues' first pennant in three decades. The new season finds them
struggling to stay in the first division as the press, fans, and front
office make Shelby's life difficult. He knows that the team's problem
is one of youth: most of the players are too young to know how to
handle the success of the previous year. Compounding Shelby's
trials is Arch Compton, a former sportswriter now employed as a
Blues PR man. Compton hates Shelby. When Compton was beginning
to make a name for himself as a journalist, a maneuver by Shelby set
his career back several years. The setback was deserved, for
Compton had proved himself an unprincipled, if not heartless, man.
He now savors Shelby's predicament, and does his best to make it
worse.

The novel focuses on Shelby's efforts to bring his team as a
whole back to a fit mental state. There are several good passages,

including one in which Shelby meditates on his team while immersed in a bathtub. Most of the emphasis is on game descriptions that O'Rourke executes with smooth capability. A season-closing series against the Brooklyn Dodgers and Jackie Robinson finds him at his best.

Extraordinary coincidence department: one of the Blues' pitchers is Herb Score, a fastballing lefthander who suffers a serious injury when struck by a batted ball. In real life, Cleveland fastballer Herb Score was struck in the eye by a line drive in 1957, a blow that came close to killing him and that cut the bloom from his career long before its time.

126.   . "One More Pennant." Saturated Evening Post 224
        (May 31, 1952): 28-29+.

A dark departure from most Post sports stories in that the hero does not triumph but instead admits defeat, and not just defeat in one game, but defeat forever at the hands of time.

Duke DiSalvo has starred in center field in the American League since the mid-1930s, but the end is near. It is, in fact, a lot closer than he is willing to admit when the story opens. Although his best friend and his manager urge him to take himself out of the regular line-up, Duke is convinced, or wants to convince himself, that the team needs his regular services to win the pennant.

Duke looks himself in the eye during a tense game with Cleveland. He makes some good plays, but his body aches, and he wishes the game were over. With Larry Doby at bat and runners on base, Duke sees the light. Doby hits a fly ball to deep center; Duke knows immediately that he has not reacted properly to it, and as he drives himself back to catch up with the ball, he "knew it was going from him in one terrible, empty-bodied moment, all the greatness and instinct and beauty that had been second nature ... gone as he ran; ran not for the ball, but for the years that were vanished, for the body that was strong, for the memories and the joys of yesterday." The ball sails over Duke's head, the game is lost, and Duke's career is done.

This is strong writing, coming to grips with what cannot be escaped. The pat little cheery note at the end is there only from obeisance to Post standards. "One More Pennant" is at heart a story about a loss that can never be escaped; it is, ultimately, a story about death.

127.   . "Terrible-Tempered Rube." Saturday Evening Post
        227 (July 17, 1954): 24+.

Rube is a hayseed pitcher with great skill offset by a temper with a short, fast-burning fuse. Opposing players, managers, his own teammates, all upset him with the least provocations, but he reserves his most spectacular tantrums for umpires. He throws his glove on the pitching rubber, flings the resin bag toward third, and screams invectives at the ump as his teammates drag him off the field (foreshadows of a certain St. Louis pitcher in the 1985 World Series).

His manager makes good on a promise to get rid of Rube after an ultimate outburst; the next season, Rube returns to lead his new team to the pennant, and humbles his old boss in the process. The reason for Rube's newfound consistency lies in his marriage, but it is not a marriage with the "Made in Heaven" stamp upon it. This story shows O'Rourke's usual skill at quick character development, and is more than usually funny.

128. Phillips, Michael. "The Class D League." North American Review 5 (May-June 1968): 13-18.
A solid class-A story set in the lowest of the low minors, narrated by a marginally-literate third baseman. The old third sacker leads off the story speaking of shortstops, and "the slickest I ever seen was a kid by the name of Julio Vasquez." Vasquez, a Cuban, joins the team in the spring, in top shape from playing winter ball in Cuba. Vasquez can do it all--run, hit for power and average, and field his position beautifully. He has one little problem, however: he listens when fans in opposition ballparks throw insults at him. A sensitive lad with a quick temper, his play at first comes undone under the taunts from the stands. In time his anger turns to determination; by the time he returns to a stadium where the fans gave him an especially rough time, he can channel his outrage into base hits and great plays. He caps his performance with a home run, followed by a slow, gloating trot around the bases. From home plate he hoists a finger to the crowd. It is not the finger used to proclaim that "We're number one."
A riot commences with various objects hurled from the stands. The upshot: Vasquez is suspended, quits the team, and flees to the sub-minor leagues of Mexico, from which he never surfaces.
A funny story, but not without sorrow, for Vasquez's chagrin is as real as his talent, and the narrator's sympathy, though inarticulate, is also real. "And besides that," he concludes, referring to his inability to keep the boy from bolting the team, "I didn't even speak the poor kid's language."

129. Plimpton, George. "The Curious Case of Sidd Finch." Sports Illustrated 62 (April 1, 1985): 58+.
An April Fool's Day ruse about a 28-year old New York Mets rookie whose pitches have been clocked at close to 170 miles per hour, over 60 mph faster than Nolan Ryan at his peak. If the claims about Sidd Finch's abilities were a little less extreme, the story would be almost believable; as it stands, it rates as a good satire on the age-old theme of the rookie that blooms in the spring, then disappears. Plimpton concocts a full biographical account (as full as possible; Finch is an elusive sort) of the pitcher, including reminiscences by his former landlady and his Harvard roommate. Numerous photos of Met personnel, and one of a locker with Finch's name on it support the tale's stab at credibility, but discussion of Finch's baseball artistry as seated in his mastery of Yoga, a picture of him astride a camel near the Egyptian pyramids, and several other absurd details provide a tip-off to the story's facetiousness.

We are eager to be gulled, however, and Plimpton's joke hauled in a fair catch of readers ready to lay aside their skepticism.

130. Pohl, Frederik. "The Celebrated No-Hit Inning." In Baseball 3000, p. 143-163. Edited by Frank D. McSherry, et al. Elsevier-Nelson, 1981. First published in Fantastic Universe (Sept. 1956).
      Boleslaw, a difficult-to-handle star pitcher, finds himself borrowed by future baseball administrators for a cameo appearance in the chronological distance. Baseball's rules and style of play have changed so much that an inning without a hit has become a thing of wonder, and two-thirds of the line-up is composed of robots. On his return to the present, "Boley" is a much more tractable man, though he refuses to take batting practice against the pitching machine.

131. Poverman, C. E. "A Short Apocryphal Tale of the Sea My Father Would Deny Anyway." In his The Black Velvet Girl, p. 229-237. Univ. of Iowa Pr., 1976.
      The narrator's brother is Ruby Whittaker, a 6'8" star pitcher for the Red Sox. Ordinarily Ruby's physician father accompanies him by yacht across the Gulf Stream, through the Bahamas and from there to spring training, where he watches his son work on his pitches. The dramatic interest of this story comes from a near-confrontation Rudy stumbles into in an out-of-the-way bar, where he has carelessly dallied with a knife-carrying man's wife. Rudy escapes, barefoot, but tears his feet apart dashing down a local road.
      Later, back at the yacht, an ominous group of villagers appear silently on the edge of the dock. One fears reprisals, but what the villagers have in mind is something more in keeping with Rudy's fame.
      An odd but interesting story, with more going on in it than the above summary suggests.

132. Powers, James F. "Baseball Bill." Collier's 119 (April 26, 1947): 102+. Also published as "Jamesie" in the author's Prince of Darkness, and Other Stories. Doubleday, 1947.
      Set in the time of Coolidge's presidency, this story features a young boy, Jamesie, who idolizes Lefty, star pitcher for the hometown team and a big-league prospect. Lefty, unfortunately, is crooked. He throws a game after betting against his own team. Jamesie can hardly stomach the talk of Lefty's crookedness, but when he visits Lefty in jail, the truth is finally too much to deny. A good study of a small-town boy whose reverence for the clean-living, square-dealing heroes of pulp baseball fiction cannot bring him through the fall of his own local hero.

133. Quigley, Martin. Today's Game. Viking, 1965.
      Barney Mann, manager of the National League doormat Blue Jays, is on the spot, his job at risk pending the team's performance

against the mighty Warriors. The Warriors are in first place, and occupy that spot in considerable measure due to Mann's trading ineptitude. He has shipped Jerry Adams, a prominent pitcher, to the Warriors in exchange for a young outfielder who has so far been a bust at bat.

Today's Game is a relatively brief, fast-moving novel, and may also be the ultimate novel about a single game. From the point at which "The Star-Spangled Banner" is played, description of the game consumes the rest of the book--nearly half its length--in detailed, inning-by-inning fashion, with the line score updated after each inning. The first half of the book sets the stage, with Mann planning his team's best possible line-up against Jerry Adams. The game is set up, in part, as a grudge match in which Adams, feeling betrayed by his old friend Mann, will do his best to set the Jays down. The game is interesting from the point of view of tactical considerations, and is well-told. Personality development is pretty thin, but here the game itself is the thing, and those with a taste for immersion in baseball detail will savor the book.

134.   Roth, Henry H.   "The Cinderella Kid."   New American Review, no. 7 (1969): 204-215.

A boy from an orphanage apparently loses his chance for baseball stardom when he suffers an early arm injury. A few years later his arm has mended, but when he looks at his old coach, he sees no happiness about his cure, only greed. He would rather be a teacher than join the organized hypocrites of pro ball. The passage in which he discovers his healthy arm is exciting, and sets the reader up well for the ironic conclusion. (This is not the Henry Roth who wrote Call It Sleep.)

135.   Roth, Philip.   The Great American Novel.   Holt, 1973.   382 p.

A frequently hilarious and imaginative but finally irritating novel. It irritates because it promises much, contains many good moments, but, long before it closes, turns into a bore that the reader finishes only from a sense of obligation. The book spends too little time at what it does best, replaying baseball history in a comically absurd style, and too much at what it does worst, expounding satirically on American political and cultural realities at large.

The premise suggests delight, if not greatness: the Ruppert Mundys of Port Ruppert, New Jersey, are exiled from their home when the Pentagon takes it over during WW II. Bereft of their fans and their home park, the Mundys, always dressed in their visitor grays, become the wandering outcasts of professional baseball, the embarrassment of the Patriot League (the now forgotten third major league, we learn). Roth's characters are a bizarre lot. They include a peg-legged catcher, a one-armed outfielder, a dwarf, a senile third baseman, and a variety of other twisted and odd escapees from the draft who form the heart of history's most inept club. The Mundys compile the worst record in the annals of pro ball, and in their disgrace lies the dissolution and the excision-from-history of the entire league.

When Roth sticks close to the game, the novel satisfies. It is rooted in a love of baseball; to make such effective fun of an institution, one must love it, or love what it was meant to be, or what mythology says it is.

The novel's narrator is Word Smith, an aging sportswriter. Mr. Smith lacks a "y" at the end of his first name, but not because he doesn't deserve it. The reader can only wish that Smith and Roth had shown a little more reticence and let the boys play ball, however lamely.

136.   Rosenfeld, Isaac. "The Misfortunes of the Flapjacks."
       Harper's 194 (June 1947): 556-561. Also in the author's Alpha
       and Omega: Stories. Viking, 1966.
       What begins as an evidently comic story shades into the pitiful, and in the end approaches the tragic. The narrator is a former trainer with the minor-league Flapjacks. Now he is but a hanger-on, though a welcome one. The Flapjacks are aptly named, for as baseball teams go, they are truly flat as a pancake. Their big hitter carries an .071 average; three of the starting pitchers are sore-armed and the fourth keeps falling off the mound owing to an ear infection that has affected his balance. The manager has lost his mind and babbles incoherent "instructions" to the boys. The club owners have abandoned the team: no one is getting paid, and it looks as though this season will be the team's last.

There are some funny passages early on, but by the time the Flapjacks are run out of a miserable "party" in a hotel and stranded in a town they travelled to by mistake, the mood is sad. The last paragraph presents Eglantine, the one-time power hitter, flailing helplessly at three nothing pitches. "God damn it," says the old trainer, "all that power and that glory gone to waste." It is a sentiment that reaches out well beyond the confines of baseball.

137.   Runyon, Damon. "Baseball Hattie." In A Treasury of Damon
       Runyon, p. 325-338. Random House, 1958.
       Baseball Hattie, a steadfast New York Giants fan--or "bug," as fanatics were termed in the old days--saves the integrity of the game by exercising a skill acquired in a shooting gallery upon her talented but corruptible husband, left-handed ace Haystack Duggeler. A nice little story with a "heartwarming" twist in the last two paragraphs.

138.   Schramm, Wilbur. "My Kingdom for Jones." Saturday Evening
       Post 217 (Nov. 25, 1944): 12-13+. Also in Fielder's Choice;
       An Anthology of Baseball Fiction. Edited by Jerome Holtzman.
       Harcourt, Brace, Jovanovich, 1979.
       For sheer nerve, few (if any) baseball stories can surpass this one. Set in the days of Tinker, Evers, and Chance, when the Brooklyn club was known as the Superbas, it features a horse who becomes the sensation of spring training by playing third base for Brooklyn, and by playing it well. That such a story could work at all defies belief, but it does, and almost as well as Jones picks off line drives with his teeth.

139. Serling, Rod. "The Mighty Casey." In <u>Baseball 3000</u>, p. 173-
      210. Edited by Frank D. McSherry, et al. Elsevier/Nelson,
      1981. Also in <u>The Stories of the Twilight Zone</u>. Bantam,
      1963.
      The Brooklyn Dodgers are playing poorly until the arrival of
pitching whiz Casey, a blank-faced boy with a smoking (literally)
fastball and a curve that takes more bends than a backwoods mountain road. A chance line drive fells Casey, and during routine
medical attention the truth comes out: the Mighty Casey is a robot.
This is a typical <u>Twilight Zone</u> episode, if lighter than most, for
its moral tag, but the story is better on paper than in its television
production. The portrait of the Brooklyn manager relishing his
club's ability to win, at last, is quite good.

140. Shaw, Irwin. "No Jury Would Convict." <u>New Yorker</u> 13
      (Oct. 2, 1937): 56-58. Also in the author's <u>Short Stories:</u>
      <u>Five Decades</u>. Delacorte, 1978.
      An amusing and at the same time sympathic look at a con-
firmed, apparently life-long, rooter for a subpar team. "The man
in the green sweater" comes "all the way from Jersey City" to watch
the Dodgers play the New York Giants, but he finds little to cheer
about, and a lot to lament. He vows to abandon the Bums, but in
the end "he went back to Jersey City, leaving his heart in Brooklyn."

141. _____. <u>Voices of a Summer Day</u>. Delacorte, 1965. 223 p.
      Benjamin Federov spends an afternoon at the local ball field,
watching the game, and especially watching his adolescent son play
center field with the same grace that characterized Federov's play
as an amateur. His son Michael shares more than his father's skill
with the glove; like his father, he can't hit.
      The game serves as a jumping-off point for a set of connected
reveries ranging across the whole of Federov's life. The shifts from
the present day in 1964 to earlier years do not take place as
smoothly as one would like, but the novel does allow for some enjoyable observations of family relations in Federov's memories. There
are some trenchant passages, such as Federov's rejection by an officious government agent during a Depression job application. The
reason: his body, trained for football and fit as possible, exceeds
by a few pounds the allowable weight-to-height ratio. "But you
have the body of a god," his mother raves. "They should be built
like you, those maniacs...."
      Father-son and brotherly relations are also well-observed. At
one point in the game Federov ostentatiously catches a foul ball.
Later Michael accuses his father of embarrassing him by showing off.
"All the fellows know it.... Nobody likes his father to be con-
spicuous." A younger Federov greets his brother Louis after playing
a particularly bad football game. Louis is bloody and bruised, the
result of a challenge to a fan who was heckling Federov.
      The mechanics of the book don't quite work, but the charac-
ters are attractive, there is enough emphasis on sport to please the

fan, and the issues raised by a man's review of his life are significant enough to deepen the book's meaning.

142. Sims, Marian. "Pitch Your Own Game." Collier's 96 (July 13,
        1935): 18-19+.
        A Depression message to stand fast on your own ground, re-
gardless of others' desires, for to stand fast means to find success
in both love and career.
        This little moral surfaces in the decision of law graduate Johnny
Cason to sign for his first summer out of school with a team in the
South Atlantic League. He signs in opposition to the wishes of his
girlfriend, Kay, and her father, a powerful lawyer. Although Johnny
plans to take the bar exam, his father is in financial difficulty, and
Johnny feels obligated to earn his own way. A decision like this in
popular fiction could have only one result in 1935: Johnny wins 20
games, and, through his courage, also wins both Kay's heart and
his future father-in-law's respect.

143. Small, David. Almost Famous. Norton, 1982. 416 p.
        An entertaining and thoughtful, if sometimes numbingly slow-
paced, novel about choice, despair, obsession, and responsibility.
The chief character is Ward Sullivan, who in his mid-30s tends a
peanut-sorting machine in a peanut butter factory. He takes good
care of his old Cadillac, shaves thoroughly, and plays a table-top
baseball game for which he keeps meticulous records. He believes
that he is trying to keep his life simple.
        He is trying to avoid life altogether. The thing he was "born"
to do, play professional baseball, was denied him by a car wreck the
night before he was to join the Boston Red Sox, a dozen years before the story opens. All that remains of his baseball career are
some minor-league trophies, a uniform in a plastic bag in his closet,
and the old Caddy, presented as a bonus when he signed with the
Sox.
        The route Sullivan follows back to the world of action with a
promise for the future makes a good story in an old-fashioned sense,
one populated by a variety of interesting characters. One of the
best-realized is Shaw, the aged, washed-up relief pitcher on Ward's
old team, a man who represents the opposite of the awareness that
Ward eventually reaches.

144. Sorrells, Robert T. "The Phone Call." American Review,
        no. 19 (1974): 125-148.
        Ferris, a talented semi-pro third baseman, makes his living
in Arkansas by running a sporting goods store. He might well have
made it to the majors, but he quit trying after an embarrassing play.
The real issue at the story's center is the conflict between father
and son, and how a father's fear of failure can keep his son from
achieving the success within his grasp. Sorrells does a fine job
here of showing how bad lessons learned early can sour a man's marriage, his talents, and his whole life.

145. Stanton, Will. "Dodger Fan." In Best from Fantasy and
     Science Fiction; 7th Series, p. 195-200. Doubleday, 1958.
     First published in the Magazine of Fantasy and Science Fiction
     (June 1957).
     Fans of the Brooklyn Dodgers were famous as a group for
their dedication to the team. Dodger fan Jerome is on vacation, doing what he likes best: watching the Dodgers on television with his
wife. The team is losing, however, and Jerome can't stand it. He
goes for a walk, and, through the assistance of an unusual travel
agent, goes to Mars. The whole of Martian culture is ready for his
inspection; all its secrets, including a method for achieving universal peace, are his for the taking. All his interest turns to
watching baseball in a stadium specially constructed by his hosts.
When he finally comes back home, his wife hardly knows that he's
been gone: she's been too busy watching the Dodgers on the tube.

146. Stein, Harry. Hoopla. Knopf, 1983. 366 p.
     A superbly-researched and engrossing recreation of American
baseball and culture at large in this century's second decade. The
tale's final focus is on the World Series fix of 1919, when the Chicago White Sox, rechristened the "Black Sox" when the dirty wash
was hung out in public, threw the Series to the Cincinnati team.
Stein guides the reader to the fateful year of 1919 through two major characters, to both of whom he permits the luxury of telling
their stories in the first person.
     The two characters share a dependence on sports, but they
are far apart from each other in both literary and worldly sophisti-
cation. We first meet sportswriter and all-around reporter Luther
Pond, "Jack Public's favorite snoop in high places," in a long
opening chapter in which he covers the Jack Johnson-Jim Jeffries
fight in Reno, Nevada, a contest "that stopped the country dead in
its tracks for three weeks."
     Narrator number two is George D. "Buck" Weaver, White Sox
infielder and one of the players banned for life for his part in the
fix. Weaver is at best mildly literate, but his narrative portions
are never dull. The book's forward momentum falters a bit at times,
especially in some of Pond's sections. But even these stretches are
interesting enough in themselves.
     Through Weaver, Stein portrays the White Sox as victimized
for years by owner Charles Comiskey's skinflint form. Whether
gypping his players in major ways (exploiting their ignorance by
paying them dirt-cheap wages during a post-season barnstorming
tour), or trivial (giving them $3 per day meal money rather than the
league's prevailing standard of $4), Comiskey rankles his players
and earns their enduring dislike. There is no financial security for
the ballplayers. Star pitcher Ed Cicotte, terrified of the possibility
that he won't be able to support his family when his playing days
end, is obsessively pursuing practical knowledge through correspondence courses. This grim concern for money, along with the occasional flirtation with gambling that has been with the game for years,
makes the Sox players' receptiveness to the fix offer comprehensible

to the reader, and not out of line with past practice for the Sox
themselves.

Luther Pond is a press fixture in the revelation of the scandal.
Buck Weaver is the vehicle for insights on the humanity of the players involved. Weaver's characterizations of his fellow players are
keen. Shoeless Joe Jackson, a heavy hitter and mental flyweight,
"could just never accept that he had no brains and leave it at that."
Pond enjoys a remarkably good relationship with the terrible Ty
Cobb, and catches his personality firmly when writing up an interview he has had with Cobb at the player's Georgia house. Pond
must write his story by candlelight, for Cobb is disputing a $4 bill
from his electric company. "The sonsobitches'll rot in hell before
they get a nickel out of me," says Cobb, a likely remark from the
game's best hitter and most committed misanthrope.

Stein's evocation of a departed time is entertaining, intellectually stimulating, and full of historical insights. The characters
are interesting, the writing adept (Stein takes a chance, and succeeds very well, in adopting both Weaver's first-person identity and
his struggling syntax). Who could ask for more? The book, whose
title is taken from a gossip column Pond writes, deserved a little
more hoopla than it received.

147.   Street, James H. "Golden Key." Good Housekeeping 119
       (Nov. 1944): 34-35+. Also in Desert Island Decameron.
       Edited by H. Allen Smith. Doubleday, 1945.
       It's time for a World Series not long after the turn of the cen-
tury, and in little Pine Hill, Mississippi, the only way for the locals
to stay abreast of a game's progress is by telegraph. An ace
telegrapher, known as such by the golden key he wears, picks up
coded descriptions of the games. These in turn his assistant calls
out to the gathered townsfolk. There is a plot of sorts to hold the
piece together, but the real stuff of the story is the well-developed
atmosphere of baseball-mad small-town America, portrayed in a form
in which it will never be seen again.

148.   Sullivan, Frank. "The Cliché Expert Testifies on Baseball."
       New Yorker 25 (Aug. 27, 1949): 22-25. Also in Fielder's
       Choice; An Anthology of Baseball Fiction. Edited by Jerome
       Holtzman. Harcourt, Brace, Jovanovich, 1979.
       If this question-answer session with a Mr. Arbuthnot does not
bring to light, and print, every conceivable cliché of baseball writing and announcing, it comes close. Should be taken as an astrin-
gent by every enthusiastic fan, and one wishes that sportswriters
and announcers would study it closely.

149.   Temple, Willard. "Good-bye, New York." Saturday Evening
       Post 230 (Mar. 15, 1958): 37+.
       Joe, a New York City auto mechanic, is crushed at the Giants'
departure for San Francisco. The loss of his favorite team preys on
him; he takes his girlfriend to a spot on Coogan's Bluff and shows
her where he and his father sat to watch the games for nothing, or

at least the parts of the games acted out by the shortstop, the left
fielder, and the center fielder, the only players visible from this
vantage.
   Springtime in New York without the Giants is finally too much
to bear. Joe quits his job, packs up, and heads for the Bay to set
things right. It is a slight story, but of some historical interest as
only a mildly exaggerated reaction suffered by many Giants and
Dodgers fans when their teams lit out for the territory.

150. _____. "The Invisible Umpire." American Magazine 162
      (July 1956): 32-33+.
   Instant video replay has brought with it the chance to see
athletic officials revealed for what everyone knew they were: fal-
lible. The distance between seeing one's team deprived of victory
by bad calls and demanding mandatory electronic surveillance of
close plays is a short one. The outcome of yielding to such a demand would probably resemble what happens in this story.
   Spike Garrett joins a minor-league collection of has-beens and
hopefuls, and, with his power hitting, soon has them near the top
of the league. Spike's one problem is an uncontrollable temper
easily set off by dubious calls from the home-plate umpire. After
shredding several uniforms and destroying his locker, Spike turns
to high tech for relief. A radar man in the service, he devises a
system to register perfect ball and strike calls. The umpire merely
loiters about to call other plays. The machine works to perfection,
but, deprived of the stimulation he finds in umpire-baiting, Spike
slides into a dreary slump.
   Stories of this sort can have none but a happy end, and this
one does; they also require a little romantic complication, and that
is here too. The point of interest is the early intrusion of technology on the game, an intrusion that has far from run its course.

151. Thurber, James. "You Could Look It Up." Saturday Evening
      Post 213 (April 5, 1941): 9-11+.
   The National League's first-place team is stumbling, and "Half
the time nobody'd speak to nobody else, without it was to bawl 'em
out." After an exhibition game loss in Columbus, Ohio, manager
Squawks Magrew meets 54-year old midget Pearl du Monville in a local bar. Pearl's humor is of Civil War vintage, but Magrew finds it
just the tonic to rescue him from his depression over the ball club's
doldrums. Before long, Magrew fixes Pearl up with a uniform, and
when a critical point arrives in a game, Magrew sends Pearl up to
bat. If Pearl had taken his base on balls, all would have been calm,
if odd. Because he cannot resist taking a swing at a three-and-oh
pitch, pandemonium breaks out. The journey of Pearl from home to
first is one of the funniest passages in baseball fiction.
   This story inspired St. Louis Browns' general manager Bill
Veeck to sign up the midget Eddie Gaedel, who went to bat one time
for the Browns in 1951. You could look it up: Gaedel's entry is on
page 184 of The Official Encyclopedia of Baseball (10th edition).

152.   Tooker, L. Frank. "A Pitcher Full of Cream." Century 84
       (Sept. 1912): 643-650.
       Members of office softball teams may recognize themselves in
this tale of men past their athletic prime fielding a baseball team
against a group of younger men. The old boys, led by the editor
Archer, are staff members of a magazine. The younger contestants
occupy menial offices for the same publisher.
       The men follow the routines still clung to by office teams.
With no opportunity to practice, they must assign positions based
on individual claims of prowess, "and modesty was in consequence
at a discount." The game, described in detail, includes a variety
of strange plays, plenty of insults, a determined fielder's dive into
the lemonade vat while pursuing a foul, and a late-inning break for
ice cream from a nearby "ice cream saloon." The ice cream gives
the story its name, upon the younger pitcher's wanton overindul-
gence and consequent miseries when the game resumes.
       A mild ribbing of both youthful arrogance and the refusal of
the aging to acknowledge the passing of their own youth.

153.   Tucker, Tommy N. "The Perfect Garden." Sports Illustrated
       55 (July 6, 1981): 48+.
       A mysterious stranger has come to a small Iowa farm community.
He's an old man named Cary. Partly because he has shown the narrator's father an uncanny acuteness for baseball details, he signs
on with the man as a hired farmhand. Cary soon assumes the umpire's job with the hired-hands' league; he lays out a diamond with
flawless accuracy, "a perfect garden," using only lime powder and
his unaided eyes.
       Cary is an unusual man from the outset, but when he confides
in the narrator that "I'm the man who settled on three outs for an
inning," we can be sure that something is going on here beyond the
unusual. Cary proves to be an arbiter of perfection, not just of
baseball games (life itself?) as they are, but of The Game as it ought
to be. The story's climax comes in a forboding atmosphere, with a
black storm building out past the drought-parched fields, lightning
flashing and wind howling. A batter hits a ball that stops short of
the centerfield fence, but Cary calls it a home run, because the wind
"wrongly blew it back." A violent scene follows, and the narrator,
describing these events of sixty years past, confides that he has
never played or attended another baseball game.
       A good story, full of things felt beneath the surface, in touch
with the inexplicable as well as the routine of existence.

154.   Ullman, James R. "I Seen 'Em Go." Scribner's Commentator
       7 (Dec. 1939): 127-132. Also in the author's Island of the
       Blue Macaws, and Sixteen Other Stories. Lippincott, 1953.
       The central characters here are a group of fans, retirees, who
sit in section 14 of the Yankee Stadium outfield. Each of them has
a different approach to the game; the story's conflict lies in the antagonism between one old fan who continually derides the players,
especially a rookie named Warner, and another rooter who insists

that these same players are worth their pay, particularly young
Warner. The climax is unexpected and violent; it follows Warner's
striking out to end a big game. The characters here are well
portrayed, with the old accountant who puts his faith in the players
notable in this respect.

155.   Updike, John. "The Slump." Esquire 70 (July 1968): 104-
       105+. Also in the author's Museums and Women, and Other
       Stories. Knopf, 1972.
       A once-feared hitter has gone into a dreadful slump, and
"dread" may be at the heart of it--that, or a complete loss of faith
in the concreteness of the game. A good, quick look at athletic
existential anguish, even if Updike does have his former slugger
meditating on Kierkegaard, an event as likely as Kierkegaard himself coming in to pinch-hit.

156.   Van Loan, Charles E. "The Indian Sign." Collier's 53
       (Aug. 1, 1914): 5-7+.
       An over-the-hill outfielder, an owner who likes to meddle in
on-field decisions, and a star pitcher who is psychologically intimidated form this story's basis. Blues outfielder Speck Adams has a
chronic charley horse. He cannot cover center field, and can barely
run the bases. Manager Joe Cotter has no choice but to bench
Adams in favor of a younger man, and he must stand up to club
owner Burgess to keep Adams with the team. Burgess, a proto-
typical Steinbrenner, has been interfering with Cotter regularly,
but Cotter has his way with his decision to let Adams ride the bench
through the season.
       The Blues are in a tight pennant race. In the game that de-
termines the pennant winner, Cotter cleverly employs Adams as a
pinch hitter against a pitcher he has "the Indian sign" on. Today's
players would say Adams has found a "cousin," a player against
whom, for no accountable reason, he performs well beyond his customary standard. Given one last chance, Adams makes the most of
it, and the process by which he and Cotter completely unravel the
opposing pitcher's nerves is quite funny.

157.   _____. Score by Innings. Doran, 1919. 349 p.
       This collection of baseball stories shows Van Loan's dexterity
at creating amusing characters and lively plots. His stories empha-
size old-fashioned virtues in an old-fashioned way, but they remain
good-humored and more readable than many stories by Van Loan's
contemporaries. "Mister Conley" is a fairly representative piece.
In it a rookie comes on too much like one of the boys before giving
his teammates a chance to accept him on their terms. His overag-
gressiveness causes frosty relations throughout the season, but an
act of selfless courage in the World Series reveals to the rest of the
team the real value of Conley as a man.

158.   Vidal, Gore. "The Zenner Trophy." In his A Thirsty Evil;
       Seven Short Stories, p. 57-80. Zero Pr., 1956.

An early Vidal story (1950), "The Zenner Trophy" concerns a
Boston prep school athlete's fall from grace, in the eyes of his
school if not in his own, over an unspecified infringement committed
with another student. Unspecified, but pretty bad, since there is
speculation as to whether the news, reported to the boy's parents
by the officious twit of a principal, will cause his mother a stroke.

The athlete, 18-year old Flynn, is the school's most accomplished sportsman in more than a decade. A baseball standout, he
"was the only possible choice" for the Zenner Trophy, awarded an-
nually. This is all out the window now, along with Flynn and his
comrade in infamy, Sawyer. The boys are being expelled with only
a week to go in their stay at the school.

Mr. Beckman, an instructor, acts as an emissary from the
principal to deliver the expulsion judgment to Flynn. Flynn takes it
calmly, and soon has obtained Beckman's sympathy. Surely the boy's
deviation from the norm is of no great consequence, in spite of the
school's self-righteous rage, a rage more adopted for effect than
genuinely felt.

The story's implied homosexual tryst will no longer shock in
most quarters, but the piece retains interest as a character study,
and further interest as part of an important writer's early body of
work.

159.   Vincent, Richard. "Bad Call." Saturday Evening Post 231
       (April 11, 1959): 24+.
When a veteran big-league umpire realizes that he has been
making bad calls with disturbing frequency, he quits three weeks
before the end of the season, disregarding the league's offer to let
him work to the end at games of no bearing on the pennant race.
He is more interested in preserving the well-being of the sport he
has served so long than in saving face. A better than usual Post
sports story, with the sentimentality kept to a minimum and the
moral points made persuasively.

160.   Wallop, Douglas. The Year the Yankees Lost the Pennant.
       Norton, 1954. 250 p.
The Faust legend is a handy little device for a writer to have
around the house, and Wallop uses it with some aplomb in this light
tale of Joe Boyd, a middle-aged man who cuts a deal with Old Nick
on behalf of the Washington Senators.

The story opens one hot July evening in 1958. The Yankees
are apparently headed for their tenth straight American League pennant, and long-time Senator fan Boyd is sulking through another
summer of foregone defeat as he follows the Nats on their annual
migration to the A.L. cellar. If you know the Faust story, you know
what happens next: Satan, known here as Mr. Applegate, turns up
on Joe's evening walk, and makes Joe an offer that means too much
to the Senators for him to turn down. Joe Boyd becomes Joe Hardy,
a mysterious 21-year old phenom from the sandlots. Following an impressive tryout with the Senators, he hits pinch-hit homers in his
first two games, and the chase is on to supplant the hated Yankees
at the top of the league.

There is a serious side to the novel; Joe learns Lessons about Life in the course of his fantastic summer. Fortunately the lessons are only heavy enough to give this frothy story a little ballast to keep it from tipping over. A pleasant way to spend a couple hours some Saturday afternoon when the home team has been rained out.

161. Warren, Robert Penn. "Goodwood Comes Back." In his Circus in the Attic, and Other Stories, p. 108-119. Harcourt, Brace, 1947.

Luke Goodwood, an Alabama boy, is blessed with a strong arm that carries him from the country to the big leagues during the Depression. He is also cursed with the drinking habit that is killing his father and ruining his brothers. He drinks himself out of baseball, then finds a way to destroy his ambition to own a little piece of land back in the country. Narrated by Luke's boyhood friend, whose tone is nearly that of a disinterested bystander watching a fore-ordained pathological event with little more than mild curiosity.

162. Whalen, Tom. "My Only Homerun." Ploughshares 9 (no. 2/3, 1983): 89-96.

This may be the only short story in captivity that juggles philosophical remarks attributed to Wittgenstein, a middle-aged man's affair with an adolescent girl, and a boy's solitary homer (off a fat, lazy knuckleball) in his organized baseball career. The narrator tells of the homer long after the fact, and, we gather, some time after he has completed his relationship with one of his students, a 15-year old who at first kissed like a fish. He hit the four-base blow in his last season; his eyes were starting to go; "books and writing are already shoving the organized activities of my life to one side."

As a boy, the narrator selects a bat; as a man, he reflects on his parents' infirmities, his mother's breakdown, his affair with the girl, the exhortations of Wittgenstein ("Don't let yourself get overwhelmed with questions; just take it easy.") Did Wittgenstein ever say "just take it easy?" Probably not, but does it matter? He also reflects on a mysterious fragment of a letter addressed to his grandmother from his grandfather in 1915.

At last the pitcher throws the ball. The batter swings, and, as the man remembers, the boy's swing against the "languorous" knuckleball turns into an embrace of the young girl now gone from his life.

The story does not work completely, but it is undeniably ambitious, and in literature as in baseball, spectacular swinging strikeouts are more interesting aesthetically than Texas-league singles.

163. Wiebe, Dallas E. "Cucumber Sandwich." In his The Transparent Eye-Ball, and Other Stories, p. 55-84. Burning Deck, 1982.

An original and peculiar tale of a farmboy who, with only a couple of years in the minors, becomes the pitching terror of the National League. The originality is hinted at in the title: this boy sees his life in vegetable metaphor. Line for line, there are probably more vegetables in "Cucumber Sandwich" than in the produce section of the nearest large market. The celery, tomatoes, squashes and onions all work together in growing effectiveness. Not a perfect story; the homosexual angle of the conclusion doesn't square with the young pitcher's busy lust for women at the beginning--but the vegetables and a riotous passage in which the boy's teammates attempt to cheer him up make this fertile reading.

164. Wier, Allen. "Mr. Ollie, Think of the Baseball." Carolina
      Quarterly 29 (Fall 1977): 1-10.
      A quirky but rather delightful story of an old man who goes
to the ballpark with a pair of friends and has a unique experience.
      Mr. Ollie accompanies Mr. Fulcher and Mr. Pell to a minor-
league game featuring the Salem Pirates. None of the men care much
about the game, but Mr. Ollie revels in the colors, the sounds, and
the smells of the stadium. He "liked just being there." When play
gets under way, after Mr. Ollie frets about whether to hold his
hand over his heart during the "Star-Spangled Banner," he thinks
little about the game, though he notices from time to time that it
has been taking place without his awareness. His attention flits
briefly, but lodges with intense momentary interest, on a succession
of subjects that have no bearing on the game and no connection with
each other. (One might think that Mr. Ollie had indulged in some
taboo substance before leaving for the stadium.) He sees outfielders
reflected in Mr. Fulcher's glasses, ponders the windows of a house
beyond the outfield, imagining what it would be like to live in that
house and to watch the game from one of its windows; he watches
the moon rise "like a seamless baseball hit up from the dark." If
Mr. Ollie is not stoned, his consciousness is that of a five-year old.
      The game's big event is a foul ball that lands in Mr. Ollie's
soft hands. He locks himself in a toilet stall to examine it, steals
a kiss from a woman who offers to trade him one for the ball, and
then rushes home to revere the ball as it sits on his kitchen table.
After the game, Mr. Ollie returns to the stadium to perform a
magical feat involving the ball and the moon.
      A story of good feelings for Mr. Ollie, and for the reader,
too.

165. Wise, William. "Glory in Bridgeville." Harper's 204 (June
      1952): 40-45.
      A sardonic story of the baseball scout's life. Former Pitts-
burgh player Ted Shane comes to little Bridgeville to try to sign
Billy Slater, a high school pitching prospect. Billy is the focus of
numerous big-league scouts. Shane expects Billy's mother and step-
father to hold out for a maximum bonus. Shane misses the old
days, when he could sign a boy for a few dollars and the promise
of an honest chance, nothing more.
      Shane does face a difficult obstacle in his attempt to sign
Billy Slater, but it is Billy himself. He exposes himself as a
greedy, conceited, rude, and otherwise wholly unpleasant young man.

A trace of the origin of Billy's foul attitude shows up in his mother, who, after Shane has signed the boy, accuses him and "men like you ... who come around with all that money" of turning Billy into the lout that he has become. Neither the scouts nor the money turned Billy into anything: he was like that before they showed up. Billy is a big hero in his hometown, but Shane has seen a side of the boy that the small-town folk have either missed, or deliberately ignored. Shane beats it out of Bridgeville before dark.

Anyone who has observed small-town sports from an objective distance will see in Billy Slater's story an example of a phenomenon that appears with tiresome regularity.

166. Witwer, H. C. "Play Your Ace." American Magazine 85 (May 1918): 26-30+.

Hector Sells is a hopeless loser in every department but food. He takes a scientific approach to his diet, and can quote the protein and calorie counts of anything edible to the exact figure. Hector is not a chef, however, but a baseball "player" of utter gracelessness. For seven years he has exhibited his lack of skill with bat and ball in the service of a friend, now a big-league manager, who also doubles as narrator. Hector supported the manager years ago in a difficult time, and has been rewarded with a sinecure.

Alex, one of the manager's acquaintances, is an automobile entrepreneur from Vermont. He bets the manager $1,000 that he can strike the fire of success into Hector. It looks like a safe wager for the manager, but Alex cleverly plays upon Hector's fear that the U.S. war effort will deny him a reliable food supply. Hector invents a new food, "a weird-lookin' slab of glue," in his manager's estimation, that "is the last word in calories, protein, and nourishment."

Like many other popular sports stories of the period, the emphasis here is on striking it rich, and Hector does. That his name is "Sells" may or may not be a conscious reinforcement of the story's main point.

II. BASKETBALL

167. Cook, Marshall. "Parting Shots." In Here's the Story: Fiction with Heart, p. 52-56. Edited by Morty Sklar. Spirit That Moves Us Pr., 1985.

Seven-year-old Johnny accompanies his father to an amateur game played before a handful of people. His father is a substitute, and starts the game on the bench. Johnny shoots baskets, or tries to, at one of the backboards on the side of the gym, then wanders around, sees his father get his feet tangled up when he is faked out on the court, and plays with a toy car he carried to the game in his pocket. Not until late in the game does Johnny's father score a few baskets, after botching several earlier chances. His team takes a pounding.

After the game, father and son walk out onto the floor in the now-empty gym to perform the ritual of the parting shot. Johnny takes three shots to sink one; his father sets up an imaginary game-winning scenario for his shot, and misses it.

This sounds like fairly innocuous stuff, but as the collection's subtitle indicates, this is definitely "fiction with heart." The link between Johnny's struggles with the basketball and his father's efforts to wring everything he can from a tiny helping of talent is subtle and touching, as is the growth of understanding between the two when they go out into the lonely gym for their "parting shots." A very tender, humane story.

168. Farber, Thomas. "The Mad Dog Instructional League." In his Hazards to the Human Heart; Stories, p. 2-18. Dutton, 1980.

One of the narrator's old friends, "Mad Dog," drifts into town. Mad Dog is a 5'8" basketball freak, as well as a self-diagnosed paranoid schizophrenic. An account of his history lends considerable credibility to this diagnosis. Mad Dog and the narrator get together nearly every day at a playground, where Mad Dog instructs the narrator in basketball's fine points. The narrator wonders why a sane man in his mid-30s "would be getting deeper into basketball.... When the prospect of being clobbered from the blind side or twisting an ankle outweighs even the possibility of dunking the ball. But there I was ... a self-confessed space-case my guru."

Farber gives an inspired and painfully acute description of playground ball, and playground players, a collection of people convinced that they are former or undiscovered stars, all intent on the maxim "I shoot, therefore I am," shunning passes, confident the other players are all clods.

In the end, Mad Dog moves east, but not before he gives the narrator a walnut plaque with a pertinent and moving inscription. This story is a fine look at pick-up basketball; it will also be of special interest to readers who have been sufficiently blessed (or cursed) to have in their lives a come-and-go, brilliant but unhinged and just below the level of the law friend like Mad Dog, who is, regardless of his craziness and his violence, a very enjoyable man. From a distance.

169. _____. "Mad Dog, One More Time." Ibid., p. 140-144.
"Of course the game went on." These are the closing words in this brief coda to Mad Dog's life and times. A year after disappearing into the East, Mad Dog comes back to town, a "wife" in tow, his beer-swilling down to a mere sixpack per day. He still plays basketball, but a cherished job in an auto shop has helped him lose some of his awful need on the court; he plays easily, without his old manic intensity.

The Mad Dogs of the world cannot enjoy their periods of serenity for long, and Mad Dog's breather from chaos comes to an end when a co-worker stirs him to violence in an incredibly mean and pointless way. Mad Dog's subsequent return to a life on the lam is a sad event, for the reader and for the narrator. "I watched his VW bug pull off into the night. I haven't heard from him since." But the game goes on. These few pages carry a lot of feeling, and from the point of thematic continuity it is important that one reads them immediately after the first Mad Dog story.

170. Farrell, James T. "Tournament Star." In his When Boyhood Dreams Come True; Further Short Stories, p. 126-139. Vanguard, 1946.
Cal Dolan is one of the finest high school basketball players ever produced on the Chicago courts. He hopes to lead his team, St. Mary's, to a national championship. The students and fans of St. Mary's give him a great salute when he takes the floor for warmups before a game against a tough North Dakota team. Cal makes many long shots in warmup, his eye is sharp, the crowd adores him, but all is not well. Cal has not yet recovered from a case of gonorrhea acquired one reckless night, and from time to time a stabbing pain cuts through his groin.

Cal plays the best he can in the first half, but with his exertions the pain worsens. At the half, Cal's coach learns the truth about his star's problem, and bastes the boy with scorn. Cal tries to play the remainder, but cannot finish. The crowd loudly cheers Cal for what appears to be his game effort to play over injury, while his coach and other school authorities inform Cal what a vile person he is. This is a story of real power. The conclusion, with Cal convinced that his life is ruined as he whips himself for his terrible "sin," hits hard.

171. Greenfield, Robert. Haymon's Crowd. Summit, 1978. 375 p.
Our hero here is a white, Brooklyn-bred player who, though

not endowed richly in the intellectual department possesses notable
athletic prowess in his 7-foot body. It carries him to a role with
the Los Angeles Lakers. The novel chronicles the passage of Haymon ("Hulky") Jacobs from the playgrounds of late-'50s Brooklyn
to an NBA championship series in the early 1970s. His "crowd" includes a former college associate who becomes the Lakers' pharma-
cological agent, and the bookie's son who first assisted Haymon
toward his current fame. The basketball action is good, and, if
the author's portrait of the effects of drug abuse and money lust in
big-time sports is not news at this point, it is at least well-informed.

172.   Greenlee, Sam. "Sonny's Not Blue." In Black Short Story
        Anthology, p. 91-96. Edited by Woodie King. Columbia Univ.
        Pr., 1972.
        A warm little story about a young boy in Chicago "who knew
just what he was going to be when he grew up"--a basketball player.
Sonny is firmly rooted in the lower class, but his mother and some
older boys look out for him and steer him right when he slips, for
example, when he starts to do badly in school. Sonny is confident--
more confident than the reader can be--that he will make the pros,
but when we last see him "practicing his moves in front of the
closet mirror," the possibility is there.

173.   Heuman, William. "Wizard of the Court." Collier's 129 (Jan.
        5, 1952): 28-29+.
        A much better than standard popular story that appeared in
the aftermath of the point-shaving scandals of the early '50s. The
title character is Amos Judson, a 66-year old coach at a large state
university. Judson earned his nickname through the many innovations he brought to the game, both in training methods and in on-
court tactics. He has been through the college athletic mill from
bottom to top: he began as a coach at a small college where he was
given a sleeping room in the basement of the library building, and
gladly tended the library furnace as part of his job. His first lesson in collegiate sports morality came in the form of his dismissal
after his initial season--a very good one--because the school preferred to reward an old alumnus with the job.
        Over the years Judson has apparently tried to run a clean
operation, but he has grown defensively cynical about college administrators, and has learned to manipulate the media with great
skill. When the story opens, Judson has just seen three of his top
players led off by the police for alleged involvement in point shaving. Judson's concerns are 1) how to handle the press; 2) how to
make the remainder of the team feel like playing the next game,
which he does not believe they can even hope to win; 3) how to
spend the rest of his life, for he has decided to resign.
        The story is full of bitterness toward the "crooked gamblers
and a high-pressure athletic board ... the money-grabbing promoters
and the publicity-seeking university men and even the hypocrytical
coaches...." These sentiments are expressed as Judson's, but there
can be no doubt that they are also the author's.

Judson is far from happy with himself; the little tricks (mild enough, actually) that he uses on his players and the press to achieve his ends leave him feeling dirty and disgusted with himself. As he looks at the wreckage left by the scandals, he sees blame to spread everywhere, but those who bear the heaviest layer of it, the players, deserve it least, for a corrupt system has made them its most disposable tools.

There is a positive ending here, but, beneath the reaffirmation of Judson's belief in the game and in his re-evaluation of his own attitudes, it is a forced ending, willed to stand in optimistic defiance against the ugly revelations of the scandals and the despair that courses through the author's tone.

174. Kaylin, Walter. The Power Forward. Atheneum, 1979. 303 p.

A novel about basketball, true, but also a novel about violence, loyalty, and broken dreams. The force around which the story turns is Isaiah "Muley" Bishop, a powerful scoring and rebounding black forward from the ghetto playgrounds of Bedford-Stuyvesant. Muley is truly more a force than a character: he moves through the book like an angry wind, dark humored, frightening, ominous.

The evident reason for Muley's seething self is his banning for life, while still a teenager, from the National Basketball League of America. Muley was implicated in a national point-shaving scandal while playing as a freshman for an obscure Ohio college, and has been forced since then to squander his great talent playing clown ball for a barnstorming team that resembles the Harlem Globetrotters.

Muley's exile in athletic side-show business is driving him to a frenzy of self-destruction when the book opens. He is especially antagonized by the coming retirement from the N.B.L. of Pete Pendleton, a former playground mate of Muley's and a star for the past decade. Muley is the same age as Pete, and sees Pete's imminent retirement as a clear sign that his own powers, though great, are doomed by time.

Through credible circumstances, Pete and Muley are reunited (in a sense), and Pete comes to believe that Muley was railroaded in the scandal, that he deserves a chance to play for Pete's team, the New York Heroes. A lengthy examination of the tangled web that led to Muley's "confession" shows that he was, indeed, falsely implicated. Pete, an extremely conscientious sort, goes on a hunger strike to force the N.B.L. to accept Muley as a player.

The novel seldom fails to maintain reader interest. Muley is an explosion waiting to go off, a point clarified by Kaylin's exploration of Muley's youth. The man has always been on the edge of violent outbursts, generally directed against the people closest to him, including Pete. By the time he reaches his thirties, his rage has shifted its target to himself. There are some very intense passages here. In one, Muley relates the way the authorities coerced him into confessing in 1964 to a part in the scandal, how he was surrounded by 40-year old men berating him and threatening him with poison: "Who are you," asks Muley, referring to himself, "Who

are you, Martin Luther King, you know how to take that shit?
What do you know? You're half their age and there's only one of
you and all you know is basketball."
     Eventually the real source of Muley's phoney confession comes
to light: the confession was extorted as retribution for an appalling
humiliation Muley forced upon a former acquaintance. This event
and its immediate aftermath are so deviant that, if the reader had
any doubt about the outcome of Muley's career, they are doused at
this point. When Muley goes completely berserk in his one pro
game, we are simply watching the inevitable happen.
     The major flaw in the novel is probably Pete Pendleton's ob-
tuseness. He is so dedicated to justice for Muley that he is blind
to the man's flagrant detachment from conventional reality and
civility, or at least blind enough that he seems convinced justice at
last will salvage Muley's life. Pete, then, is bothersomely credulous,
but he is also a very decent man, and an attractive character. To
be generous, one ascribes his surprising failure to see through
Muley not to the author's lack of skill at character delineation, but
to his interest in showing how good intentions coupled with faulty
judgment produce disaster.
     This novel is not fun. It is, rather, an ultimately grim and
depressing story, but is one well-told, and will hold the attention
of those who can take it.

175.   Koperwas, Sam. "Ball." Esquire 83 (Feb. 1975): 100-101+.
     An amazing story of a father's overpowering dreams for his
son. The narrator has yearned for his boy to play pro basketball
since the day he brought him home from the hospital. The boy has
the build for the game, but shows no interest in it. In fact, "My
son hates basketball. He reads books about blood circulation and
heart conditions." Through all his father's yammering about the
boy's glorious career in basketball ("Become a Knickerbocker....
Be a Piston, a Pacer.") the youth has eyes only on matters of
great substance, on healing the sick, bringing succor to the poor.
The major part of the story consists of the father's anguished en-
treaties to his son to heed his advice on the virtues of jump-shots,
tip-ins and rebounds, and it is a funny piece of writing. The
laughs subside when a fantastic exaggeration occurs, the father's
ambitions for his son transmogrified into something huge and horrifying.
     The father finally resigns himself to his son's humanitarian
aims, but these, too, he must push to insane extremes. "You'll
bring peace to the Mideast.... You'll grow bananas that don't
spoil." In the end, whatever laurels the boy achieves will only be
over his father's dead body. With a father like this, we must wish
him luck.

176.   Larner, Jeremy. Drive, He Said. Dial, 1964. 182 p.
     A satirical attack on the prevailing American values of the
Cold War, featuring the body, Jewish All-American basketball player
Hector Bloom, and the brains (such as they are), campus revolu-

tionary Gabriel Reuben. Like Roth's Great American Novel (item 135), Drive, He Said is at its strongest when the focus is furthest from politics. There is some beautifully-described basketball here, along with an overload of the author's commentary on everything from superpower confrontation to advertising. Turn to this novel for one fine basketball game in which Bloom scores big in an overdue release from the constipated playing style dictated by his uptight coach; for the maximum connection between politics and sport, turn to Don DeLillo's End Zone (item 337).

177. Levin, Bob. "The Best Ride to New York." Massachusetts Review 17 (Summer 1976): 267-284. Also in The Pushcart Prize, II: Best of the Small Presses. Edited by Bill Henderson. Pushcart Pr., 1977.

Noah Raezor is a good basketball player, but a little too small and too slow to make it in the NBA. That's all right: he plays the minors, doing what he likes, "living the life." When his teammate and roomie gets busted for a stupid crime, serious but at the same time so trivial that it's senseless, Noah's grip on "the life," and on life itself, begins to come undone. He blows up in an important game, and by story's end he is convinced "it's not going to work out, it's over, and that it never does for no one." A story of tragic recognition, with some very good stretches of basketball action.

Levin's themes of the bottomside of pro basketball continued in his novel, also called The Best Ride to New York (Harper & Row, 1978; 149 p.) The hero's name is now Jake Baer. Jake is another case exemplifying the athlete's difficulty in beating the odds, whether of age, superior competition, or the game's apparently built-in corruption. A former New York Knicks hopeful, Baer is nearing forty, playing ball for an obscure Pennsylvania outfit, the Ridley Gap Ghosts. Some good on-court passages help lift this short novel above the routine loser's tale.

178. _____ . "Open Man." Carolina Quarterly 28 (Spring/Summer 1976): 15-20.

Here is Jake Baer again, stopping by his father's house. We learn from a gas station attendant that Jake's father killed himself, and from a letter to Jake how he did it.

Jake's father was also a basketball player, and a good one. On his brief stop at the house, Jake shoots a few baskets, using the old hoop his father had set up. A neighborhood boy joins Jake, and the two trade shots while the boy fills Jake in on what a "neat" man his father was, without knowing Jake was the man's son. Jake gives the boy some pointed instruction in ballplaying: "Go crazy or they'll knock it down your throat."

The story's interest lies in its unfolding of the father-son relationship.

179. Neugeboren, Jay. Big Man. Houghton Mifflin, 1966. 213 p.
An attention-holding book for several reasons, both literary

and historical. The main character is Mack Davis, former college
hero and present employee of a carwash. Why would a college basketball star throw himself away in a carwash? The immediate answer
is that Mack was implicated in the point-shaving scandals of 1951,
to this date one of amateur athletics' most notorious departures from
the ideal of clean competition. The underlying answers are not that
simple, as the sports columnist Rosen well knows.

Rosen is convinced that the players whose professional careers
were derailed by their involvement in the scandal have a legal case
against the National Basketball Association, and that the case is firm
enough to allow them entry to NBA play. With this crusade in mind,
Rosen sympathetically dogs Mack Davis, urging him to open up about
his real desires. Davis hedges every bet now, afraid to admit either
his yearning for a pro career or his feelings for other people.

The one place where Davis feels free is on the playground and
local gym courts where he plays ball with pick-up teams and, later,
for a semi-pro team sponsored by the carwash where he works. If
Neugeboren has not spent some time on the court himself, he has
watched very carefully while others have played this "non-contact"
sport, and he has felt both the euphoria that accompanies good play,
and the pain of an elbow to the chest. Late in the book he pulls
out the stops in an exciting, detailed description of a game between
the carwash team and their opponents.

Much of the rest of the book concerns Mack Davis's difficulty
in getting along with others, a difficulty that grows out of his inability to acknowledge to himself how devastated he was by the effects of his foolish, if naive, participation in the fixes. Clearly,
to the reader, Mack hates himself. "Big Man" may be the traditional term for a basketball team's most valuable player, but in
Mack's view of himself these words take on tones of ugly irony and
self-mockery. There are people who hope for the best for Mack,
but something has burned and twisted permanently out of shape
within him, and few will close the book believing that Mack's future
offers more than the lot of the fading playground star.

180.   . "Ebbets Field." Transatlantic Review, no. 24
          (Spring 1967): 64-76. Also in the author's Corky's Brother.
          Farrar, Straus, & Giroux, 1969.
          Howie's friend Eddie has his about-to-bloom basketball career
nipped by an apparent "heart condition." Howie goes on to play
college ball; Eddie goes into business. They meet occasionally,
reminisce, and play a little ball. A warm, highly enjoyable story of
a good friendship that holds up in spite of time's changes. The
title refers to a nice account of a visit the two young men make to
a game at Brooklyn's Ebbets Field, shortly before the Dodgers pulled
out and moved to Los Angeles.

181.   . "Something Is Rotten in the Borough of Brooklyn."
          In his Corky's Brother, p. 129-150. Farrar, Straus, &
          Giroux, 1969.
          An arresting story of athletic frustration and self-destruction.

In grade school, Izzie Cohen plays basketball like a future All-American, but shortly after he passes a height of five feet, he stops growing. In high school he reroutes his athletic energy into literature and a nose for dirt: he exposes the school basketball coach's kickback arrangement with a local sporting goods store. There are a pair of excellent passages here. In one, Izzie waits patiently, almost happily, to receive a beating by the coach's enraged players. The other is a final scene of real pathos. The depiction of the deteriorating friendship of Izzie and Howie, the story's narrator, is also well-handled. (For another look at Howie, see item 180.)

182. Oldham, Archie. "The Zealots of Cranston Tech." In <u>Great Stories from the World of Sport</u>, vol. 3, p. 267-280. Edited by Peter Schwed and Herbert H. Wind. Simon & Schuster, 1958.

Strictly for fun, and it is fun. John Yeabsley transfers from a big midwestern university to tiny Cranston Tech. A basketball star back home, Yeabsley has a little trouble with the Cranston coach's decidedly eccentric training program, as well as with the moonstruck dietary regimen the coach's daughter tries to inflict upon him. If tales of liver-and-lung pie and mandatory 30-foot high jump shots stir your interest, you'll like this one. The author became head basketball coach at Columbia University. (First published in <u>Bluebook</u> magazine in 1956.)

183. Olsen, Jack. <u>Massy's Game</u>. Playboy Pr., 1976. 277 p.

At the front of the book a roster notes the personnel of the NBA Wasps. There is Basil McBride, the high-scoring, though easily-rattled, veteran forward; Edwin Crowder, the ill-tempered center; Conrad "Red" Green, a showboating, amphetamine-eating crowd pleaser, and, among the rest, Broussard Massy, a Cajun rookie who stands eight feet two inches tall.

Massy, a one-time junior-high star whose devotion to basketball fell to a stronger love of classical piano, joins the Wasps, a consistently losing team, more on Coach Francis X. Rafferty's hunch than on any observable promise. Massy's court moves are barely memories; he hasn't played in years, is awkward, readily intimidated, and a quick butt for sardonic sportswriters.

As the season moves along, however, Massy slowly becomes a major force as a shot blocker and all-around defensive presence. He also engages the hostility of other teams and league officials, who fear that Massy, although a gentle, introspective type who shuns meat out of a sense of "shame" at eating butchered animals, threatens the game by opening it to physical "freaks" and "goons."

A readable novel by a long-time writer for <u>Sports Illustrated</u>, <u>Massy's Game</u> is more than just fun. Olsen makes the reader think again about the relations of athletes to management and to the public at large. Some of the thoughts that flow from Massy's experience are dark ones.

Most of the characters are not overly-detailed, but are still

enjoyable in their typecasting. Coach "Butts" Rafferty furnishes
several amusing pages with his excited pitches on behalf of team
spirit and with his histrionic courtside performances. Massy himself
could have been better drawn; too often he comes across as too
much a hulking shadow than as a fully dimensioned character.

That may not matter too much. The novel scores its points at
a fairly steady pace regardless of its imperfections (including a silly
and mercifully brief subplot involving the "real" reasons for Massy's
career). Narrated by a sportswriter, a role the author knows in-
timately and which he fills in fictionally with conviction.

184.   Penner, Jonathan. "At Center." In his Private Parties, p.
        77-90. Univ. of Pittsburgh Pr., 1983.

A story that ranges in its few pages from bitter comedy to
pathos to love. Bruce, an overweight and athletically inept adolescent, is coerced by his father to accompany him on a basketball
instructional session at a city court. The session is ridiculous;
Bruce's father has no idea what to do with the ball and succeeds
first in making a fool of himself, then at bringing on chest pains
that require a doctor's attention.

Bruce joins some "friends" for a four-on-four game. Bruce
blows a pair of easy shots, bloodies his own nose, and manages to
ruin a game-winning opportunity for his side. After the game, the
boys go behind the school to smoke and brag about their amorous
adventures. Bruce is convinced that love, sweet love, will never
be a part of his life. He makes himself look like a complete incompetent when one of the boys offers to let him try a cigarette.

This is all well-described and quite miserable, yet the story
ends happily, in a sense, with a very touching scene between Bruce
and his father, who, it is plain, loves Bruce so much that he is
willing to try to do the impossible for him.

185.   Rehder, Jessie C. "Atalanta in Cape Fair." Harper's 178
        (May 1939): 588-594.

A nice study of the joy of sport, unusual in this case because
the central character is a girl basketball player, Joanna Prokosch.
The story takes place on the night of the high school team's last
game. Joanna is a superlative player, and has been since she first
stepped onto the court four years earlier. Predictably, she must
put up with skeptical, demeaning remarks from her family, implying
that her "interest in games" is somewhat infantile. Joanna herself,
listening to this carping, begins to wonder if she will ever do anything well but play basketball.

When she takes the court, her natural ability and delight in
the achievements of her body take over. The crowd exults as
Joanna seizes control of the game, but she scarcely hears the shouts.
She is so in tune with the game that she floats through it almost in
a trance. "She lost the sense of the forms of her fellow players
round her, forgot the passage of time.... She sped down the court
below the balcony, oblivious to everything but the delight that
coursed through her body."

The story includes a fine passage describing Joanna's half-time reverie about how pleasant it will be to slide into her bed when the long night is over, to let sleep come upon her as she listens to the wind in the willows outside her window. This dreamy passage ends with the whistle that starts the second half. A very fine story, ahead of its time for its focus on the female athlete and on the pure athletic sensibility.

186.   Rosen, Charles.   Have Jump Shot, Will Travel.   Arbor House, 1975.   204 p.

Another tour of the basketball netherlands, set chiefly among a group of small coal-mining towns in Pennsylvania. Bo Lassner, the main character (he is not a "hero;" in spite of its humor, this is a novel of victims, not victors or heroes), is a slightly talented second-string center for the Wellington Rifles of the Atlantic Professional Basketball Association. Play in the APBA features routine bursts of deliberate violence. Broken noses and kneed groins are not unusual. Lassner looks upon his league's departure from basketball's Platonic ideal of grace and beauty with distaste, but finds himself ultimately drawn into its rude grip.

Beneath the book's "fun" is an evident vein of sour frustration. Like their counterparts on the asphalt and concrete playgrounds of the urban ghetto, the players in this ghetto founded on coal turn to basketball as one of the few avenues available where they can assert themselves within the law. Fans as much as players are trapped in a rigidly stratified social class; they go to the games to go crazy, to escape from themselves and from the bleak routines of their lives.

Rosen is also the author of The Scandals of 1951 (Holt, Rinehart, & Winston, 1978), on the college point-shaving fiasco.

187.   _____.   A Mile Above the Rim.   Arbor House, 1976.   281 p.

The focus in Rosen's follow-up to the above novel is the conflict between the rigid, pattern-obsessed coach of the NBA's New York Stars and some of his free-spirited players. Coach Smalley's freest spirit is Silky Sims, a former Smalley protegé and ghetto player who has become the most exciting man in the NBA. Not as interesting as the earlier novel, but still worth the fan's attention for Rosen's considerable feel for the game.

188.   Rutman, Leo.   Five Good Boys.   Viking, 1982.   278 p.

For readers looking for another fictional account of the point-shaving scandal (assuming they have read Jay Neugeboren's tough and soulful Big Man, item 179), this novel may be of interest. A decade after the scandal at "New York College," a gathering of former players at a teammate's funeral serves as the take-off point for recreation of the events that did so much damage to the game's reputation, let alone the lives of the young men who were implicated in controlling final scores to suit the needs of the big-money bettors.

Rutman is at his best describing on-court (as opposed to in-court) action and at evoking a feel for the New York City atmos-

phere. His description of the players' corruption by the gambling
interests is fairly compelling.

189.   Sayles, John.   "Hoop."   Atlantic 239 (March 1977): 37+.
       Also in the author's The Anarchists' Convention.   Little,
       Brown, 1979.
       "Sport, if God didn't want them gaffed, he wouldn't of made
them fish." Following this advice from a pool hustler, Brian picks
up spare dollars in one-on-one basketball games. He never shows
more of his ability than he has to, always keeps his opponent in the
game, so Brian's victory can be attributed to luck, cheating, anything but the truth that he is the better player. Counterpointing
Brian's acumen, and his admiration for a free and easy playing
style, is his high school coach's dogged devotion to a systematic,
careful approach to basketball, an approach that other teams find
easy to anticipate, and as easy to defeat. A story that observes
sport intelligently from several angles.

190.   Shainberg, Lawrence.   One On One.   Holt, Rinehart & Win-
       ston, 1970.   216 p.
       A complex, funny, sometimes confusing, occasionally profound,
and consistently serious novel in which basketball, especially the
metaphysical purity of the jump shot, has become the chief character's last resort from the sloppy world of human emotions and inter-
action.
       The major player in this athletic psychodrama is Elwood Bas-
kin, at 6'9" and 244 pounds the most talented man to step onto the
court since Lucius McCarver, an NBA star whose career concluded
in a frenzy as he went amuck during a game, with his outburst
capped by an attempt to eat one of the nets.
       McCarver is in more ways than one an apt paragon for Baskin.
Baskin's hold on mundane reality is not much better than his hero's,
and McCarver's style delivers Baskin from a routine relationship
with basketball to a spiritual plane experienced by few players.
Studying films of McCarver at his best, Baskin finds his life changed
by the star's jump shot, a shot that affects Baskin as fundamentally
as it once revolutionized the game itself. What was once a pleasant
exercise for Baskin becomes an avenue to a Zen-like clarity. Gone
is his prosaic, deliberated set shot, replaced by the instinctive,
thought-free and performed outside-of-time jumper. For Baskin it is
not simply a new shot, "but a whole new game.... There was almost no relationship between the person I was before the jump shot
and the person I was after."
       Indeed, all that is really left for Baskin is the game. His so-
cial life is in shreds. The son of Jewish millionaires who own a
chain of restaurants (the "Smoky Pig" franchises) in the deep South,
Baskin has been in psychoanalysis since the age of 14. He is constipated, impotent, and given to long periods of silence. He elects
to play college ball for New York University so that he can be in
easy reach of his analyst, not that he doesn't carry the man around
in his head at all times. Baskin's human relationships have deterio-

rated to the point at which his parents, his girlfriend, his analyst, and even the Chinese philosopher Lao-tzu, exist as voices between his ears. Their sometimes-physical presence merely gets in the way of his focus on the battle within himself.

The real "one on one" game, then, is Baskin against the nearly white noise inside his own mind, but there are some magnificent passages when the noise subsides to let Baskin dwell on the mystic perfection of the game, of the mind-body-ball-basket continuum: "For me, you see," he reflects, "the ball is alive. It feels my hands while they feel it. I talk to it and it answers me. Its rhythm is my rhythm, its voice my voice."

One On One is a very sad book, depicting as it does the attempt of a man to hold on to one slim shard of beauty, truth, and sanity through his game. It is also, perhaps, the best piece of fiction about basketball ever written.

191. Walton, Todd. Inside Moves. Doubleday, 1978. 162 p.

Jerry, a young man with a crippled leg, works in a San Francisco box factory. The highlight of his day is a three-hour basketball session with some black men at a park. Jerry is married to a beautiful junkie. When she's straight, he takes her to pro basketball games. When she isn't, he goes with the book's narrator, Roary, a badly-crippled Vietnam veteran who hides his physical scars with long hair and soothes his emotional wounds with a junk-food habit.

Jerry and Roary set out on a campaign to raise money for surgery on Jerry's right hip. They get the money, but decide to buy a bar with it, a place that has become nearly a private club for the disabled. With Jerry in a deep depression after a pimp and his buddies beat him close to death, Roary seeks out the financial help of Golden State Warrior player Alvin Martin to finally secure Jerry's operation. After the operation, Jerry rebuilds himself, and Roary begins dating a woman who persuades him to go on a diet and to trim his hair.

This short novel is a little diamond. The title refers to Jerry's adroit moves on the basketball court, but it alludes to the internal changes of the book's characters. For all its early grimness, the book is basically optimistic, for it argues that personal change for the better is possible. It makes no easy promises that this change can be anything but hard-won; it must be fought for, and the fight can be of overwhelming difficulty. Witness Jerry's wife, who, after unsuccessfully trying to kick her drug habit, moves in with a man who will keep her supplied free of charge. She ends up a wreck on the streets.

It is a novel full of love, and with some real basketball, too. When Jerry makes a couple of good plays in his first semipro game, the reader wants to join Roary in cheering; later game action pumps almost as much adrenalin as the real thing.

192. Wilner, Herbert. "Whistle and the Heroes." Furioso 8 (Spring 1953): 1-15. Also in the author's Dovisch in the Wilderness, and Other Stories. Bobbs-Merrill, 1968.

A good character study of a working man whose only real pleasure lies in the twice-weekly basketball games in which he plays at the community center.

Marvin Wessel is close to thirty, and works at a dead-end, menial job in a department store. A birth defect that interferes with his speech has led to his humiliating nickname, "Whistle." He lives at home with his sick mother, and has no success with women. He shines on the community center court, though, where he plays with grace and with an instinctive knowledge of where the ball and the other players will be at any given time. Yet Whistle is playing against high-school boys, age is steadily creeping up on him, and he has already found out that even at the height of his court skills he was not a good match for a talented college player.

Whistle does not admit it to himself, but the reader sees that he has nowhere to go but down the inevitable decline that waits for men who do not feel themselves alive except in their obsessive clinging to the athletic achievements of their pasts.

193. Baumbach, Jonathan. "Mother and Father." Iowa Review 10
(Spring 1979): 34-39.
The narrator watches his parents compete against each other
in a game of pool. They play each night before going to bed. As
is so often true in sports between husband and wife, there is far
more going on than simply the knocking about of a few balls on a
table, or even the issue of winner and loser.
Mother plays with a certain uninformed good fortune and finds
herself ahead. At this point she insists that she plays not to win,
but for the fun of it. "Winning and losing are the same to me,"
insists Mother.
"That's a lot of shit if I may say so," says Father. In this
exchange we see the real contest taking place, although Father is
not, as a rule, quite so blunt in his dismissal of Mother's assertions.
This is on one level a funny story with Father's deadpan irony
counterpointing Mother's ostensibly air-headed (but covertly mali-
cious) remarks about his "puerile" game. On another level the tale
is fairly appalling, with the sniping commentary a painful example
of the running verbal battles that so often mark marriage.
The story closes on a pathetic note. After his parents finish
their game and leave (or, in effect, carry their real game to
another front), the narrator remains behind in a high stool, "deserted and forgotten, too small to climb down without aid, a first
and final witness."

194. Carpenter, Don. "The Crossroader." In his The Murder of
the Frogs, and Other Stories, p. 15-26. Harcourt, Brace,
Jovanovich, 1969.
It is always a pleasure to watch a clever outsider exploit
bigotry, suspicion, and plain meanness to his own advantage. That
is what happens here as a lone black man drops into an eastern
Oregon town with his billiard cue in hand, and proceeds to quietly
make fools of the locals at any game they choose. A work of western
humor with roots in Mark Twain.

195. Ford, Jesse H. "Beyond the Sunset." In his Fishes, Birds,
and Sons of Men, p. 99-117. Little, Brown, 1967.
Clarence Perks is transferred, at age 60, from his old familiar
dry goods store in East Tennessee to a new one in The People's
Dandy chain far from home. His wife is dead; his only comfort is
shooting pool. Mr. Perks, in fact, is a gifted player, but he barely
knows it, for he never plays with anyone else. An unsought match

with a farmer leads Mr. Perks to an utterly out-of-character act of
violence; the action somehow breaks the wall of strangeness standing
between him and his new surroundings. There are good passages
throughout this story, with the best covering the pool match with
the farmer and the subsequent meal at Mr. Perks's boarding house.

196.   Harrison, William. "The Snooker Shark." Saturday Evening
        Post 240 (July 29, 1967): 56-58+. Also in The Best American
        Short Stories, 1968. Edited by Martha Foley and David
        Burnett. Houghton Mifflin, 1968.
        If this story were a little funnier and a little more absurdly
tragic, it would be a print parallel to W. C. Fields's classic short
film, "The Fatal Glass of Beer." Young Sammy plays snooker, a
variation of pool, flawlessly, but the hustler's life beckons to him
less powerfully (he likes to think) than the intellectual one. His
family sends him off to college, where he hopes to find great truths
and mysteries revealed in the library stacks, but--there's this
local pool-hall dive, you see, and once it's in the blood there's no
denying it. Sammy doesn't.

197.   Lyons, Paul. "Table Legs." Pulpsmith 5 (Spring 1985): 52-
        63.
        A lively account of pool shooting and father-son relations, this
story contains humor, suspense, and emotional depth. The narrator
is a boy, probably below the age of twenty, who has been spending
a lot of time hanging out at a local pool joint, playing with some of
the old-timers for low stakes. His particular challenge is a black
pimp-manager known as Table Legs. Legs carries a fat wad of
cash, will bet on anything, and enjoys riding the boy during their
games with a steady patter of creative, but not mean-spirited, insults.
        On the night of the story the boy is late for supper; he is
about to pack up his cue when he sees his father. The boy is
stunned into stupidity: his father has never set foot in the place
before. He does not collar the boy and steer him home; he asks
him if he can beat Table Legs. "Let's see you shoot," he tells his
son. "I don't get out of the house much in the evenings." There
follows a long set of games for which the boy's father puts up the
$50 per game stake suggested by Legs. "You wanna shoot with the
great Table Legs you gonna have to play like a gentleman, you gonna
have to come up with some real money."
        The games, described in detail, close with a tension-laden, ex-
tremely difficult shot. When the boy and his father have breakfast
afterwards in a Hungarian diner, the older man begins to weep, and
his son places his hand on his father's. It is a touching moment,
and a good conclusion to a well-written story.

198.   Pronzini, Bill. "The Hungarian Cinch." In Arena: Sports
        SF, p. 195-220. Edited by Ed Ferman and Barry Malzberg.
        Doubleday, 1976.
        A fanciful twist on the tale of the hustler. Walter Tevis (next

item) would recognize the basic elements of the challenge posed in
this story, but not even Minnesota Fats has likely seen a talking
pool cue with arms and legs.

Fancy Fontana has drifted from the hustler's existence to that
of a billiard-parlor proprietor; he is too adept at the game to attract
willing opponents. When visitors of the "alien type" propose a game
for "fifty big ones," Fancy nearly salivates at the thought of an
easy win. What Fancy fails to take into consideration is the hypnotic
ability of the alien types, and the treacherous conduct of his own
trusted sidekick, No-Balls. Justice prevails, but not without some
special effects, including the walk-on bit by the talking pool cue.
For fun only, and succeeds well at its intentions. (The story's
first appearance was in this anthology.)

199. Tevis, Walter S. The Hustler. Harper, 1958. 214 p.

A fast, tense novel of the poolhall whose atmosphere is so
thick the reader can smell the cigarette smoke and feel the sweat
slide down his ribs as the players plan difficult shots. The hero
(definitely with a lower-case "h") is Fast Eddie Felson, who follows
classic hustling strategy by softening his opponents' guard with
amateurish, clumsy shooting, and then crushing them with his finesse when the money gets serious.

Eddie, unsatisfied with cleaning up among his small-time antagonists, hungers for a shot at the legendary Minnesota Fats, king
of the cuestick. In a riveting match with Fats, Eddie finds that
his speed is not quite up to the master's; he blows a huge lead and
loses miserably, and shortly afterward suffers some nasty revenge
worked on him by a victim of his hustling. Eddie bounces back
from this disaster with the help of a tough woman and a manager
who helps instill in Eddie the hardcore winner's attitude.

The love story here is fairly tired, but the pool scenes are
excellent and the feel for the poolroom is sure. Robert Rossen's
1961 film version of the novel, with Paul Newman as Eddie and
Jackie Gleason as Minnesota Fats, is another one to watch for either
on late-night television or in the videocassette rental stores.

IV. BOXING

200. Ade, George. "The Fable of the Coming Champion Who Was
      Delayed." In The America of George Ade, 1866-1944, p. 86-
      92. Edited by Jean Shepherd. Putnam, 1960.
         An aspiring prizefighter receives a painful lesson when he
enters the ring against a "has-been," a "physical wreck."

201. Algren, Nelson. "Dark Came Early in That Country." In
      his The Last Carousel, p. 1-17. Putnam, 1973.
         Roger Holly, drawn from Algren's stable of worn-out boxers,
can remember the fights he has been in, but not the names of the
men he has fought. He remembers the places where he fought, too,
"the places where I'd used up my hostility." The story tracks
Holly through a number of fights, all sleazy, up to a concluding
bout against a blind man. Holly loses, and decides to open a diner.
Algren's fight world is crooked, dirty, absurd, and, because of
narrator Holly's refusal to take any of it quite seriously, it is good
here for a few laughs.

202. _____. "He Swung and He Missed." In his Neon Wilder-
      ness, p. 157-164. Doubleday, 1947; reprint ed., Peter Smith,
      1968.
         Young Rocco, close to washed-up at 29, agrees to throw a
fight for a hundred dollars. When the fight begins, his pride in
never having been knocked out takes over, and he does his best to
win. He doesn't win, and his girlfriend Lili loses the $100 by bet-
ting on him. A taut, lean story, with effective irony and a moving
tribute to the power of self-respect.

203. _____. Never Come Morning. Harper, 1942. 284 p.
         Algren's second novel, set in North Chicago's Polish ghetto,
is populated with losers, dreamers, crooks and killers. There is
scarcely an attractive character to be found in the book, but its
strength is not in the appeal of its characters; it is in Algren's
powerful evocation of a section of the urban underbelly, in a style
that comes close to being a poetry of the gutter.
         The novel centers on the grimy adventures of young Bruno
"Lefty" Bicek, who has pretentions to the heavyweight title. Bicek
also fantasizes about fame on the baseball field. As he throws baseballs for kewpie dolls, he slips straight into a Mitty-esque trans-
substantiation of this inane feat, seeing himself "on the mound at
Comiskey park under a burning July sun with three and two on the
batter and the sun in his eyes.... Big Lefty Bicek yanked his cap
down over his eyes to see his signals better...."

The novel opens with Bicek's mentor, Casey Benkowski, bragging about his developing skill in the ring, this after he has been knocked cold. "All the time, I'm gettin' the old experience. All the time I'm perfectin' the old technique." At the age of 29, all he has left to perfect in the ring is the most aesthetic supine pose. His manager, a barber and small-time con, laughs off Casey's delusions and presses him into petty money-raising schemes.

To supplement their income, Casey and Bicek turn to burglary, stealing slot machines from road houses. Bicek's criminal ventures lead to murder, in an act that complements Bicek's basic dishonesty and cowardice. The novel concludes with a gruesome boxing match between Bicek, with Casey in his corner, and a black fighter. No one could mistake Never Come Morning for a novel of good feeling, sensitively taught moral lessons, or optimism, but it feels as real as a razor cut, and bleeds as freely.

204.   Apple, Max. "Inside Norman Mailer." Georgia Review 30
        (Summer 1976): 278-289. Also in the author's The Oranging
        of America, and Other Stories. Grossman, 1976.
        A very clever and funny fantasy in which the narrator, a writer and English instructor of modest achievements, takes on Norman Mailer in a prizefight. Literary and boxing metaphors feed off one another as tension builds toward the big fight. Mailer enters the ring in a pair of YMCA trunks and cheap sneakers, his terry-cloth robe threadbare. "The crowd loved his slovenliness." The outcome is predictable. Mailer himself says at the end, "James Jones and James T. Farrell and James Gould Cozzens ... I took them all on, absorbed all they had and went on my way...."

205.   _____. Zip; A Novel of the Left and the Right. Viking,
        1978. 183 p.
        Ira Goldstein, the 24-year old narrator, runs an automobile scrapyard in Detroit. He lacks the "zip" that would enable him to go out, find a good woman, and conceive the child his grandmother craves, but he knows talent when he sees it. He sees it in Jesus Martinez, who hires on as a battery-buster at the scrapyard. Ira recognizes Jesus's boxing ability, and assumes his ring management. Jesus's first fight is on March 15, 1965, against a man with scuffed shoes and a drippy nose. He quickly establishes a winning record, and, along with an affluent radical girlfriend, he acquires an additional name. A promoter appends the tag "Goldstein" to his original name. "It might get some Jews back into the armory," he says. "They spend a lot on refreshments."

Jesus piles up copies of Ramparts and the Daily Worker beside his bed. Ira two-times him, and goes to jail. The novel concludes, after a wild trip in which J. Edgar Hoover plays a prominent part, in a bout in Cuba against the U.S. middleweight champ Tiger Williams. Jesus now wears red trunks emblazoned with the hammer and sickle; Howard Cosell covers the fight for American television.

An excess of surrealism, too much simplistic caricature, and an awkward voice--Ira speaks as though directly to Jesus--grow irritating at times. The novel does have its share of funny passages, however, and will be just the thing for readers who always wanted to see the former head of the FBI suspended in a red, white & blue basket above a boxing ring in Castro's Cuba.

206. Barrett, William E. "The Fix Is On." Saturday Evening Post 229 (Oct. 27, 1956): 37+.

This story has some defects. The ending is too happy, the situation that puts Andy Nielsen, a college boy, into the ring sounds a little unlikely, and, worst of all, the illustrator blatantly telegraphs the story's central irony with his opening-page picture.

Even with these problems, Barrett's story is one of the most sophisticated of the mass-market magazine pieces covered here. Its real issue, aside from the corruption of big-time boxing, is how a man seeking to be honest tries to deal with ambiguity. Nielsen is a middleweight on his way toward a possible championship bout. An article in the newspaper hints that he is going to take a dive in his next scheduled fight. Nielsen knows of no such arrangement, but when he tries to explain the complexities of the game to his girlfriend, she interprets his remarks to mean that he has, indeed, agreed to a set-up. She then writes a scorching essay on boxing in her newspaper television column.

Nielsen goes into the ring to discover that a fix has been called; how he deals with the knowledge creates a passage of tension, excitement, and psychological interest.

207. Bates, Randolph. "The Gym." Ploughshares 10 (Nos. 2/3, 1985): 191-206.

Off the beaten path as boxing stories go, this one portrays the relationship of a 34-year old white teacher and a crippled old black gym manager named Collis. The teacher has decided to put "a haunting adolescent fantasy" to rest, for better or worse, a fantasy in which he sees himself as a professional fighter. He lies about his age when he enters the gym, claiming to be 29. Collis reacts to this strange white man's interest with such solicitude that the teacher senses a hustle on Collis's part. Why would the old man be so decent to him, advising him on equipment, never questioning his motives, even inviting him to his home, if he weren't trying to squeeze something out of his less than apt pupil?

The teacher eventually realizes that Collis's interior is the same as his exterior: he means what he says, he has no concealed motives for treating the teacher (who apparently never reveals his occupation to Collis) like a human being. As the teacher trains, he and Collis grow close enough that Collis confides in him some details of his personal history, about his son's stretch in the pen, about his daughter's shooting him. Collis reveals this information in a laconic way, as if he's embarrassed to mention it but feels compelled to do so.

Collis is a very sympathetic, easy to care for character. When the teacher turns down Collis's offer to come into his house for a little orange juice, we immediately sense the wrongness of his refu-

sal, which springs from self-consciousness and a failure of trust.
The teacher recognizes his error, but we fear that a second chance
may not arrive. The two men do, however, work out an amicable
arrangement for the teacher to write a story based on Collis's life.
    A boxing story that is both more subtle and more emotional
than most.

208. Bukowski, Charles. "You and Your Beer and How Great You
      Are." In his South of No North, p. 23-27. Black Sparrow
      Pr., 1980.
      Jack Backenwald, the world's 3d-ranked light-heavyweight,
comes home from a fight and breaks up with his lover. She can no
longer put up with his incessant references to his own "greatness."
Backenwald is a close cousin to the lead character in Ring Lardner's
"Champion" (item 233).

209. Burnett, William R. Iron Man; An Epic of the Prize Ring.
      Dial, 1930. 312 p.
      A tersely-written story of another man gone to the dogs that
feast on declining fighters. Coke Mason is a simple man whose
pleasures are fighting, movies, and his two (and three) timing wife.
George Regan, his manager, tries to steer him through the ring's
hazards, but Regan hasn't the ability to walk a tight line through
a decadent scene. When a corrupt manager moves in on Mason, the
end is inevitable. This story's chief advantages are its no-nonsense
style, its blunt depiction of the fighter's world, and some effectively
drawn characters, particularly Mason and Regan.

210. Carter, Rubin. "Return of the Kid." In Voices from the Big
      House, p. 43-51. Edited by Frank E. Andrews and Albert
      Dickens. Harlo Pr., 1972.
      This story should not work, so ridiculous is its premise, yet
it does work, against all reason. Manny Thomas and Charlie Higgins
are anxious for a new plan to pack the fight fans into the Millville
Sports Palace. Their steady attraction, hometown boy Kayo Keegan,
has been putting pugs away at a rate of one a week, and the suspense has gone stale. Manny reaches into the Twilight Zone to pull
out a promotional scheme: they will set Kayo up against a non-
existent fighter, the "Invisible Kid." Come fight night there is a
big turnout, and Kayo has been carefully instructed in how to take
a convincing dive against the boxer who isn't there. The reader
may guess the outcome before reaching the conclusion, but even that
does not destroy the story's effectiveness, which it owes to its unthinkable plot and its rather eerie, dreamlike execution. (The author
was better known to the public as "Hurricane" Carter, whose imprisonment became a cause célèbre for many.)

211. Coe, Charles F. Knockout. Lippincott, 1936. 319 p.
      Flash Philbin, a naïve country youth, shows potential prize-
fighting talent in his exhibitions as a carny strongman. The book
follows his career from muscular innocent to experienced ringmaster

in typical boxing novel fashion: there are the corrupt promoters,
the crooked managers, the tank artists recruited to make Philbin
look good on his way to the heavyweight title (though Philbin is a
capable fighter, and hardly requires fixed bouts). Knockout does
depart from most boxing novels in its central character's fate: when
Philbin's managers fleece him, he turns their own methods against
them.

212.   Cox, William R. "Crowd Pleaser." Collier's 135 (May 27,
       1955): 70+.
       One of the mainstays of television in the 1950s was boxing.
Something symbiotic went on between the square ring and the rectangular tube; whether it was healthy is open to question. In Cox's
opinion, the answer is no, and it is his antagonism to television that
makes this story interesting.
       Willy Czernsky, a young fighter managed by former contender
Frank Berry, rejects Frank's plan for a slow progression to title
contention when an agent from Sports Incorporated waves the promise of big television dollars at him. Frank sees nothing good for
Willy in this route: "Sports Incorporated and television had combined to ruin the breeding places for good, solid boxers--the small
clubs." Television demands broad, spectacular, and preferably gory
fights. The subtle infighting that marks the trained professional is
lost on the television audience.
       Willy garners quick celebrity through a series of televised
bouts against incompetents, and through his victories puts himself
in line for a fight with the current champion, a man who only a few
years ago beat Frank Berry badly. Sick at the slaughtering he is
certain Willy will undergo in this fight, Frank hatches a plan to
knock some sense into the boy's head, in a very literal way.

213.   Craven, Margaret. "Return to Glory." Saturday Evening
       Post 229 (Feb. 2, 1957): 34-35+. Also in the author's The
       Home Front; Collected Stories. G. K. Hall, 1981.
       Big Jim Taggart, a former heavyweight contender, has dropped
out of the fight game to seek a living in a logging camp. It seemed
to Taggart that "he had been coming here forever, so slow was the
way of bitter descent." The slide began when he could no longer
get fights under his own name. He settles into the camp's day-to-
day work, but the past plagues him. He keeps a little newspaper
clipping that calls him one of the "great old heavyweights" in his
watchcase, and takes it out from time to time to read.
       Unlike so many stories of worn-out boxers, this one ends on
a positive note, and it is a relief. Taggart heroically saves the camp
mill from a fire, and with that act he cements a respect that had
been slowly growing for him among the camp hands. Given the common fates of fictional ring has-beens, Taggart's happy resolution is
a nice departure, and Margaret Craven's gentle sense of character
is, too.

214.   Davis, Clyde B. Temper the Wind. Lippincott, 1948. 251 p.

A novel of post-war small-town America, held together by its focus on Navy veteran Cowboy Shandy. Shandy, a mechanic and an aspiring boxer, comes back to the town of Buell, Wyoming, following his discharge. The book moves forward in an easy, anecdotal style that allows observations of the various town characters, ranging from a sportswriter turned boxing manager to a reformed prostitute. The story culminates in a lively boxing match. To keep the conversation on a higher plane than one might expect in boxing circles, Davis endows Shandy with a fairly formidable intellect.

215. Farber, Bernard. "Hundred Dollar Eyes." In <u>Nelson Algren's Own Book of Lonesome Monsters</u>, p. 40-49. Edited by Nelson Algren. Bernard Geis, 1963.

"I got drunk and thought of his eyes and my hundred dollars." This closing line sums up both the mood and the point of this story. A young, novice fighter's first professional match is against a worn-down old-timer who has agreed to take a dive. The boy realizes what is happening when he looks into the old fighter's eyes during the bout. The action leading up to the fight is competent but familiar (although the boy reads <u>Madame Bovary</u>; most prize-fighters do not dally with Flaubert), but the effect developed upon the boy's discovery that the fight is his without his honest effort makes it worth reading.

216. Farrell, James T. "The Fall of Machine Gun McGurk." <u>Canadian Forum</u> 19 (July 1939): 116-121. Also in the author's <u>$1,000 a Week, and Other Stories</u>. Vanguard, 1942.

McGurk, an Irish boy from South Chicago, earned his nickname through his murderous punching style. His managers have worked him up in the ranks to within a single fight from a match with the heavyweight champion. McGurk's rise has been badly tainted, however, by a long string of set-ups with over-the-hill boxers and tank artists.

When McGurk goes up against a fighter of plodding but dedicated skill, the game is up. McGurk takes a fearsome beating. A memorable last paragraph describes McGurk as "another punch-drunk bum hanging on the edge of the sport world, broke, shabby, with a beaten and battered brain making him the butt of cruel and stupid jokes." One more story of boxing's corruption, with plenty of onus spread around to implicate the press and public as well as the fighters and their managers.

217. _____. "Twenty-Five Bucks." In <u>Stories for Men</u>, p. 179-187. Edited by Charles Grayson. Garden City, 1938. Also in the author's <u>Calico Shoes, and Other Stories</u>. Vanguard, 1934.

A beat-to-hell boxer named Kid Tucker has to fight a six-round match against a young opponent. Kid's take will be $25, if he turns in a passable performance. Kid takes a hammering from the youngster, but the crowd is so unhappy with his effort that, to silence cries of fraud, Kid's promoter refuses to give him the money. It

hardly matters. Kid Tucker is dead of a brain hemorrhage. An
atmospheric story of an ugly, cruel scene.

218.   Fay, William. "Nolan's Last Fight." Saturday Evening Post
       226 (Jan. 16, 1954): 26+.
       Willy Nolan has returned at the age of thirty-two from an un-
distinguished but profitable boxing career to work as a late-night
disc jockey. He's good at it. He has a talent for discussing serious current events in a listenable way, and also exhibits a spry
sense of humor. Unfortunately for Willy's reputation among his old
friends in the fight business, many of his on-the-air jokes come at
their expense. When he attends a reception for a French boxer,
the old boys ignore him.
       A ruse traps Willy into a comeback fight against the French-
man; Willy wants no part of it, but feels obligated to enter the ring.
The compulsion to give the game one last shot at him is one that he
must meet, or lose both his self-respect and his girlfriend. Willy
fights and loses, but puts up a brave effort. Like so many other
popular sports stories, this one is essentially concerned with the
main character's proving himself able to "take it like a man."

219.   Foley, Martha. "Glory, Glory, Hallelujah." Story 9 (July
       1936): 27-38. Also in Best Short Stories of 1937. Edited by
       Edward J. O'Brien. Houghton Mifflin, 1937.
       A sweet story, but not so sweet that the center is without a
dash of bitters. A young girl is transported into passionate sympathy for "the colored people" when a black choir visits her school
and sings spirituals. Emily vows to "do something" for the race
which hers has wronged. Her action takes the form of support for
a black fighter, Henry Theophrastus Sully, better known as "The
Black Shadow." To the dismay of her brothers, she roots for Sully
in his Independence Day bout against a white boxer that the world
at large expects to clobber him. Emily even writes Sully a letter
to let him know that she will be praying for him.
       The questions remaining after the bout are how genuine is
Emily's new commitment to racial justice, and how long it will last--
and will it find more meaningful avenues for expression than in a
romantic seconding of a black man she will never have to see in person?

220.   Ford, Corey. "The Killer Racket." Saturday Evening Post
       226 (Sept. 12, 1953): 37+.
       A grim story of greed, opportunism, and death. Jimmy Nolan
went into boxing not because he liked hitting other men, but because he wanted to make enough money to buy a new car. He dis-
liked the ring life, hated training, and had no intention of pursuing
the sport further than necessary to buy his wheels. He was a good
boy, with an innocent expression that earned him the nickname
"Babyface."
       A conspiracy of circumstances traps Jimmy into what looks, at
story's end, like a living death in the ring. He marries a woman

with an insatiable lust for the high-life that Jimmy's fight winnings
can provide; an unscrupulous manager exploits the notoriety attending
Jimmy after a punch-drunk fighter dies at Jimmy's hands. Following
the death, Jimmy says that people in the neighborhood "didn't hate
me, it wan't that. They acted, well, excited. Like almost hero-
worshipping."

Throughout the story we hear an announcer reporting Jimmy's
latest fight, one he has agreed to under duress. His wife watches
the bout on a bar television, with a smug smile on her face as she
anticipates the big money. Jimmy wins, but takes a terrible beating, his face cut to pieces, his nose mashed flat, his lips so mangled
that his speech is unintelligible.

"They used to call him Babyface," says the announcer. A
story that Dreiser would probably enjoy.

221. Friedman, Bruce J. "The Night Boxing Ended." In his
      Black Angels, p. 136-142. Simon & Schuster, 1966.
      A man recounts his experience at ringside the night the fights
stopped. An Irish boy and a Latino are engaged in the lackluster
main event when a fan begins to heckle both of them savagely. He
berates the Irish fighter for not using his right hand. "Knock his
head off. Knock his head off," bellows the heckler. The story
leads up to one astonishing paragraph, and it does pack a wallop.
It is also quite funny.

222. Gardner, Leonard. Fat City. Farrar, Straus & Giroux.
      1969. 183 p.
      This much-praised novel deserves much of its praise, but it
misses out on claims to greatness because of its characters. Gardner
treats them well, but they are such hopelessly uninteresting, even
boring, people that one hardly cares what happens to them. That
the book remains readable as a whole owes strictly to Gardner's
stylistic command and to his own sustained interest in the characters.

Who are these dull people that Gardner finds so engrossing?
They are losers and would-bes, chiefly Billy Tully, a used-up fighter
nearing thirty, and Ernie Munger, a teenager with ring ambitions but
no outstanding talent. Gardner chronicles their "careers" in Stock-
ton, California, in an economical, understated prose. Ernie pumps
gas, Tully lives in the Hotel Coma. Ernie trains to be a boxer,
Tully's wife leaves him and he takes on work as a farm laborer.
Ernie gets married to a woman he doesn't want to marry and joins
Tully in the fields. Ernie gets knocked out; Tully tries to stage a
comeback and wins $100 for ten hard rounds. Things happen, and
at the same time, nothing happens. It is the loser's life, and
Gardner puts it down just right, with some outstanding passages on
training (Ernie snorting salt water to toughen his nose, for example)
and on the men at work in the fields. The book's drawback, in
spite of its fine technical merits, is the mundane, tedious defeat that
must be its characters' lot. They have no other possibilities.

223. Gault, William C. "Title Fight." In Run to Starlight; Sports

Through Science Fiction, p. 246-262. Edited by Martin H.
Greenberg, et al. Delacorte, 1975. First published in Fantastic Universe (Dec. 1956).

Unlike another fight described here which also features a man
battling a robot (item 235), this one evokes all its sympathy for the
robot. In the end, though, the message is similar: machines
threaten the destruction of humanity.

Here, Alix 1340, made in man's image, is to go against Nick
Nolan, the champ, a man "made in His image." Alix's mechanical
backers hope that their boy (their 'bot?) will not only defeat the
offensive Nolan, pride of the white world, but will "give the word"
to the wretched of the earth that the time has come to overthrow
white society everywhere. What they only hint at to Alix is that
this revolution will be only a preliminary to the machine's complete
mastery of the human race. Alix does, in fact, defeat the human
champion, but his word to the masses is far from what his eager
mechanical mates anticipate. Given Alix's nurturing by Bach,
Beethoven, and Shakespeare, his departure from the expected may
not be too surprising.

224. Guthrie, A. B. "Independence Day." Esquire 53 (Jan. 1960):
      117+. Also in the author's The Big It, and Other Stories.
      Houghton Mifflin, 1960.

"It was July 4, 1920, and Charlie Bostwick was seventeen
years old when Bill the Butch fought the Fairfax Soldier." Thus
begins this sad story of a man who cannot recognize his own defeat,
or his own arrogance. Bill the Butch is a young German, a but-
cher's helper, and the town fighter. No one wants to tangle with
him. The locals import a good fighter, a soldier, for the Independence Day match with Bill. Bill lands a couple of early blows,
but, much to the crowd's delight, continues to receive a thorough
beating from the soldier.

The fight is a revelation for Charlie. He pities the bull-
headed young German, partly because he sees the man's obstinate
and completely mistaken insistence that he is the superior fighter.
Guthrie writes economically and perceptively in this story of an
emotional and intellectual crisis.

225. Hale, Nancy. "Waxen Man." American Mercury 30 (Sept.
      1933): 14-18. Also in the author's Earliest Dreams. Scrib-
      ner's, 1936.

A study in vindictive over-reaction. The story begins with a
woman, Gerda, lying in bed "feeling drenched and hopeless." The
source of her sorrow is her lover's marriage to another woman.
Gerda takes her rejection not just personally, but cosmically. Oh
my, my, it is a hard and heartless existence! Two of Gerda's
friends, Gordon and Williams, stop by to take her to the fights.
One of the fighters in the main event looks a lot like black-haired
Jim, who dumped her. Under the influence of alcohol consumed en
route to the fight, Gerda confuses the fighter with Jim, and savors
every punch delivered to this unwitting physical substitute. Before

the fight is over, Gerda stands up and screams for the death of
the "Jim" boxer. "Kill him!" she cries.

Gerda's behavior embarrasses her companions, but she is too
steeped in self-pity to recognize her excesses. Though narrated
in the third-person, the point of view is very much Gerda's, a fact
excusing what one would otherwise call some overly-heated literary-
ness. Gerda herself is overheated, so the prose matches and exposes her state of mind.

226. Hamill, Pete. Flesh & Blood; A Novel. Random House, 1977.
      276 p.

This boxing novel doesn't hit hard: it cuts and slices like
an edge of glass, reducing the reader to cleanly-carved pieces.
Bobby Fallon, an Irish youth from Brooklyn, carries with him, wher-
ever he goes, a barely-contained rage that, combined with his fistic
skill, makes him a serious contender for boxing laurels. In an
electrically-charged opening chapter, Fallon, offended at the treatment he and a black friend receive in a bar, all but demolishes the
place by himself. For this action, Fallon goes to prison, a stretch
Hamill describes in merciless detail. Out from behind the walls,
Fallon puts his trust in trainer Gus Caputo, who works to refine
the young man's skills and to help him learn to slow the speed at
which his temper's fuse burns.

Paralleling and partially illuminating Fallon's boxing career is
a subtheme of incest and parental desertion. Whether this part of
the story was necessary is questionable, but Hamill handles it acceptably. Where the book really shines, however, is in its description of Fallon's violent approach in the ring and toward life itself.
Hamill's tense, adrenalin-charged style is well suited to his subject.

Flesh & Blood is a novel of considerable artistry whose effect
is to some extent overshadowed by an overly conscientious effort
to show "why." The reason does not matter nearly as much as the
fact of being; Hamill's portrayal of a violent sensibility is, minus the
sociological undertow, one of the purest to be found in boxing literature.

227. Heinz, W. C. The Professional. Harper, 1958. 338 p.

Boxer Eddie Brown is a good, if inarticulate, man. Frank
Hughes, a magazine reporter, stays with middleweight contender
Brown in Brown's training camp to observe him preparing for a
fight. The book concludes with the fight, which lasts less than two
minutes, leaving Brown a befuddled and possibly doomed man.

Readers interested in either boxing or sports journalism will
enjoy this novel. In addition to providing an extended insider's
view of a boxer's training, it furnishes insights into a sportswriter's
career (perhaps at the expense of some immediacy in our sympathy
with Brown; the novel is sometimes too much like an account in the
sports section than an intimately-felt fiction).

228. Hemingway, Ernest. "The Battler." In his The Nick Adams
      Stories, p. 47-57. Scribner's, 1972.

After a brakeman throws him off a train one night, Nick
Adams stumbles onto the hobo camp of Ad Francis, a battered old
prizefighter. Initially friendly, Francis soon turns threatening
toward Nick; Francis's friend and keeper, a black man, intervenes.
Typical early Hemingway, with a lot of tension riding between the
lines of superficially innocuous conversation. Chilling moment: when
Ad Francis says, "Listen. I'm not quite right."

229. _____. "Fifty Grand." In his The Short Stories of Ernest
Hemingway, p. 300-326. Scribner's, 1953.
Jack Brennan, a poorly-conditioned fighter, confesses to Jerry, the story's narrator, that he is betting fifty thousand dollars
on his forthcoming New York bout. His bet is on his opponent--to
win. Brennan wins his bet by losing the match, but he has to lose
by refusing to admit that a deliberate low blow delivered by his opponent was a foul, a foul carefully planned by the other boxer's
managers. A story of sordid intrigue and a kind of courage, with
the fight described sharply and sympathetically. The passage in
which an inebriated Brennan reveals his loneliness to Jerry is a
high point, and the glimpses into Brennan's fundamental stinginess
lend further dimensions to the story.

230. _____. "The Killers." In his The Short Stories of Ernest
Hemingway, p. 279-289. Scribner's, 1953.
Although boxing is only mentioned briefly in this story, it is
presumably a fight-game doublecross that accounts for its events.
Nick Adams is at the counter of Henry's lunchroom one evening when
a pair of sinister men come in. They order supper, pick a moronic
argument with George the cashier, and tie up Nick and the cook in
the kitchen. They're waiting for the usual 6 P.M. arrival of Ole
Andreson, a former heavyweight boxer. They plan to greet him with
a sawed-off shotgun. Ole doesn't show up, and the killers leave.
Nick runs over to Andreson's rooming house to let him know the
killers are in town. Andreson thanks Nick for the information, but
says "There ain't anything to do."
The tension in this story is agonizing. There is good reason
to believe that the hit men will kill Nick, George and the cook
simply for being in the way. Andreson's resignation is almost clas-
sically fatalistic, and Nick's reaction--"I'm going to get out of this
town"--is absurd. How would it be different in any other town?
"It's too damned awful," says Nick, and he's right.

231. Idell, Albert E. Pug. Greystone, 1941. 245 p.
The title says it all, or most of it. Pug tracks another ac-
ceptable, if not good, boy gone bad thanks to the rotten world of
pro boxing. Idell's hero, or victim, is young Whitey Phillips, a
youth of no keen mind but with a pair of quick fists. After his
initial success, Whitey, hooked on the idolatry of the crowd, stumbles
up queer street (see item 269) looking for a glory that will continue
to recede on the horizon. Whitey's small but representative tragedy
ends in death, but for practical purposes Whitey is dead long before

his final action. An unhappy story, and a familiar one in most respects.

232. Lardner, Ring. "The Battle of the Century." Saturday Eve-
      ning Post (Oct. 29, 1921): 12+. Also in the author's Some
      Champions: Sketches & Fiction. Edited by Matthew J. Bruc-
      coli and Richard Layman. Scribner's, 1976.
      Lardner's treatment of the Dempsey-Carpentier fight, which he
considered mere hot air. He presents the fight between the American
champion and the French challenger as a carefully-manufactured big-
money fraud. One manager says, "if the public demands the match,
what do we care if the two men stack up together like a pimple and
a goiter?" The public demands the fight, it takes place, the chief
figures take their money and run, and the public goes home happy.
As the narrator puts it, "You know what Barnum said. Well, he
didn't go far enough."

233. _____. "Champion." Golden Book Magazine 19 (Jan. 1934):
      1-14. Also in the author's The Best Short Stories of Ring
      Lardner. Scribner's, 1957.
      Michael "Midge" Kelly has a great left hand. It is by far his
best feature. This up-and-coming young boxer knocks his crippled
brother cold for 50 cents, slugs his mother, beats his wife, ducks
out on his creditors and double-crosses his manager. "Champion"
is Lardner at his most bitter, showing how a vile character can win
the public's heart through clever publicity and mawkish, irresponsible journalism. If there is a problem with the story it is that
Kelly is almost too ghastly to believe, but Lardner's picture of a
worthless man publicly glorified is one of a kind frequently developed
in the mass media. Anyone who finds the story interesting will also
want to see the fine 1949 film based on it, directed by Mark Robson.
The title is the same; the lead role belongs to Kirk Douglas.

234. _____. "Frame-Up." In his How to Write Short Stories,
      p. 249-282. Scribner's, 1924.
      Lardner is in top form in this one, scoring points both with
good humor and with his usual mordant view of the sporting life.
A Michigan farm boy, Burke, turns up in a Chicago gym looking for
boxing lessons. The lad has no initial interest in becoming a pro;
he just wants to lay out a competitor for a woman back home.
Burke proves himself an accomplished boxer, and when he sees the
impression his fighting makes on women in general, he takes up the
game seriously, planning to use it to attract a wealthy, beautiful
girl. Burke has talented hands and feet, but nothing but wide open
spaces between his ears. This leaves plenty of room for his gal-
loping ego, but it also leaves him easily hoodwinked by a scheme to
make him fall for a "society girl" identified as "Esther Fester." The
mash notes to Burke, forged in Esther's name, are models of bait
for the gullible, and Burke swallows them whole.

235. Laumer, Keith. "The Body Builders." In Infinite Arena,

p. 61-90. Edited by Terry Carr. Nelson, 1977. First published in <u>Galaxy</u> (August 1966).

"Feely smelly" television with contact screens for the eyeballs
have given way to surrogate bodies, which negotiate the dangerous
world for their owners, whose organic bodies lie on file in the Mu-
nicipal Vaults. Physical fitness has turned to servotechnology.
Barney Ramm, our hero and narrator, is a prizefighter who, through
a series of miscalculations, ends up facing a humanoid robot in the
ring, but in his organic body, not that of his mechanical double.
The triumph of man over machine is exciting; it will give heart to
saboteurs everywhere.

236. Lewis, Hobart. "The Famous Dempsey Crouch." In <u>That's</u>
      <u>What Happened to Me</u>, p. 50-63. Edited by Whit Burnett.
      Four Winds, 1969.

Elmer Hoobler takes a job on a road-building crew, hoping
that the hard work will toughen him up enough to win him a spot
on his high school football team in the fall. A co-worker offers to
give Elmer boxing lessons, and soon the boy has visions of welterweight grandeur. These visions come to an inglorious end, but
Elmer still manages to make the football team. A good illustration
of the ease with which modest achievements at age sixteen become
"promises" of great things to come.

237. London, Jack. <u>The Abysmal Brute</u>. Century, 1913. 169 p.
      Also in <u>The Game and the Abysmal Brute</u>. Horizon Pr.,
      1969.

Sam Stubener receives a letter from an old fighter advising
him to investigate "Young Pat Glendon," a natural heavyweight.
The boy is that, but he also dotes on flowers and poetry, and
takes fighting less than seriously. The boy's father has brought
up Young Pat in backwoods California innocence, keeping him ignorant of the fight game's seedy qualities. Pat "don't know a man
ever lay down or threw a fight."

Pat inaugurates his career with a series of lightening knock-
outs. The fans dub him "One-Punch Glendon." In spite of his
growing fame, he still checks out novels from the public library,
and attends lectures on Robert Browning. As he works his way
through the heavyweight contenders, both Pat and Stubener grow
wealthy, "due, more than anything else, to the clean lives they
lived." Because Pat keeps to himself, seldom going out with the
fight crowd, he acquires a wholly unfair reputation as a dull-witted
ox, the "Abysmal Brute," as one sportswriter calls him.

Pat turns a corner in his relationship with boxing when young
Maud Sangster comes to interview him for her newspaper. She finds
the sensitive soul beneath Pat's crude public image. During the
interview, Maud accidentally tips Pat off to the probability that his
upcoming fight has been fixed, in his favor. Pat and Maud marry,
and he works a double-cross on the fight syndicate that leads to a
broad investigation, complete with indictments.

Not up to the psychological interest of <u>The Game</u>, but this novel is still worth reading for its revelations of London's attitudes toward prizefighting. He clearly loves the game, and just as clearly detests the squalid corruption that characterizes its management from top to bottom.

238. _____. The Game. Macmillan, 1905. 182 p. Also in The Game and the Abysmal Brute. Horizon Pr., 1969.

A short novel as subtle as a blow to the head. Upon finishing it, the reader may feel more than a little pummelled. The story is set in Oakland, California, where young Joe Fleming works as a sail-maker and club fighter. In the book's first half, we watch as Joe and a sheltered girl, Genevieve, fall in love. They meet in a candy store where Genevieve works, and each is immediately drawn to the other.

They enter upon a remarkably chaste affair, yet even in the midst of their discreet, fleeting touches, each awakens to new and disturbing sensations. Genevieve feels what is apparently a primal lust that she identifies as an impetus to "sin;" Joe feels an unaccountable and perplexing desire to hurt this delicate girl, whom he is sure he loves.

The book's second half is set in an arena where Joe fights a brute named Ponta. Genevieve sneaks into the all-male stronghold and observes the fight through a dressing room peephole. When she first sees Joe in the ring, naked but for his trunks and sneakers, "The leap of something within her and the stir of her being ... was delicious sin, and she did not deny her eyes." The fight is a pounding, animalistic encounter. Genevieve "exulted with each crushing blow her lover delivered." The bout goes back and forth between the fighters, and ends in a shocking manner that London claimed elsewhere to have actually observed in his own fighting experience.

The Game is partly about the conflict between a man's compulsion to participate in this grim sport versus his also powerful desire to please his chosen mate; it is partly about sexual relations in their most primitive form, and it is also about the realities of the ring, which London both cherished and loathed. The book is "minor" London, but is strong and memorable. In a sense, it is the boxing novel to end boxing novels: few could say (and few have said) much about the sport that this one does not.

Readers should try to find the novel in the original Macmillan edition, which, alas, will be rapidly deteriorating in most instances. It contains a large number of illustrations by Henry Hutt and T. C. Laurence, some almost joyously morbid, that bring out aspects of the story one might otherwise overlook.

239. _____. "The Mexican." In his The Night-born, and Other
     Stories, p. 243-290. Grosset & Dunlap, 1913.
     Felipe Rivera, age 18, is a revolutionary of a frightening cold
temper. He leaves his comrades for unexplained periods, but returns with large amounts of money to help finance their work. He
promises to raise $5,000 for guns. He fights a New York boxer,
Danny Ward, though Rivera has had no experience except against
a few locals. Rivera "despised prize fighting. It was the hated
game of the hated Gringo. He had taken up with it ... solely because he was starving." A potent passage describes Rivera's vision
of the people he is fighting for, to free from the grip of oppression
by Porfirio Diaz. What follows is one of the most grueling fights
imaginable, with the New York man at first sure of an easy victory,
then, with the conspiracy of the referee, seeking victory through
foul play. Rivera's dedication to his cause carries him past both
fair and foul attempts to stop him.

240. _____. "A Piece of Steak." In Jack London: Novels and
     Stories, p. 849-867. Edited by Donald Pizer. Library of
     America, 1982. Also in the author's When God Laughs. Mac-
     millan, 1911.
     Set in Australia. Tom King, a tired old fighter, must send
his children to bed hungry while his wife begs credit from trades-
men. He sits at home one night longing for a piece of steak, remembering his flush days when he threw steak to his dog without
a thought. Scheduled for a bout with a young New Zealander,
King stands to win a few pounds, if his battered, 40-year-old body
holds up. London describes the fight in careful, painful detail,
and leads the reader to great sympathy with the old fighter, who
puts his body at risk not for glory or the prospect of future wealth,
but for a chance to feed his family. When it is over, and Tom King
must make the long walk home to report the outcome to his wife, the
reader knows that this outcome was inevitable. A very strong story
that takes the reader in the grip of London's keen feelings for those
who have nothing and cannot realistically hope for more.

241. Lowry, Robert J. The Violent Wedding. Doubleday, 1953.
     255 p.
     A psychological drama with themes of race and class conflict,
but carried out with subtlety that makes it richer and more ambiguous than similar material might be managed, by, say, James T. Farrell. Paris "Baby" James is a ranking contender for the middleweight championship. He has an affair with Laine Branden, a former
Bennington art student and creatively-blocked painter. Laine is
white; Paris is black. When she first sees Paris walking up the
stadium aisle to the ring, looking like "an animated bronze statue
out of some sculptor's dream," she is hooked.
     Their affair is brief, but it rekindles Laine's artistic inspira-
tion, and she works hard at her painting. Danger signs are everywhere, in her fear of Paris and in the questions she asks herself.
Does she love him "just becuase it is such a desperate thing to love

him--such an annihilating thing?" She is closer to the truth here than she probably thinks. Their affair ends in an ugly fashion, and Laine annihilates herself with sleeping pills. Her memory near-ly drives Paris to quit the ring, and the reader wishes that he would.

There are some very authentic fight scenes, including one with a mortal outcome. Before the book's concluding fight, "Both fighters looked like brides in those towels and robes." It is a somber book without much hope held out to the reader's grasp. The fight busi-ness, however, is well portrayed, and the clash in values between an educated, artistic white woman and an unschooled (but by no means unintelligent) black man who earns his living with his fists creates a tension-filled novel.

242. McKeon, J. M. "Gladiator." Story 10 (June 1937): 29-39.
     Also in O. Henry Memorial Award Prize Stories of 1937.
     Edited by Harry Hansen. Doubleday, 1937.
     "Yih liddle bastid. I tol yih nodda come." This story of a boxing match between Tony, a prison champion, and Swede Sunjer-strom, a fighter from the outside, is marred by frequent forays into dialect writing of which the opening sentences here are typical. If the reader can overlook the "liddle bastids," the story will be a rewarding one.

The fight takes place within the prison walls, and is attended by a crowd of prisoners and farm families. The bout goes badly at first for Tony, but he draws strength from his fellow prisoners' support, and in the end soundly beats Swede. The prison atmos-phere comes through well, as does the mysterious bond between the victor and the defeated, which sets them apart from all those in at-tendance.

Better managed than the dialect are italicized flashbacks to Tony's childhood and youth; they illustrate some of the social forces that drove him to boxing, and to prison.

243. Matheson, Richard. "Steel." In Run to Starlight; Sports
     through Science Fiction, p. 265-297. Edited by Martin H.
     Greenberg, et al. Delacorte, 1975. First published in the
     Magazine of Fantasy and Science Fiction (May 1956).
     Some years after boxing between humans has been banned, two men, a mechanic and a former boxer, arrive with their robot boxer in a nowhere heartland town. They have a fight scheduled, but their robot snaps a spring before the bout. Down on their luck, hungry, anxious for funds to repair their "Battling Maxo," their choices are shaped by desperation. Steel Kelly, the former pugilist, decides to pass for a machine, and enters the ring against a powerful new model robot. The fight that follows is a work of butchery (machines may not be cruel, but neither do they show mercy). Back in the dressing room, Steel rattles on about how the couple of hundred he earned for passing as a robot will put good old Maxo back in tip-top condition.

Matheson, long a front-rank writer in the horror genre, nicely illustrates one of the prizefight occupation's most pathetic scenes, that of the beaten man who fools himself into believing that he can come back to the vigor of youth. That the youth Steel is out to restore at the price of his own body once belonged to a mechanical man makes little difference. Compare this story with items 223 and 235.

244. Maxwell, James A. "Fighter." Collier's 131 (Jan. 10, 1953): 64+. Also in Prize Stories, 1954: The O. Henry Awards. Edited by Paul Engle and Hansford Martin. Doubleday, 1954.
    The narrator looks back at when he was a small boy and his assistance in training a teenaged boxer, George Schumacher. George paid the boy for doing minor chores by giving him boxing lessons and tickets to matches. George was a fighter with some potential, but his father accused him of pursuing "kid stuff." At a charity match, George killed an opponent with a chance blow to the head. He apparently never fought again, and the narrator has not heard of him in three decades.
    The relationship between the boy and George is well-handled. Two scenes stand out, one in which George dismisses the boy from his duties, the other in which, after the fatal fight, the boy witnesses George's angry, hurt reaction to his father's treatment of him.

245. Menaker, Daniel. "The Champion." In his Friends and Relations, p. 161-167. Doubleday, 1976.
    Narrated by the brother of the world heavyweight champion, whom the narrator does not name, but calls only, with greater intimacy than a given name, "my brother." The champion, his two trainers, the narrator and the narrator's wife live in a loft in an old industrial building. The champion spurns the usual material goods favored by wealthy athletes and insists on remaining a man of the people. His only indulgence is a large television screen built into one wall of the loft so that his brother, who cannot bear to watch him fight in person, can view his bouts on the closed-circuit screen.
    The story concentrates on one fight. The champion takes on a tough, young challenger in New Delhi, and comes very close to losing. The narrator realizes when it is over that he wanted his brother to lose, "Just to have it done with, to discover what will happen to us once the burden of greatness is lifted away. I dread that he may never lose, that he will continue as champion forever, but at greater and greater cost, with more and more suffering."
    This very short story produces an effect far out of proportion to its length. The crushing sense of obligation stemming from achievement is very real; the champion's commitment to "the people" leaves him and those closest to him living the lives of tenement dwellers, with the wealth that could free them all from material want nowhere to be seen. We fear with the narrator that the champion will continue to fight, and to put himself at risk, because of a compulsion that no one can understand.

246.   Moise, L. C.   "The Last Ounce."   American Magazine 75 (April
       1913): 70+.
       A boxing story that need not hang its head in any literary
company.   Jimmy Nolan (why is "Nolan" such a popular name for
fighters?), former lightweight champion, has lost both his title and
his wife.   When "The Tornado," the fighter who absconded with
Jimmy's wife, secures the lightweight title through a string of coincidence and other boxers' lack of skill, Jimmy is sufficiently enraged to train for a bout with The Tornado.
       Jimmy has been out of the ring for some time, and his weight
has gone up.   Moise describes in arduous terms Jimmy's struggle to
pare his pounds down to the maximum allowed in the lightweight division.   The effort is costly, robbing Jimmy of his last ounce of re-
serve strength.   The only way to bring his weight down far enough
is through avoidance of liquid.   By the time Jimmy reaches the ring,
his lips and throat are parched.   The fight starts badly for him,
and the crowd expects The Tornado to put Jimmy down.   Late in the
fight, Jimmy hears laughter from ringside: it is that of his former
wife, amused at the prospect of Jimmy's defeat by her new lover.
Infuriated by her laughter, Jimmy reclaims "the last ounce," and with
it the ability to go on.
       Unsentimental and well detailed, this story will hit many read-
ers hard, whether they sense the hatred that fires Jimmy's victory,
or taste the lemon he sucks on during his "drying out," when he can
have neither milk nor water.   Bonus attraction: illustrations by the
noted artist George Bellows.

247.   Newman, Edwin.   Sunday Punch.   Houghton Mifflin, 1979.
       279 p.
       Included here only to warn away potential readers.   Television
"personality" Newman's "satire" on boxing and the world at large is
unfunny, unsympathetic with its characters, and boring.   Even the
most run-of-the-ring stories from the Post or Collier's noted here are
superior.

248.   O'Hara, John.   "The Weakness."   New Yorker 37 (July 8,
       1961): 23-29.   Also in the author's Assembly.   Random House,
       1961.
       Bob Buzzell has quit the prizefight business in his early 30s
with his wits intact and $75,000 in the bank.   He enters a good
financial arrangement with a bowling alley, but his wife, an aggressive social climber, is not satisfied.   She is convinced that her
knowledge of his "weakness," a desire to be hurt when making love,
will enable her to manipulate him as well as his former managers did.
       It is a tossup as to which character, Buzzell or his wife, is
more offensive.   He is initially at least tolerable, but proves himself
to be both sadistic and masochistic.   Perhaps the two deserve each
other.   It is, anyhow, a story that shows well how long-harbored ill
traits can bloom in the right soil, in this case, that of Buzzell's retirement from the ring.

249. Pancake, Breece D'J. "The Scrapper." In his The Stories
      of Breece D'J Pancake, p. 101-114. Little, Brown, 1983.
      A slice of southern whiskey-drinking, cockfighting, barnyard
brawling life. Skeevy, a veteran impromptu pugilist, goes up
against a local antagonist at Jeb Simpkin's barn. Skeevy is convinced that Gibson, his opponent, wants to kill him, and as the
story ends the reader fears that Skeevy's conviction will be carried
out in fact. Many motives and personal histories rumble below the
surface of this story. (Pancake, a young writer of great potential
and some concrete achievement as represented by this collection,
killed himself one night in April, 1979.)

250. Phillips, James A. "Comeback." Saturday Evening Post 227
      (Sept. 18, 1954): 22-23+.
      This novelette-length story of a former middleweight champion's
return to the ring is surprisingly good, free of the easy contrasts
between right and wrong and free of the cheap happy ending that
spoils too many popular sports stories.
      George Dolan has not fought in seven years and, though still
possessing great speed of hand and a smooth style, it is doubtful
whether his stamina is sufficient to carry him the length of a ten-
round bout. He would have no desire to put on the gloves again,
but bad investments and gambling losses have drained his once-
healthy bankroll.
      Dolan trains for a comeback against Mike Jeffray, a hard-
slugging but awkward young man. Jeffray is a stolid, colorless
man, but the author paints him as one with redeeming, humane
qualities, a nice touch that keeps the reader from a simple-minded
choosing-up sides when the fight begins.
      Following the match, there is a brief but touching encounter
between Dolan and Jeffray in Dolan's dressing room that further emphasizes the boxers' mutual humanity, and the last paragraph contains an especially good scene: as Dolan's wife drives him away
from the arena, with their small daughter in the back seat, Dolan
keeps his head averted from the little girl "because he did not want
her to see his face." A boxing story successful at both the level
of popular and literary interest.

251. Riess, Curt. "Sparring Partner." Esquire 18 (Sept. 1942):
      61+.
      Another examination of yet another seamy side of boxing. The
portrait here is of a sparring partner, an aspiring fighter who lets
a champion pummel him in practice for the sake of a few dollars.
The sparring partner is convinced, naturally, that nothing but
"bums" stand between him and the championship of his own weight
division. Little vignettes within the story--an over-the-hill boxer
with feeble, old-man's legs prepares for a fight that may put him in
the hospital; a doctor expounds on the inevitability of brain damage;
and discussion of the fight game's economics making it plain that the
boxers are nothing but property--bring home the point that this ambitious but none-too-bright youth will probably finish his career in

the same condition as hundreds of other fighters. He'll be beaten,
broken, addled, penniless, and useless.

252. Rooney, Frank. "Loser Take All." Collier's 132 (Aug. 21,
      1953): 70-73.
      An arrogant young boxer has his first meeting with humility
in this story. Arlen is an egotist and a loudmouth, easily insulted
when the papers fail to quote him accurately, jealous over the
media's attention to the present welterweight champ. Arlen is convinced that being champion means winning the championship fight
and wearing the diamond-studded belt that goes with the win. His
manager tries to persuade him to see that there might be a little
more to being a true champion, but Arlen shrugs off this counsel.
      Comes the fight, and Arlen and the champ pound one another,
round after round. Both go down, and rise again; the fight takes
on something of the dream-like quality said to characterize military
battle. Arlen defeats the champion, but the old champ still wins
the hearts of the crowd and the journalists with his gutty insistence
on sticking it out to the end. After the fight, all the attention
continues to go to the defeated man. There is a good passage describing Arlen's visit to the former champion's dressing room. No
one pushes Arlen aside; all simply flow around him and ignore him
in their focus on the beaten man. Arlen is surrounded, but in his
moment of triumph he is utterly alone. He returns to his dressing
room, where he sits in silent dejection, truth beginning to illuminate
his mind like a sliver of light under a closet door.

253. Runyon, Damon. "Bred for Battle." In his Money from Home,
      p. 83-98. Stokes, 1935.
      An early argument for genetic fine-tuning. The narrator's
old acquaintance Spider McCoy is sure that he has at last determined
the best method for selecting a likely heavyweight contender. His
secret is scientific breeding. Applying the lesson of the track,
where the wise bettor performs genealogical investigations on any
horse he pins his money on, Spider McCoy picks himself a can't-miss
prospect. His new boy is Raymond "Thunderbolt" Mulrooney, son
of a tough fighter and a tougher mother, "by Shamrus Mulrooney
out of Bridget O'Shea." That "Thunderbolt" prefers reading and
playing the zither to beating up others doesn't detract from McCoy's
enthusiasm. McCoy sets the boy up against a tank artist, Bubbles
Browning, for his first fight, and insures a win with a threat to
shoot off Browning's ears should the latter not take his scheduled
dive.
      When the bell rings, Mulrooney comes out sobbing, his face
buried in his hands. McCoy's genetic answer to the heavyweight
question may not be altogether invalid, though, for there is some
question about a possible dalliance between Mrs. Mulrooney and
a zither-playing floorwalker. A tolerable Runyon piece in which he
keeps his penchant for lippy wisecracks under better control than
usual.

254. Saroyan, William. "Dear Baby." Collier's 103 (June 24,
      1939): 12+. Also in the author's Dear Baby. Harcourt, 1944.
      A successful fighter mourns the woman with whom he lived.
She has died, apparently from the complications of pregnancy or
childbirth. In addition to feeling bereft, the fighter is remorseful
when he remembers the times he failed to treat her well. Boxing
victories now leave him empty and hopeless. The story is fairly
sentimental, but it holds up because Saroyan is tactful, and because
he shows that a boxer can be a man of sensitivity as well as one of
muscle, bone, and good reflexes.

255. Schulberg, Budd W. "Crowd Pleaser." In his Some Faces in
      the Crowd, p. 124-133. Bodley Head, 1954.
      A fight in the ring becomes a contest in the crowd as a talent-
less but dirty white fighter does his worst against a good black
boxer. The narrator sits between two other men at ringside and
describes their conduct through the fight. One of the men, who
favors the white boxer, is a crude, blustering, self-satisfied sort
named Dempsey, who years before "had appointed himself a sort of
one-man claque to urge the fighters on to bloodier efforts." The
other man, Glover, is a slightly-built male stenographer who admires
the black fighter's quick, clever style.
      As the fight progresses, Glover and Dempsey become increas-
ingly pointed in their comments; they speak as though to the boxers,
but it is obvious that they are having a verbal battle with each
other. Glover's man has by far the better of the bout until Dempsey's resorts to some patently foul tactics that the referee overlooks,
no doubt because of the victim's color. Dempsey rejoices in his
fighter's dirty win; Glover is distraught over his man's undeserved
defeat.
      Vivid and gripping, "Crowd Pleaser" is a good study of the
vicarious, yet intense, experience of the fight in which many ring
fans delight.

256. _____. The Harder They Fall. Random House, 1947.
      343 p.
      A good chronicle of prizefighting squalidness, where money
rules and where sentiments of decency and fair play are left to the
saps. The novel's focus is on its victim, Toro Molina, "the Giant
of the Andes," an Argentine who stands closer to seven feet than
six and who weighs nearly 300 pounds. Fight promoter Nick Latka
and his press agent Eddie Lewis contrive a hyped "career" for
Molina that leaves Latka the beneficiary of Molina's, and the sporting crowd's, ignorance. It leaves Molina a beaten-to-a-pulp bum.
He never did have any boxing talent. The novel plays off the ring
debacle of Primo Carnera, but it holds up well as an exploration of
big-time boxing's small-time morals. The author's eyes and ears are
sensitive: he sees and hears the authentic details of the ring, and
relays them well to the reader.

257. _____. "Memory in White." Collier's 110 (Sept. 26, 1942):

20+. Also in the author's <u>Some Faces in the Crowd</u>. Bodley
Head, 1954.

An excruciating portrait of self-delusion and personal tragedy.
Jose Fuentes, who would rather be known as Pancho Villa the Third,
worked for a few years as a club fighter. When he hung up his
gloves, he retained great ambition, but not full command of his
faculties. His scheme for grandeur calls for him to make it in the
boxing business as an announcer. To further this end, he buys
himself a tacky white linen suit and white platform shoes, and lo-
cates a beaten-up old megaphone in a pawnshop. He then hangs
around his old gym day after day, bellowing "announcements" to
the fighters and the other hangers-on. "He was the greatest announcer in the world. Only nobody could understand him." Too
many shots to the head had turned his speech into "a kind of gut-
tural doubletalk."

Another gym bum with a "califlower brain" takes much delight
in humiliating Fuentes by dirtying his suit and stepping on his
white shoes. On the night when Fuentes finally gets a chance to
announce at a fight, the conflict between him and his tormentor
takes a lethal turn. A fine and grating story; Fuentes is too far
gone to feel the embarrassment in which he bathes, but the reader
feels it, painfully.

258. Scott, William R. "They Called Him a Killer." <u>Saturday Eve-</u>
     <u>ning Post</u> 226 (Nov. 14, 1953): 34-35+.

Harve Pigeon, a Cherokee Indian and a widower, works in the
Oklahoma oil fields. Old age has turned the corner on him, and,
as he rakes leaves in his yard, he believes he has nothing left to
look forward to, not even seeing his beloved stepson, Ben. A
couple of years earlier, Ben killed another boxer with a right-hand
punch. Harve believed that Ben would quit the ring, but Ben,
though shattered by his opponent's death, put the gloves back on
and worked his way up near the top of the contender list. Harve's
desire to see his stepson come home finally materializes; Ben has, it
turns out, been fighting only from a sense of responsibility to provide for the family of the fighter he killed. A minor story with a
few good stretches, including Ben's confrontation with the family of
the dead boxer.

259. Shaara, Michael. <u>The Broken Place</u>. New American Library,
     1968. 239 p.

Tom McClain is far from the standard hero of a novel about
boxing. He spent two years in college before going to fight in
Korea, and distinguished himself sufficiently to win a Silver Star.
Back in the U.S., his physical wounds healing, his emotional wounds
are still deep and inexplicable. He knows that he craves peace, yet
he feels complete, feels himself a man, only in moments of furious
action, the kind he found in the Korean War, and the kind he found
earlier in the ring.

The first two-thirds of the novel follows McClain as he struggles to find himself, back at his old college with old friends, with

new women, off on an ill-starred trip to the Middle East with a close
friend. In the final third, McClain comes back to boxing, the only
place left where he can be himself as he must be. He is a natural
fighter, with a powerful killer instinct: as soon as he senses his
opponent's injury, he moves in and focuses on that point with deadly intensity. The crowds love it, but McClain pays a heavy price
when one of his victims dies after a fight.

McClain cannot bring himself to strike to hurt in his next
bout, and he suffers a terrible beating. After the fight, he wanders
out into the winter night, where he achieves an epiphany about the
nature of peace and man's fate, and a severe brain hemorrhage.
When the novel ends, there is no certainty that McClain will survive,
but if he does, there is little doubt that, as Hemingway put it, he
will be stronger at the broken place.

A nicely thought-out novel about violence, friendship, and the
virtues of a gentle relationship with the world. The climax is especially strong, with McClain's post-fight wandering through the dark
and the cold a very well-written and affecting passage.

260. Shaw, Irwin. "I Stand by Dempsey." New Yorker 15 (Mar.
      11, 1939): 23-25. Also in the author's Short Stories: Five
      Decades. Delacorte, 1978.
      Two friends engage in a pointless argument over the relative
abilities of the prizefighters Joe Louis and Jack Dempsey. They resolve the debate in a violent way. Worthwhile especially for Shaw's
presentation of the athletic argument pitting against each other two
figures from different eras, an argument whose like occurs with
tedious frequency among committed sports fans.

261. _____. "Stop Pushing, Rocky." Collier's 102 (Dec. 10,
      1938): 27+. Also in the author's Short Stories: Five Decades.
      Delacorte, 1978.
      The fight is on, and so is the fix, both in a Philadelphia bout
between the coming welterweight champion Joey Garr and the talent-
less Rocky Pidgeon. Joey has agreed to let Rocky look reasonably
good for ten rounds; Rocky, fired up by the hometown crowd's
adoration, becomes convinced that he is a better fighter than the
record shows. As Rocky irritates Joey with his aggressiveness, two
thugs with guns sit in the audience to make sure Joey's temper
doesn't interfere with his keeping the deal to insure Rocky's ten
rounds. There is considerable tension here as the reader waits for
the expected moment when Joey's rage over Rocky's attack pushes
him to serious retaliation.

262. Shulman, Irving. The Square Trap. Little, Brown, 1953.
      374 p.
      This novel stands with a very few others at the top of the
many written about boxing. It is the story of Tommy Kansas, born
Tomas Cantanios, son of a Mexican sandal-maker who has been forced
to abandon his craft and to work at undignified jobs. Tomas, his
father Vidal, and the rest of the Cantanios family live in Chavez

Ravine, near Los Angeles, where they eke out a marginal living. All are trapped in the relentless cycle of poverty.

Shulman writes with controlled energy and effect from the outset, when Vidal comes home from his job at the brick factory to find his modest house full of new furniture bought on credit. He must announce to his family as they display their new goods that his Anglo bosses have fired him for being "too old."

A gym manager, Pete Genusa, rescues Tomas from a probable beating in a street brawl, and introduces the ambitious youngster to the ring. Through prizefighting, Tomas, now Tommy Kansas, a 130-pound lightweight, would realize all his dreams. For his father, there would be an independent business; for his family, escape from the Ravine ghetto; for himself, fancy clothes, cars, and women.

Tommy's ambitions surpass his skills, but he is too proud to acknowledge his limitations until they are pounded into him, as they are. Tommy's boxing career ends just short of death, and the book ends with Tommy beating his fists in frustration against a wall. He is trapped, his family is trapped; there is no escape.

Shulman recreates the atmosphere of the boxer's life with authenticity and compassion. His emphasis is less on the corruption of prizefighting than on the stubborn, yet pitifully doomed, quality of individual dreams that do not connect with available opportunities.

263. Skene, Don. The Red Tiger. Appleton-Century, 1934. 196 p.

As this bibliography indicates, there is no shortage of novels and stories that peel back the outer skin of boxing to reveal the festering corruption beneath. There are very few laughs in this literature, and for that reason this novel is a relief. This satirical portrait of boxing succeeds in making the entire boxing enterprise look as dirty and fraudulent as any of the deadly earnest muck-raking jobs do, and it has the pleasant side benefit of being fun to read.

"The Red Tiger of the Rockies" is the hokey ring name assigned one Merle Gillingwater, a mild-mannered, peaceful petshop employee for whom even small, furry animals pose a threat of violence. Merle's one fighterly attribute is his size, resting securely in heavyweight territory. Under the crooked tutelage of Doc Carey, Merle climbs (through fix upon fix) to the pinnacle of the heavyweight pantheon. (That's the sort of overinflated lingo you hear in boxing; the phonier the sport, the more ponderous the terminology).

If any reader can get through The Red Tiger and two or three of the grimmer muckraking jobs discussed here, and still look upon boxing as "the manly art," that individual should prove impervious to any persuasive tactic short of an uppercut to the chin.

264. Switzer, Robert. "Death of a Prize Fighter." Esquire 31 (June 1949): 39+. Also in Prize Stories of 1950: The O. Henry Awards. Edited by Herschel Brickell. Doubleday, 1951.

Billy Murdoch, manager of fighter Tony Casino, takes heavy

criticism from the press when Casino dies from brain injuries sustained during a bout. Background information reveals that Casino
had no business being in the ring that night, owing to tell-tale head
problems and a recent severe knock-out. Murdoch fears the press,
but rationalizes his mishandling of Casino. Our last glimpse of him
comes when he joins some cronies for scotch and sympathy; it is a
lot like watching a pack of rats get together over something recently
killed. A clean jab at the sport, with Murdoch a well-conceived
example of fight-game sleaze.

265. Sylvester, Harry. "I Won't Do No Dive." Esquire 8 (July
      1937): 80+. Also in Esquire's 2d Sports Reader. Edited by
      Arnold Gingrich. A. S. Barnes, 1946.
      A boxer's manager arranges for him to throw a fight for $900
by taking a dive before the seventh round. Although he initially
rejects the deal, the fighter finally agrees. The body won't agree
with the mind's capitulation, however, and the fight fails to follow
its script. An unfortunate melodramatic ending weighs down the
story, but it is otherwise a fairly good piece of its type.

266. Thompson, Morton. "Apprentice of Manly Art." Esquire 5
      (March 1936): 89+.
      Fictional boxing seldom looks as pointless, witless, and ugly
as it does in this story. A young fighter takes on a new youth
from the CCC (Civilian Conservation Corps) camp. Both boxers are
nervous, but when they start swinging they forget their nerves and
beat each other senseless for a few dollars. The fighters are dull
and deluded; the crowd is mean and repulsive; the referee is incompetent. The "manly art" is an excuse for those with a taste for
blood of the human variety to taste it legally. A companion piece,
in this vein, to Jack London's "A Piece of Steak" (item 240).

267. Tully, Jim. The Bruiser. World, 1936. 248 p.
      Unlike most other boxing stories, this one features some know-
ing instruction as delivered by his manager to Shane Rory, a talented fighter who stays on the square in spite of the dishonesty all
around him, and who can be moved to tears by reading Helen Keller's
autobiography. Silent Tim, Shane's manager, sums up the business
when he says "It's a rough world ... as warm as the very devil when
the referee's raisin' your hand, and cold as a hangman's heart when
he ain't."
      The Bruiser follows a breakneck pace as it pursues Shane on
his career toward the heavyweight championship, a chase that concludes in a title fight that brings near obliteration to both boxers.
The denouement is a touch sentimental, but for a good 240 pages the
novel is hard and true. Early passages showing Shane and other
drifters doing their best to survive the Great Depression lend a
further valuable touch to the book.

268. Witwer, Harry C. The Leather Pushers. Putnam, 1920.
      341 p.

A fight manager takes on the contract of Kane Halliday, better known in the ring as Kid Roberts, to settle an old debt. Roberts, a wealthy expellee from Yale, looks like a tough fighter at first, but soon shows ill promise by letting a run-of-the-mill pug slice him up like a ripe grapefruit. (Bibliographic hazard: read enough of this work, and the argot will infect your prose.) From this point we take off on a trip to the kid's boxing glorification, culminating in his manager's saving him from ignominy at the hands of a man who could not only slice him to sections, but squeeze the juice from the rind.

The quality that makes this slangy book of some interest is not the story, for it amounts to little, but the author's odd motivations. In an apparently sincere introduction, he writes sarcastically and angrily of professional boxing's vileness, corruption, and appeal to the base instincts of the crowd. The reader expects, then, an impassioned attack on boxing in the pages that follow. There are moral points here, it is true, but the author takes considerable delight in describing the nastiness of the pro game, and seems at his happiest when writing of gory fights in detail. It is a strange performance from one who claims to repudiate this sport.

269.   Zinberg, Len. "Up Queer Street." _Esquire_ (Sept. 1940):
        30+. Also in _Esquire's 2d Sports Reader_. Edited by Arnold
        Gingrich. A. S. Barnes, 1946.
        Two black fighters are having a tough bout. Told from one fighter's point of view, the impression of the match is very hazy, dream-like, distant and more curious than frightening. A trainer calls this state of mind "Up Queer Street." The fighter snaps out of it late in the bout, and straight into a reflection on the racism involved in the fight game, as the all-white crowd excitedly watches the black men hammer each other. A good piece of writing, with the dreamy passages carried off imaginatively and persuasively.

V. BULLFIGHTING

It is even more difficult to rationalize bullfighting as a sport than it is to do the same for prizefighting. Like cock-fighting, bearbaiting, and other exercises in the deliberate abuse of animals, bullfighting is a repugnant pastime. It defies this bibliographer's resolve to pursue bullfight fiction in a systematic way; nevertheless, here is a quartet of good works on this singularly unpleasant "sport." The most fitting of the four is probably William Hjortsberg's.

270. Conrad, Barnaby. Matador. Houghton Mifflin, 1952. 213 p.
    This novel is one of the best-received in the bullfight genre, probably in no small measure because of the author's personal involvement with the sport. Before writing the book, Conrad was himself a matador. The story comes across as a familiar blend of blood and sand; what carries it are Conrad's energy, authenticity, and the drama lived out by his central character, the matador Pacote. Pacote, burned out but wealthy at 29, would prefer not to when the arena beckons him back, but circumstances recall him for a final meeting in Seville, where he competes against a spectacular newcomer that many expect to leave Pacote in defeat and disgrace. Pacote attempts to rescue his crumbling reputation, but he pushes farther than his power will take him. Conrad, who should know what it tastes like, effectively creates the flavor of fear with his tense, insider's prose.

271. Hemingway, Ernest. "The Undefeated." In his Men Without Women, p. 1-57. Scribner's, 1955.
    Manuel Garcia, an aging matador, believes that he still has the skill to be a success in the ring. Others know better, but Garcia either ignores them or enlists their help. Most of this story consists of a graphic depiction of a bullfight that proves a debacle, with the crowd throwing things in contempt and Garcia led off after the bull seriously gores him. Many readers will be repelled by the cruelty of the bullfight, and their repulsion is to their credit. Hemingway does describe it well, however, and puts the reader right alongside the self-deluded Garcia.

272. Hjortsberg, William. Toro! Toro! Toro! Simon & Schuster, 1974. 160 p.
    This satire treats bullfighting with the attitude it deserves: total contempt and irreverence. It is best not to dwell too long on the plot, since it exists only as an excuse for the author to cut loose a series of mocking effects, including an adolescent Irish pop

singer who persuades a bull to fall in love with her, a Gypsy girl
who likes to perform the veronica by moonlight in the nude, a par-
rot who shrieks "Long live death!" and Paco Machismo, Spain's top
matador, who agrees to enter the arena against a rhinoceros in a
scheme cooked up by a couple of crooked promoters from the U.S.

El Camion, the Irish girl's sweetie-pie bull, has a radio trans-
mitter implanted in his head, allowing his "operator" to move him
from a state of zombie-like placidity to raging fury in seconds.
One of the highlights of El Camion's career is the day he vaults into
the grandstand during a performance; the reader is hard-pressed
not to cheer the bull on as he runs wild through the crowd.

By the time we reach the grand apotheosis, a showdown in the
bullring between the rhino and Mototoro, a computerized mechanical
bull, it is clear that bullfight fiction will never be the same again.
It is just as well.

273. Lea, Tom. <u>The Brave Bulls</u>. Little, Brown, 1949. 270 p.
The "brave bulls," indeed. Do they have a choice? Do they
know what is going on? If not, then how are they "brave?" This
title alone encapsulates much of the bedrock lunacy of bullfighting,
with its sentimentality and its obtuse anthropomorphism. But on
with the book: discounting its brief preface, it takes Lea nearly
half the novel to reach a bullfighting scene, but when he gets there,
his tactics are ingenious. Rather than directly observing the action
in the stadium, he presents it through a radio broadcast. The announcer must describe a grisly accident that befalls a veteran matador, and the reader's attention, like that of the characters listening
to the radio, is rapt upon the announcer's words. "The bull has a
wet horn, ladies and gentlemen. The horn is red."

The Texas-born Lea, nearly a lifelong follower of bullfighting,
provides a colorful portrait of the sport, of the people who follow
it, and of the matadors, with a focus on Louis Bello, who has come
from a poor background to the height of his calling. The author's
bold illustrations help set the novel's tone.

274. Andersen, U. S. "Turn Ever So Quickly." <u>Saturday Evening</u>
     <u>Post</u> 235 (Nov. 3, 1962): 56+. Also in <u>Best American Short</u>
     <u>Stories, 1963.</u> Edited by Martha Foley and David Burnett.
     Houghton Mifflin, 1963.
     A salesman and his young son go on a fishing trip that turns
into a search for a "lost lake" that no longer exists. The salesman
is tired of his job, no longer believes in his dreams--but is careful
to protect his son's dreams the best he can. A rather melancholy
story; the salesman learns that his favorite fishing spot has been
ruined by developers, and his past as a whole seems to be drying
up like the "lost lake." It is not a story without hope; while the
father's past is dead, the son's future is still alive.

275. Andrews, Mary R. S. "Campaign Trout." <u>Scribner's Maga-</u>
     <u>zine</u> 48 (July 1910): 61-74.
     Oh, the innocent political days of pre-World War! The gullible
times when a politico's merit could (in the terms of popular fiction)
be revealed by his noble commitment to a trout! That is what happens here, and if <u>Scribner's</u> was willing to bet fourteen pages on it,
no doubt a good number of readers went for the bait. The politician
in question is Judge Walter Morgan. He and his younger brother
Bob have been fishing and hunting up in Canadian moose country;
their first mail in ten days brings them the news that the Judge is
on the verge of nomination to run for governor. On the heels of
the mail comes a functionary dispatched to retrieve the Judge and
return with him to the nominating convention.
     Running for governor is very fine, of course, but there is a
fish at stake here, a huge trout which the guides spotted. The
Judge does not say that he would rather cast flies than be Governor, but what he does say amounts to the same message. The message delivers him the nomination; he catches the trout, too. Given
the thirst for power associated with political office, the Judge's attitude is fairly incredible, but who can doubt that today's public is
as easily moved by irrelevant issues as the public of 1910? In many
ways, the passage of seven decades has done nothing to change our
prevailing gullibility.

276. Banks, Russell. "The Fisherman." In his <u>Trailerpark</u>,
     p. 196-242. Houghton Mifflin, 1981.
     Merle Ring, a 77-year old trailer park resident, spends every
winter in his ice fishing shanty on the nearby lake because it makes
the rest of the year "more interesting." Ring is an interesting man

himself. A former carpenter, he has built his shanty with the care
and precision ordinarily devoted to far more "important" structures.
From the time the ice is solid until spring, Ring lives on fried fish
and Canadian Club whiskey, visiting town only rarely for supplies.

When he wins the state lottery, and then the Grand Prize of
$50 thousand, Ring becomes an object of obsession for the other
trailerpark occupants. He gives away most of his initial winnings,
but keeps the $50 thousand in $100 dollar bills in a cigar box in
his shanty. Ring listens in near silence to advice on how to have
the "happy" retirement the money would give him. Why, he could
move to Florida, play shuffleboard, and make lots of friends! Ring
sees straight through this shallow business. His life is already a
well-made thing, like his fishing shanty. The big money can change
nothing for the better.

A story of wisdom and character insight, this one is also a
very well-observed account of that lonesome sport, ice fishing.
Banks's description of the shanty, the tip-ups, the ice-filtered light
that comes through the hole in the shanty floor, and other details
are both accurate and atmospheric. The story's conclusion is also
moving, as well as despairing.

277.   Beck, Warren. "First Fish." Story 24 (Mar./April 1944):
       43-49. Also in Best American Short Stories, 1945. Edited
       by Martha Foley. Houghton-Mifflin, 1945.

An effective, moody account of a boy catching and eating a
fish the day before his fifth birthday. The boy, Peter, accompanies
his father, who does the main business of fishing--baiting the hook,
putting the fish on the stringer, and cleaning it. There is a nice
contrast between the boy's innocence and the act of killing the fish.

278.   Beeler, Janet. "A Day for Fishing." In Mademoiselle Prize
       Stories: Twenty-five Years, 1951-1975, p. 76-88. M. Evans
       & Co., 1976. First published under the name Janet Fowler
       in Mademoiselle 48 (Nov. 1958): 110-111+.

Harris, his wife Eleanor, and their niece Molly, who may be
eleven or twelve years old, are on a fishing trip in the Ozarks.
Much of the story is given to Eleanor's memories of her ineptitude
on past fishing outings with Harris. She has fretted about the discomfort of the fish, has shown herself to be an incompetent in the
boat, and, on an occasion when Harris severely cut his wrist while
cleaning fish, she behaved with a rattled lack of command.

Eleanor feels her husband, who is close to forty, slipping away
from her. Her sense of impending loss is sharpened on this trip by
Molly, who seems to be everything that Eleanor is not. She is adventurous, a capable learner, unhindered by self-consciousness or
exaggerated concern for the pains of fish. Harris delights in Molly,
and on one boat ride Eleanor's perceptions of the gap between what
she believes she is and what she thinks Harris wants her to be
reach a keen pitch of intensity when she realizes that she is jealous
of her niece's rapport with Harris.

A good picture of a woman whose understanding of what is

going on may be accurate, but may also be an emotionally-overblown embroidery of fundamentally innocent circumstances.

279. Bonetti, Edward. "Beginner's Luck." In his The Wine Cellar, p. 32-36. Viking, 1977.
As in Raymond Carver's "Pastoral" (item 285), a man's outing is spoiled by ruffians; unlike Carver's main character, Bonetti's overcomes his antagonists.

Thorson, fishing for the first time in years, is having a good day on the jetty. His lures and casting techniques are working well. He looks up to see a father and his adolescent son observing him. They are ill-dressed and poorly equipped for fishing. They insult Thorson, steal his bait, and nearly hook him in the eye. He realizes that the pair hate him. When he has a large fish on his line, he tries to cut the line with his fishing knife to deny the man and boy the pleasure of detesting him for landing it. The boy reaches for Thorson's knife hand, with violent results.

A story of sustained tension from the first appearance of the man and his son.

280. _____. "Fever." New American Review, no. 13 (1971): 224-231. Also in the author's The Wine Cellar. Viking, 1977.
Crazed Nat Seever fishes in the sea surf, determined to catch everything. Dead fish pile up around his campsite, filling the air with their stench as he baits up for more. A vivid example of sport twisted in the service of personal pathology.

281. Brodeur, Paul. "The Turtle." Saturday Evening Post 238 (March 27, 1965): 42-44+. Also in the author's Downstream. Atheneum, 1972.
Two young brothers, Peter and David, often go fishing on Hiram Pond. Their bass fishing has been spoiled by turtles. An old man of their acquaintance hates turtles as a race, since a snapping turtle once bit off one of his dog's hind legs. The old man takes the boys and his .22 rifle and goes with them on a turtle slaughter, ending in a successful quest for a huge snapper that may or may not be the one with a taste for dogmeat. The old man is in a near ecstacy at his opportunity to kill the big turtle; the shell will make a nice birdbath, he thinks.

The boys at first watch the vendetta eagerly, but the snapping turtle's hopeless struggle for life leaves them both in tears. A good story of the boys' awakening to sympathy with "ugly" creatures much unlike them, with their reaction to the turtle's plight well-foreshadowed by their discovery that the frogs they use as bass bait have sometimes healed and returned to their old ways after escaping the hook.

282. Brooks, Winfield S. Shining Tides. Morrow, 1952. 281 p.
A complex if not especially well-drawn cast of characters on Cape Cod revolves around the life of a striped bass known as "Roccus." Roccus is a big one, in the neighborhood of 100 pounds.

Roccus is more interesting than the people who pursue him, but the
passages dealing with nature and fishing are written with authority.

283.   Burnett, Whit.   "Two Men Free."   transition, no. 16/17 (June
       1929): 73-82.   Also in Best Short Stories of 1930.   Edited by
       Edward J. O'Brien.   Dodd, Mead, 1930.
       Two foreign journalists working at subsistence wages in Paris
take off on a fishing trip.   The trip is ill-organized, but it allows
the men temporary escape from the newspaper, its "crummy ideas"
and its "thousands of words and none of 'em mean anything."

284.   Carver, Raymond.   "Nobody Said Anything."   In his Will You
       Please Be Quiet, Please?, p. 41-59.   McGraw, 1976.
       The narrator, a boy of perhaps fourteen, begs off from school
attendance one morning with an allegedly upset stomach.   His stomach
is not the only thing upset in the household: his parents have been
conducting a long-term battle over unspecified topics.
       After his mother leaves for work, the boy watches a little
television, smokes a cigarette, inspects his parents' room hoping to
find a box of condoms, and then decides to go fishing at a local
creek.   On the way, with his rod and creel, the boy is picked up
by a young woman in her car.   He fantasizes about her when he
reaches the creek.   The fish aren't biting, and it looks like a totally wasted day, until a younger boy attracts his attention by shout-
ing about "the biggest fish I ever saw."   The two boys collaborate
on catching the fish, not without animosity and suspicion about who
may try to claim it as his own.   The narrator finally lands the fish,
a two-foot steelhead, with his bare hands, and solves the ownership
question in biblical fashion: he cuts the fish in two.
       Returning home with the fish's front end, the narrator is
eager to show his catch to his parents.   They are carrying on another nasty round in their fight; when he shows them the fish, they
recoil from it and shriek at him to "Take that goddamn thing out of
here."   The boy takes the fish outside and looks at it lying in the
creel.   "I lifted him out.   I held him.   I held the half of him."   He
is a boy full of pride, but "nobody said anything" about his achievement in catching the big fish.   A story with a lot of hurting in it,
much of it suggested by the final paragraph.

285.   _____ .   "Pastoral."   In his Furious Seasons, and Other
       Stories, p. 79-91.   Capra Pr., 1977.
       Reminiscent in some respects of Hemingway's "Big Two-Hearted
River" (item 304), this story concerns a man, Harold, who visits an
old fishing ground in the winter off-season.   He has come without
his wife, and, though Carver does not dwell on it, there is obviously
something wrong at home, and maybe at work, too.   Harold is trying
to settle himself a little with this outing, but he is still edgy.
       When he reaches the river, his fishing is first disturbed by a
doe that emerges from the woods, one of her hind legs smashed by
the bullet of a clumsy hunter.   The doe struggles off, soon to be
replaced by a "pack" of boys, one with a rifle.   When Harold refuses

to tell them which way the deer went, they throw rocks at him and threaten to shoot him. A troubling story of a man's favorite things falling apart around him, and with reliable refuges of the past defiled beyond resort.

286. Clark, Geoffrey. "Advance Creek." In his What the Moon Said, p. 100-119. Story Pr., 1983.
    This story of an adolescent girl's introduction to a corrupt piece of life's underside is, at times, almost horrifying in its intimacy. Margot, nearly fifteen, gets up early one morning to go with her father on a smelt run in northern Michigan. Darryl, her father, is a good man who loves his daughter, and, though Margot is embarrassed by his failure to find work (he apparently uses a neurological disorder as an excuse to avoid trying), it still feels good to be out with him in the jeep in the early morning, and away from her hard-nosed mother, a school principal.
    The scene at the smelt run, seen through Margot's eyes, is far from attractive. Men swarm about, belching and cursing. When the conservation officers give the signal to begin dipping for fish, Margot and her father see a huge man holding a tub that his partner fills with fish. As Margot looks on, the big man takes one of the fish and eats it alive. A string of circumstances leaves Margot alone with the big man's partner, Smiley; he forces her into his station wagon and assaults her sexually in a manner that stops just short of rape.
    Reunited with her father, whose questions she deflects, Margot wants only to get home and lock herself in the bathroom to see if anything "really awful" has been done to her. Something "really awful" has been done, but the worst of it has been done to her mind, not her body. This is very uncomfortable but also very effective writing. Margot describes the men at the smelt run as being "like bugs crawling all over things, grabbing and tearing ... and eating things alive...."

287. Cobb, Irvin S. "The Moral Leopard." Esquire 1 (Jan. 1934): 50+. Also in the author's Faith, Hope, and Charity. Bobbs, 1934.
    Fred, a backwoods guide, reels out a story in fractured English about a pretty girl, her two suitors, and a clever old trout, the biggest ever seen in the waters of Steamboat Creek. The young lady's boyfriends seem fairly equal in almost every respect, and it looks as though the one who wins her hand will be determined by the one who proves his fishing mettle by pulling the trout, old Sitting Bull, from the water. It doesn't work out that way, and thankfully so, considering the ignominious manner in which the supposedly wily fish meets his fate. An amusing enough story, with some funny twists of the tongue and a tidy satire-in-passing on the literati who praise Nature in the abstract but who hate rain, bugs, poison oak, sun, and wind in the concrete.

288. Coover, Robert. "Quenby and Ola, Swede and Carl." In his Pricksongs & Descants, p. 150-167. NAL, 1969.

A successful exercise in impressionism, time manipulation, and
fragmentation. Carl is a businessman who has come up north for
fishing; he stays on a remote island with Swede, Swede's wife Quenby, and Ola, Swede's adolescent daughter. Told in short segments,
each focusing on a different aspect of Carl's stay on the island, the
story opens with Carl and Swede out on the lake at night. The boat
motor is dead. Swede, taciturn, works on the motor. As the
seemingly random pieces of the narrative come together, we realize
that it is Carl's mind at work in them, and that this has been far
more than an ordinary fishing trip. Carl has managed to blunder
into affairs with both Swede's wife and his daughter Ola. Threaded
through the story is Ola's account of Swede's killing the family cat
because it tracked through Swede's lemon pie. As the tale knits together, the cat's death becomes an ominous signal for what may be
Carl's fate out on the dark, cold lake, assuming that Swede's feelings
about his wife and daughter are at least the equal of his feelings
about his lemon pie. Swede has, we trust, discovered Carl's indis-
cretions, but he says nothing. The threat of violence fills the darkness.

289.   Corrington, John W. "A Day in Thy Court." In his The
       Southern Reporter, p. 93-122. Louisiana State Univ. Pr.,
       1981.
       An old attorney dying of cancer still goes out bass fishing.
As he fishes, memories flood over him: in them he sees his former
colleagues, old ones now dead, young ones now old. He is taking
a powerful narcotic for the pain, and for the first time in his life
takes liquor with him when he goes fishing.
       Throughout the story pieces of the past, especially those con-
cerning his dead wife, break into the text in sentence fragments,
surfacing like creatures from the deep. Two resolutions occur on
his final fishing trip, one regarding his memories of his wife, his
ability to enjoy her memory rather than mourning the anguish of
her loss; the other is the matter of his own mortality, his acknowl-
edgment that this particular court must adjourn. His insights take
place in conjunction with his hooking a giant bass that struggles
with great effort not to be drawn up from the water, its life.
       The sentence fragment technique is mildly annoying. Other-
wise, this is a moving, capably written story, with nice parallels
between the lives of men and fish.

290.   Curley, Daniel. "All of a Summer's Day." In his In the
       Hands of Our Enemies, p. 18-23. Univ. of Illinois Pr., 1970.
       A ten-year old boy and his father are out fishing. The day
goes badly. The boy has caught the only fish, a nice perch, and
his father casts about to no effect but growing annoyance. He
even persuades the boy to let him cut up the perch for bait, but
still draws no taker from the water. They pack up and head back
to the landing, the boy trolling with his father's rod as the man
rows. Finally, nearly at the dock, a strong strike hits the bait,
almost jerking the rod from the boy's hands. He does his best to

land the fish, tears in his eyes in anticipation of his father's disgust with him should he fail.

There is no need to reveal the success or failure of the boy's
efforts. This is a good snapshot of a moment of growing up, and
of the relationship between father and son.

291.   _____. "The Moth, the Bear, and the Shivering Stars."
Ibid., p. 135-145.

A good story of the different times of a man's life, with all
of them overshadowed by death. The narrator, Thomas, has received a telegram. He is sure that it contains news of a death, for
his family has traditionally reserved telegrams for such announcements. Thomas, an old man now, recalls the first death that came
to him by telegram, that of his cousin Charles. Long ago, Charles
and Thomas and Thomas's grandfather went out with a fishing party.
Thomas tended his grandfather's line while the old man sat ashore
and made observations on nature on topics ranging from the gaps in
the Milky Way to the eyes of snapping turtles. It is a most enjoyable time; one sees that the young cousins are very fond of the old
man. Thomas rides home with him in the evening, with "enough
robes in Grandfather's buggy to make the very cold a pleasure."

When they reach home, a telegram waits for them reporting the
death of Charles in an accident. Now Thomas, aged eighty, stands
with another telegram in his hand, one that he does not want to
open.

This story works superbly in all its parts, and the lengthy
section on the fishing trip sets a perfect tone for its concerns.

292. Dexter, Bruce. The Fishing Trip. NAL, 1966. 181 p.

A tightly-wired story of a fishing trip's effects on its diverse
party. Six men, including two guides, travel by horseback to a remote lake in the Sierra Nevadas, where they create the worst
outdoor experience the guides have ever undergone. The four clients--
a businessman and his lawyer, a doctor, and a former football
player--take part in a series of almost unbelievably stupid contests,
so without any rational qualities that the reader must look at them
for hidden meaning. It is there, and not far from the surface.
Whether catching far more fish than they can eat, setting each other
up in poker games, or exploiting one another's weaknesses for the
hell of it, the four vacationers impose on the face of nature the same
base habits that serve them in their daily lives.

The highlight of this transfer of idiotic, destructive competition is probably the passage in which several of the party, caught
in a cabin in a rainstorm, work off their accumulated rage with rifle
practice--inside the cabin. The main target for their practice, a
nude calendar foldout, may make plainer than necessary the sexual
undertone of our four fishermen's hijinks. The guides are the most
tolerable of the characters, in that one would not mind spending
time with them. Of the rest, the businessman, Sunderland, is the
most offensive, but also the most interesting.

A fairly compelling novel, with good outdoor passages and
good passages into the hearts of darkness within "civilized" men.

293. Douglas, Ellen. "On the Lake." New Yorker 37 (Aug. 26,
     1961): 35-38+. Also in Prize Stories, 1963: The O. Henry
     Awards. Edited by Richard Poirier. Doubleday, 1963.
     One August morning, well-to-do Anna Glover takes her sons
Ralph and Steve and their friend Murray on a fishing trip on Mississippi's Lake Okatukla. Just as they are about to set off in their
boat, they see Estella Moseby, "a large and beautiful Negro woman
who had worked for the Glover family since the children were small"--
until she quit to give more time to her own family. Anna persuades
Estella to come along on the trip, during which Anna awakens, apparently for the first time, to the great cultural differences between
her and Estella.
     On the way back, a storm comes up. Frightened, Estella
stands up and capsizes the boat. After an ordeal in the water, the
group is rescued, except for Estella, who is presumed drowned. She
does survive, but in the end, the gulf between her and Anna seems
larger than ever.
     A gripping psychological study with some rather eerie over-
tones, and with a terrifying effort against drowning in the open
water.

294. Duncan, David James. The River Why. Sierra Club, 1983.
     294 p.
     This serious, satiric, sometimes funny and engaging, often
tedious novel is above all ambitious. If it were less ambitious, it
would probably be better. It tells the story of young Gus Orviston,
spawn of the redoubtable fishing expert Henning Hale-Orviston
("H$_2$O") and Henning's cowgirl wife. They bring Gus up on a diet
of Izaak Walton and an ongoing debate over the virtues of fly
fishing versus worm fishing. His head all aswim over contradictions
and unanswered questions, Gus retreats to the hills, where he lives
in a remote cabin near a river. Complications and revelations follow
involving the issue of humanity's proper place in the natural order.
     The book starts far better than it finishes, with some genu-
inely funny scenes of familial contention. Before long, however, the
author's overbusy seriousness and pointlessly quirky characters defeat his purposes. The book's final third, filled with warm, sticky
philosophical rumination, is an unrewarding chore to negotiate.
Duncan quotes too many other writers, and forgets that his lead
character supposedly knows nothing but fishing when he has him
refer to the bodhisattvas. A book with some good moments, but on
the whole too self-conscious and too busy.

295. Enright, Elizabeth. "A Little Short of the Record." In her
     The Riddle of the Fly & Other Stories, p. 83-91. Harcourt,
     Brace, 1959.
     A very neat tale of a woman's cooperation in her husband's
self-aggrandizing lies, and in her own diminution. Celia and her
husband Gregg are out fishing in the Florida keys; their guide,
Captain Barker, stands in the prow of the skiff, poling the boat
stern forward. As Barker tries to find the couple some good fishing

spots, Celia reflects on her husband's disparate qualities. Perhaps
it is because he has been such a good father, because he is so handsome, because he has been brave in hard times, that she tolerates
his lies, like the one he tells Barker about the time he supposedly
caught a huge tarpon off the Cuban coast. Gregg knows that Celia
knows he is lying, but she does nothing to spoil the effect of his
dishonest boasting.

Celia hooks a big fish. Even as she struggles to land it, following the amiable Barker's advice, we can guess what Gregg will
make of the event. The guess is accurate. When Celia and Barker
repair to the lodge bar for a drink, they hear Gregg, already inside,
bragging about "catching" the fish that Celia caught. "What a fight
he gave me!" Once again, Celia does nothing to mend the truth, or,
in this case, to take credit for her own achievement, one she had
been feeling very good about until her husband spoiled it for her
with his lies. In the end, we wonder which fault is worse: Gregg's
lies, or Celia's acquiescence in them.

296. Epstein, Seymour. "Summer Place." Antioch Review 15 (Sum-
     mer 1955): 169-179. Also in the author's A Penny for Charity;
     Short Stories. Little, Brown, 1965.
     Two brothers, one sixteen, the other nine, slip out of their
summer house at dawn and take a rowboat out to deep water on a
lake. After they put their fishing lines into the water, the older
one tells his brother that their ceaselessly arguing parents have decided to get a divorce. The younger boy tries to stop his brother
from rowing back to shore after the truth is out, but he is not
strong enough.

Both boys' characters are nicely sketched, and the image of
the two out alone on the deep water is an apt one for children
facing the threat of their parents' imminent divorce.

297. Foote, John Taintor. "A Wedding Gift." Saturday Evening
     Post 195 (Jan. 13, 1923): 6+.
     A trout fishing fanatic assumes, of course, that his new bride
will be delighted to spend their honeymoon tromping through the
waters in a pair of English waders. This is not quite how it works
out. Nothing of consequence here, but Foote keeps the story going
well; anyone who has watched a spouse consumed by a hobby that
he or she believes everyone must find equally fascinating will recognize the type represented by George Baldwin Potter. For more of
Mr. Potter, see Foote's novella Daughter of Delilah (Appleton-
Century, 1936), in which Potter's wife lures him to purchase a new
house by using the trout-stocked stream on the property as leverage.

298. Ford, Jesse H. "The Trout." Atlantic 208 (July 1961): 47-
     49+. Also in the author's Fishes, Birds, and Sons of Men.
     Little, Brown, 1967.
     Eight-year-old Coy has gone fishing with his grandfather since
the age of three. His grandfather's choice as the best fish to catch

is the trout, because of the wild fight the trout puts up. Coy feels
a strike on his line; the fish breaks the boy's light pole, and Coy
plays it badly, losing it. When it jumps from the water, it proves
to be a trout. The old man tries to comfort Coy, who has never
caught a trout. This story has a good feel for the thoughts of a
small boy, beside whom few can be as certain of finality. Coy "knew
the trout would never strike again," and he wipes his tears on his
arm.

299. Fosburgh, Hugh. The Sound of White Water. Scribner's,
      1955. 192 p.
      "The river ain't nothing to fool with I can tell you," says an
old river hand a short way into this novel. He delivers his admoni-
tion to Tony Farr, the least experienced woodsman in a group of
three about to embark on a two-week fishing trip, by canoe, down
the Big River. The old man's warning is well-taken, but Tony
proves himself equal to the river's worst.
      The book features excellent descriptions of outdoors life--
fishing, canoeing, camping--and good characterizations. Some individual passages stand out, such as one of the men's cutting into
his own thumb to remove a deeply-embedded fishhook. The novel's
moral lessons are not profound; "live better by taking risks" about
sums them up, but the action is steady, the company is good, and
the scenery is unspoiled.

300. Gordon, Arthur. "The Sea Devil." In Impact: Short Stories
      for Pleasure, p. 37-46. Edited by Donald L. Stansbury.
      Prentice Hall, 1971.
      A story of relentless action on a par with that of "The Most
Dangerous Game" (item 473). The story's pulpish roots are also
common with that story. A man (nameless, always "the man") goes
out for a little late-night mullet fishing off the Florida coast.
Through an errant twist of luck, he manages to "catch" a thousand-
pound sea ray, and cleverly secures himself to the ray with a slip-
knot around his wrist. The ray pulls him out of his skiff and takes
him on a mad tour of the tide. The rope is taut; the man cannot
loosen the knot.
      It would have been a better story if the ray had pulled the
man out to sea, but it doesn't. What saves the story from mere
pulp status, aside from the author's competent prose, is his fairly
deft illustration of the thin line that separates contemporary humanity
from its primitive past, and from the elemental forces of nature.

301. Gordon, Caroline. "Old Red." In her Old Red, and Other
      Stories, p. 124-147. Cooper Square, 1971.
      Old Mister Aleck Maury, as much a part of the land as the
elusive fox, Old Red, has had to give up his beloved hunting because of physical problems. He can still go fishing, and he eagerly
looks forward to his next fishing trip. This is an effective study
of a sportsman near the end of his life; the closing passages, with
Maury lying awake in bed, visualizing familiar woods, waters, and
old times, are very well conceived and written.

302. _____. "One More Time." Ibid., p. 148-157.
    Mr. Maury describes his visit to a favorite old inn, near some
good fishing holes. When he learns that Bob Reynolds, an old
friend, is also staying at the inn, he invites him along fishing.
Reynolds can't make it; he has been ill for some time. By the end
of the story we learn how ill, and what the "odd-looking bundle"
was that Reynolds took with him when he went "to see the old place
one more time." A story of mortality and the choices made under
its pressures.

303. Graves, John. "Green Fly." In Prize Stories, 1955: The
     O. Henry Awards, p. 215-225. Edited by Paul Engle and
     Hansford Martin. Doubleday, 1955.
    Thomas Hilliard has come to Mexico seeking sanctuary where
he may work undisturbed on his doctoral dissertation. He meets
a gentlemanly Spanish doctor, a refugee from the political situation
in his homeland, and now just getting by financially with a modest
position.
    Hilliard and old Doctor Elizondo share an interest in fly fishing
for trout, and strike a tentative friendship with their hobby as the
link. It dies an ugly death when Hilliard's American friends, a professor and his wife, come to visit. The professor, Wright Forsythe,
initially took the fledgling academic Hilliard under his care, but in
Mexico he reveals himself, beneath his scholarly exterior, as an in-
sensitive, patronizing boor. He is especially uncivil toward the old
doctor, and saves his worst behavior for a time when the doctor has
given him some emergency medical attention.
    The dignity of Dr. Elizondo in the face of crude insult and
Graves's satirical rendering of a scholar who is no gentleman make
this story memorable, and the emphasis on fishing is never far from
attention.

304. Hemingway, Ernest. "Big Two-Hearted River." In The Short
     Stories of Ernest Hemingway, p. 209-232. Scribner's, 1953.
     Also in the author's In Our Time. Scribner's, 1930.
    On its surface a matchless (detailed, accurate, closely-felt,
economical) account of a one-man fishing trip in northern Michigan,
below its surface an equally-fine look at a man trying to keep his
mind in one piece after his experiences in World War I have nearly
blown it apart. Every action that Nick Adams takes, from cleaning
fish to observing grasshoppers, has the air of ritual, of a ceremony
performed in a precise manner, for only such precision will hold the
devils at bay. Much critical commentary has appeared on this story;
nothing fresh can be said here. "Big Two-Hearted River," however,
is not only one of the best stories of sport in American fiction; it
is one of the best short stories in American literature.

305. _____. "The End of Something." In his The Nick Adams
     Stories, p. 200-204. Scribner's, 1972. Also in the author's
     In Our Time. Scribner's, 1930.
    A fishing trip serves as the means for Nick to break off an af-

fair with his girlfriend Marjorie. Good description of fishing details, and a nicely understated break-up scene.

306.   _____. "Out of Season." In The Short Stories of Ernest
         Hemingway, p. 173-179. Scribner's, 1953. Also in the
         author's In Our Time. Scribner's, 1930.
         A "young gentleman" and his wife are travelling in Italy.
They have made arrangements with a somewhat disreputable guide to be escorted to a good out-of-season fishing spot. The guide shows up drunk and makes a big to-do of leading them through the town. The young gentleman's wife turns back, and he himself cannot go fishing when he reaches a good spot because he has forgotten to bring leader. He is relieved, however, because he does not want to break the law.
         As with so many Hemingway stories, there is more happening here than the reader sees in the lines themselves. Why does the young gentleman's wife turn back? Why, if he does not wish to break the law, has he arranged for this illegal fishing trip? The only easy question to answer is the one about the guide's partici- pation: he sees it as a way to escape his menial chores at the ho- tel--but his escape is likely to be brief.

307. Krekorian, Michael. "Our Collective Hearts." Iowa Review
       11 (Spring/Summer 1980): 39-47.
       A party of fishermen and one woman is off the California
coast, fishing for yellowtail. The catch has been poor. Not even Jim, the master fisherman, has been successful. At last Jim hooks something with an anchovy as bait. It's a big one, and pulls out Jim's line, up to 250 yards. The fish has plunged down a shelf, where nothing lives but a few mudcats and sandsharks.
       Jim battles the fish; his play improves following a little pep- talk (it seems) from the enigmatic Clare, who comes down from the wheelhouse wrapped in a white towel. The narrator fries up a mud- bass at the Captain's orders to feed Jim while he fights the fish. Clare pulls the mudbass from the bait tank, stepping into it herself in water up to her neck. She bashes the fish to death against the deck. "There, he's dead. Fry him honey," she instructs the nar- rator. Here is the critical passage. The narrator prepares the fish, and as it fries he meditates on the meaning of the trip: "So we come out here and it should mean something--it has to mean something ... a fat fish to take home to our wives, some new stories about sub- duing fish...." But he has his doubts about whether this event means anything at all.
       Jim lands the fish at last, with the help of Clare, who gaffs the yellowtail, and in the process stains her white towel with the blood of the fish. When the excitement has subsided, they notice that the fish has apparently pulled the boat out of sight of land, "and for an instant it shoots a pang of fear into our collective hearts." This is a moody, discomforting story with some ambiguous- ly symbolic content. Especially interesting is the role of Clare, who seems, upon reflection, not altogether human.

308. Kuhn, Robert J. "Atavism of Ralph Piscatore." Esquire 8
      (Oct. 1942): 53+.
      A story of transsubstantiation, or shape-changing. Ralph has
been pursuing the lives of fish for a long time, and in the gulf of
Mexico he becomes one himself. For him the aquatic life, even with
its dangers, is the preferred one. A nice fantasy with a violent and
miraculous ending.

309. Larsen, Erling. "The Trout of My Dreams." Antioch Review
      23 (Summer 1963): 145-162.
      This story of ambition, pride, and deception is set in the
northern Midwest at a small fishing resort. The narrator, Mr. Williams, is a writer. The trout of his dreams is his vocation, writing,
but there is another "trout," so-called, that plays a big part here.
      Williams is an experienced visitor at Charlie's camp; the two
have become less client and guide than friends. Williams brings
Charlie whiskey; Charlie lets Williams sit in his cellar or on his
steps, drinking home-brewed beer. Williams is also, from the reader's point of view, a nearly insufferable busybody and know-it-all.
When a couple, the Hendersons, and their obese son come into the
camp, Williams tells Charlie in detail how unpleasant the Hendersons
will make things for him. The Hendersons are, at first, fairly unappealing. Eva Henderson is the boss of the family, big, tough,
and aggressive. Mr. Henderson is ineffectual, and their son Bob is
snotty. They are an easy lot to dislike.
      Eva Henderson evidently longs for her husband to make a big
score as a fisherman. Charlie takes them out on the water, and,
when Henderson hooks a big trash fish, Charlie claims that he has
caught a "German brown trout." Convinced that Charlie speaks the
truth, the Hendersons begin to fry up the fish in their cabin that
night, but the foul smell of the phoney "trout" drives them to fling
the fish, pan and all, out into the rainy night.
      The reader's sympathy goes to the Hendersons. True, they
are not the sort one would choose to spend a vacation with, but
they did nothing to deserve the fraud worked upon them by Charlie.
When Eva Henderson tenderly comforts her husband after the stink
raised by the frying fish, we see that the most honest sensibility
in the situation is hers; she wishes well for her husband, and suffers with him for his failure. As for Charlie, he lets his desire to
please his clients decline into lying to them, and Williams, though he
sees through what is happening, is too self-congratulatory in his
keen perceptions for the reader to stomach. A very well worked-
out story with some subtle twists of the reader's expectations.

310. MacKuck, Peter. "Filling the Igloo." Southern Review 20
      (July 1984): 632-644.
      A funny yet pitiful story of an incredibly miserable fishing
trip. Quinn, his wife, their sons, and his brother and sister-in-
law are visiting a southern beach. Quinn, a serious fisherman from
Ohio, is not getting away from it all: he is stepping squarely into
it. His brother-in-law Henry is "depressed." Henry is a musician;

the ocean "overwhelms" him so he can't practice, but he can throw
regular barbed comments at Quinn mocking his interest in fishing.
Quinn's wife occupies herself making limp apologies for Henry, while
Henry's wife merely takes up space. Quinn's boys are whining
about having nothing to do at an ocean they have never seen before.
When Quinn takes them fishing, they grumble and pester him for
money to attend a carnival.

Quinn attempts to obtain some respite from this crew by buying
a ticket to fish off a private pier, but the pier is alive with noisy
nincompoops. One of them takes a wild cast and nearly removes
Quinn's eye with his hook; Quinn must drive off for emergency hook
removal and a set of stitches. A couple of buffoons in the parking
lot guffaw about how Quinn got himself "a big un!" When Quinn finally catches some fish to put into his Igloo cooler, the first of them
comes thanks to the assistance of one of the pier denizens that
Quinn can't stand. When the story closes, Quinn is still fishing
while an old woman raves of her religious visions.

Anyone who has seen an anticipated pleasure trip turn into
something resembling a "B" horror movie will appreciate this story,
and those who savor fishing at its best--an act performed in quiet
unity with nature--will be struck with pains of commiseration at
Quinn's predicament.

311. MacLean, Norman. "A River Runs Through It." In his <u>A</u>
      <u>River Runs Through It, and Other Stories</u>, p. 1-104. Univ.
      of Chicago Pr., 1976.
      "Something within fishermen tries to make fishing into a world
perfect and apart.... Many of us would probably be better fishermen if we did not spend so much time watching and waiting for the
world to become perfect." So reflects the narrator in this short
novel of life in the woods and streams of western Montana in the
1930s. What David Duncan tries to do in his ambitious and ultimately overblown <u>The River Why</u> (item 294), MacLean does here,
gracefully and subtly. He finds the place of the river in a man's
life, the river as a retreat, as a source of unity, of uncorrupted
being. He manages this not through high-flown, pretentious philos-
ophizing or by quoting thinkers of the past, but through rooting
his account in concrete, sensible details, such as the way, back in
those days, you could leave beer to cool in the river and no one
would steal it, how "we covered the beer with rocks so it wouldn't
wash away."

The narrator frequently makes his fishing trips with his
younger brother Paul, a hell-raiser from the time he refused to eat
his oatmeal as a baby. Paul comes to a tragic end. When the narrator looks back on the past from his vantage as an old man, he
finds himself still reaching out to his brother and to others now dead.
As he fishes alone in the Arctic half-light of a Montana canyon, "all
existence fades to a being with my soul and memories and the sounds
of the Big Blackfoot River ... and the hope that a fish will rise."
His final words: "I am haunted by waters."

And this is a haunting story, honest, moving, real. One of

the notable aspects of this collection as a whole is that it is the
author's first--not so remarkable until one realizes that MacLean did
not begin writing for publication until in his 70s. He is a very good
writer, combining depth of feeling, humor, and a discerning eye for
the natural world. (This was also the first work of fiction published
by the University of Chicago Press.)

312. Matthews, Jack. "The Sea Wall." In his Bitter Knowledge;
      Short Stories, p. 1-10. Scribner's, 1964.
      Bill is a troubled and difficult boy, recently discharged from
the armed forces, now an indifferent university student. As the
story opens, his mother urges him to take his father fishing down at
the ocean inlet. Bill tries to evade the job, but his mother prevails.
The old man is dying, and Bill knows that the trip will be important
to him.
      They drive to the inlet, out on the sand where the seagrass
brushes the sides of the car. As they fish, the old man confides
in his son how he fished this same inlet fifty years before, and now
"in a way, it seems like I'm still a boy ... and I'm just dreaming
about being an old man.... Only, in another way, it seems that I'm
just dreaming that I was ever a boy."
      The sea wall borders a walk the two fishermen take. Before
they return, the incoming tide has swept the walk, and Bill must
carry his father piggyback on their way to the car. In the end,
Bill thinks, "No matter how much I tried, I could never do enough
for him now." A good story of age and youth, with the relatively
eternal quality of nature setting both into a deeper perspective.

313. Peterson, Edwin L. No Life So Happy. Dodd, Mead, 1940.
      221 p.
      This novel is steeped in fishing lore, particularly that of
trout fishing, but it transcends its genre. It is "about" fishing,
but it is also about the inter-relation of humanity and nature, and
about the unspeakable mysteries of our place on earth.
      The narrator and his friend George go trout fishing up in the
country, in the woods, where "crazy" isolated folk live. Elaine, a
young woman reminiscent of Rima in W. H. Hudson's Green Mansions
appears to the narrator, materializing from the woods. She is an en-
chantress of a kind, and in the end leads the narrator to a vision
of the King, a giant, legendary trout.
      No Life So Happy contains good descriptions of fishing inter-
spersed with philosophical meditations on the sport's spiritual aspects; the latter are not tedious. At its best the novel evokes the
sense of wonder at nature that fills the memorable "Piper at the
Gates of Dawn" chapter in Kenneth Grahame's The Wind in the Willows, but even when not at its best it is a much more than routinely
interesting novel of fishing.

314. _____. "Parmachene Bell." Esquire 14 (Aug. 1940): 22+.
      This story begins with what seem to be light, satirical inten-
tions. A small boy persuades his mother to accompany him to the

shop of Old Solomon, a fly tier. The mother regards Solomon as a
disreputable type, and harrumphs her way out the door. Soon, however, the boy takes an important fishing trip with his father and
"Old Sol." In the story's final part the tone is somber, elegiac, as
the boy, now a man, fishes the same water he learned as a child.
Peterson works hard to give this section a poetic, melancholy tone,
and succeeds. (The story's title refers to a fish lure.)

315.   Proulx, E. A. "The Wer-Trout." Esquire 97 (June 1982):
       118+.
       Rivers has retired and moved with his wife into a rural New
England backwater where he slowly loses his retirement funds as the
proprietor of a fishing tackle shop. His wife, a "needlecrafter,"
grows disgusted with Rivers's habits and the country dullness,
packs up and moves out. Sauvage, a French-Canadian neighbor (in
this region, "neighbors" live a mile or so apart), shares Rivers's
spousal bereftness: his wife has cracked up and taken to eating
mice. She, too, has left the premises, though more in the passive
role of being packed off than in the active of packing up.
       Rivers and Sauvage head for the deep woods to do some seri-
ous trout fishing. Rivers becomes annoyed with the somewhat
younger, cruder Sauvage, who employs cheap fishing gear in a
brusque, artless fashion, and, what is worse, catches fish. Rivers
catches nothing. Under the influence of whiskey consumed on a
solo slog through the swampy terrain, Rivers tries to exploit
Sauvage's superstition by telling him a mean-spirited tale about an
alleged monster, the "wer-trout." To compound his unpleasantness,
Rivers commits a small, cruel act that will remind Sauvage of his
wife's pitiful condition. There is a real monster loose in this story,
but it is not the wer-trout. It is the worst kind of all, what E. E.
Cummings called "this busy monster, manunkind."

316.   Rogers, Michael. "Fishing." In his Do Not Worry About the
       Bear, p. 187-209. Knopf, 1979.
       A very effective story combining elements of horror, bad
dream, and psychological insight. Steven and Stephanie both like
to get away from civilization. He is a fisherman, she an amateur
biologist. They charter a plane to fly back to a remote lake in the
Alaskan wilderness; there they make camp. Steven fishes while
Stephanie studies the tundra.
       The fishing comes to a halt on the third day when Steven pulls
in a bizarre fish that looks like something from a primeval sea. Excited by the anachronism, Stephanie insists on freezing the catch in
a snowbank so they can take it back with them for scientific study.
       The strange fish's presence disconcerts Steven. He will not
say quite what bothers him, but he loses his interest in fishing, and
seems to think that something is fundamentally wrong. He begins to
doubt that the bush pilot will return to pick them up; perhaps war
has occurred in the civilized world, or something unimaginable has
happened. He tells Stephanie an unsettling anecdote about the time
he caught a bat with a fish lure.

The feeling of things not being right builds steadily through the story, until the reader's skin crawls. Steven resolves his discomfort in a remarkable way, but the reader's remains.

317. Travers, Robert. "The Big Brown Trout." In <u>Best American Short Stories, 1967</u>, p. 303-313. Edited by Martha Foley and David Burnett. Houghton Mifflin, 1967.

Clay is a dairy farmer, content to work his 80 acres and to let the wide world slide by on its course the best it can. He feels one with the land. When his Korean War buddy, Harry, now a corporate executive, visits him, Clay has to listen to Harry tell him he isn't making a real contribution to the country's needs. Harry's company, by contrast, can rapidly switch to production of armaments instead of civilian products. An experience with a large trout in a pool on Clay's farm enables Harry to see, at last, that union with the land is as important as being on the "front lines" of the international action.

Harry is for the most part so obnoxious that it is hard to see how Clay tolerates him, and Harry's awakening to Clay's point of view is not altogether convincing. Nevertheless, the story has some nice fishing passages, and the fish serves to illustrate Clay's sympathetic relationship with the earth.

318. Van Dyke, Henry. "Gentle Life." In his <u>Ruling Passion; Tales of Nature and Human Nature</u>, p. 121-139. Scribner's, 1901.

Two friends go fishing. They follow separate channels, planning to meet again where the channels join. One of them falls asleep against a birch tree. There he dreams that he has been visited by none other than Izaak Walton. Walton provides the dreamer with a moral lesson, inveighing against hurrying (it causes all bad business, from personal sorrow to war), and championing angling as the proper pursuit to put a man straight. There is a certain sweet naivete in Van Dyke's tale, but the words he puts in Walton's mouth are wise ones, and as deserving of attention today as they were in 1901.

319. _____. "His Other Engagement." <u>Scribner's Magazine</u> 41 (Feb. 1907): 167-179.

Another example of conflict between sport and domesticity. Narrated by a member of the Petrine Club, "which has for its motto the wise words of St. Peter, 'I go a-fishing,'" this is the story of Bolton Chichester's almost-wedding day. Bolton, a determined but reasonable man, is engaged to the talented and wealthy Ethel Asham. Their coming marriage is one made by the angels, but for one little detail: they disagree intensely on Bolton's hobby. As befits a Petrine Club member, he is a devoted fly fisherman. Ethel is a devoted antagonist of fishing who regales Bolton with quotations from "authorities" on the terrible agonies endured by the poor fish upon the hook. Bolton is patient, but unmoved. His response to Ethel's criticism is Van Dyke's apologia for fishing.

Bolton goes on an early-morning fishing jaunt on the wedding day. They have come to Quebec, and, in the company of a pair of French-Canadian guides, Bolton lands a big salmon. Van Dyke lavishes his attention on the contest between Bolton and the fish.

His involvement with the salmon leads to Bolton's tardy appearance for the wedding. Upon reaching town after his engagement with the fish, he finds that his engagement with Ethel has been terminated. He does not quite say "Well, that's life; hand me my rod and tackle, boys," but that is much the tone of the story's conclusion. A rather interesting look at the author's (and presumably some of the author's readers') notion of sporting values versus the responsibilities of the "real" world.

320. Waldrop, Howard. "God's Hooks." In Universe 12, p. 48-64. Edited by Terry Carr. Doubleday, 1982.

It is shortly after the Great Fire of London. The smell of smoke lingers in the air. Izaak Walton, Charles Cotton and friends are enjoying a supper together at the End of the World Tavern in Great Auk Street when wondrous news sends them scurrying for their fishing tackle. "Portent of Doom" is the cry, "Monster fish seen in Bedford."

At length Walton and crew reach the weed-choked mere north of London where the creature reputedly lurks. As they cast their lines, a preacher condemns their action, assuring them that the beast is The Beast, a harbinger of damnation. Walton ignores the preacher's counsel, baits up with a specially-grown maggot, and promptly hooks the Leviathan. A fantastic battle ensues, with demons, ghosts, and banshees flying everywhere.

This one is a lot of fun. The old English setting is persuasive, the sense of humor is true, and Izaak comes off as every bit the appealing chap one would expect. "Oh, Charles, I denied God," he laments. What is worse, ... but read the story. And don't miss the identity of the preacher who tries to deter Walton from his pursuit of the fish.

321. Watson, Henry S. "Truant Disciples." Harper's Weekly 54 (July 30, 1910): 18-19+.

A very strange story. It opens with the narrator and his wife Juliet in their home on the upper West Side of some anonymous metropolis. It is a May night, and the spring air inspires the narrator to write a fish story. Evidently he has written a good many such tales, for Juliet advises him on how to produce something fresh. The story, she insists, must have "a wonderful girl" in it.

We then move into the story proper, in which the narrator and Juliet are living in the country for the summer. One day he meets "the girl" in a village street, and, with the help of his wife, arranges to take her on a trout-fishing trip. The trip goes satisfactorily (and chastely), with the girl showing her considerable skill with the pole. The trip complete, Juliet picks them up in a surrey.

This plot makes sense only as an exercise in daydreaming on paper, daydreaming representing the middle-aged narrator's (and

author's?) fantasies about retreating to the bosom of nature with an
unspoiled country girl, a girl who does not, as the narrator's wife
does, fret about the quality of dresses available in the city.   That
a middle-class city couple in 1910 would actually enter upon such an
arrangement with an unknown country girl defies credibility; the
reader must wonder what lies below the text of this odd piece.

322.   White, Frederick.   "The Whirling Dervish."   <u>Scribner's Maga-</u>
       <u>zine</u> 73 (April 1923): 434-444.
       World War I makes itself felt in this story in a fairly clever
way.   Young Harmsworth has been invited to a little fishing inn
where a number of old habitués size him up as a prospective member
of their fly-fishing in-group.   Though congenial enough, and possessing diligence, Harmsworth suffers unaccountable bouts of clumsiness in the river.   The old fly-fishermen rudely christen him "The
Whirling Dervish" for his peculiar spells, and speculate on the
reasons for his difficulty.
       The most sought-after trout in the region, "Old Bill," eludes
all the members of this little club, but Harmsworth himself successfully hooks and lands him.   He later explains his out-of-kilter style:
his plane crashed in France during the war, and from that point on,
a detail of the crash reproduced in certain natural motions would
bring on his dizziness in the most outwardly peaceful situations.
The aftershocks of war, here as in Hemingway's "Big Two-Hearted
River" (item 304) are persistent.

VII. FOOTBALL

323. Ade, George. "What the College Incubator Did for One Modest
 Lambkin." In The America of George Ade, 1866-1944, p. 161-
 164. Edited by Jean Shepherd. Putnam, 1960.
 Young Wilbur goes off to college a rube; he comes back a full-
fledged sport, fresh from "eating Raw Meat and drinking Blood at
the Training Table." His ambition now is not learning, but football.
The moral: "A Boy never blossoms into his full Possibilities until
he strikes an Atmosphere of Culture." And the moral still holds.

324. Bailey, C. P. "The Barbed Wire." Michigan Quarterly Review 5 (July 1966): 209-213.
 Five boys, apparently all high school seniors, are sitting in
the shade of a tree waiting for football practice to begin. Two of
the boys, Dan Phillips and Billy Blake, are the team's best players,
and, although neither of them wants to admit it, they are rivals.
Billy is black.
 The boys smoke, brag about their success with girls, discuss
their summer jobs at the A & P and the ice plant. The job talk
moves the conversation to money. The boys are expecting to receive ten dollars each for each game they win; they keep this information to themselves, since it is clear that the payoff is to encourage
a good performance not for the sake of school spirit, but for gamblers' purposes. One of the chief gamblers in town is Dan's father,
a flashy n'er-do-well who "always looked and acted as if he had a
million dollars." He has left his family. Dan sees him only occasionally now, on the street.
 The boys begin some aimless horsing around as they wait for
their teammates to arrive. Billy practices his specialty, punting;
Dan runs out for passes. At one point Dan runs into Billy, possibly on purpose. The two exchange hot words, then fight. The
fight ends when Billy drags Dan across a barbed wire fence at the
edge of the field, leaving him with blood trickling down his back
into his trousers. The school principal, Mr. Rowan, breaks up the
fight and announces to the boys "I know what's going on ... I know
what all of you are doing."
 In this story the chief issue is the corruption of the boys by
the town and by the school. The high school coach scouts the surrounding country for promising players, starts slipping them money
as early as ninth grade, and finds jobs for their parents. This is
not sport: this is business, and dirty business. Small wonder,
then, that the boys smolder over their treatment. They like the
money, yes, but they know very well that they are being used by

others for unethical purposes. The fight between Billy and Dan is
a mutually destructive symptom of their awareness and resentment
of their corruption. The barbed wire surrounding the practice
field is symbolic of the inescapable institutional trap into which
these young men have fallen.

325. Bishop, Morris. "Football in the Faculty Club." New Yorker
      29 (Nov. 7, 1953): 132-135.
      A neatly-turned little satire on the habit of interpreting
phenomena according to narrow points of view, this account of a
group of college professors "explaining" football recalls the blind
men's evaluation of an elephant: one held the animal's tail and found
it like a rope, one its leg and declared it like a tree, and so on.
The Professor of Social Science sees football as a symbolic coming of
age ritual, and draws parallels between the game and primitive warriors and headhunters. The Professor of Moral Philosophy sees the
sport as a symbolic acting out of the quest for the Good, with the
end zone standing in for the ultimate Good. The Professor of
Chemistry draws a diagram of an offensive formation and sees in it
something mighty like a molecule.
      This high-level analysis breaks down into some uninspired, if
polite, quibbling about why the home team lost its latest game.
Funny and provocative, one wishes for a follow-up tale analyzing
faculty functions in a similar vein.

326. Brooks, George S. "The Last Season." Collier's 92 (Dec.
      9, 1933): 10-11+.
      One of the few football stories of any era featuring a woman
as the lead character, and one of fewer still that does not depict
women as either inevitably know-nothing about the game or as mere
trophies for successful players.
      Kitty Benton is a grandmother, married to Dad Benton, coach
at Jackson College. Benton is near retirement, and as he looks forward to the next game with Jackson's intense rival, Depew, it appears that his retirement will be hastened by a massacre at the hands
of Depew. The Depew team is big, tough, and best-suited to playing in bad weather; Benton's is light, fast, and made for dry conditions. The weekend of the game finds the weather, and the field,
a mess, and the game begins with all signs of a Jackson pasting.
      Kitty Benton attends the game, and saves her husband from
humiliation through clever observation of the opposing coach's tactics. Kitty Benton may not be in a fictional class by herself as a
woman both knowledgeable about football and able to contribute intelligently to tactical plans, but the class she occupies has plenty
of empty seats.

327. Brooks, Jonathan. "Bills Playable." Collier's 66 (Sept. 18,
      1920): 5-6+.
      A case of assumed identity provides the punch for the de-
nouement in this story of a 130-pound quarterback's ruination of an
opposing college team. Interesting chiefly for its details of early
football style.

328. Brunner, Bernard. <u>Six Days to Sunday</u>. McGraw-Hill, 1975.
      307 p.
      Begins in a slam-bang way with the once powerful Chicago
Stags busy losing their fourth straight game of the season. It is
a bloody, exhausting struggle against the Vikings, and the Stags
nearly pull it out, but an intercepted pass thwarts a Stags drive,
and locks up the game for the Vikes. It unlocks Stags quarterback
Chip Hughes's hold on his starting job. Both teammates and management are disgruntled, eager for the quick fix that will bring them
back to victory. Quick fixes after long losing streaks mean fired
coaching staffs, but after four bad games they mean, as a rule,
that the team's back-up quarterback will get a start. Stags rookie
Thomas Grover is thus on the verge of usurping Hughes. So much
for the book's dramatic focus.
      Few works of football fiction have presented their players as
such crude, witless cretins as <u>Six Days to Sunday</u>. To judge by
Brunner, the average pro football player's major goals in life are
to participate in gang rape and to become drunk as quickly, as
thoroughly, and as often as possible. We are talking here about
characters who have low-normal IQs and paranormal appetites. It
is all too much to believe. Worse, Brunner's players, on nearly all
of whom he hangs inane nicknames, never stop talking. Ordinarily
men this dull would stay with the basics, like "yeah," "huh?" and
"more beer," but they don't. Too bad. The reader able to tolerate
these crippling flaws will find some good football action.

329. Cartwright, Gary. <u>The Hundred-Yard War</u>. Doubleday, 1968.
      376 p.
      Dallas Trooper quarterback Rylie Silver is about to turn 30
with a load of trouble, including a bad marriage, a bad knee, and a
tyrannical coach. Cartwright combines these standard ingredients
of football fiction--the threat of a star's decline, sexual problems,
the effects of injuries, the conflicts between management and players,
and among players themselves--into a fairly standard outing with
better than usual attention to the social Darwinism that characterizes
the life of the team.

330. Cobb, Irvin S. "Cinnamon Seed and Sandy Bottom." In his
      <u>Those Times and These</u>, p. 258-307. Doran, 1917.
      Major Putnam Stone, for whom nothing of consequence has
happened since the Civil War, has been forced by failed investments
to take a $12 per week sinecure at the local paper, a post handed
him by the editor to return a political favor. The elderly Major
writes long, dull stories about dead heroes. He earns himself im-
mortality, as long as memory will last, by delivering a rousing half-
time talk to the home team Midsylvania football club after the big,
bad Sangamon northerners have been booting them all over the field.
The Major's "viewpoint on most subjects had not altered materially
since Appamattox," and that is how he sees the game: North versus
South. His speech, in which he upbraids the Midsylvanians for lying down and quitting before a more powerful foe, has its intended
effects.

A creditably written though essentially frivolous story. Cobb's guileless references to "little darkies" are one of the piece's drawbacks, but also one of the details that make it of historical value in obtaining an accurate impression of the times. (The title, the first line of an old song, becomes a cheer associated with the Major's memory.)

331.   Coover, Robert. "Whatever Happened to Gloomy Gus of the Chicago Bears?" American Review, no. 22 (1975): 34-110.
The time is the late 1930s, the place Chicago. Meyer, the narrator, is a socialist sculptor. He has just left a hospital; his friend Gloomy Gus has died from an injury suffered during a labor riot. Gus was once a halfback with the Bears. There are mysterious references to Gus's "spectacular career" ending almost before it began.

Meyer sculpts athletes, because for him "motion is all the magic I need," and motion is best in the athlete. Meyer makes some interesting observations on the philosophy and aesthetics of sport, especially football: "In football, as in politics, the issue is not ethical but aesthetic."

The reasons for Gus's strange collapse at football, and for his death during the demonstration, slowly become clear in an increasingly wild and funny story. Gus represents the epitome of the "trained" athlete, or trained anything: all spontaneity is gone. He is a slave to patterns, patterns of a kind that show up again in Coover's novel The Universal Baseball Association (item 32).

332.   Cronley, Jay. Fall Guy. Doubleday, 1978. 192 p.
An athletically gifted, intellectually-limited young man endures his father, his coaches, and the girls who cluster around football heroes in this passably entertaining though derivative yarn. Of some interest for protagonist Ben Elliott's happy acceptance of the perquisites granted the football hero, above-board, under-the-table, and under the covers. The mood is tempered by Elliott's rather Sisyphesian attempts to prepare himself for a stardom whose promise keeps rolling back to the bottom of the hill.

333.   Daley, Robert. Only a Game. New American Library, 1967. 313 p.
Strong throughout, this novel of a star halfback's personal crisis also contains some well-drawn secondary characters and some very good game description.

At thirty-one, former All-American Duke Craig has been a mainstay for the Big Red for a decade. A model athlete, he is unfailingly polite; he is a big draw on the rubber chicken lecture circuit, where he demonstrates a superior sense of comic timing as well as an ability to keep his speeches straight and serious when the situation requires it.

He also has a marriage that is dead on its feet. One of Daley's achievements is his portrayal of Duke as a college player, caught in the trap of ignorance and social expectations, marrying a girl for whom he feels almost nothing, but, because of his youthful limitations, impresses him as all that he should expect. This leads to a marriage only a masochist could enjoy. Duke's wife Carribel is one of the most tiresome women to bitch and whine her way through any sports novel, perhaps any novel at all. When she stages a half-baked "suicide" attempt to punish Duke for his involvement with another woman, the reader cannot help hoping that she really has taken the entire bottle of pills.

Carribel is finally too terrible to completely believe. She has no observable humane qualities. The scenes between her and Duke are, however, believable and dreadful. In one highly effective passage, Duke eats one sandwich after another, turning his rage against food, while Carribel gives him a tongue lashing.

Duke's life takes a turn for the more complicated when he falls in love with a married actress, Margie Berger. It is the first time he has felt any real spark between himself and a woman, and he quickly succumbs to emotions he never suspected were in him. This is a well-conceived, credible, and moving affair. It also brings Duke's marriage to the end of the line with Carribel's "suicide" charade, and the subsequent termination of Duke's career, thanks to his piously religious team owner who cannot brook the scandalous tales Duke's conduct has brought to hover over the team. Such narrow observation of this moral issue seems quaint today. Compared to recent revelations of drug abuse and dealing in pro football, what does a sincere affair mean in terms of moral shame? Not much, but within its own framework this aspect of the story works adequately.

The football portion works much better than adequately. In addition to good accounts of games, there are better insights on the game than one finds in most football fiction. For example, "After each other, the only men players love and understand are opponents. Opponents are themselves in different uniforms." The book also contains one of the most sensitive discussions of the effects of a serious knee injury to be found in this fictional genre. A young player tears up his knee; Duke Craig sits next to him on the flight home, trying to pull his teammate out of the depression and fear brought by his injury. This leads to a meditation on the knee injury as a thing in itself, with some lines that should penetrate any reader: "Pain is hard to remember, usually. But the pain of a knee injury to a football player lasts so long and recurs so often that he never forgets it."

Good character sketches appear frequently, such as that provided Pennoyer, the taciturn, stoical quarterback who comes to camp each year amid reports that his job is now the property of some rookie hotshot, only to end up, as usual, back in his starting position when the season takes off.

Daley, who worked several years as a publicity director for the New York Giants football team, writes of the players with knowledge and affection. Football is not "only a game" for them, and one must conclude that it is also more than a game for Robert Daley.

334. DeCamp, L. Sprague. "Throwback." Astounding Science

<u>Fiction</u>, March 1949, p. 48+. Also in <u>Apeman, Spaceman; An-</u>
<u>thropological Science Fiction</u>. Edited by Leon E. Stover and
H. Harrison. Doubleday, 1968.
Oliver Grogan, manager of the Chicago Wolves, recruits personnel at a reservation in the Ozarks whose residents are the results
of genetic fiddling. They run to a height of nine feet, and play
one-handed catch with medicine balls. Grogan signs and suits up
one of the boys. The big fellow's debut is impressive, but problems
follow in his outsize footsteps, not the least of which is his desire to
study painting at the Chicago Art Institute.

335. Deford, Frank. <u>Cut 'N' Run</u>. Viking, 1973. 248 p.
<u>Everybody's All-American</u>, described below, is the Deford novel
not to miss, but this earlier work set in 1967 has enough good pieces
to make the reading palatable, even if the pieces don't fit together
like steak and eggs. The center of this satire's crowded stage belongs to football fanatic Jerry Start, a stockbroker whose autumn
Sundays are wholly given to worship of the Baltimore Colts via the
color television down in the basement. The other major players include Jerry's sex-starved wife Rosalie (when The Game is in the air,
the mating dance must wait until the dead of winter), and Toby
Geyser, a war hero that the Pentagon allows to play for the Colts
in hopes of improving armed forces recruitment. There is a bit too
much going on here in too strained a fashion; the subplot about the
"threat" of a coup by the National Guard seems pulled out of a
brain-storming session that went awry. Still, the whole is fun.
The best section is the chapter "Double Coverage," concerning
Jerry's wild, ingenious, and successful plan to clear thousands of
dollars in stock commissions by "predicting" the winner of the 1964
NFL title game. Jerry's ruse is so outrageously conceived that the
book is worth locating for these 13 pages alone.

336. _____. <u>Everybody's All-American</u>. Viking, 1981. 314 p.
A thoughtful and alternately moody and exciting account of a
star player's unhappy collision with reality. Gavin Grey, "The Grey
Ghost," a brilliant halfback with the North Carolina Tarheels in the
early 1950s, goes on to play for a decade with Toronto in the Canadian Football League and with the Washington Redskins. After his
final college game, however, the glory is gone and life itself takes
over with disillusionment, marital problems, and betrayal by friends.
Gavin is not exceptionally bright, and isn't averse to blowing
off steam in a cathouse as he awaits his wedding to the impeccable
and virginal Babs (the North Carolina Blueberry Festival Queen),
but neither is he more than justifiably proud of himself, whether in
a footrace with a former black football star or when approached by
small boys seeking his autograph. He enjoys the public's fawning up
to a point, but after that point it makes him a little ill: "The last
goddamn place I wanna be ... is eatin' dinner at the Carolina Inn
with a bunch of alumni all liquored up comin' round makin' a mess
over me."
Deford writes persuasively here, with humor and compassion,

about both place and character. His 1950s North Carolina is fully
credible, and the relationships among the major characters are believable and touching. The book's only real flaw (like that of Peter
Gent's North Dallas 40, item 347), is its needlessly melodramatic
ending. For its great majority, this is a sports novel of the first
rank.

337. DeLillo, Don. End Zone. Houghton Mifflin, 1972. 242 p.
    Like many strong works of art, End Zone is disorienting. It
is one of those novels that, upon their closing, leaves the reader
looking about nervously for some sign of constancy in a world that
has changed too fast, and become too strange, to bear. Many fictional works about football question social values, and feature sympathetic characters in difficult situations, but End Zone is an unusually bitter, icy wind through the reader's assumptions.
    The story is set at Logos, a two-bit college in a remote,
desert-wrapped parcel of West Texas. The narrator and primary
character is Gary Harkness, a young man who has drifted through
several colleges. He has settled on Logos because no other will
have him. A running back, he plays for the Logos football team.
"My life meant nothing without football," he tells us.
    Football is often compared to war; it is a substitute for war,
a metaphor for war. As is stated more than once in this novel, we
do not need substitutes for war: we have the real thing, and the
real thing, or its threat, consumes Gary Harkness. He is an omniv-
orous reader of books on thermonuclear warfare; he enrolls in a
class on "Aspects of Modern War" in which he is the star pupil.
Through Gary's obsession, the nuclear specter raises itself again
and again through the novel, climaxing with a chilling war game conducted in a local motel; the game concludes with a "spasm" war, the
annihilation of civilization.
    Football, like all sports, is not a substitute for war. It is, in
the words of one character, "a benign illusion, the illusion that order is possible," an order safeguarded by rules, penalties, and
electronic controls. Gary Harkness's dwelling on nuclear matters (a
dwelling full of vivid and grim imaginings) may account for his resort to football. Football's sense is arbitrary, an imposition, but
nevertheless present; it is light years away in reason and justice
from the spastic genocide of nuclear war.
    If Gary turns to football as a way to salvage some sense of
order from the world, the assistance it gives him is only temporary
and superficial. A sense of chaos about to take over runs through
him and around him; it shows up in his ironic black humor. At
halftime during a big game, for example, his contribution to the
"pep" talk includes the statement that "We'll never make it. We'll
never even get out of here alive." Gary's fears are far from unique.
The whole football squad gleefully participates in a grim campus game,
"Bang, you're dead," in which they pretend to shoot each other to
death at various spots around the college. This game is funny only
at the top level; at bottom, it is horrifying. In his consumption by
the culture of violence, Gary is not alone, nor is he alone in his

locker-room pessimism. When other players say things like "They'll
kill us and eat us," we know that we have left "Win one for the
Gipper" territory far behind.

The book's atmosphere is stark, the setting flat and empty,
with the desert (strongly suggestive of a post-holocaust landscape)
playing a prominent part. Gary meditates during a desert walk:
"The sun. The desert. The sky. The silence. The flat stones.
The insects.... Blast area. Fire area. Body-burn area." He
carries with him a set of terrible visions. It is no surprise that
"In the end they had to carry me to the infirmary and feed me
through plastic tubes."

The two symbols of End Zone, both embodied in the novel's
title, are the football and the mushroom cloud. (Gary's girlfriend,
in fact, wears a little mushroom-cloud ornament on her clothing.)
The football in the book is described with intensity, but it is the
intensity of people getting hurt more than that of victory or defeat.
The "big game" comes down to the recitation of a litany of injuries;
the final score (what can it be but zero?) scarcely noticed.

Saving the novel from the relentlessly bleak is its streak of
dark comedy. Many of the laughs end in chills, but they come anyhow. DeLillo's style is distinctive and energetic, yet very tightly
controlled. He writes with a sure grasp of language--what else,
for a novel set in a place called Logos?--and with a fine sense of
the meaning of sport in a society that often seems restless to destroy
itself. End Zone is a powerfully affecting and brilliantly-executed
work of fiction.

338.   Dowdey, Clifford. "Rose Bowl Team: A Story of an All-
       American Halfback." American Mercury 36 (Dec. 1935): 414-
       422.

Al Rhordnick, a guard on a team working toward the Rose
Bowl, serves a slice of college football life that leaves a bitter after-
taste. He plays for a Montford University. Like the rest of the
players, he receives $50 a month in cash, and finds occasional en-
velopes with supplementary bills tucked under his pillow. In return
for a "free ride," he has to tolerate an athletic director with a
fascist's style. He is expected to play when hurt, to submit to cruel
workouts, and to show no respect for sportsmanship. Winning is all
that matters, because the thrill of victory is surrounded by dollar
signs.

Rhordnick is instrumental in helping the team win the big
game, but the victory leaves him unmoved. He goes back to his
hotel room; he wants to study his economics textbook, but he is
too tired.

There is nothing glamorous or of the old college spirit here.
Collegiate football is portrayed as a cheerless business whose only
purpose is to finance more of the same. It is thus fitting that the
subject Rhordnick would like to study is economics.

339.   Durand, E. A. "The Football Story." Esquire 10 (Dec. 1938):
       90+.

A nifty parody of every sentimental, hackneyed football story ever written. The "narrator" is Jack Weston, a character from a short story who finds that he has been tossed, along with the rest of the story, into the author's wastebasket. As Weston reveals the details of the story, Durand cleverly needles such conventions of the popular sporting tale as the morally straight athlete, the hard-working widowed mother, and the bold and successful reckless maneuvers on the field. Why, Weston is such a gifted young man that he plays for two different colleges, simultaneously! The groans the reader hears are stereotypes dying painful deaths.

340.   Effinger, George Alec. "25 Crunch Split Right On Two." In his Irrational Numbers, p. 65-84. Doubleday, 1976. First published in the Magazine of Fantasy and Science Fiction (April 1975).
Eldon MacDay, a running back for the Cleveland Browns, has begun having hyper-realistic flashbacks featuring his wife, dead for five years. He finds that the flashbacks' realism is further enhanced by his own pain; he goes out of his way in both games and practices to get his body slammed back to the past, to a favorite restaurant where he and his wife ate their last meal together. Like so many SF time-travel stories, this one emphasizes the traveller's inability to change the course of a particular event, though in this case seeing it all for the second time works some pronounced changes on MacDay.

341.   Exley, Frederick. A Fan's Notes; A Fictional Memoir. Harper, 1968. 385 p.
Acceding to Exley's subtitle, we can call this book a novel, although it reads like autobiography. Exley the narrator is edging into middle age, his path greased by alcohol, complicated by madness, and further complicated by the memory of a father who played football to "the roar of the crowd." The one anchor (if a poor one) in Exley's life is his emotional tie to the New York Giants, and in particular to their star halfback, Frank Gifford. Gifford represents the success that taunts and eludes Exley, not only success on the athletic field, but "success" in the American mode. A Fan's Notes reveals the made-in-the-U.S.A. brand of success as too often murderous; in the end, Exley understands that it is his destiny "to sit in the stands with most men and acclaim others. It was my fate, my destiny, to be a fan." This novel is a well-written, sometimes funny, and generally compelling look at the dynamics of neurotic fandom.

342.   Farrell, James T. "High-School Star." In his To Whom It May Concern: More Stories, p. 101-118. Sun Dial Pr., 1946.
A perceptive examination of the athlete who thinks too much about what he is doing. Tom Kennedy is a player of great natural talent, but practice bores him, and he has never, in his high school career, fulfilled the promise of his ability. His coach, who likes him personally, tells Tom what a botch the boy has made of his oppor-

tunities for real recognition. A final game gives Tom a chance to
redeem himself, if not for the sake of a college scholarship, then
for his own self-esteem. Tom's performance in the game, described
in detail, is erratic. Instead of losing himself in the play, Tom
monitors his own conduct, with the crowd occupying an excessive
role in his thoughts. Not until well into the game does Tom finally
shake free from his mental ratcheting, and for a brief spell forgets
himself and the fans, and plays up to his potential. At the height
of his performance, he sustains a crippling knee injury.

Farrell presents Tom Kennedy's psychological contortions with
the sympathy and critical sense he customarily devotes to his characters.

343.   _____. "Pat McGee." In his The Life Adventurous, and
        Other Stories, p. 190-202. Vanguard, 1947.
One of sport's saddest sights is that of the former high-school
star going back to hang around the old school, to live off memories
and a worn-out reputation. Pat McGee is one of those athletes. Although but twenty-five, he strongly suspects that the good days are
gone. He still has the build of a three-sport player, but he received his release from a minor league baseball team when his arm
went dead, and now works as a car salesman.

The story follows Pat as he spends an off-day visiting old
friends from his high school glory days. The big event is a trip
to the school's practice football field. Pat is sure that all the students will look upon him with awe. They don't know who he is, and
Pat's former coach really hasn't time to talk to him. Another old
"friend" scoffs at the idea of playing pro football, which, in Pat's
life, amounts to no more than an infrequent semi-pro game. Pat
tries to convince himself that his bad arm is coming around, but we
know that his athletic triumphs are all behind him, and he knows it
too, almost as well.

344.   Fay, William. "The Fainthearted Fullback." Saturday Evening
        Post 226 (Nov. 28, 1953): 22-23+.
Jake Gilbride is the player-coach of the New York Titans, the
team for which Jake's father played as one of pro football's all-time
greats. Even now the elder Gilbride can still kick the ball between
the goalposts from the 40-yard line and when the team owner is in a
good mood, he cajoles the old man to show his stuff.

Jake resents it. His father was a great player, but he had
no financial sense and little control over his drinking. Jake has believed for years that his father was exploited unfairly by the obese,
unattractive Titan owner, and at one point says as much to the old
man. His father is stung, and contends that no one ever tried to
hurt him but his own son.

The story's first half is promising, but the second declines into a predictable resolution. Jake sees the light, his father was
right, etc. It might make an instructive project to contrast football
executives in stories like this one with the mercenary and merciless
coaches and owners described by such contemporary writers as Peter
Gent.

345. _____. "Strictly for Sweeney." Collier's 104 (Nov. 18, 1939): 9-10+.

"He took her in his arms and kissed her fervently upon the crimson moisture of her lips. She struggled free, afire and out of breath. 'I didn't think you were man enough,' she said."

With campy lines like these, this story should provide a few laughs in spite of its sincerity, or perhaps because of it. Willy Creedon is a former University of Michigan running back and pro star who has been banished, along with his evident drinking problem, to football's minor leagues. He receives a last chance to make good (that old tale again) when the niece (she of the crimson moisture) of his former team owner calls him back to help the team in its late-season championship drive.

Some three decades later the themes in this story--sex, drug abuse, and obsession with winning--would appear in much more intense and realistic ways in football fiction. Here they are reduced to pop formula, still tied to easy moral solutions: be a man, kiss the girl, and make that point.

346. Gent, Peter. The Franchise. Random, 1983. 576 p.

"The Franchise" bears a dual meaning. It refers first to the Texas Pistols, a new pro team, and then to Taylor Rusk, the young quarterback who will take the team to the Superbowl. The Franchise is in some ways an All-American novel. Extraordinarily, often repulsively violent, riddled with drug abuse, greed, the Mob, mean-spirited sex, and a crazy obsession with football, the book is good reading in spite of these qualities. It compels because Gent never fails to give the impression that he knows what he's talking about, whether the topic is the destruction of flesh and bone on the field or the big-money manipulations in league offices.

A handful of respectable characters, foremost among them Taylor Rusk, keep the cast from becoming too loathesome to put up with. Gent's quick black humor, which surfaces in some unlikely spots, also keeps the tone from slipping too far into morbidity or self-importance. Gent does know football, from all angles. One of the most affecting passages here describes a knee-injured player's attempt to prove to management that he has full mobility in his bad knee. While the trainer is setting up a videotape to record the test, the player surreptitiously adjusts the machine he's attached to so that it will flex his knee to full extension, about ten degrees beyond its newly-curtailed capacity. The injured player goes through an agonizing session, and spends the night crying with a knee that swells to burst his pantleg--but management has a tape to prove that his knee is sound, and uses it as ammunition to help trade the player while he is supposedly still able to perform.

North Dallas Forty is a better novel; there are too many undeveloped characters here, and the violence does wear thin. Still, few readers of the book will be able to look at pro football in the same way again.

347. _____. North Dallas Forty. Morrow, 1973. 314 p.

Until the conclusion, this first novel by the former Dallas Cowboys' pass receiver is consistently readable, credible, and funny. Gent's protagonist is Phil Elliot, a marginal receiver close to the end of his career. He and many of his teammates prop themselves up with painkillers; to counteract the sedative effects of the analgesics, they pop a variety of uppers. Phil hopes for the worst from the team's starting receivers, for only when the game goes badly is Phil likely to get a chance to play, a chance to prolong his career, a chance to once again be clobbered from the blind side by a defensive back.

The humor is real and pointed. Much of the book's tone is set in an early hunting trip on which Elliot accompanies a few teammates. The hunt turns into a grotesque drunken slaughter of anything that moves, not a great deal unlike the events on any NFL playing field on an autumn Sunday afternoon. The hunt is hideous and yet funny at the same time, a tough combination but one that Gent manages to sustain through most of the novel. The relationships Gent portrays among the players, especially between Elliot and the quarterback, Seth Maxwell, are real and mature.

The book's worst problem is its conclusion, which pulls the story down from its heights of honest compassion to mere bathos. Mind this with a tolerant eye, however; the book remains one of the best works of sports fiction of recent years.

348. _____. Texas Celebrity Turkey Trot. Morrow, 1978.
239 p.
Thirty-year old defensive back Mabry Jenkins of the Dallas Colts is having his "best training camp ever." The knee injury he suffered in the previous season is still nagging him, though, and he has already sat out most of one exhibition game because of it. No worry. When coach Buck Binder calls him back to his office one day, Jenkins assumes that the issue is a minor detail in his contract. The issue is not minor: Jenkins is being cut from the team, and no one in the NFL, not even basket-case Tampa Bay, has shown any interest in picking him up on waivers.

Cut adrift, Jenkins goes on the Texas celebrity circuit, and puts in appearances of a consistently embarrassing sort at fishing and golf tourneys and other "personality"-ridden events.

The best passage in the book is the cut scene itself, when all of the player's expectations are knocked out from under him. Irony has its ways; a season later Jenkins is back in the Colts' saddle owing to other injuries and coincidences. At the book's end, Jenkins has resumed his old willful assumptions about his longevity, but it is plain to see that what came around for him once will come around again, and prove terminal.

A good venture into the life of the professional athlete trying to hang on.

349. Gerson, Noel B. The Sunday Heroes. Morrow, 1972. 288 p.
Just as his current employer, the New York Giants football club, is at the peak of its success, young executive Robin Stephens

yields to an offer to join the Chicago Cougars as assistant general
manager. The Cougars have a lot of tradition, but only a handful
of good players, an inept scouting system, and a familiar position as
the NFL's doormats.

With Chicago's regular general manager on sick leave, Stephens
sets out to cure the Cougars, and quickly. He wants a profitable
team, and a winner. These goals require a complete shake-out of
the Cougar roster, coupled with imaginative but extremely unpopular
trades. One of the most controversial trades sends a talented public
favorite to Baltimore for the notorious Fred Finch, a youthful quarterback of limitless potential, a large, economy-sized ego, and pen-
chants for illiberal doses of wine and women.

Stephens must contend with an enflamed Chicago media led by
radio broadcaster Phil Donegan, a Chicago coach who is dismayed by
Stephens's tradition-damning moves, with wildman Finch, and with the
autocratic league Commissioner.

There is some nodding aspiration to the exposé here, but the
novel is basically a titillating "behind the scenes" look at football
executives as we suspect they are, tough guys who call players
"gooks," buy, sell, and trade them like so many slabs of bacon, and
keep the dollar sign foremost in view. Taken at its own level, the
novel is satisfactory reading, and sometimes better than that.

350. Graffis, Herb B. "Homecoming at State." Esquire 14 (Nov.
     1940): 44+.

Johnny Smith, an engineering student from an impoverished
background, proves the potent blocker who can free State's running
star Pinky Fowler for long gains. Johnny gets little recognition and
minimal financial help from the school; in a big game he sustains a
serious injury. Trainers haul him roughly away. He makes a disconcerting comeback at the homecoming game years later in the
story's conclusion. The narrator is a sportswriter, and if he is just
a touch cynical about big-time college sport, he will probably become
more so after his disturbing vision of the new Johnny Smith.

351. Guy, David. Football Dreams. Seaview, 1980. 314 p.

The title mentions dreams, but the book reads a lot more like
football memories. Dan Keith reminisces about his life and hard
knocks in prep school football. This is an effective presentation of
a side of school ball that isn't obvious on the sporting pages or from
the stands. Attitudes toward winning and losing, fears that one
won't fit in, the arrogance of older boys toward newcomers, and
coaches (both stupid and decent, talented and incompetent) all come
in for attention. There are some good football action passages, but
the big concern is emotional growth.

Dan is growing up while his father's health is deteriorating.
The reader who has been through many novels of school or adolescence will recognize much familiar ground in this story, but it is
ground well-tended. The characters are real, the situations of
dramatic interest, and the style of Dan's first-person narrative en-
courages an emotional response.

352. Hall, Jim. "The Miracles." Carolina Quarterly 31 (Spring/
      Summer 1979): 59-75.
      A cheerleader's tale that begins in a funny vein but which
ends morosely. Candy Miracle is the narrator. She works as a
beautician at the Cadiz Beauty College "in a jerkwater town in Kentucky." She assures us that her life is pitiful, that this is going
to be a depressing story. Candy's husband is Elwood Miracle.
Elwood came home from college to a job working with the high school
cheerleading squad, which included Candy and several girls named
Sandra. Elwood's "cheers" involved snatches of Latin and other
foreign tongues, as well as the inventive use of mirrors. Instead
of whipping the crowd to a frenzy, Elwood's cheers reduced it to a
state of contented somnambulism, and worked the same effect on opposing teams, allowing the Cadiz Flamingoes to run up amazing
scores against their opponents. Elwood rode the team bus to away
games, slumping down in his seat with the Tibetan Book of the Dead.
      Elwood's real objectives lay in a far grander arena than high
school football, and shortly before the season's last game, he took
off for Washington, D.C., with plans for stopping war forevermore.
Elwoodless, the Flamingoes were crushed, humiliated. Elwood returned months later, a drunken, hopeless man railing against the
fools in the Pentagon. Candy took Elwood back, for in his unique
way he had given her a glimpse of something deep within her that
surpassed anything she had ever felt.
      Hall gets Candy's tone and syntax and befuddled understand-
ing down just right; it is her vision--cloudy, hurt, yet compas-
sionate--that makes this story so successful, so funny, and yet so
sad.

353. Heinz, W. C. "Man's Game." Collier's 124 (Oct. 15, 1949):
      18-19+.
      Eddie is a college coach with his job on the line. Disgruntled
alumni are fed up with him; they assign to him the blame for the
school's three straight bad years. The college president has confer-
red with Eddie in an ominous and ignorant manner; the man has no
conception of the complicated nature of coaching. All that counts is
the final score.
      Eddie is well-respected by his players. He coaches with imagi-
nation and patience, trying to draw the best from all his boys, however limited their skill or their intelligence. And he knows that they
are boys, adolescents, no matter that from the stands they look like
mature men in their helmets and pads.
      The story's main event is a critical game against the State
team, an undefeated, arrogant powerhouse. If Eddie's boys win, his
job will be safe. Otherwise, he will be sending his resume around.
The end is "happy," but is tempered by irony in a way that few
popular magazine stories are. The most admirable feature of "Man's
Game," in fact, is the irony implied by the title. Football is that
sort of game, but Eddie is fully aware that his team is a team of
boys who will not, and cannot, be men for some years to come.
This insight is a significant departure from the assumptions about

college football as a test of manhood underpinning so many popular
football stories.

354.   Herndon, Booton. "Dirtiest Game of the Year." Saturday
       Evening Post 225 (Oct. 18, 1952): 38-39+.
       Stan Slotnick is on his way to the Touchdown Club's Monday
night film of the Saturday game played by the local college. Slotnick is upset, afraid that the film will confirm that it was his son,
Stan Jr., who deliberately struck the opposition's star back,
Smathers, in the jaw.
       Slotnick dwells on his own football past, when he and the
whole town of Springdale had become incensed over a player on another opposing team, a player with a foreign, "Bolshevik"-sounding
surname. Slotnick had earned the regrettable nickname "Slug" by
breaking this "foreigner's" jaw with a punch on the game's first
play. Ever since, Slotnick has tried to live down this uncharacter-
istic moment of cowardly, dirty play; the act haunts him.
       Not until well into the story do we learn that Smathers is
black, and, like the unlucky boy of twenty-some years ago, has
aroused the entire town with a savage desire to "get" him, to show
him what happens to "uppity niggers" (though Herndon never uses
the term "nigger," he hints at it with incomplete sentences) in white
little Springdale. Herndon botches the story in spots; on the heels
of a good dramatic confrontation between father and son, Slotnick's
wife breaks in on the two angrily. "Doris is so cute when she's
mad," says Slotnick. Most readers of today will grimace at that
line, and rightly so, but remember that this was written in the early
1950s, and sexual attitudes were no more (not as?) enlightened than
racial ones. Herndon does his best, though, and the story carries
some weight beyond that of socio-historical interest.

355.   _____. "Football Punk, That's Me." Saturday Evening Post
       224 (Nov. 17, 1951): 22-23+.
       Bill Czerny, a high school fullback from a dirty coal-mining
town, sees his plans for a college scholarship smashed when his
coach, Grizer, moves him to a new position, substitute center.
Grizer is a corrupt operator hungry for a job at the college level;
he tries to coerce Czerny into deliberately flunking some of his
classes so that the boy will be available to play center another year.
Czerny, a straight arrow, will have none of this: he would rather
abandon all hope of college than compromise himself in this way.
       Can such an upright young man fail to earn his just reward in
the Post? Do footballs take funny bounces? It seems that one of
Czerny's teammates has a father who does a little scouting for an Ivy
League school. The man recognizes Czerny's spirit and devotion,
and promises him that a likely spot awaits him on the Ivy eleven.
There is, of course, no under-the-table money for footballers there,
and the boy would probably have to work in the university library
to cover his expenses.
       There is some good game action in this story, but the main
point of interest is the suggestion of widespread corruption and

illicit payments to college athletes, with the road for this evil well-paved by high school routines.

356.   Heuman, William. "Breakaway." American Magazine 152 (Nov. 1951): 26-27+.
      Susan Smythe, beauteous secretary to the Panthers' owner-coach Oscar Brunn, won't give the time of day, or anything else, to Norm Peters, the team's quarterback. Norm is quite smitten by Miss Smythe, but she considers him Brunn's lap dog, a man with no mind of his own. She wants him to take a job as a college coach. She "was out of her mind even thinking such a thing," thought Peters. "It was typical of a woman."
      Yes, yes. But as Norm and the Panthers struggle through a rough game with the Bulls, Norm seethes over Brunn's ultraconservative playcalling. Late in the game, while Brunn signals from the sidelines for running plays, Norm ignores him and goes to the air, his own man at last. It is not long before he writes a letter of acceptance to the little college that offered him a coaching job, and he and Miss Smythe leave a flustered Coach Brunn for the Marriage License Bureau.
      The theme of the submissive player under the dominant coach is well-handled, but the story is more interesting now for its portrayal of women as embodied in Susan Smythe. Norm Peters dismisses her thinking as "ridiculous," but she emerges as the one hard-headed, perceptive person in the story. No wonder Heuman felt compelled to have her ask permission to powder her nose at the story's end: he has already shown her to be a decisive, strong-minded type, and too much of this would not do for a woman in the Middle America of 1951.

357.   _____. "Fall Tryout." Collier's 138 (Oct. 12, 1956): 54+.
      Harry Marks was a gifted pass receiver who threw his pro career away with drink and carousing. His binge the night before a championship game may have cost his team the victory; it was the last game he played. The team cut him immediately afterward. He comes back in this story, in his mid-30s, five years out of the league but on the wagon, and with responsibilities in the form of a wife and two small children, unlike any he bore in his wild youth. He also stands at the edge of financial ruin, for the sporting goods business he has built up was destroyed by an act of nature.
      Will his old coach allow him a tryout, to see if one more season remains in this aging body? Will Marks succeed? The answers to these questions are probably obvious, but Heuman again handles the matter quite well. The reader finds no going-for-the glory guff here, only a man with serious responsibilities trying to meet them the best he can. A didactic tale, as are so many works of sports fiction, but one whose outlook is more mature than that of most pop fiction of the period.

358.   _____. "I'm Back, Coach." Saturday Evening Post 228 (Dec. 31, 1955): 30-31+.

Danny Forbes has just come back from a year in the Canadian Football League, following an eight-year stint with the NFL Cougars. Using an offer from the Rams as a negotiating chip, he wins back a job with the Cougars, and shows that he still has what it takes to win games. Danny's wise-cracking character and the overall wry tone create an enjoyable story free of the self-important earnestness of too many football tales. We know we're in different waters here when we learn that the fullback is preparing to be a psychiatrist! Featherweight fun.

359. Hopper, James. "He Could Take It." <u>American Magazine</u> 116 (Nov. 1933): 52-55+.

If it were not for this story's appearance at the trough of the Depression, it would be easily dismissed. With a hero named Cam Carrington who says things like "By Jove!" and who calls his father "The Governor" (his father is not, in fact, the governor), its promise is not soon apparent, but in the context of the Depression the story serves as a fairly powerful reminder to the public to keep trying, no matter how grim it looks, and as a promise that the effort may be worth its cost.

Cam drops in on one of his father's old friends, who unaccountably relates a long anecdote about how the elder Carrington held off the Yale football team in the 1890s with his valiant punting. The Yale line belted him mercilessly after every kick, but no matter how many times Carrington went down in the dirt, he got up and kept kicking.

Cam politely hears out the tale, then goes to his father's office to drive him home. Catching the old man by surprise, Cam learns that the business is teetering, and that his father has been hiding the news from his family. Cam readily offers to make the necessary sacrifices, beginning with his car, and promises to join his father as soon as he graduates; together they will "keep on kicking."

360. Inglis, William. "John Smith: Hero or Fool?" <u>Harper's Weekly</u> 54 (Jan. 1, 1910): 32.

Until rules changes reversed much of its lethal violence, football shortly after the turn of the century was approaching the possibility of an official ban. No less rough a rider than Theodore Roosevelt himself threatened collegiate functionaries with the condemnation of this popular game should they fail to control the carnage brought on by such innovations as the flying wedge formation. Over thirty players died in college ball in 1909.

It is in this context that one must place the story of John Smith, a defensive back and ball carrier. Smith, a great hero on the field, is knocked unconscious when he runs into a goalpost. Not until much later do physicians at Johns Hopkins learn that he has broken his neck. Not one to malinger with such trivial hurts, Smith wears a specially-designed headgear and continues to plow through the opposition for the school's greater glory. "Possibly the fact that he might drop dead at any moment lent an added fascination

to the game." There is no doubt about which category noted in the
title Smith belongs in, nor about the author's own opinion. "I dare
not answer the question," he writes. "But when real men are
needed, may God send us plenty of John Smiths." An interesting
point of view in a nation a few years away from joining the massacre
of John Smiths in the European trenches.

361. Jenkins, Dan. <u>Life Its Ownself: The Semi-Tougher Adven-
     tures of Billy Clyde Puckett and Them</u>. Simon & Schuster,
     1984. 316 p.
     Another installment in the rowdy, bawdy carryings-on of Billy
Clyde and company (see their first incarnation in the next item).
Billy's football playing days come to an end under a ton or so of
Washington Redskins. Billy Clyde limps into the broadcast booth to
do some work for CBS, falls for a young production assistant,
drinks, grouses, and whines. This sequel has some entertaining
and funny passages; old buddy Shake Tiller's blooming career as an
author offers a few. The plot does not amount to much, however,
and the abrasive tone is not relieved by characters with whom the
reader can feel close.

362. _____. <u>Semi-Tough</u>. Atheneum, 1972. 307 p.
     <u>Semi-Tough</u> succeeds at two things, and struggles to carry
itself all the way through to the end on their strength. It develops a credible narrator, Billy Clyde Puckett, who calls himself
"the humminest sumbitch that ever carried a football," and, chiefly
through Billy Clyde, flaunts an attitude that, were one to speak in
terms Billy Clyde would feel at home with, one would call smart-ass.
     The rationale for Billy Clyde's lengthy account of his and his
Giant teammates' exploits is a book contract. On a whim, he has
proposed a book, and now is hard at work on it, keeping a running
record of events leading up to and away from a game against cross-
town rivals the New York Jets. The game is the Superbowl, played,
with fitting absurdity, in Los Angeles rather than New York.
     Billy Clyde is a good old boy, free loving, free drinking, pro-
fane, obscene, and often funny. His journal is a loosely-constructed
assemblage of anecdotes, set-pieces, and deliberate outrages. His
use of conventionally offensive words, including "nigger," among
others, is reminiscent of Lenny Bruce's efforts to defuse such language of its power through endless repetition of it. It is, unfortunately, a lot easier to believe in Lenny Bruce's sincerity than in
Billy Clyde's.
     The book contains a predictable roster of "characters." Typi-
cal of the tone they set is that produced by T. J. Lambert, known
for his wondrous ability to fart on command. This novel has received
more than its due acclaim; there are many better novels about football and about the people who play it. <u>Semi-Tough</u> is only about
semi-successful: when the attitude wears thin (it does), and when
the cussin' good ol' boy redneck excess becomes too predictable (it
does, too), the book begins to hobble like a halfback whose cleats
caught in the artificial turf when he tried to make a cut. There is

fun and truth here, but it would have made a better story than a
novel.

363.   Kaplan, Bernard. "One of the Seas is Called Tranquility."
       Antioch Review 29 (Winter 1969-70): 461-471. Also in Best
       Little Magazine Fiction, 1971. N.Y. Univ. Pr., 1971.
       Hale, a poet (or so he believes, and is there a difference?),
lives in a Chicago-area home for mentally ill men. The men from
"the Home" go to Chicago Bears games. Some of them watch the
games; others study their potato chips or the posts. Hale develops
a crush on a 65-year old vendor named Nome. A depressing story
whose violence is far more sickening than a football game's; well-
written, however.

364.   Kinney, Robert. "The Fixed Grin." Esquire 15 (April 1941):
       58+.
       John Littlefield has recently switched prep schools. At his
new school he makes no friends, then enrages his classmates by
sitting on the opposition's side during a football game, and, worse,
by carrying water out to the other team during a time out. Littlefield receives a vicious beating for this disloyalty, a beating he
bears with "a fixed grin" and, at last, with laughter. A football
coach with Littlefield's interests at heart tries to counsel the boy,
but to no observable results. Littlefield is a born loner and antagonist, and will obviously remain that way.

365.   Koch, Claude F. "Snowshoe." Antioch Review 22 (Winter
       1962-63): 443-457.
       A disturbing story, for it suggests that a high school football
coach's cruel approach to the game is a respectable one, even one
to imitate. The coach is Sy Snowshoe, seen as the story opens in-
structing young children for the city recreation department. This
is years after his long term as coach at a Catholic high school, where
he achieved notoriety for the dirty play of his teams.
       The narrator is one of Snowshoe's players who, after an in-
jury, becomes an assistant to the coach. He watches Snowshoe
closely, does his job, and finds himself invited to the coach's house
one evening. There he meets Snowshoe's wife, an invalid with heart
disease, yet the only person able to soften Snowshoe's rough demeanor. It is evident that the character of Snowshoe's wife Ellen
indicates that Snowshoe's motives lie beyond football, that he is con-
tending not against an opposing team in his fanatic insistence on a
brute, head-on battle (he shuns all finesse on the field, and the
idea of using the pass is close to sacrilege for him), but against
death itself. If the implications aren't clear enough, Koch lays them
out bluntly when Snowshoe says that he is teaching his players "how
to die. If I thought I was teaching these people anything else, I'd
quit." The narrator seconds Snowshoe's humorless philosophy when
he hopes that his kids will fall under the guidance of someone like
Snowshoe.
       The story's climax comes with Snowshoe's intentional destruc-

tion of a talented back on his own team because the boy fails to embody Snowshoe's ruthless dedication to the "right" way to play. The
boy actually fancies the forward pass!

It is possible that the author does not share the narrator's admiration for the Snowshoes of the world, but one would welcome some
sign that he considers learning how to live a better goal than learning how to die, especially for boys in high school. In any case,
this is an interesting story for the light it throws on one unhealthy
aspect of sport.

366. Lampell, Millard. The Hero. Messner, 1949. 298 p.

The Hero joins a group of books in which the status of collegiate athletics as a business comes under attack. "The hero" is
Steve Novak, a New Jersey high school player who seeks a balance
between sport and scholarship. His sensitivity to his intellectual
needs leads him to reject the recruiting efforts of large colleges that
obviously want him only to pack a football stadium in favor of a small
Virginia school. Steve finds the path for the conscientious athlete-
scholar a difficult one to follow. Even in the "genteel" atmosphere
of a Virginia college, the sordid realities of industry masquerading
as amateurism are commonplace, manifested in greed, political opportunism, academic irresponsibility by faculty members, deliberate injury, and infantile alumni. A readable and honestly-observed book
by an author who knows and cares about his topic.

367. Lyons, Grant. "The Assistant." In 4·4·4: Short Fiction by
      Laurence Gonzales, Grant Lyons, and Roger Rath, p. 98-109.
      Univ. of Missouri Pr., 1977.

"Football was the only thing he had, the only future worth
thinking about." So concludes Ray Begnaud, an assistant summer
coach at the high school where he was a star football player only a
few years before. Now he is a marginal player in college; if he
trains very hard, and has a bit of luck, he may make the first team.
Maybe not. Pro ball is out of the question, but what else is there?

On a whim, Ray challenges a young track star to a footrace.
The boy beats Ray easily. The story ends with Ray planning on
getting into the best shape of his life for the coming football season,
but we doubt the authenticity of his intentions. A good study in
self-delusion.

368. MacAlarney, Robert E. "Aaron Luckett's Gridiron Gloat."
      American Magazine 75 (Nov. 1912): 114-123.

Buck Murchison, star backfield man for Princeton until he
graduated in 1904, is now working his way up in the banking industry. He still puts in some free time, and some not so free, as
assistant coach with Princeton. This moonlighting sits uneasily with
Murchison's crusty superior, Aaron Luckett, and Luckett issues an
ultimatum: play ball with the boys or bonds with the bank, but
not both.

Murchison gives in to Luckett's demand, until Luckett himself,
motivated by a football bet in spite of his total ignorance of the game,

orders Murchison to go back to Princeton to help the team prepare
for the upcoming Yale game. Although Luckett knows nothing of
football, on game day he readily detects a crucial deviation in Yale's
formation after seeing plays diagrammed. One among many sports
stories in which big business plays a significant part.

369. McCluskey, John, Jr. "Once a Wars' October." Callaloo 7
     (Fall 1984): 7-26.
     Considering the background events--the Cuban Missile Crisis
and the Civil Rights movement in the South--this story is surprisingly low-keyed and reflective, and may be better for those qualities
than if the author had been more aggressive with his message.
     The main character is Derrick Cunningham, the only black
player, and the quarterback at that, on the Harvard University
junior varsity. The story opens slowly, with Cunningham headed
across the campus to the fieldhouse, where the Harvard JVs are to
play a junior college from Framingham. Cunningham's mind is not
entirely on the game. A good part of it lingers on his girlfriend.
As he suits up, another player insists "that the world is heading
for a showdown." The players keep a radio on the bench during
the game, which proves to be a rout of the Framingham team. The
radio keeps them posted on the U.S.-Soviet confrontation, but Cunningham's thoughts drift elsewhere.
     After playing an outstanding first half, Cunningham is not
quite in mesh with the game. There are new things happening in
the country. Martin Luther King is pledging to build a nonviolent
army, and here Cunningham is, going to Harvard, playing football,
talking Descartes. A change is coming over him as the game pro-
gresses, and it is clear that he will soon turn his attention to matters of greater moment than JV football. For this coming evening,
however, he will meet his girlfriend, and be "grateful that he had
rescued a fleeting peace while the wars of a world spun, spun, spun
outside the window."

370. McMillion, Bonner. "The Big Win." Collier's 134 (Oct. 15,
     1954): 28-29+; (Oct. 29, 1954): 54+; (Nov. 12, 1954): 44+.
     A novella-length serial featuring several of the standard ele-
ments of sports fiction, and that contains a few passages rising
above the formulae. Paul Watson is football coach at Coulton High
School, in a small West Texas town. Paul has been career building
for several years, moving from team to team, town to town, with no
sense of loyalty but to his own plans for moving up in the coaching
hierarchy. A little intrigue, a little liberal conscience-tweaking,
and a heavy dose of team spirit prove the potion to change Paul's
mind, about the town of Coulton and about his own values.
     The two chief subplots involve a blackmail scheme to persuade
Paul to throw an important game, and the addition to the team of a
black quarterback, Donnie Quillen. Donnie's presence is more interesting than the blackmail scheme; black quarterbacks were rare
finds in the mid-'50s, and next to unthinkable in West Texas.
McMillion's point of view is that of the well-meaning liberal, but he

does a respectable job of presenting to a mass audience the very
lonely existence of a black player in a thoroughly white setting.

371.   Martin, George R. R.   "The Last Super Bowl Game."   In <u>Run</u>
       <u>to Starlight: Sports through Science Fiction</u>, p. 11-36.
       Edited by Martin H. Greenberg, et al. Delacorte, 1975. First
       published in <u>Gallery</u> (Feb. 1975).
       Want to watch the 1962 Los Angeles Rams play the 1980 Notre
Dame junior varsity in the Astrodome? Or catch the 1927 Yankees
taking on the 1968 Cardinals, with Bob Gibson pitching for the
Cards? And do you want to see this not just on paper, or in a
radio simulation, but in a holographic, indistinguishable-from-reality
production? All this and more lies at the controls of Sportsmaster,
a supercomputer that has completely ruined "real" sporting events,
with their often dull, one-sided, unimaginative games.
       Shortly after the year 2000, professional sports are dead,
thanks to Sportsmaster, which controls television, theater, and
stadium events, none real, all better than real.
       Except for some. The last Superbowl game takes place between
the Green Bay Packers and the Hoboken Jets in a rainstorm, before
a crowd of less than a thousand people. It proves a magnificent
game, with a great comeback guided by an injured quarterback. No
one cares. The stands are empty before the game ends, and the
opposing teams walk off the field in tears after their classic match.
       A well-written vision of what could come to pass, as human
beings become ever-more the subjects of computers, and the victims
of illusion. Anyone who has amused himself listening to those radio
broadcasts of "games" between teams that never played each other
should read this story before taking further steps down the road to
holographic hollowness.

372.   _____.   "Run to Starlight."   In <u>Run to Starlight: Sports</u>
       <u>through Science Fiction</u>, p. 67-106.   Edited by Martin H.
       Greenberg, et al. Delacorte, 1975. First published in
       <u>Amazing Science Fiction</u> (December 1974).
       Roger Hill, administrator of the Starport City Dept. of Rec-
reation, struggles with a request from the extraterrestrial Brish'diri
to field a team in the city's football league, a few years after the
bloody Earth-Brishun War. As a political good-will gesture, the
Brish'diri receive a berth in the league. From a heavy gravity
planet, the slow but powerful ETs wreak devastation on the human
teams. All ends happily when the alien peace faction recognizes the
importance of not whipping up the remaining martial fanatics back
home with lopsided victories. The highlight here is some amusing
description of Brish'diri/human football games.

373.   Nemerov, Howard.   <u>The Homecoming Game</u>.   Simon & Schuster,
       1957.   246 p.
       Gambling, academic politics, youthful ideals, and a history
professor's dilemma blend well in this novel. Professor Charles Osman has been forced to flunk one of his students, a star on the col-

lege's football team. Osman immediately comes under heavy pressure
from students, fellow faculty, and college administrators to give the
student, Raymond Blent, a second chance to pass an hourly exam so
he will be eligible to play in the rapidly-approaching homecoming
game. Osman is ready to yield to the pressure when he invites
Blent to see him in his office. There he learns that the issues at
stake are greater than he thought: Blent deliberately failed the
exam to make himself ineligible to play, hoping thereby to foil the
plans of gamblers into whose hands he has blundered.

This is a readable novel which deals seriously with several
topics, including personal responsibility, the value of principle versus the need to compromise, and loyalty. Nemerov has a good grasp
of small-college politics (ivory towers, indeed!); the best aspect of
the book is the character of Professor Osman, one of those fictional
souls whom one would very much like to know in person. His intelligence is keen, his temper is gentle, his humor is subtle--and he
likes football, a touch by Nemerov that helps keep Osman from seem-
ing simply a cheerless devotee of things academic.

374. Neville, James M. Mud and Glory. Duffield, 1929. 304 p.
A story of personal rivalry between two Princeton football
players. One is Terry Malone, a sensitive, thoughtful quarterback.
The other is Red Thomas, a loud, practical-joking, and occasionally
violent running back. Thomas hates Malone on sight, and inten-
tionally breaks Malone's arm in his first year at Princeton. Malone
does his best to avoid Thomas, but, owing to their respective abilities, they find themselves composing a great passer-receiver combination for the team. One expects that somehow, in the book's
closing game between arch-rivals Princeton and Yale, the feud between Thomas and Malone will be buried for good in their desire to
pull out a victory. To Neville's credit, sentiment of the sticky sort
does not triumph over the ingrained enmity between the two players.
They remain antagonists to the end. To Neville's discredit, the book
still wallows in too much sentimental muck, much of it shoveled out
in a sub-plot involving Malone's and Thomas's romantic interest in
the same girl.

At this date, Mud and Glory is interesting primarily for its
picture of the emotional atmosphere of a distant era's college football.
Since Neville attended Princeton, his portrait of the campus and its
life also has a fair resemblance to probable reality.

375. O'Hara, John. "The Tackle." Sports Illustrated 21 (Sept. 21,
      1964): 108-113. Also in the author's Waiting for Winter.
      Random, 1966.
Hugo Rainsford, a prominent tackle for Harvard in the 1920s,
married shortly after graduation and went quietly into business, apparently never regretting his departure from the football field, nor
taking any intense old grad interest in the game. His ability to let
the past lie was not shared by his friends and acquaintances, however; they seldom missed an opportunity to raise the topic of football
in his presence, or to reminisce about Rainsford's playing days.

Rainsford's put-on of a woman from Cleveland that he meets on a trip--he assures her that he has been training his daughters to play football--doubles back on him when the woman reports his remarks in complete credulity in a magazine. Rainsford's irritation at the badinage this article provokes quickly leads to a general omission of the topic of football when he is in the vicinity.

Late in the story we learn the real reason behind Rainsford's lack of interest in football; it has to do with his ambition to be considered a financial success without reliance on his athletic background. It also involves his violent reaction to a man who suggests that he could not become a success on the strength of brains alone.

"The Tackle" breaks into two parts rather than standing as a whole, but it is otherwise well written, funny in spots, and profits from a clever, subtle conclusion.

376. Olsen, Jack. <u>Alphabet Jackson</u>. Playboy, 1974. 309 p.

There are enough good laughs in the first two dozen pages of this saga of the Billygoats, champions of the NFL's National Conference, to hold the reader's worries at bay for a spell. From the narrator, A.B.C. "Alphabet" Jackson, to his best friend "the late" Robert Boggs (a black power advocate who is convinced that Alphabet is a black man masquerading in white skin), to the Coach, a raving, possessed, stroke candidate, to team owner Billy Bob Bunker, an Oklahoma oil baron pickled in Chivas Regal, the book dishes out one bizarre character after another. Unlike some sports fiction that tries to get by with eccentricity alone, Olsen's combines eccentricity with credibility (more or less), and with some very well-written dialog, a fair share of it hilarious.

Considering the novel's central predicament, the humor is an achievement. Big Luke Hairston, a certifiable madman who has bounced from team to team in his brief pro career--too crazy to stay anywhere for long--is holding the entire team in the sights of a machine gun aboard a plane bound for the Super Bowl, or, possibly, annihilation. The Billygoats have picked up Hairston as playoff insurance; what they really need is flight insurance.

Each chapter opens with a section detailing Hairston's armed and very dangerous commandeering of the jet, then digresses into an account of the Billygoats' season. The skyjack drags on for hours, with Hairston gobbling handfuls of pills and playing with his gun. By the time Hairston is shooting himself up with a hypo and threatening to shoot up the plane as well, the tension is as thick as the remaining laughter is wild. Hairston drafts Jackson as his intermediary to talk to the coaching staff and flight crew. Jackson emerges as a hero, but not without paying a price.

377. Perry, Lawrence. "Barbed Wire." <u>Collier's</u> 78 (Oct. 16, 1926): 11+.

Steve Yerkes has gone to a college that sounds a lot like Harvard, following his neighbor, Dick Groome. He hates Groome for his self-assurance, though the apparent reason is Groome's part in a foxhunt that did serious damage to the Yerkes family farm. After

the hunt, Yerkes put up a high barbed-wire fence between his land
and the Groomes' place.

Yerkes cannot find himself at college until he gets a chance to
play football. At first his only goal is to clobber Dick Groome, the
team captain, in practice, but the idea of team spirit sets in, and
Yerkes conducts himself nobly, particularly against Yale.

This is another example of football as a vehicle for proving
one's manhood and selflessness. The most important lines belong to
Groome, when he compares school pride in victory to patriotism:
"It's like love for your country; the reason men die for it." A disturbing comparison, but one that shows to what excesses athletic
enthusiasm has been taken, with complete absence of ironic sense.

378. Pier, Arthur S. "The Game by Wire." Scribner's Magazine
     42 (Nov. 1907): 562-574.
     The Harvard-Yale game forms the catalyst for the reuniting
of business partners in this piece. Young Yale grad John Stanley
has been called to Boston by his employer, Mr. Prentice; Stanley
has hurt Prentice's paving company by entering some dubious contracts out west. Stanley hopes that he will be able to see his
brother play for Yale against Harvard, but an interview with Prentice leaves his plans in shreds. Stanley leaps to the conclusion
that Prentice wants him to defraud clients. Prentice's son plays for
Harvard, and both Prentice and Stanley attend a description of the
game carried by telegraph in a crowded auditorium. The fine play
of their brother and son leads the business associates back together.

Although its plot is contrived, the story is interesting from
the point of view of both class and economic analysis; business obviously is closely tied to sport here, and at one point Stanley makes
an observation on the rooters--an observation one assumes the author
shares--that is rigid with class consciousness. On the lighter side,
the description of the telegraph-based play-by-play is detailed and
gives a good feel for the event. Compare the story in this respect
with item 147.

379. Pillitteri, Joseph. Two Hours on Sunday. Dial, 1971. 256 p.
     The narrator and protagonist of this fairly familiar but cap-
ably executed story is the aging, gimpy-kneed backup quarterback
Alex Lincoln. Lincoln was a Heisman Trophy winner at Notre Dame,
but his professional career (as has been true of so many Heisman
winners) has fallen short of glorious; his present status as backup
QB was preceded by a tour of duty in the Canadian Football League.

When the book begins, Lincoln is warming the bench as usual,
while his team, the Normandy Hawks, runs out the clock for a win
against Joe Namath and the Jets. He expects to do nothing but sit,
since the Hawks regular QB Johnny Tiebor is a master of the position. Master or not, a blindside tackle knocks Tiebor out of the
game, and puts Lincoln onto the field.

Lincoln performs creditably in relief, but management has so
little faith in him that his newfound status as starter is in danger
before he has played a full quarter. The book's subsequent action

focuses on the week before a game against the Kansas City Chiefs that will determine Lincoln's fate. Will he finally shake off his also-ran status, or will he quickly disappear down the old quarterback memory hole?

Lincoln's off-field problems give further substance to his character. His obstetrician brother sponges off him; his parents cannot fathom his choice of careers, and a divorce and remarriage have thrown a large rock into the center of his domestic pond. The novel is not overly original, but is solidly performed, with competent characterizations and some good game narrative.

380.   Pye, Lloyd.   That Prosser Kid.   Arbor House, 1977.   238 p.

An engrossing study of college football as played at a small Louisiana school. Narrated by the team manager, the novel's emphasis is on the redshirt squad, which supplies the varsity with an "opponent" for practice during the week. Among the redshirts is Pete Prosser, a running back with an attitude the coaches can't bear: he makes it clear that he thinks they are all cretins. Prosser is probably the most talented player on the team, but his regard of the coaching staff all but guarantees him a career wasted on the practice field.

The novel has several winning features. The author, a former member of the Tulane team, knows football. He also writes good dialog, keeps the action moving forward at a smart pace (the book's chronology spans eight days), and manipulates the reader's emotions skillfully. The coaching staff offers the man we love to hate, and Prosser's be-damned attitude in the face of the organization is one many readers would like to imitate. These qualities, with sufficient dramatic events to keep one's interest at a steady level, make it a very good reading experience.

The novel concludes with a game against the Texas Longhorns. Prosser finally gets to play, and though Texas wins easily, Prosser and his teammates acquit themselves well. Formerly spurned, Prosser is named a permanent member of the varsity. What he does next maintains his reputation and makes a fitting ending to a better-than-average football novel.

381.   Reynolds, Quentin.   "He Could Take It."   Collier's 90 (Nov. 12, 1932): 18-19+.

A taste of Depression-era disillusionment marks this story of a football hero who goes on to become a head coach, and who learns some angles of the game that did not occur to him when he was a player.

Benny Burns was a top quarterback, an all-around player for State College. His father had coerced him into football from an early age, and he finished his playing career as an All-American. He finished his playing career in more ways than one by refusing to leave the field when he broke his ankle in his last game.

Little Wayne College hires Benny as head coach, strictly for the gate appeal of his name, and because his presence will help Wayne obtain a spot on the State College schedule. Benny cruises

through a good season with Wayne, playing small schools. He harbors hopes that his boys might knock off the powerful State team.
They don't. State College tears Wayne apart. The large crowd
hoots at Wayne's ineptitude, and Benny Burns sits on the bench,
full of hatred for his old school, aware now that football is no gentleman's game but "cruel, grim warfare."

Late in the story we learn that the narrator is Benny's father,
who was once so happy to live vicariously through Benny's athletic
achievements; he is now a chastened, guilt-ridden man. This is one
of the few popular magazine sports stories whose point of view is so
dark, so far from literary cheerleading. (Reynolds was a tackle for
Brown University in 1924).

382. Runyon, Damon. "Big Shoulders." In his Take It Easy, p.
      195-215. Stokes, 1938.
      Zelma Bodinski, daughter of bookie Blooch Bodinski, falls for
Charley, a Yale boy who assures her that Yale will win its next game
against Princeton. Blooch is under pressure to add football to his
roster of betting possibilities, but he turns down the proposition,
lacking any insider's knowledge of the game. "What do I know about
prices on the big shoulders?" he asks.

The narrator, Zelma, and Bloocher attend the Yale-Princeton
game; Zelma secretly bets a large sum of her father's money on Yale,
and, with a great debt to Zelda's vocal abilities, Yale pulls off an
amazing 2-0 upset over Princeton, with the only score a safety.
When he learns of the bet, "Blooch falls in a dead faint," but his
shock wears off. When we leave the now well-to-do bookie, football
is his specialty, and his chief dopester is Zelda's dear Charley.

This story is in a better mood than some of Runyon's, but his
hard-boiled attitudinizing is still present. In the story's opening,
for example, a young girl is weeping in Mindy's restaurant; the narrator is "about to call a waiter and have her chucked out of the
place as her sobbing interferes with my enjoyment of the gefüllte
fish...."

383. Sayre, Joel. "Rackety Rax." American Mercury 25 (Jan.
      1932): 7-47. Also published as a book, Rackety Rax. Knopf,
      1932. 147 p.
      One of football literature's premier satires. Knucks McGloin,
an enterprising New York City racketeer, maintains a stable of fighters and wrestlers during prohibition. When he learns of the tremen-
dous crowds attracted to college football, he assumes there must be
some easy money action available in that racket. A highlight of the
story is one of his underlings' attempt to explain the financial side
of college ball, covering such fine points as who gets the take,
"where the dough goes," and what it takes to muscle in on this football territory. McGloin devises an inspired, if demented, scheme to
get in on the bucks: he and his syndicate will open their own university, complete with a team populated by "that mob of palooka
fighters and wrasslers I got eating their heads off." Canarsie University is born, and so is one of the best-humored fictional stabs at

football and colleagiate athletics in general. It comes to a sad end,
however, through an old gag but an effective one: a car bomb,
which explains the absence of a Canarsie team "for the last couple
of seasons."

384.   Shaw, Irwin. "The Eighty-Yard Run." Esquire 80 (Oct.
       1973): 292-295. Also in the author's Short Stories: Five
       Decades. Delacorte, 1978. First published in Esquire in 1941.
       Christian Darling's life has been a slow decline since he made
an 80-yard run in football practice for his college team. His wife,
once his college sweetheart, grows away from him when she enters
the magazine business. Darling loves her, but cannot keep up with
her intellectually. What once was love in her eyes has been fogged
over with a "patient, kindly, remote boredom."
       This is a story of considerable sadness and regret, but it is
also one of dignity. Darling makes respectable choices, even brave
choices, and perseveres, though he has lost the things that otherwise mattered most to him. The concluding passage, in which Darling re-enacts his 80-yard run fifteen years later, strikes the heart.
Set in the late 1920s through 1940.

385.   _____. "Full Many a Flower." Playboy 25 (Jan. 1978):
       170+. Also in the author's Short Stories: Five Decades.
       Delacorte, 1978.
       An "unutterably rich" Vermont oilman ruminates on what he
considers his wholly unfair dismissal, years earlier, from a National
Football League training camp. The reason for his cut, explains a
former coach, is that the man is a "gypsy." Believing that the
NFL's player-selection system is a joke, albeit a time-honored one,
the oilman creates his own league, the Players' League, manned
entirely by NFL rejects. His league features many excellent innovations, ranging from coaches elected by players to the omission of
"The Star-Spangled Banner" from pre-game foolishness.
       "Full Many a Flower" is a delightful and funny tale; it speaks
to every reader's secret dream of throwing out all the rules, all the
accepted standards of behavior, and going on from there. Shaw's
description of the ultimate championship game, between the NFL and
the Players' League, is a gem.

386.   _____. "Whispers in Bedlam." Playboy 16 (Feb. 1969): 75-
       78+. Also in the author's Short Stories: Five Decades.
       Delacorte, 1978.
       Hugo Pleiss, an honest, clean-living, but barely mediocre NFL
linebacker, is close to losing his football career because of encroach-
ing deafness. A sub rosa operation repairs the damage, and then
some: Pleiss acquires the ability to hear plays being called in the
opposing team's huddle. This gift enables him to react with astounding grace in critical situations. Before long, his "hearing" extends
to ESP: he is able to read the opposing quarterback's mind. This
new capacity at first furnishes Pleiss with unprecedented rewards
and pleasures, but his gift eventually turns to a plague, ruining his

life, giving him not an heroic season but, as he calls it, "a season
in hell." An often humorous yet serious treatment of a familiar fantasy theme, the curse of unnatural talent.

387. Silvers, Earl R. "Forever Yours." American Magazine 126
      (Dec. 1938): 48-50+.
      A sentimental Depression tale, but even as one recognizes its
sentimentality, its effectiveness as popular magazine fiction is apparent. Red Barnes is a football hero, first in high school, then
in college. He marries his high school sweetheart, Laurel, who
promises to stand by him, no matter what. What neither of them
anticipated in the "no matter what" category were the effects of
trying to raise a child on next to nothing, especially when Laurel's
father offers to take her and the little boy in and see to their
needs.
      Red's football scholarship and part-time jobs just allow the
young family to get by, but there is nothing left for luxury. When
their son's birthday is at hand, Red and Laurel cannot afford even
a pint of ice cream and a cake to celebrate, much less the pedal-
driven toy car that the boy craves. It looks as though this may be
the end of the line for their marriage, with Laurel turning to her
father for the sake of her son. Red's teammates intervene, save his
son's birthday, and his marriage. There is a lot of football played
in this story, but its real subjects are money and loyalty.

388. Spinrad, Norman. "The National Pastime." In Run to Star-
      light: Sports through Science Fiction, p. 39-64. Edited by
      Martin H. Greenberg, et al. Delacorte, 1975. First pub-
      lished in Nova (March 1973).
      Those who do not cringe but instead salivate when an unpro-
tected, 180-pound pass receiver gets hit while in the air by a couple
of defensive linebackers running at top speed will find their eyes
lighting up at the prospect of Combat Football. In this satire on
our national thirst for violence, Spinrad posits this spin-off on football as a way for a flagging television network to improve its ratings.
Combat Football, though very similar to the original version, features
such lively rules variations as legalized punching, no protective gear,
and sympathetic slugfests in the stands. The game is a major success, and why not? With teams like the Golden Supermen, the Hog
Choppers, and the Psychedelic Stompers--along with thousands of
casualties in the stands--what could satisfy the appetite for violence
more effectively short of total war?

389. Taylor, Robert L. Professor Fodorski. Doubleday, 1950.
      250 p.
      Professor of engineering Stanislaus Fodorski immigrates to the
U.S. after WW II. He moves in with his old colleague Afton Cartwright, and obtains a position at the Southern Baptist Institute of
Technology. Fodorski is a great hit with his students because of
his innocent concern for them and his gentle manner, but look out:
attending his first SBIT football game, he falls prey to the "fanatic

devotion to a sport that was plainly larger than education." The game, in fact, attracts Fodorski like "a new religion," and in class he begins to draw parallels between bridge design and football plays.

Fodorski buys dozens of books on football, and sits on the bench during games. The team's big lack is kicking, but the Professor has an answer: he instructs a mathematically-gifted student in a novel approach to kicking that involves slide-rule calibrations on the boy's shoes.

When the SBIT coach dies, students stage a sit-down strike in an effort to have Fodorski named the replacement. The movement succeeds, and Fodorski, after trouncing Notre Dame in something called the "Finger Bowl," signs a 10-year coaching contract. He has been Americanized and athleticized so thoroughly that it is hard to tell him apart from his deceased predecessor.

A pleasant, gentle satire of collegiate sports excess; so pleasant, and so gentle, that today the book is almost quaint.

390. Temple, Willard. "A Bench Warmer Named Smith." Saturday Evening Post 227 (Oct. 9, 1954): 37+.

Smith, a perpetual bench-warmer for his college team, at last receives a chance to fill in at quarterback when his best friend Kobaleskie turns his ankle. Kobaleskie is a whiz; Smith is convinced that he'll disgrace himself on the field in the upcoming nationally-televised game. He nearly succeeds in fulfilling his own prophecy when he throws an interception that an opposing player returns for a touchdown, but the breaks turn Smith's way in the second half. A standard bit of college football formula writing, complete with a subplot concerning a sorority girl with "the bluest eyes I'd ever seen."

391. Toomay, Pat. On Any Given Sunday. Donald A. Fine, 1984. 287 p.

Because Toomay, like Peter Gent, played the pro game for a long stretch, his view of the game merits attention. As exemplified by his hero, Brad Rafferty, it is a view that could lead to a cold sweat. Rafferty, a Washington lineman, is convinced that the fix is on for a forthcoming game. His doubts about the integrity of his sport mushroom until nearly everyone but the waterboy seems culpable. The novel's strength is Toomay's knowledge of the game and its attendant phenomena (drugs, pain, the mass media); some of his game descriptions are quite original. The novel is less interesting, however, when it dwells on Rafferty's effort to dissect the fix.

392. Watson, Emmett. "The Quarterback Who Couldn't Take It." Saturday Evening Post 227 (Sept. 25, 1954): 31+.

A story of a man's overcoming his fear. Joe Mitchell is a college quarterback who has quit the game. A crushing tackle from his blind side did more than shake him up: it put a gnawing rat of anxiety into him. When he looks at the team's substitute QB, who cannot use his passing arm properly due to a pointlessly aggressive hit in practice, he sees nothing that makes him want to return to the

field. A postgame conversation with the sub quarterback in a restaurant helps Mitchell understand his fear, and take his first step
toward conquering it: he rejoins the team. Anyone who has carefully watched what often happens to quarterbacks after they throw
the ball will feel some sympathy for Mitchell, and possibly wonder if
his decision was the right one. Sometimes it is easier to be thought
brave and take a beating than to be brave and refuse one.

393. Weaver, Gordon. "Hog's Heart." Antioch Review 37 (Winter
      1979): 48-64. Also in the author's Getting Serious; Stories.
      Louisiana State Univ. Pr., 1980.
      Hog, a college football coach in Mississippi, is convinced that
he is about to die from a bad heart, a "bad heart" his doctor cannot
detect. Hog is under the accumulating pressures of his job and his
frustrations, including a pro career cut short by injury. There is
something wrong with Hog, all right; he has no faith in having been
a good son to his parents, or a good brother; vague religious yearn-
ings beset him (his mother is fervent to the point of frothiness in
her Jesus talk), and at the height of his career, with his team
poised to defeat Bear Bryant's awesome Alabama aggregation, Hog
checks out for a transcendant experience. Is--is he dead? It's
hard to say, but one gets the feeling Hog has thrown in the coaching
towel. This story is amusing and provocative, and ambiguous enough
to start a lot of arguments.

394. Wilder, Robert. Autumn Thunder. Putnam, 1952. 344 p.
      "A solitary figure dwarfed against the sky, sitting alone in an
empty stadium." It is a pathetic, lonely picture, and Larry Summers, the former "Big Six" for his college team, has become at the
leading edge of middle age a fairly pathetic man. He still lives in
the town where he starred as a player, and still works at the same
restaurant and college hangout where he took a part-time job twenty
years earlier. He is manager now, but when he meets old acquaintances who ask what he's doing, his reply, "Oh, I'm still at Marty's,"
leaves a sour taste in his mouth. He used to sit on the team bench
during games after his graduation, but the new coach sent him to
the stands and kicked him out of the locker room. His wife is difficult to understand, and insists that he remove his football trophies
from the living room.
      All Summers seems to have left are memories of his youth.
They are memories brought to a point every time he looks out the
bedroom window. There in the middle distance are the college build-
ings, changeless and timeless, and now closed to him. Everything
is slipping away except the memories, and the memories only make
the losses worse.
      With this much established fairly early in the book, it does not
leave the novel a choice as to where to go next, so it goes the only
place it can, two decades into the past, to the time when Larry was
just preparing to enter the University. He went in with ill-formed
ideas of preparing for law school, but feared that whatever he did
would be wrong. One of the first people who furnished Larry a no-

tion of what lay ahead was the original Marty, who, while making
Larry a sandwich, reflected on the destiny of college athletes: "I
hate to see a good kid spoiled and that's what the system does to
them. They never recover. After they get out of school they expect people to stand up and cheer every time they go to the bath-
room."

A personal tragedy must intrude upon the lives of Larry Summers and his wife before they finally cut the psychological cord
that has bound them to the University. Autumn Thunder has some
very good pieces. The tone of melancholy yearning for the hopelessly lost years of Summers's athletic life is effective and touching.
The accounts of his relationships with women, whether his wife or
that of a wealthy alumnus with whom he has an affair, are far less
so, and consume too much of the book.

395. Williams, Ben A. "Scapegoat." Saturday Evening Post 198
     (Nov. 7, 1925): 10-11+.
     Owens, a college hockey player, also a star running back for
the football team, seriously injures an opposing player. Rumors fly
that Owens has lost his nerve, that the accident has made him draw
back from giving his best effort. The rumors give the football coach
an opening to inspire his team--a skilled but cool bunch--to greater
intensity. A not-bad story of psychological manipulation.

396. Williams, John A. The Junior Bachelor Society. Doubleday,
     1976. 247 p.
     This novel is one of the best to cast its attention on the lives
of former black high school and college athletes. The story's nucleus
is Chappie Davis, now a 69-year old stock supervisor in an old hotel.
Davis lives pretty much for the weekend, when he sits down in front
of his television with a half-gallon of milk and a sweet potato pie to
help him through the weekend's football games. Years before,
though, Davis took a direct hand in athletics as the coach and mentor of a group of urban youths who looked upon him much as sons
upon a father.

In the 1940s, Chappie's protegés won high school champion-
ships in football, basketball, baseball, and track. Now they work
at diverse occupations--factory hand, actor, writer, college professor, city housing supervisor; most have been successful, but all
have known the necessity of compromise and the taunting of dreams
that cannot be realized.

Chappie's boys, who long ago formed a club, the Junior Bachelor Society (JBS), have decided to give him a testimonial dinner for
his 70th birthday. As plans for the dinner come together, Williams
turns first to one man, then another, to show the effects of aging
and of different career choices, and of their athletic memories. Williams does an exceptionally good job of reaching into the hearts and
minds of the old JBS members, several of whom still get together for
touch football games. Some of the local youth smirk at the sight of
the "old men" on the playground, but the old men have not forgotten
the moves that Chappie Davis helped them learn.

One shadow falls on the planned dinner, and it is a heavy one.
Moon, a JBS member who has enjoyed a "successful" career as a
pimp, decides to put in an appearance. This plays into the dirty
hands of Swoop Ferguson, a local cop, who aims to blackmail Moon
using an old murder as leverage. Ferguson, rejected for membership in the JBS as a young man, feels no chagrin at spoiling the
party.
    The book's conclusion is violent and sad, and shows that how-
ever Chappie Davis may have improved individual lives through his
selflessness, the world remains the same. With strong characters,
deep emotions, and good writing throughout, this is an absorbing,
memorable novel.

397. Wilner, Herbert. "No Medal for Sonny." Saturday Evening
      Post 239 (Nov. 5, 1966): 58-60+. Also in the author's Dovisch
      in the Wilderness, and Other Stories. Bobbs-Merrill, 1968.
    An unhappy story of a young man who tries to bury his daily
fears with angry tackling on college football fields. Sonny Schaefer
plays for a small college, and plays with great intensity. On play
after play, it is Sonny who makes the tackle, often knocking himself
into a near-stupor by halftime. The narrator describes Sonny on the
day after a game as leaning on his fragile girlfriend for support.
She cannot bear his playing, but she understands its motivation.
Sonny is afraid of elevators, afraid of subways, afraid of staying
overnight in the woods. Only on the football field can he ignore his
phobias, and perhaps, at the same time, punish himself for having
them.
    Sonny dies in WW II, in a sense getting himself killed more
than being killed. He seeks his own death in war in the same way
he abandoned all sense of personal survival when he threw himself
at opposing ball carriers. A good story of mental games played with
the self, and with some detailed football action.

398. _____. "The Quarterback Speaks to His God." Esquire
      90 (Oct. 24, 1978): 88-90+. Also in Best American Short
      Stories, 1979. Edited by Joyce Carol Oates and Shannon
      Ravenel. Houghton-Mifflin, 1979.
    A retired pro quarterback, a noted technician of the game, is
betrayed by his own body. A viral blood infection seriously damages
his heart, and, after much agonizing, he submits to open-heart surgery, with his German wife insisting that he doesn't know who his
real enemies are. There are many good passages here, some in which
the quarterback, Bobby Kraft, reflects on the intricacies of football,
some in which he swims in the dread evoked by his operation. A
fine story of a man forced to make major adjustments in the way he
sees himself; whether he will make those adjustments is by no means
a sure thing.

399. Abbott, Lee K. "The Valley of Sin." <u>Carolina Quarterly</u> 37
(Winter 1985): 14-18.
A most enjoyable story, Abbott's tale of a wronged golfer turning to the links to obtain a very peculiar vengeance succeeds in several ways. The most noticeable is the style, featuring deliberately
over-literary language inflated just enough to bring an air of high-
toned absurdity to the proceedings. The story also works in the
message beneath the playful surface: what is presented "seriously"
in a sophisticated, comical manner, thus rendering the story faceti-
ous, is, at bottom, genuinely serious.
The hero is Mr. Dillon Ripley, a New Mexico golfer who knows
absolutely everything about the game and its history, though a
mediocre player himself. As his daughter says following one of
Ripley's soliloquies on the game, "Jeez, Dad. You know some awful
dumb stuff."
It is no doubt in large measure Ripley's obsession with golf
that leads his wife to abandon him for Ivy Martin, the local club's
resident pro. Ripley must be hospitalized upon this shocking incident, and, following his release, his friends question him on his
plans for returning to the fairways. He returns, but in a form
skulking and terrible.
The troubles first crop up on the 10th and 11th holes, where
a groundskeeper finds the flagsticks twisted into outlandish shapes,
"one, it was said, an idea of horror made steel." Next, cryptic
notes tinged with visions of religious judgment appear within the cups
on the greens. "We are a breed," reads one, "in need of fasting and
prayer." And then there is the awful specter sighted by Tommy
Steward on the 14th green as he and his girlfriend neck by midnight.
"It was in skins, yes.... One fist was shaking overhead and in the
other, like a cudgel, hung a golf club heavy with sod." A thousand
ideas come to Tommy, "none concerning humans."
Dillon Ripley sells his house and moves to a place where there
is no sport but hunting, and where the winds "blow as if from a
land whose lord is dark and always angry."

400. Ade, George. "The Fable of the Caddy who Hurt His Head
While Thinking." In <u>The America of George Ade, 1866-1944</u>,
p. 106-107. Edited by Jean Shepherd. Putnam, 1960.
The moral of the fable is one of Ade's best-remembered lines:
"Don't try to account for anything." A caddy sits near the 9th
hole, speculating on the unfairness of a life in which his father, an
informed man, must "shove Lumber all day," while the club members
play golf all the time and have money to throw away.

401.   Castle, Everett R.   "Customer Golf."   Saturday Evening Post
       206 (Nov. 4, 1933): 18-19+.
       One of sport's dreariest perversions is the frequent transfor-
mation of golf from a game pursued for its own sake to an adjunct
of business dealing.   In retrospect, this light story of business-golf
and duplicity says more than its author intended about American
values.
       The plot concerns a young advertising agency vice-president,
Brodie, and his effort to retain the good will of his client, Mr.
Bullfinch.   Bullfinch is an atrocious golfer who ascribes his failures
on the course to little errors easily corrected.   Brodie and Bullfinch compete against another ad man and his partner in a match
spread over several tours of the course.   Brodie and Bullfinch fall
far behind, to Bullfinch's extreme annoyance, and it looks as though
Brodie may lose his client in spite of his own exemplary play.   Only
by resorting to a ruse, abetted by the club pro, does Brodie salvage
the match and his client's account.
       The most interesting angle of the story is the author's easy
acceptance of both the mis-use of golf and of victory through cheating.   The approbation given such themes in a popular magazine is
bothersome.   On the story's plus side, however, there is an excellent paragraph mocking Bullfinch's elaborate address of the ball, a
procedure much-favored by countless duffers.

402.   Chapin, Anna A.   "Straight Golf."   Century 83 (Nov. 1911):
       22-27.
       "No man can play straight golf and live crooked," declares
one of the characters in another story joining business and golf.   It
is probably an accurate declaration, too, and regardless of the
story's roots in capitalism at its purest--the whole is set in the
executive offices of a bank--it will still have an impact on the reader
who does his or her best to play honestly at a game which, possibly
more so than any other, offers a multitude of havens for the cheat-
er.
       The crisis hinges on the discovery of a missing thousand dol-
lars from the Cosmopolitan Bank.   The bank's directors have con-
vened in their hot, miserable meeting room (in 1911, even bank of-
ficers sweated through the summer) to study the evidence.   All
signs point to young Teddy Thornton, an unassuming college graduate who works as a cashier.   Thornton's account of the matter is
straightforward, but only serves to confirm his guilt.   After sending
Thornton from the office, the bank's directors listen to an anecdote
one of them relates about an example of noble truthfulness he witnessed in a golf match.   The result of this anecdote is the board's
enthusiastic reversal of Thornton's "guilty" verdict.   Utterly contrived though this story is, it rests on an assumption that few
golfers who have successfully resisted the temptation to cheat would
deny: one who plays by the rules of golf will also probably play
by the rules of life, both legal and moral.

403.   Dulack, Thomas J.   Pork: Or, the Day I Lost the Masters.
       Dial, 1968.   209 p.

If W. C. Fields could update his immortal portrayal of the golfer to the print medium, it might read something like this babes & booze account of a young player's life on the tour. Fields, of course, would play "Pork" Waller (at least it wasn't "Hog"), with Mae West as one of the lubricous links followers. Pork can belt the ball, but equally impor- tant, in his estimation, is his sartorial style, designed to draw as many gasps as his prodigious drives. Pork is no stranger to suspect events in motels, nor to domestic strife and strange bedfellows. Through it all, he keeps teeing them up. Not a book to be mistaken for anything approximately serious, but good for not-quite clean fun.

404.   Fish, Robert L. "To Hell with the Odds." In Run to Star-
       light: Sports through Science Fiction, p. 217-239. Edited
       by Martin H. Greenberg, et al. Delacorte, 1975. First pub-
       lished in the Magazine of Fantasy and Science Fiction (Feb.
       1958).
       Another variation on the Faust theme, with a clever twist at
the end. Marty Russell has drunk himself from the top of the pro
golf ranks to near oblivion before the age of forty. As he steeps
himself in alcohol one day at the Nineteenth Tee bar, a shadowy
figure at his side proposes a deal: Russell's soul in exchange for
a victory in the forthcoming Open. Marty agrees, without being
clearly aware of the terms to which he has committed himself. By
the time he realizes the earnestness of the bargain, he holds a
good lead over a hated opponent, but also fears the consequences
should his lead hold up. He devises what he believes will be a fool-
proof plan to avoid both defeat and the Devil's due.
       The Faust story is one that many writers have run through
their mills, but why not? It's a great one, even when played for
fun, as it is in this story.

405.   Fox, William Price. Doctor Golf. Lippincott, 1963. 176 p.
       Easily one of the funniest, and best, fictional treatments of
golf. "Doctor Golf" is the head of the Eagle-Ho Sanctuary, a club
in Arkansas. The book is a collection of letters to Dr. Golf, together with his replies, from golfers all over the country. They
seek his advice on every detail of the game. Dr. Golf reveals himself in his answers as a self-important, prissy, arch-conservative
guardian of the great game. His answers are as amusing as they
are absurd, and the queries from concerned golfers are equally so.
A typical request for assistance comes from a golfer whose fellow
club member hanged himself in the bootblack's closet after a slice-
plagued round. The correspondent's concern: what is it, Doctor,
that causes a sliced shot?
       Doctor Golf's shameless huckstering of Eagle-Ho products
lends another satirical edge to the book. Numerous cartoons by the
corrosively-gifted Charles Rodrigues expertly illustrate the good
Doctor's points. Any golfer with even a vestigial sense of humor
will count as well-spent the time used in locating this volume.

406.   Fullerton, Hugh S. "Pay to T. Hartley, Good Sport, $10,000."
       American Magazine 90 (Nov. 1920): 40-42+.

The conflict between golf and religion takes place routinely on summer Sundays, and reverence for a good drive or a clean iron shot often pushes formal piety aside. Prayers uttered in sandtraps are frequently superior in sincerity to many mouthed in a pew, and curses delivered in the rough are equal to any promised from the most fundamental of pulpits.

Here Rev. Hartley enlists the aid of his parish and golf club in raising money to build a new church. Rev. Hartley is a serious young minister, and, though a poor golfer, a devoted student of divots and dubs. All are pleased to have him in the local club except the irritating old millionaire, "The Motor Boat," so-named for his habit of putt, putt, putting on the greens. The Motor Boat is convinced that Rev. Hartley is not a true sport, and that he will spoil everyone's fun with sermons on the evils of Sunday golf.

Sport, religion, and money all coalesce into a happy ending when Rev. Hartley shows that he is a sportsman beyond question. Could there be any other kind of ending in a popular American magazine (the "American Magazine," no less) in 1920?

407.   Gallico, Paul W. "Golf Is a Nice Friendly Game." Saturday Evening Post 214 (May 30, 1942): 22-23+.

A. R. Mallow, president of Mallow & Co. golf equipment, has challenged a rival manufacturer to a grudge match. At stake is either company's entire supply of the rubber allotted by the government's wartime rationing. The match is to pit Mallow and his business competitor, with a professional representing each company as the presidents' partners. It is Mallow endorsement recruiter William Fowler's job to find a fit partner for A.R.

There is the rub of the green. A.R. is a boor, an obnoxious man who thinks nothing of insulting his employees and the golf pros who use his products. He is also a very bad player. Luckily (predictably?) love itself finds a way to win: Fowler learns that A.R.'s niece is in love with young Mallow pro Jimmy Lane, who will put up with any abuse to please his beloved's uncle. All ends justly, with Fowler reminding the two presidents that (in the dark times of early WW II), these are days "when we all ought to be pulling together and trying to help each other out."

408.   _____. "Golf's a Big Business." Saturday Evening Post 209 (Sept. 19, 1936): 10-11+.

A Depression fantasy that contemporary readers will still find heartwarming, as well as sociologically interesting. Our old friend William Fowler (see the preceding item) attends a mythical National Open, hoping to sign some new players to contracts for use of their names in promotions. He has little luck; arriving late, the only player he signs, for the price of two ham sandwiches, is a country boy named Jet Scraggins. Scraggins survives the field cut more by luck than skill, and Fowler expects nothing from him, though he likes the boy and his fiancee.

Here the Depression theme kicks into gear. Fowler learns that the young couple have been spending their nights sleeping in Scrag-

gins's dilapidated car. His finacee blurts out that he has played
badly because he has not eaten for three days. All their spare
cash went into car repairs en route to the Open.

After Fowler sees to it that the couple have a decent meal,
Scraggins goes wild in the Open's final round, coming from far behind to win on the last hole. His victory brings him not only tournament prize money, but a hefty annual stipend from A. R. Mallow.

To the many Post readers who were just beginning to stagger
up from the depths of the Depression, this story must have served
as something more important than mere light reading, with its promise that honest, hardworking people could find a fit reward for
their efforts. Maybe this promise was not true, but who would
throw it away in favor of hopelessness?

409.   Gunn, James E. "Open Warfare." In Science Fiction A to Z;
       A Dictionary of the Great SF Themes, p. 468-485. Edited by
       Isaac Asimov and Martin H. Greenberg. Houghton-Mifflin,
       1982. First published in Galaxy Science Fiction (May 1954).
       Slim Jim Pearson is the man to beat in the U.S. Open. As he
rides a wave of tournament wins, it looks as though no golfer can
prevent him from taking this one, too; furthermore, if he does win
the Open, he will also win the approval of his beloved Alice Hatcher's
father. Hatcher can't abide the thought of Pearson marrying his
daughter, so he throws a ringer into the tournament, a golfer whose
every move is perfect. Not until well into the tournament does
Pearson discover that his awesome opponent is more (or less) than
human: he's a robot with individual aspects of his game patterned
after the game's greatest players.

In SF so light, there is no room for defeat of the just. It
betrays little to report that Pearson wins; the matter is how, and
the moral is that humanity will eventually prevail.

410.   Hall, Holworthy. "Consolation." Century 94 (June 1917):
       268-282.
       Love, golf, and square play form the skeleton of this story,
and, if there is no excess of meat on its bones, it still illustrates
the lip service paid to certain ideals.

Richard Meredith, a former college player, has not struck the
ball in four years when he takes a long-planned vacation at Pinehurst, North Carolina's famous golf spa. His ambition is to win the
St. Valentine's tournament, and he trains for it methodically. His
concentration on the game wavers when he falls for the delectable
Miss Winsted. Miss Winsted knows nothing of golf, and cares less,
but she covets the prize--a silver tray--that will go to the tourney's
runner-up. She urges Meredith to win her the tray, and it is only
after terrible vexation and a spot of luck that he is able to play to
his best, and not offend the desires of Miss Winsted. It is barely
conceivable that any woman brighter than a five-watt bulb could be
as obtuse as Miss Winsted about athletic competition, but that idea,
along with Meredith's agonizing over whether he will play a square
game or not, lies at the tale's center. Miss Winsted does, in the end,

turn to golf herself, and presumably will thus be saved from a life
of sporting mindlessness. A useful story for the analysis of popular
misconceptions, myths, and stereotypes.

411. Jacobi, Carl. "The Player at Yellow Silence." In his Dis-
     closures in Scarlet, p. 11-23. Arkham House, 1972.
     In the distant future, genocidal war looms between the human
race and the Yansis, who "migrated" to Earth in 1984 and soon
demonstrated their conquering ambitions. Yellow Silence is a golf
course where players perform with electronic clubs and balls, contend with time-warp hazards, and face holes over a thousand yards
long. Joseph Forbes, a stranger, appears at the height of war
preparations, and stuns the club with his record-breaking scores on
the course. Forbes, we learn, is an interplanetary agent whose
assignment is to show the possibilities of peace through gentle competition, in this case in the form of golf between humans and aliens.
By no means a stylistic success, this story is still of interest for the
author's faith in sport as an alternative to armed conflict.

412. Jenkins, Dan. Dead Solid Perfect. Atheneum, 1974. 234 p.
     "A golf course always looked like a better place for a man to be
than underneath a car with a wrench in his hand, or behind a desk
trying to read the fine print on something that had to be notarized."
This is how golf pro Kenny Puckett looks back on his first infatua-
tion as a nine-year old with the professional golfer's life. Kenny has
never made a big impression on the tour, but, after nearly a decade
at it, he has managed to earn a comfortable living by doing something
that few would describe as "work." The novel lays out the major
frustrations of Mr. Puckett, the majority of them concerning his three
wives (one at present, two former), during his surprising run at the
National Open title in Heavenly Pines (Pinehurst?), North Carolina.
His chief opponent in the Open is his semi-friend and total rival,
Donny Smithern, a sanctimonious, grasping creep. His chief concern
is the serious illness of one of his former wives.
     A number of individual passages shine in this novel. Smith-
ern's mealy-mouthed invocation of "the Man upstairs" as the One Who
will decide the Open winner is a nice cut across the throat of this
familiar and fairly nauseating piece of athletic cant. The good parts
do not add up to an altogether happy whole; the female characters
are two-dimensional and raise neither the reader's real compassion
nor anger. Some laughs, some insights on golf, and a pretty credible character in the person of Puckett make the book worth a quick
reading.

413. Johnson, Owen. "Even Threes." Century 84 (July 1912):
     415-426.
     Booverman, a golfer of potential but cursed by lifelong bad
luck on the course, shoots a club record 54, witnessed by his friend
Pickings. Back at the clubhouse, Booverman's luck finally reasserts
itself: no one will believe his score, and both he and Pickings are
discredited. The conclusion is predictable, but Pickings's reaction to

his friend's record-in-the-making rescues the story from the file of
merely competent golf tales.

414.   Kessler, Jascha. "A Round of Golf." In his <u>An Egyptian
        Bondage, and Other Stories</u>, p. 161-172. Harper & Row,
        1967.
            It is the Fourth of July Golf Tournament at the hotel. John-
son, a pro preparing for the match, is overweight, surly, out of
shape. He has been drinking too much, and gambling. In his foul
humor he works hard trying to hit his caddy with his practice shots.
Johnson plays poorly as the tournament begins, and injures his
caddy when he carelessly tosses him a club. He concludes his round
wretchedly, with a stunning tantrum on the last green. Later he accuses his caddy of not caring. A good sketch of an athlete whose
life is coming undone, along with his game.

415.   Lardner, Ring. "A Caddy's Diary." <u>Saturday Evening Post</u>
        194 (March 11, 1922): 12-13+. Also in <u>The Best Short Stories
        of Ring Lardner</u>. Scribner's, 1957.
            A 16-year old caddy, convinced that he is about to turn pro,
wants to learn to write so that he can record his exploits for the
newspapers. This is Lardner's excuse for the boy to start a diary
of events at his course. His entries are mildly illiterate, but full
of stinging truths about the lying, cheating, and stealing that
characterize the play of nearly every club member. The crossover
from cheating on the course to cheating in life itself is clear here,
and Lardner doesn't let the truth-telling caddy escape without having
to look his own deceit in the face. A good story about both golf
and honesty.

416.   _____. "Mr. Frisbie." In <u>The Best Short Stories of Ring
        Lardner</u>, p. 75-85. Scribner's, 1957.
            "Mr. Frisbie," a wealthy retired businessman, reached his
sixties before playing golf. Raw luck made his first shot a beauty,
and this "first perfect drive made Mr. Frisbie a slave of the game."
He plays daily on the 18-hole course on his estate. His caddy, the
story's narrator, quickly learns that the way to secure desired goods
from Mr. Frisbie, whether a vacation or a player piano for Mrs. Frisbie, is to subtly tamper with the boss's game to improve his score.
Mr. Frisbie, a very bad golfer, becomes malleable as warm clay when
he apparently achieves a modest triumph on the course. The story
is much heavier on character than plot; many golfers will recognize
themselves in it.

417.   Lincoln, Joseph C. "The Old Hooker." <u>Saturday Evening
        Post</u> 202 (Oct. 19, 1929): 18-19+.
            Time does change the mother tongue; what magazine editor to-
day would publish a golf story with this title? The Sunset Cove Golf
Club finds a legendary champion in the person of Reginald Greenleaf
Hickson, a young man with mathematical talent who has been helping
the club pro, McDermott, balance the accounts. Hickson catches "the

golf bug," and dedicates himself as astutely to the links as he does to numbers. His one flaw is an exaggerated hook on drives made with an old brassie, also known as "The Old Hooker." When McDermott can't play in a match, Hickson substitutes for him, and saves the day with a spectacular shot from the brassie, though not before certain intrigues place Hickson's honor and the club's future in doubt.

This story's complications and resolution are too pat and its characters too flat to reach the Post's best standards for fiction, but it does have some very attractive illustrations.

418. MacPyke, Douglas B. "Bumblepuppy's Revenge." Harper's Weekly 53 (July 3, 1909): 25.

This one-page story relates the contest between "two old duffers--they were forty and fat" to determine which of them is the club's most incompetent golfer. Blunderby secretly magnetizes all the cups, and plays a ball with a steel core, a ruse that produces some wonderful effects when he strokes his putts anywhere near the holes. Bumblepuppy discovers his opponent's ploy, however, and at their next meeting has arranged a little surprise for the man with the seeing-eye ball.

On a par with most dumb golf jokes (e.g., have you heard the one about the man who while putting on the first green held his hand over his heart when a funeral passed on the road? his wife, you know), "Bumblepuppy" shows that silliness has long been a part of the game.

419. Marquand, John P. Life at Happy Knoll. Little, Brown, 1957. 167 p.

A collection of letters by various members of the Happy Knoll country club dealing with topics of acute and chronic concern. Some of the letters are quite wonderful; the first, for example, from the Chairman of the Emergency Membership Drive to a newly-arrived, obviously affluent resident, is a paragon of two-faced pleading and back-stabbing, the back belonging to the area's other country club, Hard Hollow. Other letters on the "Caddie Crisis," "Locker Room Trouble," and "Breakage" satirize the fairly idiotic tribulations of country-club life, a life the club's president emeritus justly calls "a superficial manifestation of bourgeois culture." The book is not a novel, but a group of pieces which first appeared in Sports Illustrated. Marquand carries his satirical shaft lightly, but it does have a barb.

420. Marquis, Don. "Rattlesnake Golf." American Magazine 107 (June 1929): 22-25+. Also in the author's Sun Dial Time. Doubleday, 1936.

A Major Stacey relates to the story's narrator an account of an attempt by his business acquaintance, the duplicitous "Colonel" Elwood B. Sanford, to unload a piece of land forty miles from Los Angeles. The narrator is an easterner, new to the West, and one suspects that the story Major Stacey tells is woven of something other than the stark truth.

A "boob" from New England, or maybe England itself, showed
some interest in the aforementioned land, a desolate piece populated
by gila monsters, rattlesnakes, and coyotes. According to the Major, he and the "Colonel" took the "sucker" out to play a round of
golf on a course the Major had improvised on the desert land, since
doing business on the golf course had become quite the fashion.
The round the Major describes is one of the most fantastic ever re-
corded. The players go up and down gulches swarming with var-
mints and blast 600-yard drives across bare rock. Everything on
the course, including a mirage of Los Angeles, turns into a selling
point. This is a good satire on both gullibility and on that routine
insult to the sporting sensibility, golf's use as a business tool.

421.   _____. "The Rivercliff Golf Killings." In his Sun Dial
         Time, p. 215-239. Doubleday, 1936.
         The golfer who does not laugh aloud at this story must have
just blown a dozen three-foot puts. Cast in the form of a trans-
cribed courtroom interrogation, the story reveals the rank unfairness perpetrated on the gentle philosopher Professor Waddems, a
calm man, a man of peace and reason. Don't get the wrong idea
about this humanitarian when the D.A.'s questioning unveils the
trail of violence that follows Waddems around the Rivercliff course.
The body buried in the sand, the caddie first chased up a tree,
then driven from its uppermost branches by hurled clubs, the
"suicide" on the 15th hole helped along by "a little pat of approval" on the back as the unfortunate stood at the edge of a deep
pool ... yes, the Professor was there, and it is true that he forced
his opponent to eat his scorecard on the third hole, but, well, "If
I hit him they might make me add another stroke to my score," and
besides, even the bullfrogs at the water holes "have been trained
by the caddies to treat me impertinently." Poor Doc Waddems.
         Any golfer who has received unsolicited advice during a round
will roar at this exercise, and find the D.A.'s surprising summary
completely justified.

422. Pickens, Arthur E. The Golf Bum. Crown, 1970. 223 p.
      Bud Parker is the product of a working class family. His
father "never owned a jacket that matched his pants," and supported
his family making automobile tires in Akron. Parker found his first
set of golf clubs in a wealthy man's trash can, and from that point
on the game owned him. The Golf Bum is a contemporary Horatio
Alger tale. Parker spends a lot of time plodding and struggling,
picking up expense money hustling suckers, comforting himself with
strange women. Things look pretty grim, and, though he aspires to
glory, Parker's money worries are close to driving him permanently
out of the PGA tour. At the bottom of the barrel he meets a high
school coach who saves him from despair with a lead to a job working
with poor city children. From here, Ragged Bud is bound to rise,
and a PGA championship and true love lie ahead. Corny enough, to
be sure, but the author was a producer of the television program
"World Series of Golf," so he does know the game, and his game

descriptions are detailed. Otherwise, his literary game spends too
much time in the rough.

423. Tarkington, Booth. "Desert Sand." Ladies' Home Journal
      42 (June 1925): 8-9+. Also in the author's Women. Double-
      day, 1925.
         A funny tale of over-enflamed post-adolescent romantic angst.
      Lily Dodge, a highly-talented golfer, has given the gate to her boy-
      friend Henry; she confides to a friend that her love life has burned
      out forever, and her heart "is desert sand--desert sand, my dear!"
         Emotion blooms again in Lily's heart in a roundabout way when,
      while playing the local country club by herself one evening, she ac-
      cidentally beans a man on the green ahead of her with her drive.
      The victim proves to be James Herbert McArdle, newly-arrived in
      town to take over management of his wealthy family's nearby factory.
      Word goes around that Lily, who is a consummate golfer, deliberately
      conked McArdle with her drive as an excuse to meet him. Before
      the complications unravel, McArdle has asked Lily to marry him, and
      Henry--also an adept golfer--learns of Lily's true feelings, to his
      delight.
         Very much a story of the 1920s; the milieu is one of wealth
      and leisure. Even those who are described as no-accounts, like
      poor Henry, are members of the country club. There is no indica-
      tion that anyone in the story has to do menial chores, such as get-
      ting up in the morning to go to work. For a contrast in golf story
      themes, read this one in conjunction with item 408.

424. Tousey, J. S. "A Day with Colonel Bogey." Harper's Weekly
      54 (June 4, 1910): 25.
         This good-humored little sketch, complete on one page, shows
      that in many ways little has changed in amateur golf since the cen-
      tury's first decade. Tousey describes the Saturday noon rush to
      the "green country," where office workers attack the courses in an
      attempt to escape the trials of their daily work. Anyone who has
      played in a golf league will recognize the characters here: there
      are the equipment fetishists, who are convinced that a new putter
      or bag will deliver them from dufferhood to good scores; there is the
      liar whose scores tallied in solo play square rather oddly with those
      he makes in company; there is also that bane of the fairway, the
      foursome that takes forever to play, and the hacker who chops the
      turf to bits with his irons. There is also an interesting young lady
      who belts a solid 200-yard drive, a thing of beauty and a joy for at
      least the length of its flight to the men gathered around the tee. In-
      cludes some good little illustrations by the author.

425. Tuttle, Anthony. Drive for the Green. Doubleday, 1969.
      341 p.
         This overlong and talky novel follows three professional golfers
      on the tour, with their personal dramas coming down to resolution at
      the Masters Tournament in Augusta. Includes the inevitable romantic
      interests; manages to miss most of the inner drama of golf, possibly

the most internally-determined of sports. Only for those who cannot
get enough golf fiction to satisfy them.

426. Updike, John. "Intercession." <u>New Yorker</u> (Aug. 30, 1958):
      24-27. Also in the author's <u>The Same Door.</u> Knopf, 1972.
         Paul, a young man with a family, has recently taken up golf.
He plays with the usual beginner's clumsiness. On a summer day he
unhappily plays part way around the course with another beginner,
an offensive adolescent who freely criticizes Paul's form and then
cheats wantonly at his own game. At first intimidated by the youth's
aggressiveness, Paul begins to see the cracks in the boy's defenses.
In mid-round, out of sight of his unwanted partner, Paul walks off
the course and back to his car, thinking of supper and family. All
the action in this story takes place on the golf course, and illustrates
the doomed purposelessness that sometimes invades an athlete's perceptions of his or her performance. The last phrase is especially
telling: "a fatiguing curse seemed laid on everything."

427. _____. "The Pro." <u>New Yorker</u> 42 (Sept. 17, 1966): 53-
      54+. Also in the author's <u>Museums and Women, and Other</u>
      <u>Stories.</u> Knopf, 1972.
         A nice illustration of a teacher-pupil relation in which the
teacher needs the pupil more than pupil needs teacher. The story
includes a subdued but comical and insightful passage with the student, a veteran of over 400 lessons, supine on the 18th green as
the pro questions him much as a psychiatrist would interrogate a
client.

428. Van Loan, Charles E. <u>Fore!</u> Doran, 1918. 328 p.
         A pleasant collection of golfing stories told in the author's
relaxed, conversational style. The best of the lot may be the first,
"Gentlemen, You Can't Go Through!," about four incorrigible duffers who hold up other players without mercy. Long-term partici-
pants in most sports will share the suffering of "The Man Who
Quit." Robert Coyne, a better-than-average golfer, is in a miserable slump; it gets so bad that he swears off the game. As it does
for most golfers who make the same oath, the game draws him back.
         Times have changed, of course, since Van Loan flourished,
and some of his touches--a stereotyped black clubhouse man, for
example--may distress contemporary readers. We are all prisoners
of our own times, however, and will do best to read Van Loan for
his solid storytelling--unless the point of reading is, in fact, a
critical exploration of the assumptions of the times in which Van
Loan worked.

429. Van Wert, William F. "Putting & Gardening." <u>North American</u>
      <u>Review</u> 267 (June 1982): 22-28. Also in <u>Prize Stories, 1983:</u>
      <u>The O. Henry Awards.</u> Edited by William Abrahams. Double-
      day, 1983.
         A moving, gracefully written, at times humorous study of a
man who, in his 42nd year of marriage, can free himself from

thoughts of his wife's terminal illness only on the golf course. The
story is more than one of escape, though; it is also a close look into
the depths of this man's relationship with his son, who accompanies
the old man to the golf course, "because it's my only chance to see
the boy in my father, and he's happy I've come with him to share
his passion." Among the several good passages is one in which
father and son turn their anger at fate against their golf balls:
"And we just banged away all day, like terrorists." Perhaps the
best is the final paragraph, when the son turns to see why his father, a farmer by birth, is not following him off the 18th green.
"I ... see him on hands and knees, lovingly replacing my divot on
the magic carpet, this essence of the green, the only garden that
is left for him."

430. Whitlock, Brand. "Doting Fathers." American Magazine 77
      (April 1914): 56-60.
      Paternal devotion leads to filial failure in this story of a golf
elimination tournament. Teddy Landon and Perk Staymate, two old
companions on the course, have bequeathed both their names and
their interest in golf to their sons. Teddy and Perk the younger
are developing into excellent players, and both their fathers look
forward to the forthcoming tournament with excitement and high
expectations. They have been cautioned, however, to stay out of
sight when their sons play. Dewar, the club's Scottish pro, knows
that the presence of fathers adds too much tension to the already
tough atmosphere of a golf confrontation. The boys' elders initially
heed the old Scot's advice, but when both boys defeat all the competition, except each other, the lure is too strong: the men creep
out onto the course to observe their sons' climactic head-to-head
match.
      The consequences are grave. The outcome of the match de-
pends not on one player's superior skill, but on the fathers' lack
of discretion. A tolerable story that touches on some nearly universal truths about fathers and sons. (The author, says his by-line,
was "formerly Mayor of Toledo.")

431. Wilson, Robley. "Fathers." Ploughshares 9 (no. 4, 1983):
      131-136.
      A sweet-tempered little story in which golf provides the uni-
fying link between generations, and, though sweet, is not without
a dash of bitters to keep the whole from being too sugary.
      An older man and a young woman, whom we readily assume are
father and daughter, are out on the front nine of the course. The
man plays; his daughter accompanies him around as an observer.
Things have not been going well. When the story opens, the man is
scouring the rough looking for a sliced drive. His daughter refers
to his "hooked" shot; irritated, he says "You should learn to tell a
hook from a slice." To her, there is no difference: "Either way,
you can't find the ball." Shortly afterward, he expresses doubt as
to whether she really likes the game, although one senses that at
this point--he has just double bogeyed a hole and is playing much
worse than usual--he is not overfond of it himself.

The high point comes on a par three hole, one on which the green is out of sight of the tee. The daughter takes a forward position behind a tree, from which she watches her father's drive take a number of crazy bounces and roll into the hole. Upon retrieving the hole-in-one ball, her father flings it into the trees behind the green. She takes this as "an expression of joy," but it seems to be one of disgust over an otherwise best-forgotten round. In the clubhouse, the father describes his first set of clubs, the old hickory shafted, gutta percha wound models inherited from his father, and reminisces about his father's rather hapless, if sincere, attempts to teach him the game. The story's tension melts away in the final lines into a very tender moment between father and daughter.

432. Wolff, William A. "A Rub of the Green." Collier's (June 10, 1916): 11-13+.

Women on the pro tour exposed to this story might well lapse into shock, so emphatic is its demeaning of a woman golfer. Mary Crandall is both a stunning beauty and one of the local club's top golfers, with a berth in an upcoming tournament. Burnett, a lawyer in his thirties, has lost his heart to Miss Crandall, but she has eyes only for the lads capable of breaking par. Believing it his only route to his beloved, Burnett takes up the game. He ingratiates himself sufficiently with Miss Crandall that she allows him to carry her clubs during the tournament. She plays an uncharacteristically erratic round; Burnett allows her to dodge the consequences of her poor play by leading her off the course to announce their engagement. Surely a girl excited about marriage cannot be expected to play capable golf! This is insulting enough, but is nothing compared to the revelation--withheld from Miss Crandall--that Burnett attempted to sabotage her clubs to insure her poor performance. This information comes out with complete approval by the author of Burnett's tactics.

IX. HORSERACING

433. Algren, Nelson. "Bullring of the Summer Night." In his
The Last Carousel, p. 314-351. Putnam, 1973.
Jockey Hollis Floweree is being plagued by a gifted Mexican
jockey, Casaflores. The "bullring" is a track where pretty much
anything goes: horses too ill to race race anyhow, riders bet on
their competitors and help them win. As is standard in Algren's
sports tales, something underhanded is going on: Floweree plans
to win a race by using an electric prod on his mount.
Algren's grasp of the inside of horseracing is sure and compelling. He takes us in among the ill-paid track workers, shows
just enough of behind-the-scenes money action to let us know that
he is thoroughly conversant with it, and that what we are reading
is true. This story also contains some convincing pre-race tactical
planning that shows there is more to a horserace than simply lighting out for the finish line at the fastest clip possible.

434. _____. "I Never Hollered Cheezit the Cops." Ibid., p.
37-44.
A jockey "so confident that he was smarter than anybody,
while all the time he was dumber than anybody" manages to get his
one friend into serious trouble with the law through a betting
scheme. As in many Algren stories, everyone comes out looking
stupid, corrupt, or victimized--or all three at once.

435. _____. "Moon of the Arfy Darfy." Ibid., p. 352-366.
Also, in an earlier form, in Saturday Evening Post 237 (Sept.
26, 1964): 44-45+.
Hollis Floweree, a one-time winner, has been reduced to
scavenging the track grounds for $5 winning tickets accidentally
thrown away. Much of the action takes place in a seedy losers'
bar, where Floweree stumbles into a plan to con a few hundred dollars out of an easily-duped bettor. The story ends with a poem
about "Christ's poor damned cats." Grim stuff, for sure.

436. Anderson, Sherwood. "I Want to Know Why." In The Sherwood Anderson Reader, p. 86-94. Edited by Paul Rosenfeld.
Houghton-Mifflin, 1947. Also in the author's The Triumph of
the Egg. Huebsch, 1921.
A boy of fifteen and some friends from the Kentucky horse
country follow a couple of their locally-trained horses to the track
at Saratoga. The boys hop freight trains to get there. The narrator is in love with horses, especially a beauty named Sunstreak.

His love extends to Sunstreak's trainer, but when he sees the
trainer in a brothel following a victorious race, something of the
race game is spoiled for him forever. Hew could the trainer be involved with something as clean and innocent and beautiful as Sunstreak, and then spend his time with "rotten" women? "What did
he do it for? I want to know why." A story of an end to innocence, and a good one; the boy keeps putting off telling us what
he has learned about the trainer, and the delay works to good effect.

437. _____. "I'm a Fool." In The Sherwood Anderson Reader,
      p. 380-390. Edited by Paul Rosenfeld. Houghton-Mifflin,
      1947. Also in the author's Horses and Men. Huebsch, 1923.
      A young man, already a veteran of the track, takes a job in
Sandusky caring for the horses of a delivery business. On an off
day he goes to the races and tells a pretty girl he meets in the
grandstand about his father "owning" one of the race horses. He
lies about his name and about his home to impress the girl. After
all the lies, he realizes that he could have told the truth in the first
place; she likes him, and not because of his bogus claims. By this
time, though, he is too embarrassed to confess his false front, and
she leaves by train, never to see him again.
      The poor boy is a fool, just as he says, and that he knows it
doesn't make it much better. This is a painful, remorseful story--
"Even yet sometimes, when I think of it, I want to cry or swear or
kick myself."--and it is one of the author's best.

438. _____. "The Man Who Became a Woman." In The Sherwood
      Anderson Reader, p. 128-156. Edited by Paul Rosenfeld.
      Houghton-Mifflin, 1947. Also in the author's Horses and Men.
      Huebsch, 1923.
      Herman Dudley, a young drugstore clerk, shucks conventional-
ity and lives the track habitué's life, hanging out with the touts and
grooms and gamblers. His best friend becomes Tom Means, an aspiring writer and a groom. Tom moves on, and Herman, a shy,
lonely boy, tends a horse himself. Herman forms almost a spiritual
link with the horse, a link that helps him bear his loneliness and his
fear of women.
      The events of this story funnel around like a whirlpool, coming
down to a nightmarish conclusion. Herman visits a bar by himself,
witnesses an act of violence, and looks into the bar mirror at his re-
flection only to see what seems to be the face of a young girl, the
kind of innocent girl he has dreamed of. From this point intimations
of homosexuality and possibly bestiality are prominent, and the almost surreal climax sees Herman running naked through the night to
fall in a tangled embrace with the bones of a dead race horse.
      Anderson may take a bit long to get to the point, but the
story is full of effective imagery and some good ideas.

439. Bukowski, Charles. "Pittsburgh Phil & Co." In his South of
      No North; Stories of the Buried Life, p. 87-92. Black Sparrow
      Pr., 1973.

Hank yields to his friend Joe's nagging and takes him to the Santa Anita track one January day. Joe knows nothing about horses, but begins an astonishing string of betting wins. He buys new clothes, new women, a black Cadillac, and vanishes from Hank's life. He resurfaces years later, busted, but hooked on gambling and still convinced that he has the sure touch. He doesn't. A good sketch of the compulsive gambler.

440. Caputi, Anthony. "The Derby Hopeful." Cornell Review, no. 3 (Spring 1978): 69-76. Also in Prize Stories, 1979; The O. Henry Awards. Edited by William Abrahams. Doubleday, 1979.

Clyde Simmons, now a research assistant at Michigan State, visits old friends near Decatur, Indiana. The friends, father and son, are horseracing fans, and it is clear that they have put more into their fanaticism than into their decaying farm. They stake their hopes--quite imprudently, it turns out--on a chestnut horse they have been raising to be a good runner in the mud. Their pipe dream about working the horse, Marvin's Tip, up to a slot in the Kentucky Derby nearly takes in Clyde, but a minor race shows how feeble is the basis for their hope. A well-presented story of empty dreams.

441. Cheever, John. "Tomorrow Is a Beautiful Day." New Yorker 16 (Aug. 3, 1940): 15-16. Also in the author's The Way Some People Live. Random House, 1943.

Joe Walker and his wife have been suffering a tough run of luck at the track. Life in general has been difficult since they told Joe's mother-in-law about their marriage. She promptly booted her daughter out into the snow, and appropriated a quantity of the girl's clothing.

The way grows no easier through the story. Joe loses his lucky silver dollar, and places a bet on a sure thing that loses disgracefully. Mr. and Mrs. Walker leave the track with $13 (a lucky coincidence, no doubt) and some change to their names.

This story joins several others of the track with its knowing look at losers busy denying their condition. Two critical events take place: Joe goes into a frenzy at the disappearance of his precious (and, as we can see, completely luckless) "lucky dollar," and, shortly after discussing their remaining pawnable possessions, Joe discovers a four-leaf clover. "Isn't that swell?" he exults. "God, that makes me feel good! We'll lick them tomorrow." And if not tomorrow, then some day, somewhere, there will be a win, place, or show for Mr. and Mrs. Walker. But don't bet on it.

442. Davis, Richard Harding. "The Man Who Could Not Lose." Collier's 45 (Aug. 20, 1910): 17-19+; (Aug. 27, 1910): 15-17+. Also in the author's The Man Who Could Not Lose. Scribner's, 1916.

In 1910 the wide-eyed belief in the riches of the future that this story suggests might have been taken to heart by its readers.

Today we read the story with our contemporary expectations of irony and disappointment, and are surprised that what the piece claims to be about _is_ what it is about, namely, a man who cannot lose.

Champneys Carter is a poor young writer trying to write "the great American novel" (Yes, the phrase was alive even in 1910.) He and his bride are nearly broke, but a succession of vivid dreams brings Carter foreknowledge of the outcome of horse races. Betting everything they have on their faith in Carter's dreams, the young couple soon win a small fortune. Part of it goes into promotion of Carter's novel, which has been received unenthusiastically by his publisher--and soon he scores in the literary races, too. The public adores him, clings to his prognostications, and he serves them up with winning consistency.

The story itself is much like a dream. It is a record of impossible events, yet stated with such matter-of-factness; what burns beneath it is an intense lust for wealth and fame. Whether this emotion is all the author's, or whether it is a manifestation of public consciousness, is a topic of some interest.

443.   Effinger, George Alec. "The Horse with One Leg." In Worlds Near and Far, p. 139-148. Edited by Terry Carr. Thomas Nelson, 1974.

An incredible story told so sincerely that the reader can do nothing but accept it as true, while it lasts. A young girl has been left at home on the farm when her mother and father are away. In their absence, the horse Calpurnia gives birth to a fine foal whose only flaw is that he possesses but one leg. Through the girl's loving care, Lucky the colt not only learns to stand on his solitary limb; he learns how to hop about, and at considerable speed. Lucky eventually enters a major race at the urging of a prominent stable owner. There is no need to give away the ending, but in spite of the premise the story works as an example of the power of love to overcome handicaps.

444.   Farrell, James T. "Sport of Kings." In his $1,000 a Week, and Other Stories, p. 21-40. Vanguard, 1942.

Harry and Sarah, a married couple, have a little problem. Sarah is a compulsive gambler, addicted to playing the horses. She and Harry have full-blown fights over the issue, followed by days of silence. Sarah promises repeatedly that she will never bet again, but she does, and Harry finds her dope sheets and calculations tucked inside her True Confessions magazines. The story closes with Harry's recognition that nothing he can say or do will keep Sarah away from the bookies, and that divorce is out of the question because he can't afford it. As he sometimes does, Farrell tells too much and shows too little here, but the story is not a bad look at one of the unsavory corners of this sport.

445.   Faust, Irvin. "The Year of the Hot Jock." In his The Year of the Hot Jock, and Other Stories, p. 1-27. Dutton, 1985.

Once into its rhythm, and once the reader catches up, this jockey's tale turns quite gripping. Initially the style is difficult to adjust to: it is compressed, abrupt, and propelled with a whip hand, a textual parallel to a hard race. Conjunctions and verbs disappear in stacatto sentences, but the omissions add to the story's momentum.

The story takes shape as the speeding, autobiographical account of jockey Pablo Diaz, a man of much success, a man who always wants more; not more money, he rolls in it, but <u>more</u>. The reader follows Diaz through a succession of tracks and races. "Terrific week. Typical. Fifteen winners 6 days." Diaz has trouble relaxing, as his narrative tone suggests. Only when he visits an old friend in the barrio does he come down from the supercharged high that keeps him going.

There are two crises, one coming when Diaz's old friend tries to use him in a crooked scheme, the other when his mount apparently breaks a leg and throws him at the end of a race. It is a measure of the story's merit that the reader cares a good deal about what happens to Diaz at the end, when at the beginning he sounds simply like a man with a high opinion of himself and a recent dose of amphetamines.

446. Foote, John Taintor. "'Class' to Both the Horse and the Jockey." <u>American Magazine</u> 76 (Oct. 1913): 27-33.

Trainer Blister Jones illustrates his idea of what constitutes "class" in both men and beasts through the exploits of Hamilton, a two-year old who looks to most track men like an unmanageable animal. Hamilton has a wild look in his eye, and cannot control himself in the starting gate. Young Mickey Mulligan, as brash and easily-provoked as Hamilton, takes over as the horse's rider when others fail.

Blister Jones claims that Hamilton has "the look of eagles" in his eyes, a sign that he was born to be a winner. He wins one race, but, following an accident before that race, both horse and rider perform so bravely that one win is enough. Hamilton, though crippled, is auctioned off for stud service at a high price, and jockey Mulligan receives a fat contract to ride for a major stable. The lesson is that class will tell. It is an entertaining story, with very good illustrations and some unfortunate casual racism.

447. Fuchs, Daniel. "The Apathetic Bookie Joint." <u>New Yorker</u> 14 (Aug. 20, 1938): 14-18. Also in the author's <u>The Apathetic Bookie Joint</u>. Methuen, 1979.

A young man visits a bar which features a bookie operation. He has come to place a small bet on a horse running at Saratoga, but it is not such an easy transaction. Barlow the bookie, a bald accountant unable to pass the CPA exam, tries to argue the bettor out of it, telling him he doesn't like to see "a nice American kid with a college education" become involved with gambling and its attendant lowlife.

The bet goes on, and the rest of the story records the exchanges among the operators and clientele of this strange dive. The bartender grouses, the bookie's assistant treats his boss rudely, and a languid lady comes in to drink rye whiskey with a beer chaser. Barlow laments his sad place among the dregs. When a detective walks in to make a bust, Barlow manages to humiliate himself in front of the rest; his parting line is "I don't care if I live or die."

    This story is both funny and pathetic, but it is not at all apathetic in its examination of this gloomy set of horse followers.

448.   _____. "The Man from Mars." New Yorker (April 8, 1939): 20-21+. Also in the author's The Apathetic Bookie Joint. Methuen, 1979.

    Johnny Bluestone, his wife, his father, and the unidentified narrator are among the ten or twelve thousand people attending the Hialeah track one afternoon. Everyone is excited about the races and is busily laying bets, all but the older Mr. Bluestone. Mr. Bluestone is more than a little out of "synch" with both the events of a day at the races and with those of life on earth. "Ever since I retired," he says, "I achieved a perspective, a long-range view. I feel like a man from some other planet looking down...."

    Mr. Bluestone looks around at the crowd and announces that it all adds up to "a squirrel cage, yes." A squirrel cage allows the squirrel to walk in alone, but once inside there is no way for him to get out.

    Mr. Bluestone's harsh judgment on the track and on life itself does not convince his son, who calls him "a regular Schopenhauer." It doesn't convince the reader, either: Bluestone sounds a lot more like a man who has given up than like one who has found "a perspective."

449. Heimer, Melvin L. Penniless Blues. Putnam, 1955. 311 p.

    A group of friends who share an interest in the track pool their money to purchase the book's title character, a horse who goes on to bring most of them fortune in the areas they most cherish. Unfortunately for the syndicate, the newfound wealth from their ironically-named horse drives wedges into their friendship. Light, but not without insight.

450. Hemingway, Ernest. "My Old Man." In The Short Stories of Ernest Hemingway, p. 191-205. Scribner's, 1953. Also in the author's In Our Time. Scribner's, 1930.

    "My Old Man" follows Joe Butler and his jockey father from Milan to Paris. Butler is clearly involved in some shady dealing at the tracks, but young Joe, because he loves his "old man so much," does his best to ignore the obvious signs of corruption. In the end Joe must face not only death, but the undeniable truth of what his father has been. Concludes with one of the most chilling and hopeless lines in Hemingway's work: "Seems like when they get started they don't leave a guy nothing."

451. McCullers, Carson S. "The Jockey." New Yorker 17 (Aug.

23, 1941): 15-16+. Also in the author's Ballad of the Sad Cafe. Houghton-Mifflin, 1955.

A rich man, a bookie, and a trainer are eating an expensive meal in a Saratoga hotel. A jockey approaches them. He is in a state of cold rage over an injury sustained by a friend at a track in Miami. He stands at the well-laden table like a column of ice. It is impossible to believe that he will not allow himself an outburst, that he won't tip the table over and throw dishes across the room, but he doesn't. He chews a mouthful of French fries, spits them out on the carpet, and calls the three diners "libertines." From this jockey's lips it sounds like the dirtiest word in the language. The story is made by the atmosphere of barely-contained anger that McCullers creates in a few brief, carefully-chosen scenes.

452. McGinnis, Joe. The Dream Team. Random House, 1972. 213 p.

There are some funny passages in this novel of obsession, but their tone is black. Dreams are the topic at large, dreams of wealth, of beating the system, of fame and glory. All the dreams are empty.

The narrator, a young best-selling author burned out from a publicity tour for his book, flees to Florida with a woman reporter he has known for a day and a San Francisco radio interviewer whose real life is the track. They spend a week at Hialeah, losing badly in spite of the interviewer's allegedly fool-proof system. As they lose, tempers run short, the drinking gets heavy, and ugliness takes over.

Best known for his book on Richard Nixon (The Selling of the President, 1968 Trident, 1969), McGinnis creates an authentic track atmosphere, with some well-written racing passages. Two of the best describe a 19-year old jockey's determined, and ultimately cruel, efforts to win, whether the race matters or not. The characters are not particularly attractive, but they sound true. Blaine, the interviewer, is the most interesting of the three: he devotes "eighty, ninety, sometimes a hundred percent" of his creative energy trying to perfect his system.

453. Malzberg, Barry N. "Notes Just Prior to the Fall." In The Best from Fantasy and Science Fiction, 19th Series, p. 161-173. Edited by Edward L. Ferman. Doubleday, 1971. First published in the Magazine of Fantasy and Science Fiction (October 1970).

Simmons the horseplayer is on a bad losing streak when someone, or thing, that doubles as the story's narrator gives him a tip. Simmons takes him (it?) up on the information, and lays his money down on a 90 to 1 horse. Simmons is a nicely-imagined gambler, and the tout is, well, unique. The story's final two paragraphs are so remarkable that they bring laughter, not only because they are funny (though they are funny), but because they are so out-of-tune with expectations. Seldom has the cliché "You can't win 'em all" meant so much.

454. Mankiewicz, Don M. <u>See How They Run</u>. Knopf, 1951.
     307 p.
        The author, a knowledgeable denizen of the track, turns in a
     believable behind-the-scenes examination of the sport's effects on a
     small group of main characters, a trainer, a gambler, and a jockey.
     Jockey Nick Bragg is nervous before the big race; he has ridden
     a long time without injury, and fears that his good luck is bound to
     reach its limit. Trainer Sam Gleason, "dean" of American horsemen,
     has a "consuming passion" to breed and train a Kentucky Derby win-
     ner. John Van Alstyn (Commodore) Terhune is a clubhouse regular
     at the track, situated in the second tier of the aristocracy, which
     translates into a table in the second row from the window. The
     horse the trio put their bets on, literally and figuratively, is Red
     Apple. The book's coverage of the race in question from different
     characters' points of view is an interesting one, and the race itself
     bears out jockey Bragg's sense of ill to come.

455. Runyon, Damon. "All Horse Players Die Broke." In his <u>Take
     It Easy</u>, p. 1-29. Stokes, 1938.
        Unser Fritz, an aging horse player and former big money win-
     ner, has run into threadbare days. He still believes that he will
     draw his old flame Emerald Em to his side when he once again dopes
     out the horses adeptly, but she has not looked his way in nearly
     thirty years. "But wait until I get going good again and you will
     see," he says. Luck dictates that Fritz hits one more hot streak,
     and in a short time he accumulates slightly more than $100,000 at
     the track. He makes one last bet, planning to pick up another
     $1,000 with which to buy the almost mythical Em the perfect piece
     of jewelry.
        He bets at thousand to one odds, with the thousand on his
     side, i.e., he must bet $1,000 to win one dollar, so certain is every-
     one that Fritz's horse of choice will finish in the money. Is it really
     necessary to say that Fritz's horse steps in a hole in the track and
     fails to finish? That Fritz loses everything? Fritz kills himself in
     a vacant lot, "a bullet hole smack dab through his pimple." At
     least he spares himself from witnessing Emerald Em's arrival on the
     scene. A grim Runyon story, told in his characteristic go-to-hell
     fashion.

456. _____. "Lemon Drop Kid." <u>Collier's</u> 93 (Feb. 3, 1934):
     7-9+. Also in the author's <u>Blue Plate Special</u>. Stokes, 1934.
        So-named because of his habit of eating lemon drops, the Kid
     is a young tout. One day he swindles wealthy Rarus P. Griggsby
     of a hundred dollars at Saratoga. Running from Griggsby, he meets
     a lovely young girl in a small town, marries her, and goes to work
     in a store. It is his first honest work, and though his wages are
     small, he is also happy, briefly. His wife is pregnant, and the Kid
     can't afford the medical treatment she requires. Their baby is born
     dead, and the Kid's wife dies shortly thereafter. This is bad
     enough, but when the Kid finally returns to the horses after a
     stretch in prison for robbing a hotel in an attempt to raise money

for his wife, he learns some news that lends a far more bitter taste
to an already unpalatable life.

Runyon can present the most abysmal tear-jerker in such a
flippant, apparently indifferent manner that the misery he documents,
instead of losing the reader's sympathy because of its excess, actually engages it more than it would if Runyon told the tale soberly.

457.   . "A Story Goes with It." In his Money from Home,
      p. 121-141. Stokes, 1935.

A good place to get a sense of Runyon's impression of race-
track lingo. A group of jockeys conspire to throw a race so that
the has-been nag Never Despair will win, furnishing the horse's
owner with enough prize money to send his crippled daughter off
for an operation. A story at least as funny as it is sentimental;
"any one of the other five horses in this race can beat Never Despair
doing anything from playing hockey to putting the shot...."

458.   . "That Ever-loving Wife of Hymie's." In his Blue
      Plate Special, p. 25-50. Stokes, 1934.

The narrator accompanies his friend Hymie and Hymie's
"stable," consisting of one worn-out horse named Mahogany, to
Miami for some winter racing at Hialeah. Their accommodations are
nothing less than elegant: they share one end of a boxcar, with the
horse. Hymie's wife 'Lasses (short for Molasses), also makes the
trip, in a drawing room on the Florida Special. 'Lasses lives in
luxury in Miami while Hymie sleeps in a garage with Mahogany.
'Lasses can often be seen in the company of a certain track swell,
as Hymie hustles to secure his miserable horse a slot in an upcoming
race. Through the narrator's generosity, Hymie procures the $10
entry fee for the race, but lacks anything to make a bet. Almost
anything, that is. He bets his wife 'Lasses against $500 put up by
the swell. Mahogany wins, as 'Lasses feverishly cries out for the
jockey Frankie to bear down and win. Frankie is not Mahogany's
rider. The light telling of this story contrasts with its themes of
greed and faithlessness.

459. Saroyan, William. "Little Miss Universe." Esquire 2 (Dec.
      1934): 37+. Also in the author's Inhale & Exhale. Random
      House, 1936.

Next to boxing fiction, no genre in sports literature is so pre-
occupied with losers, dreamers, and self-deluders as the fiction of
the track. Here the narrator, a young writer, describes the variations on these thematic types as found in a San Francisco bar called
the Kentucky Pool Room.

There is Willie, with his ridiculous system: he looks for the
horse with the longest losing record because, by a measure visible
only to Willie, losing consistently promises imminent victory. Willie's
current horse of favor is Miss Universe, who bears out at least the
first half of Willie's system; she has been losing with reliable monoto-
ny.

Then there is Mr. Levin, who also has a system, in which the horses are mere puppets in a global scheme whose every event, no matter how remote from the issue at hand, in fact bears its weight on the outcome of the races. San Jose Red's system is infallible: immediately after each race, he writes the winner's name on a sheet of cardboard, then circulates among the crowd, claiming that he had picked the horse the night before.

The narrator himself gives in to the blandishments of Willie's unique system, and lays his last dollar on Miss Universe, who is running at Arlington. After the race, the narrator walks out of the Kentucky Pool Room with empty pockets, thinking about what a beautiful name Miss Universe has, and how he will make his remaining half loaf of rye bread last out the week.

A funny story with a heavy layer of pathos.

460. Shipman, Evan. "Combination." Scribner's Magazine 96 (Sept. 1934): 169-174. Also in the author's Free for All; 8 Stories. Scribner's, 1935.

This story of trotter racing, thick with track parlance and an assumption that the reader is already an initiate to the tongue may leave non-racing devotees a touch confused; it is interesting, however, to see how tightly-focused an audience Scribner's was willing to reach for with this detailed and unsentimental story.

The focus is on stable caretaker Will Broderick's work with an old but tough horse, Stamina. Trainer Fred Dunbar assigns Broderick to the horse, without real confidence in the animal's ability to pull any more victories from his frequently-tapped reservoir. Stamina's legs are nearly shot; only an elaborate routine of ice packs, ether, and rubdowns enables him to get up for his races. Stamina's one enthusiasm, aside from an occasional burst on the track, is a nice chew of tobacco. He disdains sugar.

Thanks to Broderick's knowledge and dedication, Stamina does draw one more win from his apparently exhausted allocation. The big victory does not seem to impress Broderick in any notable way. He simply continues doing his job, rubbing down Stamina. In the conclusion, Broderick and a friend fix up cots under the stable awnings, where they smoke and pass a bottle back and forth. There is a good sense here of work having been done right, with more of the same to follow. (The title refers to the men responsible for caring for a horse or a group of horses.)

461. _____. Free for All. Scribner's, 1935. 319 p.

A collection of short stories about harness racing, of which the story described above is a good example. Shipman demonstrates a well-informed eye for the details and characters of the racing life. Several of the stories are more concerned with off-track activities than with the actual moment of the race, but others do render the tension and drama of the races.

462. Van Loan, Charles E. "The Last Chance." Collier's 55 (Aug. 28, 1915): 7-8+. Also in the author's Old Man Curry. Doubleday, 1917.

Jockey Gillis, better known as "Little Calamity," is a thieving, lying, "sniffling, whining, half-portion of hard luck." L.C. takes a job as a trainer for Mr. Hopwood, who has purchased an old, hopeless, wild-eyed chestnut horse named "Last Chance." Before Last Chance completes his career pulling a delivery wagon for Hopwood's grocery store, Little Calamity leads him to a single victory, with the assistance of an electrical option. Typical Van Loan material, light, amusing, with characterizations good enough to do the job. Old Man Curry himself, who puts in an appearance, is good for a laugh with his incessant biblical quotations.

463. Annixter, Paul. <u>Pride of Lions, and Other Stories</u>. Hill &
Wang, 1960. 177 p.
Few readers of outdoors tales will have gone far without meeting the work of Paul Annixter (pen name of Howard A. Sturtzel).
Annixter is the author of hundreds of stories and several books, including <u>Swiftwater</u> (A. A. Wyn, 1950), <u>The Hunting Horn</u> (Hill &
Wang, 1957), and <u>The Devil of the Woods</u> (Hill & Wang, 1958).
Annixter's forte is the animal story; that genre is outside the scope
of this bibliography. He also writes capably of hunting, and <u>Pride
of Lions</u>, a collection of stories whose publication dates range from
1930 to 1958, is a good introduction to a cross-section of his work.
His ability to translate the hunter's world into good fiction owes
much to his skill with words and to his broad knowledge of the
woods and its denizens.

464. Benedict, Dianne. "Crows." in her <u>Shiny Objects</u>, p. 1-20.
Univ. of Iowa Pr., 1982.
A crow hunt becomes the focus of a mistaken attempt at re-
venge, followed by the killing of a young woman. Eugenia is the
woman who, at the end of the story, lies dead in a blanket in the
back of a pick-up truck. Earlier she goes with a younger man, Jim
Wesley White, to a bar. There she meets used-car dealer Rich
Stutts, with whom she carried on an affair of a not altogether healthy
sort some ten years ago.
Eugenia and Jim leave the bar, Jim quite drunk. They share
one of the adjoining cabins, though the sharing is relatively chaste.
Jim passes out as soon as he hits the mattress. Circumstances convince Eugenia that Stutts spied on her and Jim in the cabin (shades
of the Bates Motel in "Psycho"), and at the next day's crow hunt one
of Stutts's hired hands is obliged to shoot Eugenia before she can
kill Stutts.
The only character here one can like is Jim. Stutts, Eugenia,
and the rest are all either sleazy, crass, or warped. The crow hunt
is an orgy of killing carefully foreshadowed early in the story. As
the pick-up drives off with Eugenia, Jim holds her body in its bed.
When the shotguns bounce near him on the rough ride, he picks
them up and throws them over the side. There are some effective
symbolic touches, not overplayed in this story.

465. Bradbury, Ray. "A Sound of Thunder." <u>Collier's</u> 129 (June
28, 1952): 20-21+. Also in the author's <u>The Stories of Ray
Bradbury</u>. Knopf, 1983.

An exciting, tightly-written story in which a dinosaur-hunting safari is the vehicle for speculation on that familiar science fiction theme of fiddling with the past: if we made changes in it, what would happen to the present? Includes a riveting confrontation with a charging Tyrannosaurus Rex.

466. Brautigan, Richard. "Elmira." In his <u>Revenge of the Lawn</u>, p. 30-32. Simon & Schuster, 1971.
A moody piece in which the narrator returns "as if in the dream of a young American duck hunting prince" to the town of Elmira. It is late December, cold, raining, and he carries a double-barrel sixteen-gauge shotgun that he uses to annoy high-flying ducks. He hitches rides, and carries his gun at an angle, "so the barrels point toward the passenger side of the roof, and I'm always the passenger."

467. _____. "The Post Offices of Eastern Oregon." In his <u>Revenge of the Lawn</u>, p. 90-96. Simon & Schuster, 1971.
A boy and his uncle, on a hunting trip in eastern Oregon, stop at a post office where a copy of a famous Marilyn Monroe nude photo decorates a wall. Some time later, a newspaper photo of Marilyn, dead from pills, leads the narrator, a boy no longer, to remember details of the trip, including a macabre practical joke involving a pair of dead bear cubs.

468. _____. "A Short History of Oregon." Ibid., p. 105-107.
Another gloomy but pointed Brautigan short-short: a boy deer hunting in some unknown Oregon backwoods passes a wretched shack. Shoeless, coatless children come out of the shack and watch him pass in the cold rain, carrying his .30-.30 rifle. "I had no reason to believe," he concludes, "that there was anything more to life than this."

469. Brown, Morris. "Snow Owl." <u>Quixote</u>, no. 6 (Spring 1955): 32-43. Also in <u>Best American Short Stories, 1956</u>. Edited by Martha Foley. Houghton-Mifflin, 1956.
An excellent story of freedom and conduct under extreme pressures. A dozen men on a surveying expedition in the Arctic try to relieve their cabin fever with a little hunting trip. One of them shoots a great snow owl, and confines the wounded bird to a cage with the idea that he will nurse it back to health. The narrator detests first the shooting--owls are of no use to the camp cook--and then the cruel imprisonment of the wild bird. He believes that he will have to end the owl's suffering by shooting him dead, then suspects that the owl may survive if turned loose.
The parallels between the men's isolation, their near-entrapment by the alien landscape and the owl's shooting and caging give the story a special depth. Most readers will readily identify with the narrator's struggle to make the responsible choice in the question of the owl's freedom or death.

470. Caldwell, Erskine. "The Negro in the Well." In his Erskine
      Caldwell's Men and Women, p. 277-287. Little, Brown, 1961.
      Jule Robinson, of Georgia, dotes on fox hunting, as do many
of his neighbors. One morning as he prepares for the hunt, he
hears a strange sound from his shabbily-covered well. A black man
has fallen in while following his own hounds. Jule proposes a deal:
he will help the wet hunter out in exchange for two of the man's
hounds. The conclusion indicates how far both men are from a sensible assessment of the situation; both are victims of fanaticism.

471. Chappell, Fred. "Inheritance." In Under Twenty-five; Duke
      Narrative and Verse, 1945-1962, p. 180-190. Edited by Wil-
      liam Blackburn. Duke Univ. Pr., 1963.
      A young man named Locke goes deer hunting with his father,
an old woodsman called Anson, and a know-it-all acquaintance named
Max. The story opens with Anson bemoaning the passing of the old
days, how hardly anyone cares any more about guns and hunting.
The dramatic high point comes on the next day's hunt, when Locke,
concealed in a blind, nearly fires at Max, who has foolishly removed
his red cap and is crawling through a thicket. Locke's reaction to
his near-shooting of Max is what one would expect of any hunter of
some sensitivity: he nearly passes out. Max conducts himself with
perfect stupidity, and it surprises no one, reader included, to learn
of his death as reported in the sports section later in the year. His
carelessness in hunting would not yield to the lesson of the close
call with Locke. The next hunt convenes with Locke, his father,
and Anson. Locke kills a buck, but there is no joy for him in his
success; more important matters than hunting are pressing on him
now.
      A very capably-executed story of changing values.

472. Clark, Walter Van Tilburg. "Buck in the Hills." In his
      Watchful Gods, and Other Stories, p. 93-109. Random, 1950.
      Also in O. Henry Memorial Award Prize Stories of 1944. Edited
      by Herschell Brickell. Doubleday, 1944.
      Arguments about the fundamental ethics of hunting aside, a
responsible hunter does his or her best to avoid inflicting more pain
than necessary on the quarry. The good hunter shoots to kill, and
knows how to shoot to kill. When the kill shot fails and leaves the
animal wounded, the good hunter tracks it down and kills it as soon
as possible.
      This story tells a tale of sickening cruelty to an animal, and
of two men's coming up against one of humanity's ugliest sides. The
narrator is alone in the western hills, enjoying a swim in a cold pool,
looking forward with happy anticipation to his planned solo sojourn in
the hills. The mood changes when his friend Tom appears, hiking
towards him. Tom is troubled and tentative; after a swim and a
meal, Tom tells why he left behind his hunting companion, Chet
McKenny. To make it easier for himself to get a fine buck back to
their camp, McKenny deliberately shot to maim the animal, shattering
one of its forelegs. He then drove the injured buck eight miles

back to the camp, laughing at the suffering animal's clumsy move-
ments.

The men conclude that McKenny is "a first-rate bastard."
They go back down the trail the next morning, and "There was
something listening behind each tree and rock we passed...."

A superbly-written story; the reader feels like a third party
beside the campfire when Tom confides in the narrator rather than
like a stranger looking into a book. (First published in the Rocky
Mountain Review.)

473.   Connell, Richard E.   "The Most Dangerous Game."   Collier's
       73 (Jan. 19, 1924): 5-6+.

On a hunting trip in South America, Sangor Rainsford of New
York City falls off his yacht and finds himself the guest, once he
swims ashore, of a Russian Cossack on an isolated island. The Cossack likes to hunt, too, but his favorite game goes on two feet. It
is no surprise when Rainsford is soon transformed from hunter to
hunted. Strictly pulp fiction, this frequently-anthologized tale misses
most of its opportunities to transcend its limitations, but it is still
entertaining. For those interested in this theme, the 1966 film "The
Naked Prey," with Cornell Wilde, is probably as good a treatment as
it has received.

474.   Eddings, David.   High Hunt.   Putnam, 1973.   384 p.

A very solid novel of outdoor adventure and interior emotional
strain. Dan Alders, just back from a tour of duty with the Army in
Germany, goes on a mountain deer hunt in Washington with his
nearly-estranged brother Jack, an ex-Marine named McKleary, and
some other acquaintances. It takes half the novel for the hunt to actually get under way, and, though the book's non-hunting portion is
enjoyable reading, the approximately 140-page section dedicated to
the hunt is better.

As so often happens in stories dealing with close interactions
of the members of a small group in an isolated setting, High Hunt emphasizes the way the situation brings out the strengths and weaknesses, or worse, of the group's members. McKleary is a nucleus
for trouble. He drinks heavily, screams in his sleep, and shows
signs of mental disorientation. The badly overweight Cal Sloane op-
presses the group's spirit with his come-and-go symptoms of an approaching heart attack. Dan's brother Jack looks his life squarely
in the face and sees it for what it has become, a downhill slide.

Dan, the only member of the party who actually enjoys the
trip, insofar as pleasure is possible in generally unpleasant circumstances, finds himself caught in the middle when his brother and
McKleary develop an insane competition to see who will be able to
kill an albino buck spotted early in the hunt. In a space of fifteen
minutes Dan is within a hair of two murderous confrontations, first
with McKleary and then with his own brother.

Eddings handles his portrayal of the mountains and woods well;
his descriptions of hunting are detailed and informative. The characters, Dan and Jack in particular, are believable and interesting,

192

The Sports Pages

and the story proceeds with a steadily-building tension. A subplot concerning Dan's relationship with a peace activist does not succeed entirely, but it does allow Eddings to include a funny passage in which Dan passes himself off as a draft resister recently released from Leavenworth.

Eddings's interests are in proper conduct, an adult frame of mind, and respect for nature (at one point Dan apologizes to a wounded deer for having taken longer than he intended to put the animal out of its misery; at another, a guide condemns the idea of fishing for mere sport: you fish for what you'll eat, and leave the rest alone). High Hunt, the author's first novel, is superior to most first novels, and to most hunting stories.

475. Ellison, Harlan. "Final Trophy." In his Stalking the Nightmare, p. 171-186. Phantasia Pr., 1982.

"The word hunter seemed weightless when applied to Nathaniel Derr; perhaps agent of destruction might have approached the reality." Derr has left 13 million dollars to the Trottersmen, his old huntsmen's club. He has also left to the club the final trophy of his last kill, from his last hunt on the planet Ristable. This is the story of that hunt.

Derr has taken every trophy on earth, and has gone into space in search of more exotic game. He finds it on Ristable, a planet "where the rubble of the glorious ancient cities lay at the edges of the grasslands, slowly dissolving into the land from which they had come." The only residents of the planet are a race of gentle farmers. Derr is about to give up on Ristable; the planet is so peaceful and empty of challenge to the hunter that it bores him. Then he learns about "Kill Day," a day on which one of the natives sacrifices himself to a bull-like creature. Derr jumps to the conclusion that the natives don't know how to fight the beast, and nominates himself to take the victim's seat of honor at the next Kill Day, though he has, to be sure, no intention of allowing the creature to dispose of him. Derr carries out his plan, but learns a deep-seated cultural secret of the Ristable folk, a secret that leads to the most unusual trophy that now decorates the Trottersmen's clubroom.

Ellison is provocative as usual, and slips in some nice insights on the mind of the big-game trophy hunter.

476. Emshwiller, Carol. "Hunting Machine." In The Arbor House Treasury of Modern Science Fiction, p. 557-562. Edited by Robert Silverberg and Martin H. Greenberg. Arbor House, 1980. First published in Science Fiction Stories (May 1957).

High-tech hunting techniques and an ordinary, if large, bear produce a confrontation sometime in the future. A man and woman are going hunting with the help of their faithful "hound dog," a machine that tracks down animals. The encounter between the bear and the machine is frightening and depressing, the latter because of the story's ominous sense of the helplessness of nature when pitted against technology that knows no humane limits. The reaction of the hunters to the dead bear offends the reader, but the offense rises from the truth of the situation.

477. Faulkner, William. "The Bear." In his The Big Woods, p. 11-
     97. Random House, 1955.
        This short novel functions effectively on several levels. It
     works as a hunting story, as a coming-of-age story, and as a far-
     reaching commentary on the clash between traditional and contempo-
     rary cultures. Young Ike McCaslin goes out every year in search
     of Old Ben, a big, tough, clever bear who has been helping himself
     to area livestock for a long time. Under the guidance of Sam
     Fathers, an old Indian, Ike learns the secrets of the woods, and
     following Old Ben's death he grasps the unity of Nature.
        Even in some of his "easier" stories, reading Faulkner is some-
     times like cutting one's way through a fastgrowing thicket with a
     short, dull blade. Patient readers will be rewarded for their effort,
     however. "The Bear" contains very good descriptions of hunting
     life, a brief but dramatic final confrontation between Old Ben and
     his pursuers, and many other fine passages. One of the best por-
     trays the aftermath of Old Ben's killing, when the men long victim-
     ized by the bear's rampages come by to view his body.

478. _____. "The Old People." Ibid., p. 113-138.
        Further description of Ike McCaslin's introduction to hunting,
     deer hunting here, under the eye of Sam Fathers. (See above item).
     Faulkner uses the story, in part, to dwell on the theme of the
     land's permanence and the interflowing of human generations, both
     backward and forward in time. The story ends with a vision of a
     great buck appearing to Sam and Ike, a vision tied to the continuity
     of the earth. Another story that succeeds on multiple levels.

479. _____. "Race at Morning." Ibid., p. 175-198.
        Another deer hunting tale, and again an opportunity for Faulk-
     ner to consider the meaning, and the necessities, of life. Narrated
     by Mister Ernest's 12-year-old human hearing aid (Ernest, deaf, can
     only follow the hounds with the boy's help), the action involves the
     attempted chasing-down of an elusive old buck. The hunt tails into
     a meditation on the relationship between farming and hunting, between
     responsibility and freedom. The boy concludes that these "wasn't
     two different things at all--they was jest the other side of each
     other."

480. Ford, Corey. Minutes of the Lower Forty. Holt, 1962. 159 p.
        A collection of a couple of dozen short stories that originally
     appeared in the author's regular column in Field & Stream magazine.
     The unifying element in these humorous tales of hunting and fishing
     is the Lower Forty Shooting, Angling and Inside Straight club, a
     group of varied men who meet in Uncle Perk's store to swap lies amid
     the smells of ground coffee and harness leather and kerosene. The
     characters who appear in the stories are members of the club; Ford
     casts himself as the recording secretary.
        There are some passably funny pieces here, but the collection
     may be of most interest as an example of the kind of homage to good
     old boy fellowship that appeared in a decidedly non-literary sports

magazine. Women, and men sensitive in any respect to the portrayal
of women in fiction, will be repelled by Ford's crude, allegedly "funny" treatment of his female characters. In one story ("Seat of Justice"), the laughs are purchased through jokes about a man beating
his wife with a canoe paddle; in another ("Women Are All Alike"),
Ford amuses himself with lighthearted comments about a man's possible plans to shoot his wife, followed by an embarrassing passage
in which this woman becomes weepy and hysterical over a dead
squirrel.

It isn't fair to expect a collection of magazine pieces to be
gems without exception, but there isn't much excuse for the anti-
woman attitudes manifested here.

481. Ford, Jesse H. "The Savage Sound." Atlantic 220 (July,
      1967): 41-44+. Also in the author's Fishes, Birds, and Sons
      of Men. Little, Brown, 1967.
      Two men go out rabbit hunting, one with a pair of young
whippets yet to learn how to kill the quarry. The first rabbit they
run escapes when the whippets lie down beside it after winding it,
then watch it run off. The next is different. The dogs catch on
to their work, and go at it vigorously, until rabbit blood flies and
the carcass is ragged. Their owner is uneasy. He had always
done the killing in his hunts, but now he is "left with nothing but
the awful blame." This story has some Faulknerian overtones in its
treatment of nature, but it stands on its own as a thoughtful piece
of writing.

482. _____. "To the Open Water." Atlantic 214 (Nov. 1964):
      82-85+. Also in the author's Fishes, Birds, and Sons of Men.
      Little, Brown, 1967.
      Another tale of cold death at winter sport (compare with item
489). A man who has hunted ducks almost his whole life goes out
with a boat on icy waters. Recklessly he leaves the boat to walk
on a stretch of ice; it fails beneath him, and in his effort to save
himself he capsizes the boat. The end is inevitable. The story
contains good descriptions of both man and nature; one almost feels
the freezing water, the numb fingers, the futile cries for help form-
ing in the lungs.

483. Ford, Richard. "Communist." Antaeus, no. 55 (Autumn 1985):
      28-42.
      This story, set in 1961, is a good departure from many hunting
tales, whose themes so often concern young men coming of age in a
male-dominated world. "Communist" is about growing up, but the
most important relationship here is that of a 31-year old woman and
her 16-year old son, Les, the story's narrator.

The woman, Aileen, is a waitress. She and Les live in a little
house in the wilds west of Great Falls, Montana. Their husband and
father is dead. Glen Baxter, somewhat younger than Aileen, sometimes spends the night with her. Glen is a Communist with a capital
"C." He likes to hunt; killing animals--pheasants, ducks, deer--is

something special for him. He has been out of the state for a few
months, but shows up one day and offers to take Les hunting, out
of season, for migrating snow geese.

All three characters drive up to a meadow near a lake where
the geese land, and there Les and Glen kill a half dozen geese. The
passage describing the geese taking off at the sound of gunfire is
quite impressive, as is Ford's development of a mood of tension and
foreboding in the killing of the geese. Immediately following the
goose shoot, a good-natured meeting between Glen and Aileen de-
teriorates to the edge of violence when Glen refuses to put a wounded
goose out of its misery. The violence is just barely skirted, and in
its face Les recognizes some truths about both adults. He no longer
cares for Glen, and his mother becomes much more of a human being
for him. This comes out well in a gentle scene in which Aileen asks
Les if he thinks she is still attractive. "I felt the way you feel
when you are on a trestle all alone and the train is coming, and you
know you have to decide," he says.

484. Fosburgh, Hugh. The Hunter. Scribner's, 1950. 233 p.
      Monk Taylor, scion of a millionaire, throws over the life of
leisure to live in the mountains of New Mexico, where he occupies
himself as a hunter. Taylor is a violent character whose toughest
game is not the mountain lion, but his own inner being. Fosburgh
writes in a style with obvious antecedents in Hemingway, but it is
a style that suits his story. Ironically, perhaps, the narrative's
sympathies with animals are stronger than those with its human
characters. Contains excellent hunting passages.

485. Gonzales, Laurence. "A Bowl of Texas Red." In 4·4·4;
      Short Fiction by Laurence Gonzales, Grant Lyons, and Roger
      Rath, p. 20-43. Univ. of Missouri Pr., 1977.
      Steve, a Boston artist and sometime outdoorsman, is making a
bowl of chili of the "Texas Red" variety. As he works on the meal,
using a knife of unusual sharpness, he thinks about the knife's origin. He obtained it indirectly from an old man in Yellowknife who
had been making superior hunting knives for over six decades.
Steve learned of the old man, Marshall Briar, from a mutual friend
who worked as a northwoods guide until freezing to death after the
wreck of his small plane. Steve paid Briar for the knife with one of
his prints and a large pack of expensive artist's paper, for Briar is
also an amateur painter.

Now, years later, as Steve makes his chili, Briar shows up at
his door. They are face-to-face for the first time, but their common
interests have already given them a sense of comfort in each other.
Briar describes the brave and intelligent way their friend the guide
fought against his death, and as a parting gesture gives Steve another hand-made knife.

Most of this story takes place indoors, and most of that in
Steve's kitchen, but the presence of Briar's knife puts the distant
wilds always at hand. A very nice story of friendship and shared
experience.

486. Gordon, Caroline. <u>Aleck Maury, Sportsman.</u> Scribner's,
      1934. 287 p.
      Aleck Maury learns the classics at his father's knee, graduates
from the University of Virginia, and goes on to pursue a career in
academia as a classics instructor himself. His profession, though, is
almost an afterthought compared to his avocations of hunting and
fishing in the South. Told in the first person by Maury, this novel
reads like an informal autobiography of a man born to the woods and
streams. The tone is civilized, almost genteel; "Aleck Maury, Gentleman," might well have been the book's title. Through Maury, Gordon
gives the reader a good feel for the outdoors and for both broad and
narrow aspects of the sportsman's life. A typical passage illustrating
Maury's character concerns his reaction to a favorite shotgun's return
to him by its borrower in a damaged condition. He buries the piece
in his garden, almost as though it had possessed a life of its own and
deserves fitting interment. "Even to this day," says Maury, "melancholy steals over me when I think of its fate."

487. _____. "The Last Day in the Field." In her <u>Old Red and
      Other Stories</u>, p. 158-167. Cooper Square, 1971.
      Aleck Maury tries to ignore the pain in his bad leg as he
makes one last trip afield to hunt birds with a young companion.
Gordon's description of natural details on a frosty fall morning is
adept, as is her subtle portrait of a man who knows that, for him,
the autumn hunt is nearly over.

488. Guterson, David. "Three Hunters." <u>Iowa Review</u> 15 (no. 1,
      1985): 58-70.
      Sixteen-year-old Roy Ferris and his younger brother Lane are
out camping and fishing. Roy is fishing, anyhow; Lane plays soli-
taire and eats blackberries back at their camp. Roy is brooding and
dreaming. The Game Department man has assured him that the fish
are biting in Echo Creek, but the fish are nowhere to be found. We
join Roy as he hikes back to camp along a dusty road, hot and
peeved, thinking about the way his father abandoned the family.
      Tired out, Roy lies down beside the camp firepit, and dreams
of a country where the fish are plentiful, where no mosquitoes pester
the fisherman, and where no other fishermen can spoil Roy's private
pleasure. Roy's dream evaporates with the arrival of three men,
hunters, who carry big-game rifles. The atmosphere is immediately
charged with apprehension. One of the hunters seems on the precipice of violence; the threat resides in his sarcastic attitude, in his
off-center statements to the boys. When he turns his rifle on Roy,
death seems imminent. The three hunters finally leave, but their
taste stays with Roy. He can't get them out of his mind. He takes
a last pass in the creek, lands a big fish, but everything is ruined,
and the fish only reminds him of the three hunters.
      Back in town, hatred for the hunters consumes Roy. A brief
conversation with his mother leads to a revelation about his departed
father. "There are evil men in the world, Roy," she says. "Jesus
Christ save us there are evil men." The reader's sympathy is with
Roy entirely; Roy's dreams will never again be innocent.

489. Hall, Lawrence S. "The Ledge." Hudson Review 11 (Winter
      1958-59): 554-569. Also in Prize Stories, 1960. Edited by
      Mary Stegner. Doubleday, 1960.
      This story rolls over the reader like an inexorable thing, like
the tide itself. On Christmas morning, a man takes his son and
nephew out for duck shooting on the sea. They travel by boat,
and then by skiff to a ledge of land only slightly above the water
at low tide. From there they shoot their ducks, and it is there
that they meet their end at the freezing high tide, for the skiff
goes adrift, trapping them on the ledge. The inevitability of absurd death gives the story a powerful quality, and arouses both
sympathy and fear in the reader.

490. Hassler, Jon. The Love Hunter. Morrow, 1981. 311 p.
      This novel has all the elements required to make a satisfying
whole. It blends an interesting structure, attractive characters,
lively action, and mature reflections on issues of love and death.
It also contains the occasional unexpected bit of humor to season the
mix.
      Two men, Chris and Larry, are leaving their northern Min-
nesota home for a duck hunting trip in a remote part of Canada.
They have been friends for close to twenty years, and worked at
the same college, where Chris is a counselor and Larry was a history professor. Chris is in love with Larry's wife, Rachel; the
feeling is apparently mutual, though they have refrained from anything more demonstrative than a careful embrace. Chris envies
Rachel's leading men in her dramatic work, for they have kissed
her more intensely than he has.
      Larry is dying of a rapidly-progressing case of multiple scle-
rosis. The disease has forced him to early retirement, and it has
all but destroyed his opinion of himself. He can get about with a
walker, but the prognosis is bleak. Only Larry's sardonic wit
seems to sustain him in the novel's early going.
      Chris has concocted a scheme in which he will murder Larry
in the wilderness. The scheme amounts to little more than half-
baked fantasizing; when Larry is actually in danger, Chris is afraid
for Larry's life. What happens in the wilds on the hunting trip not
only reveals to Chris the lack of substance in his homicidal ambitions, but brings Larry, in a sense, back from the dead. Through
an act of heroism, Larry regains his self-respect. His disease will
bear him down, but he will go through the final phase of his life
far stronger than he has--perhaps--ever been.
      This is an intense story, for it brings the reader into intimate
and sometimes wracking identification with the two central characters. It is also a story in which love and courage are portrayed
with honest complexity, and in which the wilds play a vital part.
A potent, thoughtful, and extremely moving novel.

491. Hemingway, Ernest. "The Short Happy Life of Francis
      Macomber." In The Short Stories of Ernest Hemingway, p. 3-
      37. Scribner's, 1953.

On safari in Africa, Francis Macomber loses his nerve to a
charging lion, and his wife to Wilson, the white hunter. Macomber
regains his respectability by conducting himself bravely a short time
later. Thus, his life is happy; his life is short, however, for his
wife's aim is poor. Deliberately poor? Possibly. Hemingway's ruminations on American women in this story, through his mouthpiece
Wilson, are too sweeping to be credible, and are, in the end, annoying. The issue of Macomber's conduct is much more interesting;
the emphasis, as in so much of the author's work, is on taking pains
to do the job properly.

492.   Hershenow, Nicholas. "Opening Day." North American Re-
       view 270 (Sept. 1985): 53-55.
       An unsettling horror-satire of ecological revenge. The anony-
mous narrator opens with a brief evocation of the long tradition of
deer hunting, "what the old men remember, and what the children
imagine." From this he slides into another discussion of the changes
that have taken place in hunting, with a lightly-veiled condemnation
of the annual slaughter by city dwellers of the scientifically-managed
deer herds.
       The story moves another notch down into the sinister with a
description of this year's herd, starving in the pre-season, moving
into the suburban fringe in the quest for food, sleeping in the
graveyard. Soon the locals find signs that something is very wrong;
fresh graves are dug up, wooden coffins shattered, and bodies de-
voured. Children are found killed, their flesh eaten. The truth
about the deer becomes undeniable, and the outrage of their human
victims grows severe. "How are we to comprehend their vicious in-
gratitude, what are we to make of deer who are traitors...?" Let
alone deer with long pointed canines, mutants fitted out for foraging
on the weak and the sick in an urban setting.
       A grim but neat inversion of the roles of hunter and hunted,
with humanity still "prevailing" in the end. The descent of this
story from what opens like an encomium to hunting to a satire of
frightening effect is expertly paced and plotted. "Perhaps we should
find a new quarry, an animal more compatible with our time in history...." But perhaps we already have.

493.   Horgan, Paul. "The Huntsmen." In his The Peach Stone;
       Stories from Four Decades, p. 179-202. Farrar, Straus, &
       Giroux, 1967.
       Twelve-year old Madison goes out duck hunting for the first
time with his father. His father is mortally wounded by a discharge
resulting from Madison's careless handling of the shotguns. The
accident leaves Madison numb. It remains for his 18-year old brother
to restore Madison's belief in himself. He does this with great tact,
sensitivity, and imagination, leading to one more hunting trip with
Madison. A good story, written with deep feeling both for human
nature and for Nature itself. The characters, especially Madison
and his brother Edwin, are fully believable.

494. Humphrey, William. "The Shell." In <u>The Collected Stories</u>
of William Humphrey, p. 68-79. Delacorte, 1985. Also in the
author's <u>Last Husband, and Other Stories</u>. Morrow, 1953.
   An effective coming of age story. Young Joe's father was the
best wing shot in town. He died before Joe reached his teens, and
since his father's death Joe has been waiting for the day when he
can wear his father's hunting coat and shoulder the big shotgun his
father used.
   He is sixteen now, and suddenly the coat fits, the coat that
still smells of the dried game blood and gunpowder his father left
behind. Beyond the coat and the gun, there is a talisman, a magic
shell filled with number 8 birdshot. It is magic for it is the one
shell Joe found that his father had not used, and it stands for Joe
as a symbol of his father's whole being: his discretion, his responsibility, his skill.
   Joe believes that he must fire this shell, and not miss. Each
day of the quail hunting season he takes his dog into the field,
with the shell in the gun, but he cannot bring himself to fire for
fear of failure. At last he works up his nerve to pull the trigger,
and what follows frees him from his oppressive obligations to his
father's memory, though not in the way he or the reader anticipated.
There are many good details here, both of hunting and of father-
son psychology.

495. Hyman, Mac. "The Dove Shoot." In <u>Under Twenty-Five;</u>
<u>Duke Narrative and Verse, 1945-1962</u>, p. 9-18. Edited by
William Blackburn. Duke Univ. Pr., 1963.
   This is an affecting story of a young boy's initiation to hunt-
ing, and to the racism present in his own family. Paul's father gets
him out of bed about four A.M. on dove shoot day; they meet Jim,
their black helper, at the back door, and head out on their hunt.
Jim is an expert shot, and treats Paul with consideration. The hunting goes well: Paul shoots enthusiastically, and hits a few birds.
When Jim compliments him, "I looked at him and my face got hot and
I thought I was going to blush. I was really proud of myself."
   Paul's elation does not last. Another hunter comes up to him
and Jim while Paul's father is occupied elsewhere. The man berates
Jim for shooting, accusing him of stealing his shots, of being "a
pretty goddamned fresh nigger." Paul's father breaks up this scene,
but the ugliness isn't over. When Paul protests against the other
hunter's obviously untrue and mean accusations, his father fails to
acknowledge Jim's rights.
   "I never have known Daddy to be wrong about anything much,"
says Paul, "but no matter how I looked at it, it just didn't make any
sense."

496. Kantor, MacKinlay. <u>Daughter of Bugle Ann</u>. Random House,
1953. 122 p.
   This worthy successor to <u>The Voice of Bugle Ann</u> (below) lacks
some of the first book's dramatic intensity, but still carries itself
well. Most of the novel concerns a crisis in a young couple's mar-

riage brought on by the woman's fondness for a mutt dog who comes romancing Little Lady, Bugle Ann's daughter. She and her husband separate after a dreadful fight over the dogs, and remain unreconciled for years. If this sounds astounding, one might reflect on the countless absurd contentions that have torn marriages apart, and note that this one, at least, involves sincere interest in sensitive creatures.

Hunting plays a background role in this novel, but remains an essential issue, for it is the hunt that spurs the commitment to the hounds. Baker Royster narrates the novel in the first person; as in the earlier Bugle Ann book, Kantor does a first-class job of evoking the Missouri folk and their fox-hunting ways. The first few pages, which describe a prehistoric man's relationship with his dog, are also especially striking.

497.   _____. The Voice of Bugle Ann. Coward-McCann, 1935.
128 p.

An engrossing story of men, women, and foxhounds set in Missouri. Bugle Ann is old Springfield Davis's dog; she has a unique voice that cannot be mistaken in the distance when she is on the trail of a fox.

The hunting favored by hound-dog men described here is a bloodless sort: they raise the dogs to chase the foxes, but the chase is all that counts. They never kill the fox, but let it go to run again. Trouble comes when a disreputable, sour neighbor strings up a wire fence to keep the hounds off his land. The trouble leads to a killing, and to Springfield Davis's imprisonment. Bugle Ann dies, but not before giving birth to her successor.

The novel's plot is fairly slight, though enough to keep the reader's interest. The book's chief virtue is its depiction of a way of life, and a kind of people, that even at the time of the story's publication were on the way out. At one point the narrative mentions what would have been done fifty years ago in a situation calling for swift justice. That is now one hundred years ago, leaving us that much further away from the traditions remembered by these people. The Voice of Bugle Ann is not just a good story: it keeps alive a segment of vanished Americana.

498.   Kranes, David. "Hunt." In his Hunters in the Snow; A Collection of Short Stories, p. 69-76. Univ. of Utah Pr., 1979.
Portrays a couple so wrapped up in their own marital and aesthetic torment that they are incapable of humane, practical action. The setting is New Hampshire in deer season. Gunshots echo in the woods. The November cold is like mid-winter. Leah and her husband Hunt, with their children, are visiting his parents. Hunt apparently informs Leah that he is going to move out, though the narrative beats around the bush in such an artsy way that the reader cannot be certain. Whatever the content of his announcement, it tortures Leah. She is a sensitive thing anyhow. The deaths of innocent deer at the hands of hunters bother her. Hunters? Is there a connection there with her husband Hunt? Is he a killer, of sorts?

Leah flees out into the woods in a fit of misery. Hunt tracks her down, and, in the process, comes upon a female deer that has been crudely shot. The deer is still alive. Does Hunt mercifully put the animal out of its pain? No, he uses the wounded deer as an excuse to brood on the work of the painter Brueghel. Why not? Leah, the tender, wounded one, does no more than her husband for the injured animal.

It would be nice to assume that the author intended to hold these two characters up for examination as representatives of over-intellectualizing, irritating self-consciousness, but grounds for this assumption are slim; the story itself shares its characters' most notable features.

499. Lytle, Andrew. "The Guide." Sewanee Review 53 (Summer 1945): 362-387. Also in O. Henry Memorial Award Prize Stories of 1946. Edited by Herschel Brickell and Muriel Fuller. Doubleday, 1946.

A boy goes out duck hunting for the first time with his favor-ite uncle. The trip represents an important point in his adolescence, an admission to one of the rites of men, including staying at a rough inn and plenty of casually obscene conversation. There are two hunting guides, one a drunk, the other a would-be innkeeper, but the real guide is the boy's uncle, and the path he takes the boy on leads not to ducks but to adulthood. The story features good hunt-ing action, and good depiction of a boy who wants to be sure not to embarrass himself by acting too boyish.

500. McKinley, Georgia. "The Elders." Southwest Review 44 (Winter 1959): 12-19. Also in the author's The Mighty Dis-tance. Houghton-Mifflin, 1965.

A new England couple, the Bolgers, visit acquaintances in Texas for a hunting outing on the plains. The woman, Anita, is fond of animals and is a member of the SPCA. She would rather sit in the car reading than hunt. The Bolgers' hosts, old-time Texas gentlemen, seem to penetrate Anita's independence and budding feminist sensibility with their gracious, courtly manners. This is in spite of their patronizing attitude and their thoughtless cruelty (they starve their dogs weeks before the hunting season to make them more eager for the field.) An ambiguous story with a lot of room for varying interpretations.

501. Mathes, William. "Swan Feast." In New American Review, no. 1 (1967): 109-121.

A story very close to the surreal. A group of men on a duck hunt are moved by a sexual exhibition to perverse slaughter of a flight of swans. Their obscene revelry with the dead swans is halted by a lethal fire. Hunting details are good, but the weight of the story lies in suggested links among racism, antagonism toward nature, and displacement of healthy emotions into violent outlets.

502. Mosher, Howard F. "First Snow." In his Where the Rivers Flow North, p. 26-38. Viking, 1978.

Few events are more distressing than those which cause hard feelings between neighbors. When the neighbors are close relatives, as they are in this story, the effect passes distress and becomes positively chilling.

Walter and Eben are brothers. Walter, the narrator, describes his neighbor Eben's ill-kept house and his lazy habits; Eben knows the mountain they live on, "every foot of it," but he is no hand at farming, and he drinks too much. Nevertheless, Walter willingly helps Eben out around his place, and even takes him on as a hired hand from time to time.

What he won't do is permit two of Eben's cousins to hunt on his land in deer season. Eben takes unkindly to this prohibition, and evidently counsels his cousins to hunt on Walter's property anyhow. They kill a doe out of season, and Walter confronts the three men. "It was full dark and snowing hard" when the story closed, and the wind of a permanent rift was blowing between the two brothers. The story gives a full sense of the woods, the falling snow, and the unhappy end to the brothers' formerly tolerable relationship.

503.   Pollack, Merrill. "Tale for a Frosty Morning." Antioch Review 22 (Fall 1962): 353-363.

Thirty-six year old Ben Newman is alone in his house, his wife and children are visiting relatives in New York City. Newman lives an hour from the city, in a house in the woods he purchased only a few months ago. The house is far from the advance of urban development. Newman, a peaceful man who likes to feel close to nature, typifies the long-confined city man's sudden rush of sympathy for anything of the wild, whether rabbit, pheasant, or flower.

On this nippy morning, Newman's peace breaks when the sound of a gunshot awakens him. He has posted his land against hunting, and is angered to see a hunter stalking pheasant a few hundred feet from his house. He orders the man off his land, but, while shaving later, he again hears the gun. He goes out to confront the hunter. On the way, he finds the hunter's work, a pheasant with a torn-up wing flailing on the ground. He picks up the terrified bird, and, when the hunter appears, refuses to hand it over. The hunter points out that it will die, regardless; Newman swears that the hunter will either have to kill him or knock him unconscious to wrest the bird from him.

"You're crazy," says the hunter, and walks away. Newman carries the pheasant back to the house with vague notions of nursing it back to health, but realistic evaluation confirms the hunter's words: the bird is dying. Ironically, Newman cannot bring himself to break its neck to spare it from further suffering. "All he could do was remain with the bird, stroking it sorrowfully, for as long as it would take for its life to end."

This is an effective example of sentimentality producing the opposite of its intentions. Newman "loves" the wild creatures, but is so transported by his identification with them that he cruelly elects to let the wounded bird suffer pointlessly. There is some subtle

foreshadowing of his dilemma in his reaction to the failure of some
roses to grow on his land. He absolves the very soil of responsibility. He believes his wife didn't plant the roses correctly.
Death cannot come out of the perfection of nature, to believe Newman's view, but it does, and Newman can't handle the fact.

504.   Schaefer, Jack Warner. "Enos Carr." In The Collected
        Stories of Jack Schaefer, p. 468-484. Houghton-Mifflin, 1966.
        A human-interest story set in the modern West. Enos Carr is
a local man, an expert trainer of horses and a fine hand with a gun.
He has some unusual ideas about hunting, though; about men as
predators competing unfairly and greedily, always ready to take
more than they can use. A gun writer for sports magazines spurs
Enos to reflections on his philosophy of hunting, and though everyone in the vicinity considers Enos a crank, what he says makes a
lot of sense, and touches on issues that have never occurred to the
local hunters in the way Enos presents them.

505.   Stuart, Jesse. "King of the Hills." Esquire 17 (April 1942):
        73+. Also in the author's Save Every Lamb. McGraw-Hill,
        1964.
        Black Boy, an old hound, is on the verge of his nineteenth
birthday. He has trouble standing up. On a whim, two brothers
mix a pint of moonshine with a gallon of sweet milk and give it to
the dog; he laps it up and spends most of the day leading the boys
on a wild hunt of 'possums, skunks, and one red fox. Drunk, the
dog has reverted to his youth, but this hunt is his last: the next
day he dies. A good-natured story whose happy attitude is barely
diminished by the old dog's death.

506.   _____. "Thanksgiving Hunter." In his Save Every Lamb,
        p. 247-255. McGraw-Hill, 1964.
        A boy goes out on his first hunt with his uncle, who has
promised to make the boy "a great hunter." The boy sits on a
rock and thinks, his shotgun at his side, while his uncle shoots
doves some distance away. The boy is overcome by the presence
of death in this late autumn wood. "Everything was dead and dying
but a few wild birds and rabbits." The boy meets a dove, blinded
in both eyes by an errant shotgun blast. The bird's wounds have
healed, and now it calls to its mate in a nearby tree.
        A calm but affecting story of the boy's inner conflict over the
expectations of tradition and family versus his own inclinations,
which would take him far from being "a great hunter." There is no
bluntly-stated moral here, only a presentation of the boy's predicament.

507.   Williams, Ben Ames. "The Eftest Way." Saturday Evening
        Post 199 (Nov. 6, 1926): 24-25+. Also in the author's Frater-
        nity Village. Houghton-Mifflin, 1949.
        This story takes some time getting to its point, but the round-
about manner of its telling is in keeping with that of backwoods tale-

telling in general. An old man and a friend go out on a hunt,
which proves to be the last for one of them. Williams's main
strength in his stories of the Maine village of Fraternity, which he
began writing in 1919, is an ability to effectively delineate character and local settings. By the time he wrote the last of the Fraternity stories in 1940, approximately one hundred had been published, the majority in the Post.

508. _____. "Mine Enemy's Dog." Collier's 65 (Jan. 10, 1920):
      5-6+. Also in the author's Fraternity Village. Houghton-
      Mifflin, 1949.
      Nick Westley, a game warden, pays surly old Proutt to train
his English setter, Reck, as a bird dog. Acting on a grudge against
Westley, Proutt deliberately tries to corrupt Reck by turning him into
a deer-chaser, not a bird hunter. (In Fraternity, Maine, a dog that
runs deer is shot on sight.) Proutt's plan fails, and its failure
takes on unexpected, though foreshadowed, dimensions.
      Williams is skilled at giving the reader a sense of intimacy with
these small-town hunters, and this story also packs a fair amount of
dramatic tension, as well as compassion that saves it from becoming
only a well-written tale of justice prevailing.

509. _____. "Old Tantrybogus." Saturday Evening Post 192
      (March 6, 1920): 8-9+. Also in the author's Fraternity Vil-
      lage. Houghton-Mifflin, 1949.
      A touching story of a middle-aged bachelor and a favorite bird
dog, originally called Job, then Tantrybogus. It is, in effect, a
short biography, for it follows the dog from puppyhood to death,
and always in relation to the man's attitude toward the dog. The
story is free of anthropomorphism; this is a dog, not a creature of
human sensibilities with four feet and a tail. This authentic
canine-ness lends greater strength to the story's best passages, both
humorous and sad. Only readers with hearts chipped from granite
will be able to finish the last few pages without growing misty-eyed.

510. Wolff, Tobias. "Hunters in the Snow." Triquarterly, no. 48
      (Spring 1980): 225-240. Also in the author's In the Garden
      of the North American Martyrs. Ecco Pr., 1981.
      Frank, Kenny, and Tub go hunting in winter. Tub takes a
lot of mean kidding because of his obesity. On a farm where they
have secured permission to hunt, Kenny shoots and kills the farmer's
dog, then indicates that Tub will be his next target. Tub shoots
first. The rest of the story follows Frank and Tub as they pur-
portedly take the dying Kenny to a distant hospital. As Kenny lies
freezing in the back of the pickup, Frank and Tub repair their own
friendship with confessional conversation. The idea of two men
seriously discussing their eating habits and their girlfriends while
their wounded companion is busy dying sounds as though it defies
credibility, but here it doesn't. It is an eyebrow-raising premise,
but with Wolff's handling it works.

511. Wozencraft, Kimberly. "Backstrap." <u>Northwest Review</u> 23
       (no. 3, 1985): 38-42.
       The narrator lives with her husband Gavin out in the country.
Gavin is a retired policeman; his wife saved his life once by slowing
his bleeding following a gunshot wound. Life in the country is lonely, and both Gavin and the narrator look forward to a visit from
another married couple, Steve and Susan. It is evident early on
that the narrator takes a more intense interest in Steve than her husband does; in the end she wonders how her life might have been had
she not saved Gavin's life.
       What makes this story more than yet another tedious matter of
domestic tension and frustrated affairs is the symbolic function of
the illegal night deer hunt that the four characters engage in. They
drive a pickup out to the deer fields, immobilize their quarry with a
spotlight, and kill a doe with a single shot to the throat. They
dress it out back at the ranch. "The smell filled the barn.... It
was blood smell mostly, but also something else, maybe the way it
smelled that night Gavin got shot." To compound the symbolism, the
doe turns out to have been pregnant. The story ends with the narrator sticking her arms up to the elbows in steaming, sudsy hot
water in the kitchen sink. One cannot help but recall Lady Macbeth,
frantically trying to wash away the "blood" from her hands.

512. Arthur, Elizabeth. Beyond the Mountain. Harper & Row, 1983. 211 p.

Here the web of human relationships is overshadowed by the author's lively, evocative depictions of mountaineering. Chief character Artemis Phillips has been driven to escape and self-testing in the mountains of Nepal. The specter she seeks to lose half-way around the world rose from a disconcerting decision she made when a Wyoming avalanche buried her husband and her brother. Forgetting her husband, she fought to rescue her brother, without success. In Nepal, she moves out with an eight-woman expedition, still trailed by her memories.

Arthur's presentation of the outdoors is good, sometimes powerful; her background as a mountaineering instructor shows in the authenticity of her prose. Her people are less interesting than her mountains.

513. Boyle, Kay. "Maiden, Maiden." In A Treasury of Mountaineering Stories, p. 93-113. Edited by Daniel Talbot. Putnam, 1954. Also in the author's Thirty Stories. Simon & Schuster, 1946.

An excursion in the Alps provides the catalyst for a young woman's awful insights into the absence of substance in the relationship she has maintained for several years with an English doctor. She falls in love with her climbing guide, a character as attractive to the reader, in his workmanlike humility, as he is to her. The conclusion had to be tragic and ironic, and it is. A story of brooding self-consciousness, with some good details of late summer mountain climbing.

514. Bretnor, R. "The Man on Top." Esquire 36 (Oct. 1951): 102+. Also in 100 Great Science Fiction Short Short Stories. Edited by Isaac Asimov, et al. Doubleday, 1978.

An elegantly crafted little piece whose surprise ending is in good keeping with clues laid earlier. Everyone believes that it is Geoffrey Barbank who conquered Nanda Urbat, the world's toughest mountain. The narrator knows otherwise, and proceeds to set the record straight. He was a member of Barbank's climbing party, all of whom felt the heat of Barbank's contempt. Barbank is the prototypically obnoxious Westerner, full of arrogant confidence in the technology at his disposal, brimming with condescension for his Sherpa assistants. When a holy man visits the village the climbers are to depart from, Barbank scoffs at him. The holy man's reaction, though gentle and polite, is certain: Barbank needs his help to climb the mountain. Barbank laughs. The account of the climb is brief, since the author's point is to show what happens at the top. Few readers will fail to be both amused and satisfied by the incident at the top of Nanda Urbat.

515. Ellison, Harlan. "The Goddess in the Ice." In his Stalking the Nightmare, p. 319-324. Phantasia Pr., 1982.

Ellison strikes again. Three men, Scotti, Kirth, and Rennels, are "somewhere near the top of the world," climbing a glacier. They come upon an inexplicable object, a woman frozen in a block of ice. Rennels, with his degree in archaeology, recognizes her dress as Phoenician. The woman is incredibly beautiful, with a body that "would have made Helen of Troy jealous."

The men prepare to spend the night in a cave after chopping a portable chunk of ice encasing the woman from the block. The night does not go well. The woman in the ice exercises a strange power over the men, drawing each of them into a psychic union with her. And a sweet union it is, so desirable that it drives the men to a homicidal fury against one another. Fortunately for the woman in the ice, Rennels walks away from the carnage with an ice pick in hand, and she walks away into the stormy mountain night to "complete her destiny." "And there was no man born of man-and-woman who could say no to the terrors and passions of her body." Best not ask what happens to Rennels.

516. _____. "Tiny Ally." Ibid., p. 313-317. First published in Saturn Science Fiction and Fantasy (October 1957).

A mountaineering tale that few but Ellison would have imagined, and that fewer still would have had the nerve to write. An expedition of climbers is a few hundred yards short of the 18,000 foot mark on Mt. Annapurna, following in the tracks of the French group that reached the summit of one of the highest mountains on earth. Here the party makes a wonderful discovery, "a miniscule climber ... no more than three inches high, with a tightly-belted anorak jacket, a pike, tiny crampons, and a face quite red from exertion."

This little fellow also has a knife in his back. A very small knife. One of the party makes a reckless move toward the little man, and both go over the edge of a precipice for a very long fall. The remaining members of the party, shaken by death and weirdness, push on; at 18,000 feet they find the little man's origin, one as astounding as he was himself. A violent scene ensues, with death its end, but it would have been worse without the warning presence of the little man, "that tiniest of allies."

517. Ferber, Edna. "Ain't Nature Wonderful!" In her Gigolo, p. 188-221. Doubleday, 1922.

Florian Sykes has never seen a mountain. To him, the West is New York City's Eighth Avenue. At a tad over five feet, Florian does not appear the popular he-man sort, but neither stature nor experience stands in the way of his passing himself off as an expert

outdoorsman to the clientele of the department store where he reigns
as manager of the sporting goods department.

Florian's claims about his mountaineering exploits lead him into
a trap: he must accompany his boss's daughter and others on an
expedition to the Rockies for "three weeks of torture" on the climbing trails, capped by Florian's inconceivably inept act of getting
lost.

Back in New York, blessedly relieved of the obligation to live
out the mountaineer's life that he has so long claimed as his own,
Florian faces the future free of his fixation on false fronts.

518.   Helprin, Mark. "The Schreuderspitze." New Yorker 52
        (Jan. 10, 1977): 26-39. Also in Best American Short Stories,
        1978. Edited by Ted Solotaroff and Shannon Ravenal.
        Houghton-Mifflin, 1978.
        Wallich, a Munich photographer, has been devastated by the
deaths of his wife and son in a car crash. He travels to an obscure
mountain town hoping to collect himself. He tells the railway ticket
agent that he is going mountain climbing, though he has never
climbed before. Lodged in his hotel, he exercises intensively and
studies texts on mountain climbing, his seemingly casual fib to the
agent transformed into an obsession. As he prepares himself for
his mountain ascent, he begins a series of revealing dreams about
his dead family.

This is a strong psychological tale in which the author expertly blends details of mountain climbing.

519.   Salter, James. Solo Faces. Little, Brown, 1979. 220 p.
        This red-blooded (a little too red-blooded) novel opens on the
high roof of a church, where Vernon Rand saves a co-worker's life.
Rand is at his best in high places, and so is the book. Several
climbing passages read with the flavor of authenticity. Aside from
the mountainside action, the story offers a tale of macho friendship
between Rand and Jack Cabot, and a chronicle of Rand's relationships with women. The women here are dull, and Salter writes
them with arty seriousness. One of them "wanted to be happy but
could not be, it deprived her of her persona...." Heavens. When
life off the cliff doesn't parody an Ingmar Bergman movie sired by a
Hemingway reject, it gets into high-gear hard-guy scenery. The na-
dir comes near the end, when Rand and Cabot stage a Russian rou-
lette caper. Presented as high drama, this passage is ridiculous.
Even more laughable is the "legendary" status ascribed to Rand in
the conclusion, when he becomes a total isolate, wandering the western mountains, gaunt, mysterious, unheard from.

Some good climbing here, though.

520.   Sandberg, Peter L. "Calloway's Climb." Best American Short
        Stories, 1974, p. 217-243. Edited by Martha Foley. Houghton-
        Mifflin, 1974.
        Nils Johnson senses his marriage falling to pieces as he, his
wife Elizabeth, and a young stranger named Calloway are trying to

make a mountainside rescue. Understated parallels between the
climbing of the rocky wall and the negotiation of a crumbling marriage make this an interesting story, and the details of climbing are
plentiful.

521. Sturgeon, Theodore. "Suicide." In his Sturgeon Is Alive
      and Well ... A Collection of Short Stories, p. 212-221. Put-
      nam, 1971.
      A one-character story in which the one character, Boyle, finds
fate (chance, or something more sensible?) intervening between him
and his intended destination. When the story begins, he has already stepped off the side of a mountain, under the influence of
marital and career sorrows. His "whole life" does not pass before
his eyes on the way down, but he does see through certain personal phenomena with a clarity never-before known.
      Rather than plummeting to his death, Boyle hangs up on a bit
of rock. His suicide has been thwarted, and, when he recognizes
his second chance at life, the recognition comes as a sweet surprise.
The rest of the story describes his efforts to regain command of the
mountain, and control of his life. A nice piece of non-science fiction
by one of the SF genre's masters.

522. Ullman, James Ramsey. And Not to Yield. Doubleday, 1970.
      432 p.
      Eric Venn first learns of Dera Zor, an isolated mountain in the
Himalayas, when he comes across a description of it in a book in an
obscure corner of the University of Wahsington library. He is already past the novice stage in climbing, and Dera Zor soon displaces
Everest as the chief objective of his climbing life. Before he can attempt Dera Zor, WW II takes place, and Venn serves with the Army's
mountain troops. He performs with distinction on dangerous climbing
assignments.
      Following the war, Venn spends a long hiatus in Europe, climb-
ing, getting to know Paris, writing, and incurring the disfavor of
his brother, a successful businessman who thinks Venn is living the
bum's life, "chasing around after rainbows."
      While slowly preparing an assault on his nearly magic mountain
(the slowness is aggravated by months consumed in correspondence
with the government of Nepal), Venn works as a ski instructor.
Finally, in 1950, he and several companions approach the mountain.
The climb ends in tragedy, with the deaths of two of Venn's friends.
He blames himself, believing that it was his fixed, selfish desire on
the mountain that was responsible for the deaths. This is a fresh
layer of guilt to add to the one set down in Venn's adolescence,
when, as he led his eleven-year old sister on a climb, she disobeyed
his instructions and fell to her death.
      Venn finally climbs Dera Zor, but the nature of his success is
not what he had sought twenty years earlier. Ullman writes of
mountaineering with great authority, and of human relations with
something less, though he is earnest. And Not to Yield is, in spite
of some flaws (the chronological treatment is needlessly strained), a
generally interesting, involving novel.

523. _____. "An Easy Day for a Lady." In his Island of the Blue Macaws, and Sixteen Other Stories, p. 285-300. Lippincott, 1955. Also published as "The Deadly North Face." Saturday Evening Post 224 (Sept. 8, 1951): 35+.
    The American George Wilson returns to the Alps after WW II for the first time in fifteen years. With his former guide he climbs the same mountain the two of them climbed before the war. The guide, whose family suffered greatly in the war, now views the relatively untouched Wilson as a soft, happy, and contemptible American. Shared danger reaffirms their friendship.

524. _____. "The Mountains of the Axis." Saturday Evening Post 212 (Dec. 30, 1939): 10-11+. Also in the author's Island of the Blue Macaws, and Sixteen Other Stories. Lippincott, 1953.
    It is August, 1939. Anton and Rene, two Frenchmen, go mountain climbing in Switzerland. Two Germans are attacking the same mountain, but plan a gratuitously difficult ascent in honor of Hitler and the Fatherland. The story's chief point of action is a gripping rescue performed by the Germans on behalf of the French; the chief moral point is the rescuers' dedication to a self-destructive ideal.

525. _____. "Top Man." Saturday Evening Post 212 (Feb. 24, 1940): 14-15+. Also in the author's Island of the Blue Macaws, and Sixteen Other Stories. Lippincott, 1953.
    A group of climbers is making a difficult ascent of a previously unclimbed peak in the Himalayas. The two best climbers are a middle-aged Englishman and a young American. Their different styles and personalities are the fulcrum for the story's complications and its tragedy. Tension and suspense aplenty.

526. _____. The White Tower. Lippincott, 1945. 479 p.
    On the level of straightforward, observable reality, this novel is a success, sustaining considerable tension throughout. A very mixed group of a half-dozen climbers gather to see if they can overcome the Alpine mountain referred to in the book's title, one never climbed by the route they choose. Details of mountaineering are well-rendered as the climbers work their way up the peak, meeting a variety of hardships.
    On the level of social significance the novel is less persuasive, partly because it tries too hard to address "great issues." The effort for Great Significance is a minor fault. Ullman knows mountaineering so well that his descriptions of the sport may have seemed to him simply a matter of course, but they make the book.

527. West, Ray B. "The Ascent." Epoch 1 (Winter 1948): 78-87. Also in Prize Stories of 1948. Edited by Herschel Brickell. Doubleday, 1948.
    The "ascent" alluded to is not the routine climb in the Rockies taken on by a small party of amateurs, but the spiritual change undergone by one young woman in the group, who chooses to come

down from the peak alone, by a dangerous route. Her action at
first seems foolhardy, but it becomes evident that the risk was one
she had to take to affirm the strength of her will, if not her worth
as a person.

528. Bambara, Toni Cade. "Raymond's Run." In Ethnic American
      Short Stories, p. 25-34. Edited by K. D. Newman. Pocket
      Books, 1975. Also in the author's Gorilla, My Love. Random
      House, 1972.
          Hazel Elizabeth Deborah Parker, also known as "Squeaky," is
      the best runner in her New York City neighborhood, and proves it
      by winning a 50-yard dash. There is some good description here
      of a young girl's sense of freedom in running, but the story wins
      special merit because of the author's portrayal of Squeaky's relation-
      ship with her not-quite-mentally-right brother Raymond and her
      chief track competitor, Gretchen Lewis.

529. Bradbury, Ray. "The Anthem Sprinters." In The Stories of
      Ray Bradbury, p. 569-578. Knopf, 1983. First published in
      Playboy (June 1963).
          This whimsical tale provides a look at a curious form of com-
      petition that has become the abiding interest of the unemployed in
      Dublin. "Anthem sprinting" is a race to see who can bolt from a
      theater first in the brief interval between the end of a film and the
      house habit of playing the national anthem to close up the show.
      Told from the viewpoint of a visiting American, who enters the
      spirit of the locals so thoroughly that he, too, yields to the power-
      ful effects of an old Deanna Durbin film. Strictly Bradbury country,
      and quite amusing.

530. Brown, Barry S. "The Wheelchair Racers." Pulpsmith 5
      (Spring 1985): 116-126.
          Reminiscent of the gruesome climax of Todd Browning's film
      "Freaks," as well as of the retribution visited upon the villains in the
      EC Comics' horror issues of the early 1950s--but unfortunately lack-
      ing the moral underpinning that justified the consequences in either
      Browning's or EC's visions. Brown's story is one of mere absurd
      viciousness, and in that respect may be a perfect tale of the late
      20th century, when absurd viciousness seems to be a standard to
      which many aspire.
          The victim here is Alan, a dedicated jogger out for a three-
      mile run one evening at a local track. The run is going fairly well;
      the only oddity comes from a group of wheelchair racers across the
      track, who warm up by "calling each other every obscene name I
      had ever heard." Alan continues to run his laps in the gathering
      darkness; he passes the wheelchair racers several times, and wor-
      ries about what sort of attitude he should display. He doesn't

want to show them up by running at top speed, but doesn't want
to make them feel pitied by slowing down.
    His concerns are misplaced. He realizes this when he finds
his way down the track blocked by a phalanx of wheelchairs, and,
upon seeking an alternate route, finds that also blocked. The ending is melodramatic, but not inconsistent with the editorial ambitions
of a magazine in the pulp tradition.

531. Cheever, John. "O Youth and Beauty." New Yorker 29
      (Aug. 22, 1953): 20-25. Also in the author's Housebreaker
      of Shady Hill, and Other Stories. Harper & Bros., 1958.
    Cash Bentley, a balding former college track star, can bring
meaning to his life only by re-enacting his past hurdling triumphs
through vaulting furniture at suburban parties. Time insists on its
rights, however, and when Cash makes one too many party runs, he
falls and breaks his leg. He embarks on a pernicious depression,
seeing signs of his own physical decline in everything around him.
His brief resurgence following a last successful hurdling exhibition
comes to an explosive halt, thanks to his wife's dexterity with a
starting pistol.
    Cash Bentley, an utterly unappealing character, is the prime
example of the athlete who cannot surrender the past. The reader's
sympathies are with his wife, and when she solves her husband's
obsession, the reader's reaction is less shock than delight.

532. Corpora, James. "Tortoise and Hare." The Paris Review, no.
      63 (Fall 1975): 94-103.
    An enigmatic and somewhat confusing story, but one which
succeeds at creating an air of something very wrong in the main
character's life, wrong not only in the relatively brief span the
story consumes, but wrong fundamentally.
    La Palladio is out for his usual ten-mile jog by the river. A
lawyer in his early thirties, he has been training for some time, and
reached the ten-mile standard in a systematic fashion. His run, however, has become an ordeal, not a pleasure, thanks to a man in gray
sweat clothes who rows a scull along the river, racing La Palladio
both coming and going. "At first they had had a kind of friendly
rivalry ... but then the rivalry turned to contest, the contest to
struggle, and the struggle to a fight."
    As the fight between La Palladio and the man in the scull pro-
gresses, we see that in La Palladio's mind there is an ominous parallel between the sculler and La Palladio's father, who, we can guess,
is or has been involved in some very big-time crime. La Palladio is
haunted by his knowledge of his father's real occupation, and it may
be this knowledge that he is, in effect, trying to run away from
through his jogging.
    There is an interesting use of numbers in this story. Corpora
frequently notes the strides and oar strokes per minute of his characters, along with pulse rates. The effect is one of over-meticulous
concern with the peripheral, a habit common among those with no
real power to affect the fundamental. Thus, La Palladio cannot do

anything about his father, but he can keep track, pointlessly, of
his own pulse.

533.   Coxe, George H.   "See How They Run."   Saturday Evening
       Post 214 (Aug. 16, 1941): 22-23+.
       Another good father-son study.   Today's runners will find
this story, which employs the Boston Marathon as its centerpiece,
a good look at the sport long before marathons became almost as
common as track shoes.   Johnny Burke enters his first marathon,
continuing a tradition started by his father, who ran in the previous nineteen races.   Johnny initially considers the race a bit of a
joke, open as it is to all comers, but its running brings new understanding to him.   There is an especially good passage in which he
realizes the importance, whether they finish first or far back, of
the need the runners feel--as "all men of heart and spirit" feel--for
the "bit of acclaim" to be won through honorable participation in
the race.

534.   Dennison, George.   "Larbaud; A Tale of Pierrot."   In his
       Oilers & Sweepers, and Other Stories, p. 37-70.   Random
       House, 1979.
       Minot Larbaud, of a French industrial town, develops (or
discovers) an eccentric high-jumping style that brings him victory
in international competition.   He obliterates the previous world
record.   Public reaction to Minot's stupendous feat is at first exu-
berant, but soon turns sour and skeptical.   Minot is so downcast
by his foolish critics that he refuses to jump again and hides from
the public with a disguise and a new identity.   He eventually under-
goes a sort of metamorphosis, emerging from an intellectual cocoon
to become a highly-respected author on scientific topics.   "Larbaud"
is an elusive story that raises many questions; from an athletic point
of view, the public's rejection of Minot even in his triumph is a telling look at the stubborn hold our preconceptions exert on us.

535.   Farrell, James T.   "The Fastest Runner on Sixty-First Street."
       In his An American Dream Girl, p. 14-27.   Vanguard, 1950.
       Set in Chicago just after WW I, this story shows once more
Farrell's understanding of the effects of great social issues on those
who barely glimpse the meanings of those issues, yet who are caught
up in them and dashed about like so many leaves in a wind.   Morty
Aiken, a grammar school boy, is one of the fastest runners in South
Chicago.   He wins medals in playground tournaments, and has many
ambitions, not only regarding high school track meets, but also college and the Olympics.   His boyish dream is to become nothing less
than "the world's greatest runner."
       Morty's best friend is a tough, slow-witted Polish boy, Tony.
Tony salves the sting of the inevitable "polack" epithets by calling
those who trouble him "niggers."   When racial antagonisms in the city
turn to outright violence, Tony proves himself to his friends by beating
up black youths.   Morty has no real interest in this business, but because he is so fast he finds himself leading the hunts for Tony's next

victims. Morty chases them down in the city parks, and holds them
for Tony to pound.

In the summer of 1919, roaming bands of white thugs scout
the Chicago streets, looking for blacks to attack. Once again, Tony
enlists Morty to help him and his cronies chase down a victim.
Morty chases a black boy down an alley, well ahead of Tony and
crew. "Never had he run so swiftly." It is Morty's last run. When
his friends catch up to him, they find him dead in the alley, his
throat slashed. "And they stood in impotent rage around the bleeding, limp body of Morty Aiken, the fastest runner on Sixty-first
Street." Farrell's style is as flat as a dime run over by a locomo-
tive, as prosaic as a stop sign. He rarely produces a memorable
line or striking image, yet the cumulative weight of his work, informed by political understanding, human sympathy, and complete
sincerity, strikes much harder than its often humdrum vehicle would
suggest.

536.   Fessier, Michael. "That's What Happened to Me." Story 7
       (Nov. 1935): 54-60. Also in Stories for Men. Edited by
       Charles Grayson. Garden City, 1938.
       High school loser Bottles Barton, laughed at by his entire
class, tells us how he became the school hero through his astonishing prowess at the high jump. (In this respect, the story bears
an uncanny resemblance to item 534). It isn't long before we realize
that poor Bottles is spinning out a daydream, the daydream of a man
who has probably never enjoyed any real victory in his life. High
school engenders many fantasies of heroism; for most adults they recede into the unconscious. For Bottles, they are fresh as a cheer-
leader's cheeks. A sad story, but amusing in its way.

537.   Gilchrist, Ellen. "Revenge." Prairie Schooner 55 (Spring-
       Summer 1981): 36-50. Also in the author's In the Land of
       Dreamy Dreams. Univ. of Arkansas Pr., 1981.
       A ten-year old is the only girl among "a house full of cousins"
staying with her grandmother in the Mississippi Delta one summer
during WW II. Her older brother supervises construction of a broad
jumping and pole vault pit, and threatens the girl with abuse if she
gets in the way. One night she sneaks out to the pit, and after
several tries manages to clear the bar. "Sometimes I think whatever
has happened since," she says, "has been of no real interest to me."
Compare with Harlan Ellison's "The Cheese Stands Alone" (item 45),
another story of one outstanding achievement in childhood.

538.   Goodman, Paul. "A Cross-country Runner at Sixty-five."
       In his A Ceremonial; Stories, 1936-1940, p. 19-32. Black
       Sparrow Pr., 1978.
       Perry Westover, sixty-five years old, has signed up for his
forty-sixth annual participation in the Winchester Borough Cross-
country, a race he has won five times. His wife is embarrassed at
what the neighbors will say about Perry running when, according
to popular opinion, he should be settling down to senescence.

Perry's children share their mother's disdain for his dedication to
the run. When Perry claims that he runs to see and appreciate the
land, one son offers to give him a quick tour in his Stutz. He
would see so much more in such a shorter time!

Great speed does not, however, improve sight or understanding. The faster one goes, the less one knows. Perry's final argument on behalf of his running comes from his interpretation of a
biblical passage. This is an awkwardly written story with some very
stiff dialog, but Perry Westover and his ideas about the fit use of a
man's time make it worth reading.

539.   Goodwin, Stewart. "The Promise." Antioch Review 37 (Spring
       1979): 234-241.
       Is it a ghost story? An account of psychological overload
tailing into delusion or hallucination? In either case, it is a good
story.

Forty-year-old Jerry Rossman is preparing for his regular run
at the university athletic fields, a "six-mile ordeal" that he forces
himself through "to offset indulgences in his diet, his passion for
beer and cigars." This is only the second week that he has returned
to jogging after the death of his wife Kathy, some fifteen years his
junior. It had been her idea that he take up jogging, and they
routinely accompanied each other on this run. On one occasion she
made him promise that he would always run with her, "no matter
what happens."

All the promises between them appeared to be off upon Kathy's
death in a car accident. His friends' urging led Jerry to return to
the fields, where he might run off some of his sorrow. On this foggy
morning, he starts down the customary route. A good distance into
the run, he becomes annoyed when he sees another runner ahead of
him, breaking in on the peaceful setting. As he continues running,
several yards behind the fog-shrouded figure, Jerry sees that the
runner is a young woman who looks remarkably like Kathy. At first
he regards this as the effect of his grief; it leads him to impose his
dead wife's person on this innocent young girl.

As the course passes, however, and as Jerry reflects on his
earlier promise to Kathy about always running with her, the nature
of the phenomenon becomes more questionable, and a lot more disconcerting. There is enough ambiguity in the story to let the reader
reach his or her own conclusions; it recalls, in a way, some of the
supernatural tales of Hawthorne in its process of slow discovery and
the absence of a clear line between what is and what might be.

540.   Kram, Mark. Miles to Go. Morrow, 1982. 203 p.
       Given the ordinary diversity of jogging enthusiasts, is it very
strange that the three main runners of the 1983 Boston Marathon ex-
hibit 1) the perfect embodiment of communist high-tech athletic training; 2) Zen mysticism; 3) the all-American crack-up and subsequent
devotion to an essentially meaningless goal? The goal is to run the
Marathon in under two hours. American Roy Holt, trying to bounce
back from emotional trauma in the wake of defeat, has fixed on the

two-hour mark as something almost sacred. Pushing him are the
East German Franz Overbeck, precision-tuned to the maximum of
Marxist-Leninist skills, and the Japanese Kanji Sato, who has nearly
broken the two-hour marathon barrier himself. There are some sub-
sidiary matters here, but the novel's real meat is the run, whose intellectual and physical dimensions the author treats well.

541. Nelson, Kent. "Every Day a Promise." In his The Tennis
     Player, and Other Stories, p. 79-88. Univ. of Illinois Pr.,
     1977.
     McCallum Pillsbury, known as "Uncle Mac" to the small chil-
dren of Hillary, the woman he lives with, is close to a decade past
college, but longs for one last shot as a high-jumper in the Olympics. "Every day was a promise" for McCallum, a promise to do for
others something they wish. Even when he keeps the promises,
there is doubt about the sincerity of his actions; the one passion
that seems most true is open to question: his jumping itself seems
to hardly matter. There is "the notion that what he did was absurd." He wins his event in a meet, soaring over the bar, yet the
victory leaves him feeling empty.
     On his return to Hillary's house, he at first attempts a lie
about the meet, claiming that he lost. The lie dissolves, but the
reader senses that McCallum would have been more comfortable had
it held up. Like Nicky in the author's "The Tennis Player" (item
605), McCallum has neither faith in himself for what he does best,
nor any commitment to others save one of manners and superficiality.

542. Osborn, Carolyn. "Running Around America." Antioch Re-
     view 36 (Winter 1978): 9-20.
     "Every morning between seven-thirty and eight Martha Adams
pushes her front door open, hits the button on top of the stop
watch, and begins running a circular mile." This, the first sentence of the story, captures a good piece of its heart. There is
Martha's punctuality, her consistency (if not her rut), her ambition
to improve on past performance, and her direction, which brings
her right back to her point of origin.
     Martha is a scriptwriter for a PBS station in the Southwest.
She married a radio executive. The story tracks her through one
of her regular morning jogs around the neighborhood, and it's an
interesting trip. Martha doesn't spend much time thinking about
running while she is at it. Instead, she dwells on the residents of
her neighborhood, some whom she knows well, others whom she
identifies only by simple attributes, such as "The Man in the Red
Robe," "The Man with the Hat," and "The House of the Shouters."
Martha speculates on each in detail. She is a woman who pays attention to her surroundings.
     Whether she pays as much attention to herself is questionable.
She does not seem to recognize the existential absurdity of her daily
run against the clock. Although her reflections on her neighbors
and friends, and the State of the Union, show considerable seriousness, the real state of Martha herself eludes her.

543. Tabor, James. "The Runner." In Prize Stories, 1981: The
      O. Henry Awards, p. 52-58. Edited by William Abrahams.
      Doubleday, 1981.
      A horror story about the worst sort of horror, the kind men
make from natural ingredients. A runner jogging along a country
blacktop in Maryland has to contend with the occupants of a passing
Cadillac, who first throw a bottle at him, then try to hunt him down
with a shotgun. The central truth of this story turns up in the
early line about the runner, "An eternal innocent, he existed in a
state of near-constant amazement at the flaws in his universe."
Many quiet, solitary athletes--runners, bicyclists, hikers--will recognize their own fantasies in this violent story. First published in the
Washingtonian Magazine in 1979.

544. Tarnawsky, Yuriy. "The End." In his Meningitis, p. 134-
      141. Fiction Collective, 1978.
      A strong story of a man who almost literally runs himself to
death. On a Sunday in early summer, Jim Morrison and his girlfriend
go to an ocean beach on an island. After they establish themselves
at a spot on the long, nearly empty beach, Morrison, a runner, takes
his stopwatch to go off on a long run down the sand. On the way
back approximately an hour later, he wades out to a sand spit that
parallels the island. Here the running is very good, the sand hard-
packed by the ocean. Morrison notices that the spit does not per-
fectly parallel the island; as he runs, it veers off at a slight angle.
When the spit ends, without warning, Morrison is well over a hundred
yards from shore, too far to swim, and he realizes now, angry at
his stupidity, that the sand is hard-packed because the ocean covers
it at high tide. Morrison is in trouble, and when he doubles back
his problems do not recede.
      This story's plot is as simple as a bit of driftwood on the
sand, but it is a riveting piece, the more so the further it goes.
The author, born in the Ukraine and now a U.S. resident, employs
a microscopically-intense style, without a moment's relief; there is
not a single paragraph break in the length of the story. An eccentric style, certainly, but one in perfect mesh with this story's subject.

545. Warren, Patricia N. The Front Runner. Morrow, 1974. 346 p.
      Warren succeeds against heavy odds in this novel. She tells
her story from the point of view of a male track coach approaching
middle age; if that isn't enough of a challenge for her, the story's
theme of a gay love affair between the coach and one of his runners
should be. Warren pulls it off with well-drawn characters, a good
sense of history, adequate dialog, good pacing, and a conclusion
that, in an age of the ready assassination for absurd reasons, escapes melodrama and produces real dramatic effects.
      Harlan Brown is a politically conservative former Marine who
builds an outstanding career as a track coach. Along the way, he
slowly recognizes his homosexuality. When an unfounded rumor about
his involvement with a male student forces him to resign from his job

at Penn state, his life takes a temporary nose dive. His wife di-
vorces him, and he feels compelled to work as a hustler, in large
part to make an outsize alimony payment. As his understanding of
his own sexuality grows, his political ideas change. When New
York's gay community turns against police harassment in the Stone-
wall riots of June, 1969, Brown is on the scene, throwing rocks
and being trampled by a policeman's horse.

   A small, liberal college hires Brown, and he buries his feelings
in four years of hard work as track coach. These feelings come
back to the top when he admits to his team three young men kicked
out of another school's program for their homosexuality. Of the
three, Brown is immediately overwhelmed by 22-year old Billy Sive,
a "front runner" who likes to lead all the way in his races. Inevitably, Brown and Billy consummate their mutual attraction. Their
forbidden relationship becomes grist for the rumor mills and finally
reaches the mass media. At this point the nation's amateur athletic
governing bodies do their best to deny Billy opportunities for
further competition. Billy reaches the Montreal Olympics in spite of
these efforts; he turns in a superb showing until a man with a gun
cuts it short in the belief that he is doing God's will.

   An interesting novel written with good faith and feeling.
Warren, who has written for running magazines, knows the sport and
portrays it effectively; she also knows some of the complexities in the
hearts of men, and treats them well, too.

546. Weeks, Carl. "The Gemini Run." Carolina Quarterly 29 (Fall
      1977): 76-88.
   Identical twins, Jason (Jake) McAllister and his brother David,
have been living a life of almost completely mirrored behavior. Both
are swimmers, and have worked out a precision diving routine. The
focus of their differences rests on David's work to train himself to
match his brother's daily jogging distance. The middle of the story
contains David's dated journal of his struggle to equal Jason's performance. After a little more than a month, he makes the mark, and
then, instead of continuing to participate in David's adherence to
running, he plays tennis the day after his ten-mile achievement.
David is crushed and angered by Jason's refusal to make a permanent
commitment to their shared athletic pursuits, and goes off to sulk in
self-conscious loneliness. His snit turns suicidal when he climbs out
onto a diving board and threatens to launch himself into the
completely-drained pool below.

   This story takes turns being interesting and needlessly dense.
Several badly-done stream-of-consciousness passages succeed at little
but getting in the story's way. Plenty of arty ambiguity on hand,
though; more than enough to serve as a dubious model for Creative
Writing 101.

547. Adams, Glenda. "The Circle." In her <u>Lies and Stories</u>, p. 41-48. Inwood Pr., 1976.

An unnamed young woman joins her lover Pete and a number of others on a skiing outing. They stay in a small lodge in the mountains. Each day the woman sets out on her own, walking in a circle through the valleys and hills on her skis rather than joining the others in their downhill skiing. Pete cannot understand her refusal to join the group, and she makes no effort to explain. The story creates an effective mood with its combination of natural details (ice, snow, geographical distance) and the young woman's emotional state (removed, unassailable, chilly). Initially the reader may sympathize with her desire to go off on her own, but this sympathy grows steadily harder to support as her quest for isolation moves her to more extreme measures.

548. Banks, Russell. "The Defenseman." In his <u>Searching for Survivors</u>, p. 111-120. Fiction Collective, 1975.

A good story of a man's relationship with his past, held together by its description of his learning to skate as a child. The narrator's father was a tough, reckless defenseman in Canadian hockey. The narrator, who grew up in Canada and the northeastern U.S., became a defenseman like his father, a slow but determined skater, and willing to do anything to break up a rush. The story's main portion relates the events of the day when the narrator's father took him out to skate for the first time. It must be a common fantasy among children who first lace up a pair of skates that the moment they touch their blades to the ice they will fly, free of gravity. The real experience of the story's narrator is a lot harder, colder, and more embarrassing. Banks describes with exquisite fidelity to how it really is the novice skater's hapless combat with those thin, unforgiving blades and he shows the father's emotional support of his son in a moving, restrained way.

The story ends with the narrator, a man apparently well past his hockey days, going skating on a pond, alone; "...I am on the ice, moving across the pond's black surface like a man running slowly through a dream ... like a dancer sliding against the felt measures of time."

549. Broderick, Richard. "Brother Wolf." In his <u>Night Sale</u>, p. 125-135. New Rivers Pr., 1982.

A group of friends are on a camping and skiing trip in northern Minnesota. One of the party, Jack, is still tormenting himself

for his failure to properly assist his brother, who died as a result
of a canoeing accident in the area years earlier. Jack's brother
Phil always encouraged Jack to make the extra effort when they
stood on the brink of a dangerous act, and now, besides feeling at
least partly responsible for Phil's death, Jack is bereft of his
brother's reassuring presence.

On a sudden urge, Jack straps on his skis and follows the
tracks of a wolf that has wandered past the camp. He goes alone,
into the desolate night, following the wolf across a frozen lake.
Fears of becoming lost, of dying out on the ice, plague him, but
Jack shakes them off and pushes on to an eyeball-to-eyeball confrontation with the wolf. Neither one of them blinks; rather, their
brief meeting seems to embody a mutual insight. Back in camp,
Jack is exhausted, but his fear is gone. This is a story about
skiing, but it is ultimately about a man's effort to overcome his
self-doubt. The theme is well considered, and the passages in
which Jack pursues the wolf are exciting.

550.   Brodeur, Paul A. "The Spoiler." New Yorker 41 (Jan. 8,
       1966): 28-34. Also in the author's Downstream. Atheneum,
       1972.

Stephen Drew and his wife, in their mid-30s, have recently
lost their first child in a freak accident. This has made Stephen especially protective of their infant son, and it represents a major advance from fear when he is willing to let a babysitter tend the child
at a mountain chalet while he and his wife go skiing.

Fear reasserts itself in the forms of some shaggy-haired young
men who have apparently broken into the neighboring chalet, which
they use as a base for their irresponsible activities, including wild
skiing, drinking, and firing a rifle near the Drew's chalet. Unable
to tolerate the young men's behavior, afraid that they threaten his
child, Stephen confronts them violently.

The story's effectiveness is enhanced by Stephen's worrying,
early on, about how he has lost his youthful spontaneity and indifference to possible danger.

551.   Clayton, John Bell. "The Man Who Looked Like a Bird."
       In his Strangers Were There; Selected Stories, p. 107-110.
       Macmillan, 1957.

A beautiful little story about a timid, submissive man who
shows that he is made of far better stuff than anyone in his little
village of Cherry Glen thought. His name is Antietam Blankenship.
He is almost too afraid to cross the road from his house to the
Piggly Wiggly store. One day a freezing rain covers the town, and
the highway, with ice. To everyone's amusement, Antietam straps on
an old pair of skates. The reaction turns to amazement when Antietam streaks down the highway, pausing only to execute stunning
pirouettes and figures. After the show he steps into the Piggly
Wiggly to buy "a good nickel cigar." The once derisive crowd
"stood around him very respectfully. We felt crippled and earth-
bound."

552. Hall, Oakley. The Downhill Racers. Viking, 1963. 308 p.
Like The Pleasure Garden (see next item) this novel is at its
best when the principal characters are on the slopes. When they
sort out their problems anywhere else, especially when the problems
don't directly concern skiing, the novel drags. The plot follows
four skiers--Jack Roche, his friend and rival Chris Leavy, and two
women companions who are also in competition--through a season
from Europe to Stowe to Sun Valley to Aspen, skiing, talking about
skiing, getting hurt, fretting.
   The chief character of the lot is Jack Roche, who is full of a
need to defeat everyone in sight. In an early race, he surprises
himself by placing third, but there is no joy in it for him, "as there
would have been no joy for me," he informs us, "in a second." Accidents and tragedy are required for Roche to see through to the
root of his victory obsession, an insight that he must obtain to free
himself not only from the fear of defeat ("I don't have to beat everyone any more. It's like being out of jail.") but to free himself in
such a way that he will be able to ski his best, without a dark
tangle of mental busy-ness to hold him back.
   Hall does show us the downhill racer's life in a persuasive
fashion. It is easy to believe, for example, in one character's obvious relief at having broken an ankle, for that break frees her from
at least several months of emotionally intense competition, and also
means that she has met with an accident that has not killed or permanently maimed her. Too much of the novel, however, is devoted
to talk; talk that is too infrequently interesting to justify the space
it consumes: up to twenty pages at a stretch is dominated by
dialog. The reader who glides lightly over these passages in favor
of close attention to the skiing portions will not miss much.

553. _____. The Pleasure Garden. Viking, 1966. 377 p.
   Although set in a High Sierras resort, this novel's forays on
the slopes are only sporadic. Most of the important action takes
place indoors among a variety of lodge guests and employees, from
folk singer to ski patrol chief, who are gathering for the lodge's
anniversary. It is possible that the reader will find the characters'
self-consciousness and the author's seriousness compelling; it is also
possible that he or she will root for a major avalanche to catch the
lot of them navel-gazing around the lodge fire.

554. Hemingway, Ernest. "Cross-country Snow." In The Short
      Stories of Ernest Hemingway, p. 183-188. Scribner's, 1953.
      Also in the author's In Our Time. Scribner's, 1930.
   Nick and his friend George are skiing in Switzerland. When
they stop for wine at an inn, what seemed at first to be a purely
enjoyable outing proves to be something else, a taste of something
that cannot fit with the press of their responsibilities. The truest
line is Nick's, delivered when George wants to make a promise that
they will ski together again: "There isn't any good in promising."
In addition to Hemingway's skillful, economical psychological touch,
he provides some excellent skiing impressions here, too.

555. Nelson, Kent. "Incident in the High Country." North Ameri-
     can Review 259 (Fall 1974): 55-58. Also in the author's The
     Tennis Player, and Other Stories. Univ. of Illinis Pr., 1977.
     Thirty-year old McKay's private worries have driven him once
again to turn to his cousin Hildy as an antidote. Her good cheer
brings him out of his funks; on this weekend, he tags along with
Hildy and her boyfriend Leland as they ski cross-country up to a
remote mountain cottage.
     On the first day out they sight a red-suited figure far in the
distance, a lone man on snowshoes. The next day, they see him
again, and have the privilege of witnessing the man's suicide when
he leaps from a ledge to the snow-covered rocks far below. McKay,
driven by a feeling for the man whose devils were as vicious as his
own, strikes out to retrieve the body. His companions call him
crazy, and assure him that if he does not turn back, he will also
die in an approaching snowstorm.
     A striking story. Nelson's picture of the high mountain
country is fine and cold, the link between McKay and the suicide
is both strange and revealing, and the concluding paragraph closes
with a haunting, powerful image.

556. Rogers, Michael. "Skiing the Inkwells." In his Do Not Worry
     About the Bear; Stories, p. 61-73. Knopf, 1979.
     A young man and woman have left San Francisco behind for a
skiing trip in the mountains. He, a photographer, is eager to show
her a geological find from one of his earlier trips, the evidently
bottomless but very closely circumscribed pools called "inkwells."
She, a successful boutique operator, is paying for the trip with her
credit cards.
     The sun is hot on the skiers when the story begins. The
young woman removes her parka. It was a bad night; she told the
photographer that she had been seeing another man, her lawyer.
The photographer is upset. He likes things neat and orderly. They
eat a lunch on the trail, then press on to the inkwells, supposedly
a constant 38 degrees, according to the photographer. It isn't so.
When they reach the inkwells, they are beginning to freeze over.
His expectations smashed, the photographer breaks up the ice on the
inkwells, and in the process ruins his ski poles.
     The skiing passages in this story are passably done, the ideas
are fairly interesting, but the characters are too banal to help the
story mean as much as it might have.

557. Schmidt, Carl F. "Ancestral Voices." Story 4 (1953); 47-58.
     Henry Wagner, a former member of the U.S. occupation forces
in Germany, recalls the time five years ago when a German ski instructor taught him the sport. The German, Lothar, congratulated
Henry on his brave attack of the slopes, and compared skiing to music. The two went skiing extensively, and at one point drank to
their brotherhood. Beneath the friendship ran an ominous undertone
of Lothar's resentment over Germany's defeat. He berates the Bava-
rians for their alleged softness, claiming that they need to be

"strengthened by strong men." He confided in Henry that he was
writing a musical piece to tell the tale of the defeated Germany's
suffering.

Now, five years after these events, Henry is back in Germany
on business, and slips in some skiing on the side. A newspaper
notice alerts him to the first performance of Lothar's concerto, and
Henry attends the concert. It proves to be a ringing musical docu-
ment of martial ambition, and ties Henry's stomach in knots. Beneath the brotherhood, beyond the shared pleasure in a graceful
sport, lies the sick desire to defeat one's neighbors, not in a harmless athletic competition, but in blood.

558.   Shaw, Irwin. "The Inhabitants of Venus." Saturday Evening
       Post 236 (Jan. 26, 1963): 44-51. Also in the author's Short
       Stories; Five Decades. Delacorte, 1978.
Not long after WW II, a large group of Germans behave dis-
tastefully at a Swiss ski resort. Paris-born Robert Rosenthal, now
an American citizen, feels obligated to physically chastise a German
who has been making crude remarks about the American women
present. The German proves to be the same one who, having discovered Robert injured on a slope in 1938, stole his skis and left
him to die because he was Jewish. Robert plans to kill the German,
but his essential humanity will not allow him. A good story of both
skiing and moral conflict.

559.   _____. The Top of the Hill. Delacorte, 1979. 346 p.
Overprotected to the point of neurosis as a boy by his widowed
mother, Michael Starr as a man feels compelled to assert himself
physically in dangerous, even life-threatening pursuits. On his
honeymoon with his wife Tracy, he hurts himself skiing by taking
foolish chances in a downhill race. He spends his weekends sky-
diving, against Tracy's wishes. Soon after the wedding, he enters
on affairs with other women and finds his memory failing in his work
as a New York business consultant. The marriage falls apart, with
Tracy convinced that Michael's commitment to dangerous sports, or
to making ordinarily safe sports dangerous with his recklessness,
proves that he wants to die.

Separated, near divorce, Michael spends ten days in a hospital
after a savage beating in a bar. In the hospital he decides to quit
his job and New York to head for the hills of Vermont, where he
once spent a short but satisfying stretch as a ski instructor. Returning to the same locale, he promptly engages in an affair with
Eva Heggener, a married hotel keeper, goes hang gliding in the
mountains, and resumes his ski instruction.

And he salvages himself. He cuts off the affair when he meets
Eva's husband Andreas, a man in his early fifties reportedly suffering incurable tuberculosis. Michael grows very fond of Andreas,
and oversees the older man's return to health by encouraging him to
pick up his skis and set out on the hills once again. In the end,
Michael has made a new pact with life; no longer, it seems, will he
feel obligated to risk his life to justify it. Good characters, es-

pecially Michael and Andreas, along with effective skiing passages, make this a readable, enjoyable novel.

560. Thompson, Willa. Garden Without Flowers. Beacon, 1957.
      186 p.
      Helen Duvier, a New Englander steeped in traditions of Puritanical virtue, has been sent to Switzerland on a skiing vacation by her husband. He hopes that this respite in the Alps will relieve her of her desire to end their decade-long marriage by divorce.
      To say that this scheme goes badly understates it by several degrees. Helen continues to want a divorce, and begins an affair with a Swiss skier. From this point, things go badly rapidly. Helen finds a tree in her path on a slope, and receives the worse end of the collision when she runs into it. Her Swiss lover brings her flowers in the hospital, but flowers do not suffice to forestall an encroaching madness. By the time Helen "sees" evil little creatures running about her bed, the end is in sight, and when last we see her, she appears to be preparing for suicide.
      The divorce-scandal aspect of the novel is badly dated, but much of the action takes place on the ski hills, and the outside air is clearly felt. A cheerless but artful novel recommended for ski and sanitarium fans.

561. Updike, John. "Man and Daughter in the Cold." New Yorker 44 (March 9, 1968): 34-36+. Also in the author's Museums and Women, and Other Stories. Knopf, 1972.
      A man and his early adolescent daughter ski down a mountain on a painfully cold day. During the outing, the man sees the promise of the future in the girl, and later sees in her something joyous, "a pageant that would leave him behind." The reader nearly shivers with Updike's description of the mountain cold, and feels touched in a spot that hurts by this glimpse into a good father-daughter relationship.

562. Williams, Thomas. "The Skier's Progress." New Yorker 38 (Feb. 2, 1963): 34-40+. Also in the author's A High New House. Dial Pr., 1963.
      A long domestic drama set against the slopes of a New England ski resort, starring Japhet Villard, his daughter Margaret, his grandson Billy, Margaret's ex-husband Herbert, and ski instructor Bucky. The story presents alternating focuses on the thoughts of all these characters. Japhet, whose idea of himself has been that of "a clean, brave man" conquering a mountainside, has been reduced by the pain following a prostatectomy to an undignified reliance on painkillers and enforced indolence. Bucky, a brilliant skier, is edging into an uncomfortable middle age full of doubt about his own real value. Margaret must contend with Herbert's desire to return to her for safekeeping; he is so insecure that a ride in a ski-lift leaves him petrified with fright. Billy tolerates his mother's athletic prowess, and daydreams about being marooned in the mountains with a beautiful classmate.

An effective study whose only sense of freedom and space lies in the snow and the mountains to which the principals bring their hemmed-in concerns.

563. Caldwell, Erskine. "Vick Shore and the Good of the Game."
      In his Erskine Caldwell's Gulf Coast Stories, p. 23-31.
      Heinemann, 1957.
      Vick Shore, small-town barber, is also the local baseball um-
pire. He is known for his willingness to put up with any amount
of abuse from players, "for the good of the game." He never ejects
a player. Vick's patience meets its ultimate test when he presides
over a game between two women's softball teams; it appears to him
that one team's eagerness to win takes precedence over a concern
"for the good of the game." Feminists probably won't like this story,
but Caldwell's larger point (aside from the different approaches of
men and women to sports), about the nature of rules disputes within
the context of the game, is still worth considering, and Vick Shore's
reaction to the crisis on the softball diamond is undeniably original.

564. Cooney, Ellen. All the Way Home. Putnam, 1984. 207 p.
      The intimate feeling among a group of women gives this novel
a warmth and depth of a kind absent from most works of sports fiction. Set in a small New England town, the story details the uniting
of these women, young, middle-aged and beyond, into a softball
team, the Larkspurs. They come together under the guidance of
Gussie Cabrini, a former professional softballer who shattered a leg
in a motorcycle accident. The team coalesces in spite of the town's
skepticism. Gussie, an ordinarily laconic woman, fell in love with
softball as a child, and in a speech two-thirds of the way through
the book she talks of softball, but also of much more: "All I can
say for sure is that it feels good when you play it, and it feels good
when you watch it, and it feels good when you think about it. With
softball, see, it's all in the team. It's all in the idea of a team."
      The book's crisis is a concluding game between the Spurs and
their main rivals, the Belles, a telephone company team. It is a
good book for softball buffs, for women who want to see women
treated well in an athletic context, and for men who would like to
obtain a better understanding of the way women work together at
their best.

565. Keillor, Garrison. "Attitude." New Yorker 55 (Aug. 27,
      1979): 34-35+. Also in the author's Happy to Be Here.
      G. K. Hall, 1983.
      Keillor laments the absence of a winning attitude on a certain
softball team. Why, the batter who struck out to end the game actually lay in the dirt and laughed! He then offers some pointers

on techniques of proper attitude. These entail such elements of
form as assuming one's stance, spitting, involvement with dirt, conduct after committing an error, etc. More an essay than a story,
but included here because it's too funny to leave out.

566. _____. "How Are the Legs, Sam?" In his Happy to Be
Here, p. 129-135. G. K. Hall, 1983.
It is always said that for an athlete "the legs are the first to
go," and this story of an old softballer recalling both his failures
and his glory--a great running catch in center field in a pick-up
game--shows how they go. The final claim here about being "in
fine shape in the spring" is empty self-delusion. More melancholy
than Keillor usually is, but any aging weekend athlete will feel
some sharp sympathy pains.

567. Lorenz, Tom. Guys Like Us. Viking, 1980. 255 p.
This is both a funny and sad book about a man who cannot
grow up. At thirty, Buddy Barnes is bright enough, but whatever
sense he has is submerged in a character of confusion, indecision,
impulsiveness, and impatience. His one source of joy is his position
as left fielder for the Sticks, a Chicago softball team. His marriage,
however, is disintegrating, he's in debt to a bookie, and when the
book opens he has lost his job with the parks department for jumping into a tree from his mower. Fed up with Buddy's oblivious and
infantile behavior, his wife Jo drives him from their apartment and
throws all his possessions out after him. Buddy hooks on for a
losers' tour with his old ballmate Herman Glick, a man nearly as
worthless as Buddy; together, they pursue the city softball championship.
Lorenz mixes a superior comic sense--there are some very
funny passages in the novel--with a notably warm feeling for his
characters. He likes them, no matter how feckless they are. He
also turns out some excellent, tight lines, such as this one, describing Herman's and Buddy's life minus their wives: "They were
squires of leisure, gents of ease."

568. Sayles, John. Pride of the Bimbos. Little, Brown, 1975.
258 p.
The Brooklyn Bimbos are a five-man softball team affiliated
with a carnival. Sayles follows them on their circuit of the South,
and involves the reader with a spectrum of freaks, losers, dreamers,
and drunks. Pogo Burns, a midget shortstop for the Bimbos, is a
former detective now being trailed by Dred, a pimp who bears Pogo
a lethal grudge. The story bounces from Dred to Pogo to Pogo's
protege, young Denzel; the themes turn on matters of self-respect,
integrity, and facing the truth.
The novel sometimes slips into inessential diversions from the
main story, such as one relating some team members' trip to a diner
whose menu includes something called "hambuggers," along with
"sordid beverages" (Sayles uses local dialect with unusually good
results). Another runs a witty diatribe against the crassly goofy

ads in low-rent "men's" magazines. These stretches are fun, however, and the reader hardly cares that they do not move the story
along. Some sections at first do not seem to mesh with the story's
main gears, but prove in the end more integral than they looked.
In one of these, Dred searches through "Spook Hollow," a black
ghost town, trying to find a lead on Pogo Burns; it's an eerie passage, followed by a confrontation with an old black go-fer named
Bugbear, who pierces Dred's supercool pose with some telling
criticism.

Sayles is a writer of feeling; his heart is in the job whether
he's describing a boy's attempt to join a pick-up baseball game, or
a carnival stripper's reflections on her grocery shopping list as she
does a mechanical bump & grind to a sleazy version of "Night
Train." It is this caring, his compassion for ordinary people, even
for low-lifers, that makes Sayles worth reading. Couple his caring
with his sense of humor (Dred's giggling epiphany as he creeps up
on the carny, hurt, pig-bit, burned, one shoe gone, to be greeted
by a monkey in a safari jacket and two-tone shoes, is a wonderful
piece of comic prose), and you have a writer able to pull his readers
up and down the emotional route with great dexterity.

569. Weaver, Gordon. "Gold Moments and Victory Beer." Decem-
     ber 9 (no. 2-3, 1967): 47-55. Also in the author's Such
     Waltzing Was Not Easy; Stories. Univ. of Illinois Pr., 1975.
     George Thibault, known to his fast-pitch softball mates as
"Ter-bow," is a man of few evident accomplishments. He can't hold
a regular job; his last employed stint, as an encyclopedia salesman,
came to an end when the company canned him. George has one
sphere of prominence, that of the softball field. Though he is slow,
he is a dangerous hitter and a good thrower. He likes to savor the
memorable moments of his playing, and likes to share a few beers
with his teammates at a local bar after a win.

This may not be the perfect life, but it will do, until a man
named Smitty shows up to puncture some illusions. Smitty is a
fairly no-account man, and admits it; he gets his truth-tipped
needle out when the team pitcher starts whining about having wasted
his "million dollar arm" on amateur games. He accurately characterizes two of George's teammates as bullies. After Smitty risks a beating for the sake of his vision of the truth, which includes deriding
the entire puffed-up importance of the softballers' avocation, George
takes him across the street to buy him a drink in another bar, his
own estimation of the game's consequences seriously changed. Good
characters and an effective setting give this story its high marks.

570. West, Jessamyn. "Public Address System." Harper's 197
     (Oct. 1948): 93-102. Also in the author's Love, Death, and
     the Ladies' Drill Team. Harcourt, 1955.
     "Amplification--well, I don't know--it just seems to suit me,
somehow." Leonard Hobart, electronics technician turned softball
announcer, is ordinarily a quiet, private man. He becomes a force
of raw power when he covers the home team's games on the new P.A.

system. Dizzy with his amplified voice, Leonard develops a taste
for calling the play before it happens, and when reality fails to
blend with his prescriptions, he ignores the disparity, until he's
hustled off for some psychological tinkering. A story of pitiful
events in the life of a meek man for whom a dollop of power proved
not corrupting, but dementing. Still, the reader's feelings are with
Leonard. He called 'em as he thought they ought to be. One could
do worse. Compare with "The Perfect Garden" (item 153).

XV. SWIMMING AND BOATING

571. Charyn, Jerome. "Race Day at Hiawatha." In his The Man
     Who Grew Younger, and Other Stories, p. 159-175. Harper
     & Row, 1967.
     The time is shortly before the end of WW II, the place is a
summer camp. Two competing groups of campers, carrying on a
long tradition, are about to engage in their annual canoe race. The
outcome looks predictable: for seventeen straight years the Mac-
cabees have defeated the Hiawathans. They have the better canoe
and the better team. What they lack this year is a dirty trickster.
Hiawathan Ascher conducts a nocturnal sabotage mission on the
Maccabee's craft; when he returns to his bunk, he leaves behind
some carefully-drilled holes, concealed with packed mud, that nearly
penetrate the hull of the enemy canoe. In the next day's race
water pressure will do the rest of the job.
     Even subterfuge almost leaves the Hiawathans in the wake:
not until their rowers completely strip on the way across the lake
do they lighten their own canoe enough to overtake the foundering
opposition. A well-wrought story of summer camp and adolescent
antagonism, complete with the inevitable strongarm counselor unaf-
fectionately known as "The Destroyer."

572. Cheever, John. "The Swimmer." New Yorker 40 (July 18,
     1964): 28-34. Also in The Stories of John Cheever. Knopf,
     1978.
     Another Cheever excursion in suburban affluence, with the
expected dark currents tapped. Neddy Merrill, a slender, athletic
man of middle age, decides to swim home from a party, a distance
of several miles, by using the various private and public pools that
more or less form a waterway to his own house. He undertakes this
feat with the idea that it will make him "a legendary figure." The
swim becomes progressively more surreal, and Merrill is reminded
that his life is not in good shape. Stories of his family and money
troubles come to him from the acquaintances whose pools he crosses.
The concluding image, with Merrill pounding on the door of his
locked, empty house, is frightening and well-planned. Burt Lan-
caster starred in a good 1968 film adaptation, with the same title,
directed by Frank Perry.

573. Choy, Wayson S. "The Sound of Waves." Prism 2 (Summer
     1961): 4-16. Also in Best American Short Stories, 1962.
     Edited by Martha Foley and David Burnett. Houghton-
     Mifflin, 1962.

On a warm spring Sunday, two boys debate the possibility
of swimming a wild river. The older, seventeen-year old Bob,
thinks he can make it. His fourteen-year old best friend thinks
Bob is crazy to try. The reader expects Bob to make the effort;
his history, as recounted here, is full of crazy tries. What the
reader may not expect is the story's bleak conclusion, but reflec-
tion suggests that this conclusion had to be. A good picture of
adolescent friendship and loneliness, with some effective swimming
passages.

574.   Colwin, Laurie. "Wet." In <u>Bitches & Sad Ladies</u>, p. 283-
       290. Edited by Pat Rotter. Harper's Magazine Pr., 1975.
       Also in the author's <u>Passion and Affect</u>. Viking, 1974.
       Lucy Wilmott, a swimmer since her early childhood, continues
to swim daily, and alone, after her marriage. When her husband
Carl learns from a friend that Lucy has been swimming every day
throughout the Chicago winter (she uses a university pool), he is
shocked; he cannot understand why she has kept this fact a
"secret" from him. An interesting portrait of a woman's maintenance
of her own private self in an innocent, uncalculating way, and of
her husband's difficulty in accepting that "Every day of her life,
she would be ... for one solid time every day, as long as she lived,
wet."

575.   Creal, Margaret. "Inland Beach." In her <u>The Man Who Sold
       Prayers</u>, p. 102-115. Harper & Row, 1981.
       A day of swimming at an inland ocean beach turns into a fight
for survival, then a revelation of at least a portion of life's meaning.
Monica has cautioned her nine-year-old son Ben to avoid the water's
deeper places, where powerful outgoing currents run beneath a de-
ceptively tranquil surface. Monica looks up from shell-gathering to
see that Ben has strayed out, and though not far, still farther than
he should. She calls for him to come back, but he cannot: the
current has seized him, and the best that he can do is to maintain
his place.
       There follows a rescue effort by Monica that may make the
reader's mouth go dry with apprehension. Back on the beach after
an ordeal that sees her look forward almost with desire to drowning,
Monica realizes "How little it takes to satisfy us ... life itself is
enough."
       A thoughtful, nicely-written piece. Some readers will find it
especially appealing for the author's notions of the sympathy between
women and the feminine understanding of life and death.

576.   Drake, Carlos C. "Last Dive." <u>Transatlantic Review</u> 2 (no.
       1, 1924): 60-63. Also in <u>Best Short Stories of 1924</u>. Edited
       by Edward J. O'Brien. Small, Maynard, 1924.
       In what is closer to a vignette than a story, Drake reveals
the critical moment at which a high-diver, "the greatest diver in the
world," first has second thoughts about his pursuit. Clearly, as he
emerges from the water with his face "positively green," he will
never again know his previous confidence.

577. Eaton, Charles E. "The Naked Swimmer." Southwest Review
      61 (Summer 1976): 280-294.
      On the place of a kidney-shaped swimming pool in a marriage
in decline, and in the ultimate reversal of that decline. Elaine
Morrison and her husband Gus, a lawyer, are a New England couple
who started with very little, but who now employ yardmen. Earlier
in their marriage Elaine blew an inheritance on construction of the
pool, and, although it never met the promise of its glorious first
spring and summer, "she would always say that the pool gave her
the best ten years of her life," seeing her through a variety of
crises.
      On her fifty-second birthday, Elaine announces to Gus that
she wants to "redo" the pool, call in the excavators and enlarge it.
This ambition is one manifestation of her restiveness and marital
torpor; her reliance on sedatives and amphetamines is another.
Husband Gus's plan to restore Elaine's zip involves the rented services of a comely youth whom Elaine will discover in a nude night
swim. The plan works, it seems, though one wonders why. There
is plenty of fodder for analysis (what, e.g., is the significance of
the couple's preferred nude swimming in their materialistic surroundings?) and debate about male-female roles, though a little less
emphasis on intellectualism would have made the story better.

578. Fitzgerald, F. Scott. "The Swimmers." Saturday Evening
      Post 202 (Oct. 19, 1929): 12-13+. Also in Bits of Paradise.
      Edited by Matthew J. Bruccoli. Scribner's, 1974.
      Henry Marston, an American of 35, is an officer of a Paris
bank. He arrives home unexpectedly one afternoon to find his wife
Choupette in a compromising situation. Henry succumbs to an attack
of the vapors upon his discovery, and, on his release from the hospital, goes with his wife to the beach for restorative recreation.
Henry cannot swim, but gamely throws himself into the water to
"rescue" a young American overcome by cramps brought on by a
surfeit of ice cream. Henry himself must be pulled from the deep.
In appreciation of his selflessness, the American girl teaches Henry
to swim. His newfound aquatic ability serves him well when he, his
wife, and her lover are adrift in a boat, with Choupette and her
lover about to carry out a nasty plot against Henry.
      Far from a great story, and marred by a final section that
hangs out the end like a flagged length of two-by-four from a pick-
up truck, yet it is amusing to see Fitzgerald publishing a story in
October, 1929, in which he, through Henry, opines with great optimism about the immediate future of the United States.

579. Gold, Herbert. "Susanna at the Beach." Atlantic 193 (May
      1954): 48-51.
      The setting is a beach, where an adolescent girl practices
diving "from the end of a breakwater into the oily, brackish waste-
ridden substance of Lake Erie at Cleveland, Ohio." The girl dives
time after time, concentrating on her form, oblivious to others on
the beach. They, however, are transfixed by her: young men, old

men, old women, young women, all fix their attention on the diver
with a singular interest. Lurking beneath their attention is an ero-
tic craving, but one a long way from good, healthy lust. It is,
rather, one situated in frustration, in lechery, in a squalid hank-
ering after the unobtainable. When the girl's suit begins to rip,
the beachgoers all gather nearby in a silent, if heavy-breathing,
vigil, anticipating the black suit's disintegration. The girl goes on
diving, her mind entirely devoted to the perfection of her art, to
"a deep communion with belly-smash on the shore of Lake Erie at
Cleveland."
　　The story achieves an unpleasantly crawling sensation rather
like that produced by the "organisms" said to populate the filthy
lake water. An enigmatic yet provocative ending gives further
point to the tale.

580.　Helprin, Mark. "Palais de Justice." In his Ellis Island, &
　　　Other Stories. Delacorte, 1981.
　　　　An outstanding story of courage, perseverance, and character. An elderly attorney who has, over a half century, spent a
great deal of time in rowing shells on Boston's Charles River, heads
for his favorite sport again one impossibly hot summer day. He
finds the river all but deserted in the heat; his only company on
the water is a young and extremely unpleasant man in a new, lightweight shell. Tradition calls for a race between the two. In spite
of the heat and the obvious physical superiority of the younger man,
the attorney turns to the task. The story carefully examines his
thoughts and tactics as he works to win what, on its face, is an absurd match. The race, however, becomes something much more than
a contest of no particular point: through some expertly measured-
out glimpses of the attorney's past, it becomes a symbol of his
ability to endure emotional and physical pain and remain a decent,
honorable man.

581.　Keillor, Garrison. "Drowning 1954." In his Happy to Be
　　　Here, p. 294-300. G. K. Hall, 1983.
　　　　Following the 1954 drowning of his cousin, the narrator is en-
rolled in a YMCA swimming class conducted in the fascist style so
strangely cherished by so many swimming instructors. Fed up, the
boy plays hooky from the class. Guilt soon follows him everywhere.
He sees in the eyes of the town winos "a look of fellowship." Finally he teaches himself how to swim, and now, as he ponders "the
imperial swimming instructor[s] at the Y.M.C.A.--powerful people
who delight in towering over some little twerp"--he is filled with
certainty that all these tyrants will one day pay their just dues.
　　　　Anyone who as a seven- or eight-year-old endured swimming
lessons at a dark, cold, noisy public pool, presided over by an unforgiving Prussian with a whistle around his neck, will nod in approval all the way through this story.

582.　Kranes, David. "Diving Lesson." Western Humanities Review
　　　24 (Autumn 1970): 333-343. Also in the author's Hunters in

in the Snow; A Collection of Short Stories. Univ. of Utah
Pr., 1979.
     A father and his eleven-year old son drive out to a nearly
deserted Atlantic Ocean beach one evening. They are going not
only for a swim, but also for an opportunity to live together in a
world of their own, a private place apart from the rest of the
family. They race to a raft about sixty yards from shore, and
there the man instructs the boy in diving. All goes well until, in
a moment of separation and confusion, the boy jumps to the conclusion that his father is drowning. Frantic, he swims to the bottom
himself; by the time his father realizes what is happening, the boy
has nearly drowned.
     The story shows an unusually close father-son relationship
effectively; the boy is learning far more than how to dive off a raft,
or even how to come back from a near-disaster without letting its
memory intimidate him.

583. Levin, Jenifer. Water Dancer. Poseidon Pr., 1982. 368 p.
     David "Sarge" Olssen is a master trainer of long-distance
championship swimmers. He is also responsible for his own son's
death, through a stupid refusal to allow the young man to abandon
an attempted swim in cold water. It was more than stupid: it was,
in every sense but the formal one, criminal.
     A young woman named Dorey Thomas comes to his swimming
camp and asks him to help her train for the same swim that killed
his son, 32 miles of cold, treacherous water off the Washington
coast. Dorey has a love affair with Olssen's wife, a former cliff
diver; Olssen also finds a romantic interest in her. The novel is
at its best by far when Dorey is in, or preparing for, the water;
much of the emotional baggage that litters the terrain could have
been omitted to the story's benefit. The last chapter, though,
which covers Dorey's successful swim of the San Antonio Strait in
just over 26 hours, is especially good.

584. Long, Robert E. "Champion." In Aphrodisiac; Fiction from
      Christopher Street, p. 271-282. Coward, McCann, & Geoghe-
      gan, 1980.
     Doug Farrier, a gifted swimmer, would rather turn his atten-
tion to art and music than follow his father's selfish plan to prepare
him for the Olympics. The conflict between Doug's inner drives and
his outward dedication looks as though it will be resolved through
the assistance of Jeb Nearbin, a motorcycle-riding free spirit. Nearbin represents both the escape from his father's compulsion for victory and the uncritical affection that Doug has never been granted
by the man. A good, simply-written story with a very well-conceived
conclusion.

585. Mountzoures, Harry. "Swimming Lessons." McCall's 107 (July
      1980): 112-113.
     A short short story that compresses some major topics into its
attenuated length. A father, Brian, is out at the apartment house

pool with his five-year-old son Chris. The two play in the pool,
and Brian watches while Chris holds on to the side and lets his
body float. In an unguarded moment, Chris goes under, and Brian
must haul him from the water. The incident haunts them both.
Chris refuses for a long time to go back into the water and Brian
has nightmares about watching the boy drown while he can do
nothing.

When a science show on television provokes Chris to ask some
big questions, his last is the biggest a five-year-old can ask: "When
am I going to die, Daddy?" The story has a happy ending, but it is
an honest and moving one. The author knows the minds of young
children: his portrayal of Chris is faultless.

586.   Poverman, C. E. "Sports Illustrated." In his The Black
        Velvet Girl, p. 182-192. Univ. of Iowa Pr., 1976.
A college swimming meet is the featured event in this story,
narrated by one of the competitors, a nineteen-year old boy who, it
seems, has at least as many problems as most boys his age in deciding what he wants or who he is. He is, among other things, already a good swimmer, with the potential for better. Yet his aptitude in the water does not fill him with delight; as he describes his
preparations for his race, he sounds detached, distant from himself.
He does well in the race, but feels no elation; on returning to his
dormitory, alone, he reacts more like a loser than one with valued
achievements within his grasp.

This is a troubling story of a boy's uncertainties about himself, his father, and women. It also gives a palpable sense of the
chlorinated, bleached, and watery atmosphere the swimmer occupies.

587.   Purdy, James. "The Lesson." Mademoiselle 56 (Nov. 1962):
        108-109+. Also in the author's Children Is All. New Direc-
        tions, 1962.
Mr. Diehl, the club's champion swimming instructor, has
scheduled a private beginner's lesson in the pool for the son of "The
Commander," the club's most influential member. Polly, an adolescent
whose grandmother owns the pool, has erroneously informed a woman
that she may use the pool at the same time as the Commander's son.
This leads to a strange and lengthy argument at poolside between
Polly and Diehl. Diehl points out to Polly that the woman has no
right to enter the pool at this time (she isn't even a club member);
Polly refuses to tell the woman that she must wait until the lesson is
over. The argument ends with Polly pushing Diehl into the pool,
then nearly drowning herself as the Commander's son looks on from
the shallow end.

The argument is not really about the question of the woman's
admission to the pool: it is about power and sex. Polly apparently
feels a strong attraction to the muscular, authoritarian Diehl; her
previous reaction to him reveals her consternation at his presence:
"She had always lowered her eyes when she met him in the hall,
avoiding the sight of his wet, dripping quality...." Her challenge
to Diehl's authority, capped by physical assault, constitutes both a
rebuke to Diehl and an attack on her own incomprehensible sexuality.

588. Rule, William. "Leo, The Christian Lifeguard." <u>Michigan</u>
      <u>Quarterly Review</u> 10 (Summer 1971): 200-206.
      On the conflict between rules and fun, between authority and
freedom, as acted out in yet another YMCA pool. "The pool was
where the dungeon should have been.... It was isolated, foreign,
magic, evil-smelling, appealing and repelling." A group of boys has
been hanging out at the pool for several years, long enough to make
the big cross-over from using the boys' locker room at the pool's
shallow end to the men's locker room at the deep end.
      The pool users have various specialties they perform in the
pool and locker area. Slippery Sid does a spectacular slide on the
seat of his trunks through the shower room, out the doorway, and
into the pool. Boom-Boom Paul, an older man, has perfected a mar-
velously loud sound effect produced with his hands in the water.
Everyone devises creative bouncing on the diving board. It is a
good place, touched with harmless, gentle anarchy.
      The fun stops when the new lifeguard comes on duty. Leo,
"the Christian lifeguard," approaches his task with the joyless and
rigid repressiveness that gives a bad name to good Christians. For
Leo, rules of YMCA pool conduct are sacred script, as requisite of
heed as the Ten Commandments. Slippery Sid's act gets shelved
when Leo invokes the Y's rule banning trunks; sliding across the
tiles on one's bare backside is too much even for Sid. The hi-jinks
on the diving board are also forbidden; from now on, only one
bounce per dive is allowed.
      The greatest obstacle to Leo's total control is Boom Boom Paul's
noisemaking. The fight is a protracted one that Leo cannot win
simply by citing Y regulations; he must learn to exceed Boom Boom's
own talent. "It was the end of an era. Leo had defeated us all ...
we filed out of the pool forever." And so the world of institutions
acts once again to crush spontaneity and innocence. A fine story.

XVI. TENNIS

589. Angell, Roger. "Tennis." New Yorker 26 (July 8, 1950):
      24-26.
      Angell gives away too much, too easily in this story's conclu-
sion, but it remains a fine study of restrained father-son conflict,
a man's struggle to stay young, and a boy's struggle to grow up.
Lifelong tennis games between father and son furnish the opportunities for glimpses into the dynamics of these subjects. Any father
and son who have pursued a competitive sport together will recognize aspects of their own experience in this story; the son's inability to play his best against his father is particularly well illustrated.

590. Barker, Robert. Love Forty. Lippincott, 1975. 216 p.
      "That old line runs around the world like the equator weaving
in and out of everybody, and in the end there they all are, the winners on one side and the losers on the other. That's what this
thing is all about, old buddy." So thinks tennis player Stephen
Mitchell after beating his opponent with a good shot in a practice
game. Mitchell, age forty, shares a problem common to many athletes, both professional and amateur: play without victory is no
fun. A stockbroker with no nest egg of his own, Mitchell has had
to play tennis in his off hours; though nationally ranked, his ranking has never been high enough for him to easily crack the top
tournaments. Still, he believes that he could have been better had
the necessity of earning a living not interfered with his athletic aspirations.
      The book spans just over a year in Mitchell's life, a year in
which his marriage goes to hell while he obsessively trains for a
tennis comeback; as he works toward a big match, he ignores signs
of heart trouble, and, when the match arrives, all but kills himself
in his thirsting after victory. He wins at tennis, but loses at
everything else. The author, an accomplished player himself,
delves deeply into the mind of the possessed athlete, and shows how
the obsession with winning can destroy one's life.

591. Baumbach, Jonathan. "The Return of Service." In Best
      American Short Stories, 1978, p. 354-362. Edited by Ted
      Solotaroff and Shannon Ravenal. Houghton-Mifflin, 1978.
      Also in the author's Return of Service. Univ. of Illinois Pr.,
      1979.
      Part fantasy, part straight narration of "real" events, this
story describes a tennis match between a man and his aging father.

It is more than a tennis match, though: it is a study in generational conflict in which, as usual, the father not only plays the game, but makes the rules. No athlete as reflective as the narrator is during competition can expect to win, but he wins anyhow, and pays a price (of sorts) for defeating his father.

592. Boyar, Jane and Boyar, Burt. <u>World Class</u>. Random House, 1975. 402 p.

Tennis lovers should find this novel a treat when it sticks to tennis; others may laugh in the wrong places. At over 400 pages of small, close-packed print, there are a lot of wrong places.

The novel is of the world tennis tour. It explores the lives of a variety of star players from different backgrounds, ranging from wealth to poverty, and from diverse nations. The book is also, naturally, the story "of the women they love," and the level at which this story is told is suggested by the book's closing sentence, spoken by the central star's inamorata: "Come into my arms. Come into my life." This woodenness is far from unique in the book, although the authors did a lot of research as they trailed the touring pros for two years. The tennis is tolerable and plentiful; the book also contains a lot of sweat, push-ups, and passages set in italics.

593. Brennan, Peter. <u>Sudden Death</u>. Rawson, 1978. 335 p.

A familiar premise here, treated in most areas of sports fiction, that of the confrontation between the seasoned, knowledgeable professional, long at the top of the game, and the youth who would seize the old man's crown. The old pro here is Alex Wrangler, a tough, no-holds-barred competitor; his challenger is Fletcher Sampson, whose boyish naivete yields to his desire to win, through any means necessary. There is nothing new in the tale, but the game accounts are good, and with the author's characterizations of the two competitors give the novel its measure of value.

594. Brinkley, William. <u>Breakpoint</u>. Morrow, 1978. 324 p.

Robert Catlo, one of the greatest tennis players of all time, completed his career shortly before the big money tournaments began. Retired from competition, when he was lucky to clear $30 for a day's work, he now teaches middle-aged women pitty-patty tennis at a Florida club.

Narrator Brinkley (the author gives him his own name) writes for a sports magazine, and is covering Catlo on assignment. He saw Catlo in the star's final match at Wimbledon, where, after difficult, gamely-played sets, he lost to Jack Tillotson, thirteen years Catlo's junior and now the king of the courts. Catlo is training his son Billy, a polite though very reserved youth, for a possible shot at Wimbledon; to improve his son's chances against Tillotson, he assumes Tillotson's distinctive style in their practice games. Tillotson, a brilliant player, makes the psychological manipulation of officials and opponents almost as much a part of his game as his famous drop shots. His comment on his tactics: "Why do tennis players have to be such mama's boys that they fall apart if someone sneezes in the stands? What is this, a game or a religious service?"

The book concludes with a long, exciting account of a Tillot-
son/Billy Catlo match at Forest Hills. The outcome is probably inevitable, given the universal truth of competition that youth must
eventually displace age, but Brinkley the author (and Brinkley the
narrator) describe the games with vivid detail, and, though we anticipate the outcome, its way of coming supplies a rich diet of tension
and reader involvement. One of the novel's finest aspects is its
presentation of sport at its rare best, with outstanding players
exerting themselves to such a limit that there is little difference
between victor and defeated: the contest occurs on a higher court
than usual, where it is truly the game that is the thing. Losing
is seldom beautiful, but both Tillotson and Catlo the elder lose
beautifully and heroically. There are veins for speculation in this
phenomenon leading to the deepest reasons for athletic competition.
Brinkley may not have intended this much; with its obligatory bows
to gratuitous love affairs, the book is solidly entrenched in the pop
novel genre, not one of great seriousness, yet it delivers more than
the pop genre ordinarily promises.

595. Brown, Rita Mae. Sudden Death. Bantam, 1983. 241 p.
    A bad novel included here strictly as a consumer warning.
The book follows a young Argentine, Carmen Semana, on her tour of
the pro tennis circuit and on her quest for the Grand Slam--victories
in the same year in the French Open, Wimbledon, the U.S. Open,
and the Australian Open.
    The novel falls flat everywhere. The tennis, which constitutes
a fairly negligible portion of the book, is particularly lifeless. It
conveys none of the excitement generated by the game itself.
Brown's use of words like "electrifying" to characterize her matches
pumps no juice into them, but does point out how drained of real
adrenalin these scenes are. The characters are as two-dimensional
as the tennis. Sex scenes between Carmen and her lover Harriet
reach an emotional pitch on the comic-book level. The narrative re-
lies on stilted explanations of characters' strengths, weaknesses,
and feelings, rather than revealing them through action. The consistently wooden prose hits bottom with some ungainly metaphors.
One character, for example, possesses "breasts heaving like a flight
deck."
    If this is not enough to deter potential readers, beware the
pet cat named "Baby Jesus," also known as (believe it or not)
"Beejee Weejee." Beejee Weejee receives more than his due share of
cloying commentary, in spite of the fact that he, like most cats, does
not play tennis.

596. Bryant, Matt. "Tennis Bum." Collier's 126 (Sept. 9, 1950):
      24-25+.
    Jonathan (Johnny) Temple has been a fixture on the amateur
tennis circuit for a dozen years, minus a hitch in the Navy. He has
come into town for a tournament, expecting to find the same local
sponsor as in the past, the wealthy Mrs. Townsend, whose daughter
Tina provides Johnny a little off-court entertainment. Johnny's

expectations don't match reality. He has been in a slump, and Mrs.
Townsend has offered to take on the expenses of a younger, more
promising player. Left to scramble for a room, Johnny finds an attic that he must share with Pete Kilmer, another player making his
tournament debut. Pete idolizes Johnny; he has Temple's picture
pinned to his wall, along with photos of other great players of the
past.

A fairly interesting story of the older player's ultimate willingness to assist the younger on his way; although Pete cannot win the
tournament because of his inexperience, Temple does what he can to
assist the boy, and, in the process, cuts himself off completely from
any possible hospitality from the Townsends.

597.   Clark, Valma. "Young Man's Game." Scribner's Magazine 88
       (July 1930): 91-98.
       Too breathless with exclamation points, and too contrived (the
lead character's heart condition and his protegé's love interest are
unnecessary to the story's point), but still a passable example of the
aging athlete's step down from the top. Samuel Cochrane is the
center of attention at the French national championship matches. He
has won every major title over the past eight years except this one.
At 34, he has held on to his spot at the top longer than one could
expect, but time and his health are not on his side. He must play
one of his earlier students, Leo Meyer, in a preliminary match. Leo
is a boy of talent, but inadequate confidence. The manner in which
Cochrane draws out Meyer's belief in himself, and his motivations for
doing so, are the core of the story.

There is one rather nice metaphor in the piece comparing a
tennis career to the flight of a well-struck lob, "rising bravely,
flashing in the sunlight, falling away."

598.   Dixon, Harry V. "Tennis Bum." American Magazine 127 (Feb.
       1939): 16-19+.
       Chet Clark is a cynical but talented tennis pro at a club in
Mill Valley, California. A college champion, he was forced out of
school by the Depression, and lost all his innocence in a succession
of scrabbling jobs. Now, though he makes no friends at the club,
he earns his keep through excellent teaching and flawless judgment
of the potential of players who aspire to championship matches.

The complication is Chet's relationship with Ann Fleming. Ann
is not only beautiful, but is also the most talented woman player on
the club. The one failure in her game is that of nerve: she is
afraid of the ball. Against a strong opponent, she avoids pressing
the play or charging the net, fearful of being hit. Chet surreptitiously works to free Ann from her fear by making her angry at him.
He deliberately sets her up so that he can smash the ball at her, and
after a few days bruises from hard-driven balls cover her body.
She enjoys her moment of revenge when she catches Chet squarely in
the face with her own shot, and from this point on she plays without
fear.

Though softened by the obligatory romantic subplot, this is an

interesting story touched by athletic sadism. The passage in which
Chet stands stunned and bleeding from the nose while Ann laughs
hysterically on the other side of the court probably says more than
the author intended about men and women at play.

599. Fadiman, Edwin. The Professional. McKay, 1973. 314 p.
      The best portions by far in this book are the early accounts
of tennis great Jeff Williams's training. We meet him as a boy named
Pedro, living in the vilest of the San Juan, Puerto Rico, slums. He
builds himself a wood-floored tennis court on a deserted beach, using
scavenged and stolen materials. There he sustains an "incredible
and grotesque" training program for over a year, playing only
against himself.
      He hustles a job as a ball boy at a club. Bill Williams, the
club's aging pro, sees in Pedro's raw, untutored ability the gleam
of future greatness. Williams teaches Pedro the game; as he does,
Fadiman does a good job developing the relationship between the two.
The boy's fear that all the good things Williams has given him--time,
knowledge, and steady meals--will be swept away by chance is completely believable, given Pedro's wretchedly poor background.
      Williams becomes Pedro's legal guardian and changes his name
to Jeff Williams. The two travel to Los Angeles, where a wealthy
businessman agrees to sponsor Jeff, who immediately adopts a training regimen of great intensity. One memorable passage describes his
hatred of the ball-serving machine that he must work against for long
periods. Jeff Williams trains so thoroughly that he almost transcends
humanity in his game; he comes to be known, in fact, as "the tennis
machine." During this part of the novel, which takes a third of its
length, the story is engrossing, the premise of an ambitious slum kid
with an athletic gift well carried out.
      The book promises to become more than it does. When Jeff
goes on tour, the interest level drops, and no number of sex scenes,
no matter their serious literary intentions, can pull it back. The
tension of the story lies not in Jeff's professional career, but whether
he can become a professional in the first place. With that question
answered, the novel remains readable, and at times very good, but
after the first hundred pages the excitement is manufactured rather
than grown organically from the main character's circumstances.

600. Farrell, James T. "Ray Taite." In his Childhood Is Not For-
      ever, p. 205-221. Doubleday, 1969.
      Ray Taite is a privileged boy with fine athletic gifts, especially
in tennis. Farrell traces Ray's career, from boyhood afternoon sets
with his friend Sad-Puss to his college play. Farrell wanders all
over the map with this story, as he often does, and he isn't content
to let an event speak for itself, but must make blatant statements to
be sure the reader does not miss the point: "They, two boyhood
playmates, were travelling separate roads toward a future that controlled them."
      Nevertheless, Farrell's class consciousness does permit him to
look at sports in a way too seldom taken. Sad-Puss is also a talented

player, with a potential almost the equal of Ray's, but he is con-
demned to a loser's life because of his origins in poverty. His hard
luck has afflicted his spirit too severely to allow him to realize his
athletic possibilities. The story goes beyond issues of class and
sports, however, with strong overtones of a determinism lying in
wait for everyone.

601. Ford, Corey. "Tennis Racket." Saturday Evening Post 205
     (May 20, 1933): 6-7+.
     Another Depression-era tale of sport twisted to the service of
business. Here Jerry, an ambitious young movie studio hand, par-
lays his skill at tennis into a series of ever-cushier, better paying
posts with the studio. Through flattery and an ever-ready boyish
smile, he exploits one executive after another. All are easy game
for Jerry because of their own exaggerated notions of their tennis
acumen.
     A crisis comes when Jerry and his girlfriend Connie are paired
in a tournament against Jerry's boss, Mr. Boomer, and his partner.
Boomer has offered Jerry a job as associate producer if he will throw
the match, and, if Ford stayed true to his characters, that is the
way it would go. At Connie's goading, Jerry plays it straight.
Ironically, he still profits in a career sense from his victory over
Boomer. In spite of Jerry's late-blooming "honesty," Connie's early
characterization of him still rings true: "I think you're all ambition
and nothing else."

602. Gilchrist, Ellen. "In the Land of Dreamy Dreams." In her
     In the Land of Dreamy Dreams, p. 60-71. Univ. of Arkansas
     Pr., 1981.
     Roxanne Miller, regardless of a crippled foot, has become an
excellent club tennis player. LaGrande McGruder, herself a capable
player, cannot stand the thought of losing to Roxanne, and so wins
by cheating. Repelled more by the necessity of cheating than by
the act itself, she takes all her tennis equipment and dumps it into
the Mississippi River from the Huey P. Long Bridge. There are no
attractive characters in this story; Roxanne is merely on the make.
It is satisfying, however, to watch the smug LaGrande lose in effect, if not in the score.

603. Hannah, Barry. The Tennis Handsome. Knopf, 1983. 170 p.
     A collection of stories loosely connected by the reappearances
of various characters. The main men in this department are French
Edward, a beautiful tennis pro rendered relatively simpleminded (apparently from oxygen depletion during a near-drowning), and his
manager, a slimy physician named Baby Levaster. Reactions will
range widely to this one; there are some amusing passages, but
others seem only cruel, and pointlessly so. One might defend the
vague connections in the name of experimental fiction, or dismiss
them as the result of indifference pretending to be something superi-
or. Not for all tastes, then, but some palates will be tickled.

604. Hermann, John. "Ignoramibus." Carolina Quarterly 27 (Fall
      1975): 83-93.

A set of doubles is at the heart of this story of a man possessed by thoughts of the past, both of the actual past and of the
past anticipated. He has been a tennis player for a long time; he
and his wife have worked out a little ritual in which he announces
his intentions regarding his play on any given day. On the day of
the story he will go off to the courts. Too old for singles play, he
pulls into the parking lot hoping he will not be paired with Mike,
who, in spite of some ability, makes far too many bad shots. When
he spins rackets for partners with some of his acquaintances, his
partner is, of course, Mike.

On the court, he reveals an ugly streak. There is no reason
to believe that Mike is not trying, but he speaks abruptly and mean-
ly to Mike upon Mike's fluffed shots. He becomes so angry with
Mike's play that he will not even say good bye when Mike leaves the
park. He is convinced that he and Mike "should" have won, if only
Mike had been able to keep the ball in play.

Back home he watches his seven-year-old grandson light a
charcoal fire for grilled chicken, and imagines the boy recording the
memory for recall at a time many years later, when he himself is long
dead. This little reverie dovetails with several earlier recollections
of his dead parents and brother. He cannot seem to live in the
present; current events are not to be known for their own merits,
but as references to things dead and gone, or to death imagined.

Only in his tennis does this man live for the moment, and it
is, perhaps, this exclusivity which drives him to such concern for
winning, since only winning will make this present moment satisfactory and complete.

605. Nelson, Kent. "The Tennis Player." Michigan Quarterly Re-
      view 14 (Spring 1975): 137-149. Also in the author's The
      Tennis Player, and Other Stories. Univ. of Illinois Pr.,
      1977.

Nicky is a top tournament tennis player who has come back to
the everyday world from an apparent stay in a mental hospital or
asylum. He no longer feels the game as he once did; he plays more
from muscle memory than from conscious application. He wants not
much more than to be by himself, but allows his friends to talk him
into a position as a tennis teacher. He gives in "to telling people
what they wanted to hear." He doesn't mind the work; "It was the
feeling he got from it that he could not stand." His girlfriend
Caroline wants him to love her, so he tells her he does; he doesn't,
and dislikes himself for yielding to her, but he cannot stop himself.

Yielding again, he agrees to enter a minor tournament. In
training, some of the former spontaneity and vitality of his game return, but when he tosses the ball up for his first serve of the tournament, it looks as though he is going to lose a lot more than game,
set, and match.

A sensitively written story with Nicky reminiscent of Hemingway's Nick Adams of "Big Two-Hearted River" (item 304); he is

another young man fighting to keep his mind together after a dis-
astrous experience.

606.   Scott, Leroy. The Trails of Glory. Houghton-Mifflin, 1926.
       206 p.
       Presents the dilemma of Jerry MacAllister, a young tennis star
patronized by a businessman interested in seeing the U.S. prevail
in international competition on the courts. MacAllister, though "employed" in his patron's firm, is in a real sense a kept man. He
chafes under this arrangement; his window-dressing "job" has not
given him an opportunity to learn the realities of an occupation that
must sustain him when his tennis days are done. Though dated in
some respects, the novel remains pertinent given the role of the
amateur athlete today, whose "amateur" status must often be surrounded by quotation marks, and who is frequently ill-prepared for
a career in "real" life should his or her athletic skills prove inadequate.

607.   Shaw, Irwin. "Mixed Doubles." New Yorker 23 (Aug. 9,
       1947): 19-23. Also in the author's Short Stories: Five Dec-
       ades. Delacorte, 1978.
       A superior illustration of the way a supposedly friendly tennis
match can point out the faults in a man's character and the probably
fatal cracks in a superficially sound marriage. Shaw does a very
neat job of translating errors on the court into their domestic equiva-
lents through the mind of one of the players.

608.   Sklar, George. The Promising Young Men. Crown, 1951.
       304 p.
       This novel follows Steve Kropa from shy schoolboy raised in
poverty and violence to international fame as a tennis star, down a
moral slide to squandered talent and love, and back up again. The
novel echoes Dreiser and Farrell in its sociological underpinnings;
Steve's early childhood haunts him through all but the book's final
pages. The route of his "fall" is traced with a dogged determinism,
though if the fall were complete (as it would be, possibly, in the
hands of a slightly more serious novelist), there would be no redemption for Steve. The one Sklar furnishes is a bit too sentimental to
accept. The book is dated, with passages intended to shock, such
as the revelation of the homosexuality of Steve's roommate-coach,
now devoid of most of their punch. Still, Sklar works hard in this
novel, and does not fall short by much of producing a fairly memorable account of an athlete's corruption by the attending elements
of his sport. There are some passages, such as those detailing
Steve's slipping away from the bonds of his early friends and lovers,
that are quite well managed. The book deserves a better fate than
the one assigned the copy obtained for this bibliography, displacement to a public library's basement storage room.

609.   Sorrells, Robert T. "The Blacktop Champion of Ickey Honey."
       In Best American Short Stories, 1978, p. 136-162. Edited by

Ted Solotaroff and Shannon Ravenal. Houghton-Mifflin, 1978. Also in American Review, no. 22 (1977).

Set in South Carolina in a backwater town whose odd name appears in the title. County Agent Lodi Poidle is called upon to prepare his friend Hoke Warble for a grudge tennis match with a $1,000 stake against Newton Slock. (Sorrells obviously stayed up late to think of these characters' names.) Hoke is as unlikely an athlete as one could imagine with his short, squat, toad-like stature. Newton looks as though he's ready for Wimbledon. The match, played on an asphalt court beneath a broiling sun, turns into a debacle of melted tar and an apparently endless series of tie-breakers. Sorrell's description of the peculiar spectacle is both knowledgeable and hilarious, and he serves up a hard-to-beat ironic ending.

610.   Tilden, William T. Glory's Net. Doubleday, Doran, 1930.
       296 p.

Tilden's concern in this novel of a tennis star on the rise is the hypocrisy he sees as too evident in the game. Young David Cooper, an American champion and a Wimbledon contender, is co-opted by a wealthy stockbroker who pays Cooper a handsome salary to "sell" bonds. The stockbroker also happens to be an official of the U.S. Lawn Tennis Association. His cognizance of Cooper's asset as a publicity acquisition does not quite square with his "commitment" to the purity of tennis. The big advantage in the novel is Tilden's description of tennis action; as a three-time Wimbledon champion, he uses his intimate knowledge of the game to good effect.

611.   _____. "The Phantom Drive." In The Omnibus of Sport,
       p. 305-316. Edited by Grantland Rice and Harford Powel.
       Harper, 1932.

An old tennis champion goes A.W.O.L. from Heaven and helps a young challenger at Forest Hills, until the "modern game" proves too much for the invisible visitor. Insubstantial but fun, and the issue of a treasured racket will draw sympathetic responses from any athlete who has long-employed a favorite club, racket, or bat. Readers interested in more of Tilden's net tales will find them in his collection It's All in the Game (Doubleday, 1922).

612.   Tunis, John R. "Husband of the Champion." Collier's 93
       (May 26, 1934): 14-15+.

A good Depression story whose major issues are loyalty and integrity. Hank Fields, a modestly-paid engineer, owes his place in the slick world of high society to his wife, Gracie. She is a tennis champion, and by virtue of her athletic skill draws the well-heeled to her. Her best "friend" is Dorothy Sands, a department store advertising manager whose income far exceeds that of Hank Fields. Dorothy and Hank detest each other; she considers him a needless burden to Gracie, an embarrassment in her social circle; he sees her for what she is, an insincere woman who uses her alleged friendship with Gracie to bring herself a little further up the ladder.

An old friend offers Hank an engineering job in South America. The pay will not be great, but Hank will no longer have to ride along uncomfortably on the strength of his wife's forehand. In a nicely-written passage following a tournament match, Gracie sees through Dorothy's shallow opportunism, and willingly walks (or runs) away from Society to join her husband in humble but honest circumstances.

613. _____. "Mother of a Champion." Harper's 158 (Feb. 1929): 275-289.

The press calls her "The Girl with the Laughing Voice," but tennis champ Florence Farley's rise to the top of her sport is a case study in greed and exploitation, first on the part of those around her who use Florence's talents for their own social and financial benefit, and then by Florence herself, who learns to manipulate press and public with the flair of--of a champion. Acid drips from this piece; Tunis's examination of sport's rotten underbelly will be easy for readers to fit into their view of contemporary athletics. For an expanded look at dear Florence, turn to Tunis's novel, American Girl (Brewer, Warren, 1930). Many observers interpreted Florence as a transparent take-off on the real-life Helen Wills Moody, who was sometimes known as "Little Poker Face," on which nickname "The Girl with the Laughing Voice" is a nice twist.

614. Wallop, Douglas. Mixed Singles. Norton, 1977. 185 p.

A fast, entertaining satire on affluent suburban life and sports as a filler for the spiritual vacuum that has developed among those sharing the hollow accomplishments of materialism. Jack Bigelow is a well-to-do radiologist living in an exclusive area; his wife Franny is bored. Collecting antique milk cans and bed warmers no longer seems to satisfy her. On the advice of a psychologist, she turns to tennis, and, in the opinion of her gold-toothed, gold-earringed pro, is "a natural" at it. She challenges Jack to a match, and humiliates him.

Jack seeks instruction himself, and tennis becomes for him and his wife not a pastime but an object of fanatic devotion. The court, compared at one point in its rectangular shape to the outline of a marriage bed, turns to a battleground. As the tennis games advance, the Bigelow marriage retreats. In the final conflict, Jack has lost his wife, and must choose whether to yield to her frightening need to defeat him in a match of mixed doubles.

There are a number of good passages in this light but well-mounted attack on aimless discontent.

XVII. WRESTLING

615. Davis, Terry. <u>Vision Quest</u>. Viking, 1979. 197 p.
This short novel follows high school wrestler Louden Swain as
he readies himself for a big match. The challenge lies not only in
his opponent's strength and skill, but in the necessity of losing a
few pounds to reach the proper weight for his class, without losing
his stamina. Interspersed with passages of training and practice
are Louden's adventures with his friends and family, and chiefly
with his live-in girlfriend Carla. The two of them spend a lot of
time out appreciating Nature in the western mountains, when they
can take a break from their keen interest in appreciating each
other.
The temper of the book is a touch too sweet, particularly in
Carla's character. Louden, who narrates, spends far too much time
talking about the books he has read, but aside from this fault
(which is probably the author's, not his), he is an enjoyable character. Terry Davis, a former wrestler, knows the sport, and produces
a good number of both comic and tender scenes. It is a competent
novel of growing up with a great final line.

616. Elkin, Stanley. "The Transient." <u>Saturday Evening Post</u>
237 (April 25, 1964): 54-60+. Also in <u>Best American Short
Stories, 1965</u>. Edited by Martha Foley and David Burnett.
Houghton-Mifflin, 1965.
A young man chronically aware that death lurks for all culti-
vates his body as a refuge from the inevitable. His over-developed
muscles lead him to pro wrestling, sport's only true theater of the
absurd, where he assumes the identity of "The Masked Playboy."
His first main event, which he is supposed to lose, is against the
"Grim Reaper," an old man who, win or lose, always inflicts severe
pain on his opponents. The story builds tension with the Playboy's
steadily increasing anxiety before the match. The match itself,
described in bloody detail, comes to a predictable end as the Reaper
pounds the Playboy into a coma, and perhaps into death itself. The
Playboy's last thoughts complete the story's point: there is "something off-center and sappy and insane in heroes.... It was better,
finally, to be a non combatant, a serene Switzerland of a man, ac-
complice to one's own death." A first-rate story.

617. Hecht, Ben. "Champion from Far Away." In <u>A Treasury of
Ben Hecht; Collected Stories and Other Writings</u>, p. 167-188.
Crown, 1959. Also in the author's <u>Champion from Far Away</u>.
Covici, Friede, 1931.

Vanya Kovelenko, a veteran of WW I and of the Russian Revolution, becomes a professional wrestler under the "guidance" of a
con man. Following a ghastly match against Metzger, a German
champion, Kovelenko is promptly dismissed from the memory of a
public that previously held him in heroic regard. He is "buried in
that limbo into which Babylon disgorges its Seven Day Wonders."
An effective story of the crass manipulation of a simple man and
the cheapness of public sentiment, with a wrestling match described
so vividly the reader feels the canvas shaking.

618. Idell, Albert E. Mighty Milo; A Series of Incidents in His
      Now Famous Career by Fred Anspach, Also Known as Honey-
      boy Hackenschmidt. Hermitage House, 1954. 191 p.
      Milo Paulus may not be a Greek god, but he makes a good
Greek satire. At five feet three and 230-plus pounds, Milo looks
nothing like an athlete, but he is a formidable wrestler, as the
book's narrator, Fred Anspach, discovers. Fred, just out of high
school and a wrestler himself, works in a grocery store where Milo
comes to buy the ingredients of his original diet, which includes un-
cooked oatmeal taken with milk and a head of lettuce before bed to
promote sound sleep. When Milo shows Fred his wrestling prowess,
he also converts Fred to his diet.
      Fred slowly abandons his college football plans and, under
Milo's guidance, becomes a pro wrestler. From this point, whether
it means wrestling in molasses or the Mud Battle of the Century,
Milo and Fred cut a swath across the finest wrestling canvasses,
and complete their ascent to the top with regular television appearances.
      A gentle satire with some quite amusing stretches, the whole
helped along greatly by Milo, a sensitive, lovable, and nearly in-
vincible practitioner of the flying head scissors.

619. Lasky, Laurence. "The Cement Truck." In That's What Hap-
      pened to Me, p. 131-136. Edited by Whit Burnett. Four
      Winds, 1969.
      A high school wrestler fears his upcoming match against the
county champion. His apprehension so thoroughly wraps him in knots
that by the time he steps onto the mat, he is incapable of trying, let
alone winning. A neat little story rooted in honesty and personal
chagrin.

620. Stark, Sharon S. "A Wrestler's Tale." Antioch Review 39
      (Fall 1981): 476-487.
      Bobby, a fifteen-year-old high school wrestler, is in a match,
and working to avoid a pin as the crowd roars. From the noise he
hears his mother's voice, calling his name in encouragement; her
voice truncates in mid-syllable, and, while Bobby is eager to continue
his match, his mother is dead in the stands of a stroke. The rest
of the story details Bobby's reaction to his mother's death. The narrative is in the third person, but the sensibility is very much Bobby's, and it is one in a turmoil that a series of sessions with a
psychologist does nothing to relieve.

Bobby aims most of his anger at his father, who buries himself in drink, work, and television; Bobby blames his father for his mother's death, and makes no effort to see that, although his parents' marriage was far from perfect, his father has a right to a grief of his own.

Bobby insists on being called by his other name, "George," to avoid being reminded of his mother's cry of "Bobby." He loses himself in his wrestling, has bad dreams of Oedipal content, and seeks solace from his authoritarian, but not unsympathetic, older sister. The tale ends with Bobby-George in another wrestling match, before another crowd. Even as he is on the edge of defeating his opponent, "Grief begins at his fingertips and fills him swiftly," and his victim becomes his conqueror. The sense is, however, that because Bobby now feels real grief, rather than rage, he may be on the way out of the worst period of his grappling with his mother's death.

621. Aandahl, Vance. "Beyond the Game." In Arena: Sports SF,
p. 187-193. Edited by Ed Ferman and Barry Malzberg.
Doubleday, 1976. First published in Magazine of Fantasy and
Science Fiction (May 1968).
This masterful story will reawaken old anxieties and touch the
heart of anyone who has come under the thumb of that peculiar
breed, the phys. ed. tyrant. There is a game known innocuously
as "dodge ball," also (and more accurately) as "slaughter ball,"
in which the members of a gym class divide into two groups, whose
objective is to strike those on the other side with thrown balls of
various kinds. The last side with members who have not been hit
"wins." It is a sport that bullies and budding terrorists thrive
upon, and that instructs the slow and the weak in their laughable
vulnerability. Some gym teachers love it.
      In this story, a small boy named Ernest does his best to avoid
being hit during one of these exercises in unnatural selection through
fascism. At first he hides behind a pair of overweight boys, but
they are soon painfully struck and must go to the sidelines. Ernest
finds that he can transport himself mentally from the scene, a talent
that will stand well by him when the gym teacher, Miss Argentine,
becomes infuriated at him and sets him on one side against the entire
class.
      Aandahl's sympathy with this imaginative, beleaguered boy is
brilliantly put, and the boy's tactics for freeing himself from his torment the work of a gifted mind under great duress. In spite of the
story's sources of publication, it is not science fiction: it is a
realistic psychological study, and it illuminates one little-noted but
very unpleasant corner of juvenile indoctrination to a twisted understanding of "sport."

622. Deford, Frank. The Owner. Viking, 1976. 280 p.
      Sports mogul Duncan Radnor is a case in himself--he is crafty,
sneaky, ingenious, insightful--and he provides Deford a good vehicle for some satirical swipes against the excesses and avarice in
professional sports, particularly as found in the management sphere.
      Radnor, a porcelain and enamel tycoon, becomes a multi-sport
wheeler-dealer in a grubby manufacturing town. Whether the pursuit
is hockey or basketball, Radnor is there, pulling off transactions
that leave rival owners gasping (literally) for air. A case in point
is his deft handling of the Toronto team in the National Hockey Association, from whom he wrests the great Tommy Haley. It's an easy
job, once Radnor has in hand information about Haley's history of

game fixing. Radnor grabs basketball star Trevor Pardue with
similar aplomb.

The best portions of the book, which contains almost nothing
resembling a plot, are Radnor's commentaries on various aspects of
the sporting life. Speaking of civic pride, for example, he says
that "Ball clubs are the best things cities have now. In some ways,
they're the only things that still hold cities together. I swear to
God, a lot of people don't think of this as a country any more.
They just think of it as a goddamn league."

This and other Radnor-isms, including a wonderful anecdote
in which he uses his experience with a wrestling bear to illustrate
"what people are like after they get you playing their game," make
the novel fun to read, as well as occasionally thought-provoking.
The absence of a plot is not intolerable, given Radnor's ideas and
Deford's characters. When Radnor is not saying his piece, however,
the book is merely marking time waiting for him to mouth his aggressive opinions.

623. Koperwas, Sam. "Winner in All Things." Esquire 82 (Oct.
     1974): 179-181+.
     Either the narrator of this wild piece of braggadocio is as
good as he claims to be, or he is a 97-pound weakling hunkering
down in a corner of his room, engaging in a litany of overcompen-
sation. One suspects the latter. The story is chiefly composed of
the narrator's recitation of his athletic triumphs. This is no ordinary bar-room swagger, but a truly transcendant work of self-
glorification. There is nothing this man cannot do, from knocking
down his own father for a few extra feet in touch football to beating
the socks off his near-sighted wife at table-top hockey. He is class
president, a deadly outside shot in basketball, an infielder who
doubles as relief pitcher with an unhittable curve, a killer handball
player, a specimen, in short, that would have humbled Nazi dreamers
of Aryan supremacy. "I win in weight lifting, win in skiing, in
Ping Pong. I don't lose. Never. I win in shuffleboard. I win in
polo.... I wrestle alligators, rope steers. I win in logrolling. I
win in barrel jumping."

There is a rhythm of boasting in the story almost like a basketball's as a guard dribbles it the length of the floor. The narrator's real nature, however, lies not in his bragging but in his
father's exhortations and in his wife's eyes.

624. Kosinski, Jerzy. Passion Play. St. Martin's, 1979. 271 p.
     Central character Fabian drives a nine-axled motorhome, com-
plete with integral horse stable, around the country. He carries
with him his polo gear and a who's who of polo, pursuing pick-up
games of one-on-one. Kosinski achieves his best passages in those
dealing with the mind-body, man-horse dynamics of polo; readers
whose sporting taste runs to conventional sweaty pursuits and who
see polo as the suspect indulgence of an effete leisure class will find
more than they expected in the sometimes bone-crunching contests
described here.

Fabian looks to both his polo and his women as means of proving his own vitality, a vitality whose permanence is coming into some question as the book opens. Gray hair here, a dollop of fat there, and a bit of blood in the stool all signify that even this self-contained athlete's life must have an end. The novel is far more interesting when Fabian is on his horse than when he is adding to his stable of women, a pastime nearly as dear to him as polo. The sex scenes, described in Masters & Johnson clinical detail, are chilly and passionless; the polo action is, however, satisfactorily steamy.

625.   Sayles, John. "The 7-10 Split." In his The Anarchists' Convention, p. 59-68. Little, Brown, 1979.
A good bowling story is hard to find, but here is one, and it's very good. A group of women have been bowling together for a long time. When one of them decides to quit the group to join the Seniors' League, it puts them all off their game. They feel depressed, old, hopeless. Playing the game turns into an undesirable chore. At the bottom of this trough one of the group finally converts a 7-10 split for a spare, after failing at this difficult shot for years. Her success will set the tone for renewed pleasure in the game. It isn't just a casual metaphor when one of her partners describes this woman, following her triumphant spare, as looking "like a little girl who just done her First Communion coming back down the aisle."

626.   Sheckley, Robert. "Game: First Schematic." In his Can You Feel Anything When I Do This? p. 46-51. Doubleday, 1971.
It is some time in the nonspecific but evidently distant future. The Smithsonian has been keeping records on the game back to its earliest days, so one must assume that it has been around a long while. But what game is this? It suggests a hybrid of tennis, roller derby and volleyball; players dress in gym clothes, and may elect to wear roller skates upon the tiled court. The ball comes in various sizes and shapes, and changes each frequently during the game. Top players show up to play every day, but may complete no more than a dozen matches in a year.
Against this background the chief character walks into an arena for the game. It is for him as though he is expected to play a game whose rules are utterly alien to him; what is more, he lacks a game plan. "Like any professional he could play with or without a plan, he could play drunk, sick, or half dead." But "Why had this contest come to epitomize his entire existence?"
This story is a bit like those dreams one has of waking up and pursuing some inscrutable business, only to wake up in reality and find the world even more bewildering, for a few seconds, than the dream itself.

627.   Simak, Clifford D. "Mr. Meek Plays Polo." Planet Stories (Fall 1944): 56+. Also in The Infinite Arena: Seven Science Fiction Stories About Sports. Edited by Terry Carr. Thomas Nelson, 1977.

Out Saturn way, some of the boys in the far sectors go gunning for each other from boredom. Henrietta Perkins, a social worker for the Solar government, thinks it would be a good idea to divert their aggressiveness into healthier activities, especially of an athletic sort. What begins as a do-good project quickly takes on the dimensions of a feud, with the outcome of a game of space polo to finally settle the question of whether Sector 23 or Sector 37 is supreme. Mr. Oliver Meek, a vacationing bookkeeper, unwittingly finds himself drafted as the coach for the 23s. Mr. Meek, a ten-goal man in his youth, emerges in glory, thanks to the surprising assistance of some mathematically gifted bugs.

628.   Sturgeon, Theodore. "How to Forget Baseball." Sports Illustrated 21 (Dec. 21, 1964): 84+.
The main premise of this story is close to that of the 1975 film, "Rollerball." Future society has banned violence, but channels its aggression and hatred into a gory and sometimes deliberately lethal sport. The time is 40-some years after a 12-hour war; it took those four decades to restore pieces of the planet to something like civilization. We learn about the game of Quoit through the eyes of Mr. Ourser, a "Primitive" come to the city to do some trading. The Primitives, the people of the wilderness, still play the traditional sports, but the urbans have eyes only for the spectacular game of Quoit. The Quoit is a great saucer-like device with a cutting core that sounds like a laser, according to Sturgeon's description. A flak takes Mr. Ourser to the Quoit stadium, where he watches a game of blood: the losing player is sliced in half from groin to crown by the Quoit. Outraged at the loss of their local champion, the fans storm the field to continue the carnage as the Quoit carves its way among them.
Sturgeon describes the game in a way that allows the reader to visualize it quite adequately; the ironic conclusion leaves that reader with little hope for humanity, "Primitive" or not.

629.   Toombs, Charles. "Master Timothy." In The Indiana Experience, p. 293-296. Edited by A. L. Lazarus. Indiana Univ. Press, 1977.
Until the last paragraph, this story of an eleven-year old black child who wants to become a karate master is very similar in style to much of James T. Farrell's work. It presents the tale less as fiction than as a case study outlining the circumstances that lead the main character to his destiny.
Timothy Baker cares for his four younger siblings while his mother goes off to her nightly work as an hotel cleaning woman. Timothy is a good, reliable boy; he wants very much to spend more time with boys his own age, but he heeds the duties of babysitter, even as he practices karate kicks on cockroaches on the walls of his apartment. At length he obtains a job as a cleaning boy in the local karate studio, and it looks as though he is at last on his way, until one evening he fails to come home, and his mother learns that there has been "a very serious accident here at the School of Martial Arts."

Then comes the last paragraph, and this case study suddenly vaults into the fantastic, making much more of an already good story.

630. White, E. B. "The Decline of Sport." In Great Stories from the World of Sport. Vol. 1, p. 271-274. Edited by Peter Schwed and Herbert W. Wind. Simon & Schuster, 1958.

The peerless essayist turns in a fanciful "history" of sport in the 20th century U.S., which he portrays in the grip of an athletic mania so powerful that the workweek has been shortened to allow easier attendance at games. Some of White's projections are almost on the nose, such as the use of video images to permit stadium crowds to watch games other than the ones on the fields before them. Certain "tragedies," including the assassination of the famed right end Ed Pistachio by an enraged fan, are also part of the new history. To be read before sitting down to watch the endless parade of holiday football bowl games. It might lead to alternative action, like rediscovering "the charms of old twisty roads," main streets, and barnyards.

631. Wright, Gary. "Mirror of Ice." In Arena: Sports SF, p. 61-73. Edited by Edward L. Ferman and Barry Malzberg. Doubleday, 1976. First published in Galaxy (June 1967).

In this story of an athlete's confrontation with his own limitations, bobsledding has undergone dramatic changes. The sleds are now equipped with blade runners enabling them to achieve great speed; the world's best drivers meet to test themselves on a murderous Alpine run known as "The Stuka."

The story opens with a sled driver poised at the start of the run, making the mistake of asking himself why he persists at this dangerous game. He reflects on the many members of the sled-racing "Kin" who have died in accidents. Thinking about it turns to doing it. Within seconds of his start, the racer is moving a mile a minute, and gaining speed. Tearing downhill on the icy embankments, he barely avoids the disasters that strike several other drivers. When his own sled finally goes out of control, he realizes why he cannot quit the sport: "No matter how many times you faced yourself it had to be done again.... And again. The Self was never satisfied with victories...."

An exciting story, and the racer's realization of his motives would fit many athletes, regardless of the sport.

APPENDIX:

SOME RECENT CRITICAL STUDIES AND ARTICLES

Baker, James A. and Rog, James A. Sports and the Humanities: A Symposium. Univ. of Maine at Orono Press, 1983. 126 p.

Berman, Neil D. Play, Sport, and Survival in Contemporary American Fiction. Ph.D. dissertation, Ohio State University, 1975. 202 p.

Burke, William. "Football, Literature, Culture." Southwest Review 60 (1975): 391-398.

Burt, David J. "The Helmeted Hero: The Football Player in Recent American Fiction." In Proceedings of the Sixth National Convention of the Popular Culture Association, St. Louis, Missouri, March 20-22, 1975, p. 1298-1311. Edited by Michael T. Marsden. Bowling Green State Univ. Popular Pr., 1975.

Candelaria, Cordelia C. Baseball in American Literature: From Ritual to Fiction. Ph.D. dissertation, Univ. of Notre Dame, 1976. 200 p.

_____. "Literary Fungoes: Allusions to Baseball in Significant American Fiction." Midwest Quarterly 23 (Summer 1982): 411-425.

Cashill, John R. "The Life and Death of Myth in American Baseball Literature." The American Examiner 3 (no. 3 1974): 24-37.

Francis, Dick. "Can't Anybody Here Write These Games? The Trouble With Sports Fiction." New York Times Book Review, June 1, 1986, p. 56.

Golubcow, Saul. Baseball as Metaphor in American Fiction. Ph.D. dissertation, SUNY-Stony Brook, 1975. 234 p.

Graber, Ralph S. "A Goal-Line Tackle with a Broken Shoulder Blade: Early Football Fiction." Markham Review 9 (1979): 1-5.

Guttmann, Allen. "Out of the Ghetto and on to the Field: Jewish Writers and the Theme of Sport." American Jewish History. 74 (March 1985): 274-286.

Harrison, Walter L. "Baseball and American Jews." Journal of
    Popular Culture 15 (Winter 1981): 112-118.

_____. Out of Play: Baseball Fiction from Pulp to Art. Ph.D.
    dissertation, Univ. of California-Davis, 1980. 172 p.

Higgs, Robert J. Laurel & Thorn: The Athlete in American Liter-
    ature. Univ. Press of Kentucky, 1981. 196 p.

Keller, Richard. "Sport and Fiction." Journal of Sport History 6
    (Summer 1979): 81-86.

Kerrane, Kevin. "Reality 35, Illusion 3: Notes on the Football
    Imagination in Contemporary Fiction." Journal of Popular Culture
    8 (Fall 1974): 437-452.

Knisley, Patrick A. The Interior Diamond: Baseball in Twentieth
    Century American Poetry and Fiction. Ph.D. dissertation, Univ.
    of Colorado at Boulder, 1978. 275 p.

Merrill, David B. "Take Me Out to the Ballgame": Baseball as De-
    terminant in Selected American Fiction. Ph.D. dissertation, Texas
    A & M Univ., 1979. 196 p.

Messenger, Christian K. Sport and the Spirit of Play in American
    Fiction: Hawthorne to Faulkner. Columbia Univ. Pr., 1981.
    369 p.

Oriard, Michael. Dreaming of Heroes: American Sports Fiction,
    1868-1980. Nelson-Hall, 1982. 382 p.

Palmer, Melvin D. "The Heyday of the Football Novel." Journal
    of Popular Culture 16 (Summer 1982): 48-54.

Porter, Dennis. "The Perilous Quest: Baseball as Folk Drama."
    Critical Inquiry 4 (1977): 43-57.

Reynolds, Charles D. H. Baseball as the Material of Fiction. Ph.D.
    dissertation, Univ. of Nebraska, 1974. 272 p.

Stein, Harry. "Baseball on Their Minds--The Lure of the Diamond,
    the Pace of the Plot." New York Times Book Review, June 1,
    1986, p. 3+.

Umphlett, Wiley L. The Sporting Myth & the American Experience:
    Studies in Contemporary Fiction. Bucknell Univ. Pr., 1975.
    205 p.

Vanderwerken, David. "English 4503: Sports in Modern American
    Literature (a.k.a. Lit. for Linebackers)." College Literature 3
    (1976): 130-138.

_____. Sport Inside Out: Readings in Literature & Philosophy.
Texas Christian Univ. Pr., 1985. 512 p.

Webb, Max. "Sunday Heroes: The Emergence of the Professional
Football Novel." Journal of Popular Culture 8 (Fall 1974): 453-
461.

Young, Eugene O. Keepers of the Faith: Sports from the Wilderness to the Space Age in Selected Modern American Novels.
Ph.D. dissertation, Univ. of Tennessee, 1979. 244 p.

TITLE INDEX

AUTHOR INDEX

THEMATIC INDEX

This index is a very broad guide to some of the topics dealt with in the novels and stories discussed in the bibliography. It is by no means intended to be comprehensive. Science fiction and fantasy, two techniques rather than topics, have been included here for the benefit of readers who prefer these types of fiction.